PROGRESS

OF

THE UNITED STATES

IN

POPULATION AND WEALTH

IN FIFTY YEARS,

AS EXHIBITED BY THE

DECENNIAL CENSUS FROM 1790 TO 1840.

BY GEORGE TUCKER,

LATE PROFESSOR OF MORAL PHILOSOPHY IN THE UNIVERSITY OF VIRGINIA, AND FORMERLY REPRESENTATIVE IN CONGRESS FROM THE SAME STATE.

WITH

AN APPENDIX,

CONTAINING AN ABSTRACT OF THE CENSUS OF 1850.

New York:

PRESS OF HUNT'S MERCHANT'S MAGAZINE.

1855.

PREFACE.

The writer of the following pages being desirous of further gratifying the curiosity he had always felt on the subject of the census of the United States, was induced to make a thorough analysis of it from 1790 to 1840. The result of his inquiries decided him on giving them to the public. They have conducted him to important inferences on the subjects of the probabilities of life, the proportion between the sexes, emigration, the diversities between the two races which compose our population, the progress of Slavery, the progress of productive industry; and on one point they have disclosed an interesting fact which seems never to have been suspected. They conclusively show that, as the number of children bear a less and less proportion to the women, in every State of the Union, the preventive checks to redundant numbers have already begun to operate here, although there is no increased difficulty in obtaining the means of subsistence. From this fact we are able to ascertain the law of our natural increase, and thus, in the estimates of our future progress, correct some prevalent errors.

To the Tables and Estimates the author has subjoined comments to aid those who were not familiar with statistical inquiries; for he wished the general reader to see and understand on what solid basis rest the hopes of the Anglo-Saxon race on this continent. And though these explanations were unnecessary to the scientific statist, they may often suggest to him valuable hints and reflections.

1*

In his estimate of the annual products of the States, which most will deem rather under than over the truth, by showing how ample are the means to pay their public debts, he has taken away the only ground upon which the base doctrine "of repudiation" could have found countenance with any large portion of the American people.

Both in his estimates and speculations the writer has studied brevity, as he wished to make his little work a sort of hand book to the legislator, the statesman, and to all who are conversans with political arithmetic. To these it is more particularly addressed by

THE AUTHOR.

University of Virginia, *July* 1, 1843.

CONTENTS.

PROGRESS

OF

POPULATION AND WEALTH

IN THE

UNITED STATES IN FIFTY YEARS,

AS EXHIBITED BY THE DECENNIAL CENSUS TAKEN IN THAT PERIOD.

CHAPTER I.

INTRODUCTION—THE CENSUS OF 1790.

As soon as the framers of the Federal Constitution had decided on giving to each State a representation in Congress in proportion to its numbers, and that direct taxes, whenever resorted to, should be in the same proportion, it became necessary to take an exact enumeration of the people. Such an enumeration was accordingly directed by the Constitution; and, as it was known that the progress of population greatly varied, and would continue to vary in the several States, it was further provided that similar enumerations should be taken "within every subsequent term of ten years."*

This census of the people at stated periods, which was thus subordinate to a particular purpose, was soon found to have substantial merits of its own. It has furnished an authentic document which

* The provision of the Constitution referred to is in the second section of the first article, and is in these words: "Representatives and direct taxes shall be apportioned among the several States which may be included within this Union, according to their respective numbers, which shall be determined by adding to the whole number of free persons, including those bound to service for a term of years, and excluding Indians not taxed, three-fifths of all other persons, [meaning slaves.] The actual enumeration shall be made within three years after the first meeting of the Congress of the United States, and within every subsequent term of ten years, in such manner as they shall by law direct."

is invaluable to the philosopher and political economist, as well as to the statesman and legislator. By the evidence it affords they are enabled to deduce truths of sufficient importance to justify the trouble and expense it involves, though it were not necessary to the just distribution of political power, and to equality of taxation; and its benefits became so obvious, that the most enlightened nations of Europe have followed the example, and now take periodical censuses of their inhabitants solely for the valuable knowledge they convey. As the numbers of a people are at once the source and the index of its wealth, these enumerations enable its statesmen to see whether national prosperity is advancing, stationary, or retrograde. They can compare one period with another, as well as different parts of the country with each other, and having this satisfactory evidence of the facts, they can more successfully investigate the causes, and apply the appropriate remedies, where remedy is practicable.

They also furnish occasions for obtaining other statistical information on subjects that materially concern civilization and national prosperity. The same means taken to ascertain the numbers of the people may be used to distribute them into classes, according to sex, ages, and occupations, and different races, where such diversity exists. Accordingly, the United States, and all the European nations who have profited by our example, have thus improved their respective enumerations of their people. Six censuses have now been taken in this country in the course of fifty years, during which period many new items have added to our knowledge of the progress of social improvement. By their aid, speculations in political philosophy of great moment and interest may be made to rest on the unerring logic of numbers.

This knowledge, so indispensable to every government which would found its legislation on authentic facts, instead of conjecture, is peculiarly important to us. Our changes are both greater and more rapid than those of any other country. A region covered with its primeval forests is, in the course of one generation, covered with productive farms and comfortable dwellings, and in the same brief space villages are seen to shoot up into wealthy and populous cities. The elements of our population are, moreover, composed of different races and conditions of civil freedom, whose relative increase is watched with interest by every reflecting mind, however he may view that diversity of condition, or whatever he may think of the comparative merit of the two races.

It is the purpose of the following pages to profit by the information which the several censuses have furnished, so as not only to make us better acquainted with the progress of our Federal Republic during the half century it has existed, but also to give us a glimpse of the yet more important future which awaits us.

Before we consider the inferences to be deduced from all the censuses together, let us take a brief notice of each of them in succession.

The first census was taken in 1790, and its enumeration referred to the 1st of August of that year. It distributed the population under the following heads:

1st. Free white males, sixteen years of age and upwards.

2d. The same under sixteen.

3d. Free white females of all ages.

4th. Slaves.

5th. All other persons; by which was meant free persons of colour.

The result is exhibited in the following

Table of the Population of the United States on the 1st of August, 1790.

States.	White Males of 16 and upwards.	White Males under 16.	White females.	All other persons.	Slaves.	Total.
*Maine,......................	24,384	24,748	46,870	538	......	96,540
New Hampshire,..........	36,089	34,851	70,171	630	158	141,899
Massachusetts,.............	95,383	87,289	190,582	5,463	......	378,717
Rhode Island,..............	16,033	15,811	32,845	3,469	952	69,110
Connecticut,................	60,527	54,592	117,562	2,801	2,759	238,141
Vermont,.....................	22,419	22,327	40,398	255	17	85,416
New York,..................	83,700	78,122	152,320	4,654	21,324	340,120
New Jersey,.................	45,251	41,416	83,287	2,762	11,423	184,139
Pennsylvania,..............	110,788	106,948	206,363	6,537	3,737	434,373
Delaware,....................	11,783	12,143	22,384	3,899	8,887	59,096
Maryland,....................	55,915	51,339	101,395	8,043	103,036	319,728
Virginia,......................	110,934	116,135	215,046	12,766	293,427	748,308
North Carolina,............	69,998	77,506	140,710	4,975	100,572	393,751
South Carolina,............	35,576	37,722	66,888	1,801	107,094	249,073
Georgia,.......................	13,103	14,044	25,739	398	29,264	82,548
Kentucky,....................	15,154	17,057	28,922	114	11,830	73,077
Tennessee,...................	6,271	10,377	15,365	361	3,417	35,791
Total,...............	813,298	802,327	1,556,839	59,466	697,897	3,929,827

* Maine was then a part of Massachusetts, and so continued until 1820, but as its census was taken separately, it has always properly held a separate place in statistical tables.

By this census the population of the United States was first ascertained by actual enumeration, together with its several parts, white and coloured, free and servile, and the comparative numbers of the different States. As the result somewhat disappointed expectation, the census was supposed by many to be inaccurate, and the assumed error was imputed, I know not on what evidence, to the popular notion that the people were thus counted for the purpose of being taxed, and that not a few had, on this account, understated to the deputy marshals the number of persons in their families.* But the general conformity of this census with those subsequently taken, in all points where the discrepancy cannot be satisfactorily explained, shows that the errors could not have been considerable.

The census showed that the population of this country had been overrated at the revolution, for, supposing the rate of increase to have been the same before the census as after it, the people of the thirteen colonies, at the time of the stamp act, fell considerably short of two millions, and at the declaration of independence, they did not reach to two and a half millions.

The items of the first census were unfortunately too few to furnish much materials for comparison. The most important facts it discloses are the following:

			Per cent.
Of the whole population, the whites were	3,172,464	=	80.73
The free coloured,	59,466	=	1.51
The slaves,	697,897	=	17.76
	3,929,827		100.
Consequently, the whole free population, white and coloured, were			82.24
And the whole slave population, ...			17.76

The number of white males to that of the females was as 103.8 to 100; or, for every 10,000 males there were 9,636 females.

It deserves to be remarked that the age of sixteen, which was adopted by Congress to divide the male population into two parts, with a view probably to ascertain the number of men capable of bearing arms, made an almost equal division between them. Thus, of the whole male white population, the part over sixteen is 50.3 per cent, and the part under sixteen 49.7. The age of twenty was thus found to divide the male population of England into two equal parts, by the census taken in that country in 1821.

It will be perceived that, at this period, every State in the Union,

* It is certain that this supposed source of error was credited by General Washington, usually so cautious, and almost unerring in his judgments, and that on the faith of it, he expected that the second census would show a much larger amount of population than proved to be the fact.

except Massachusetts, contained slaves. But, as in several States the number was few, and slavery was there subsequently abolished, in tracing the progress of the slave population, it has been thought best to confine our views to those in which slavery still exists, and where it constitutes a large, or at least not an inconsiderable part of the population.

The proportion of the white, the free coloured, and the slave population may be seen in the following table:

STATES.	Whole populat'n.	Whites.	Free col'd.	Slaves.	PER CENTAGE OF		
					Whites.	Free col.	Slaves.
Delaware,................	59,096	46,034	4,177	8,887	77.9	7.1	15.
Maryland,................	319,728	208,649	8,043	103,036	65.3	2.5	32.2
Virginia,................	748,308	442,115	12,766	293,427	59.1	1.7	39.2
North Carolina,........	393,751	288,204	4,975	100,572	73.2	1.3	25.5
South Carolina,.........	249,073	140,178	1,801	107,094	56.3	.7	43.
Georgia,..................	82,848	52,886	398	29,264	64.1	.5	35.4
Kentucky,..............	73,077	61,613	114	11,350	84.3	.2	15.5
Tennessee,..............	35,791	32,013	361	3,417	89.4	1.	9.6
Total,..........	1,961,374	1,271,692	32,635	657,047	64.8	1.7	33.5

It thus appeared that in these States, then constituting nearly one-half the Union, the number of slaves was a little more than a third of the population, and that the whites were nearly two-thirds.

CHAPTER II.

THE CENSUS OF 1800, BEING THE SECOND ENUMERATION UNDER THE CONSTITUTION.

The act of Congress which directed the second enumeration added some new divisions of the white population to those of the first census. It discriminated between the sexes, and it distributed each under the five following heads, viz:

Those persons who were under ten years of age.
" " ten, and under sixteen.
" " sixteen, and under twenty-six.
" " twenty-six, and under forty-five.
" " forty-five and upwards.

This census, besides informing us of the actual numbers then in the United States, made us further acquainted with the rate of our increase, and which proved to be somewhat greater than it had, on the authority of Dr. Franklin's opinion, been previously estimated.

The whole population was thus distributed:

White males	2,204,421	
" females	2,100,068	
		4,304,489
Free coloured		108,395
Slaves		893,041
Total		5,305,925

The increase in ten years was—

Of the whole population	35.02 per cent.
" whites	35.68 "
" free coloured	82.28 "
" slaves	27.96 "
" whole coloured population	32.23 "

The following table shows the whole population of the United States on the 1st of August, 1800.

TABLE OF THE POPULATION OF THE UNITED STATES ON THE 1st OF AUGUST, 1800.

STATES AND TERRITORIES.	WHITE MALES.					WHITE FEMALES.							
	Under 10.	*10 and under 16.*	*16 and under 26.*	*26 and under 45.*	*45 and upwards.*	*Under 10*	*10 and under 16.*	*16 and under 26.*	*26 and under 45.*	*45 and upwards.*	*Free col'd persons.*	*Slaves.*	TOTAL.
Maine	27,970	12,305	12,900	15,318	8,339	26,899	11,338	13,295	14,496	8,041	818	......	151,719
New Hampshire	30,594	14,881	16,379	17,589	11,715	29,871	14,193	17,153	18,381	12,142	856	8	183,762
Vermont	29,420	12,046	13,242	16,544	8,076	28,272	11,366	12,606	15,287	7,049	557	......	154,465
Massachusetts	63,646	32,498	38,305	39,729	31,316	60,920	30,674	40,491	43,833	35,381	6,452	......	423,245
Rhode Island	9,945	5,352	5,889	5,785	4,887	9,524	5,026	6,463	6,919	5,647	3,304	381	69,122
Connecticut	37,946	19,408	21,683	23,180	18,976	35,736	18,218	23,561	25,186	20,827	5,330	951	251,002
New York	100,367	44,273	49,275	61,594	31,943	95,473	39,876	48,176	56,411	28,651	10,374	20,343	586,756
New Jersey	34,780	15,859	16,301	19,956	12,629	32,622	14,827	17,018	19,533	11,600	4,442	12,422	211,949
Pennsylvania	103,226	46,161	54,262	59,333	38,485	99,624	43,789	53,974	53,846	33,394	14,561	1,706	602,365
Delaware	8,250	4,437	5,121	5,012	2,213	7,628	4,277	5,543	4,981	2,390	8,268	6,153	64,273
Maryland	35,852	17,392	21,234	22,778	13,394	33,796	16,437	22,367	21,170	11,906	19,587	105,635	341,548
Dis't of Columbia	1,588	671	1,178	1,332	539	1,577	663	1,027	1,028	463	783	3,244	14,093
Virginia	92,438	40,500	48,708	50,262	30,221	87,323	38,835	50,730	47,810	27,453	20,124	345,796	880,200
North Carolina	63,118	27,073	31,560	31,209	18,688	59,074	25,874	32,989	30,665	17,514	7,043	133,296	478,103
South Carolina	37,411	16,156	17,761	19,344	10,244	34,664	15,857	18,145	17,236	9,437	3,185	146,151	345,591
Georgia	19,841	8,470	9,787	10,325	4,957	18,407	7,914	9,248	8,835	3,894	1,019	59,404	162,101
Kentucky	37,274	14,045	15,705	17,699	9,233	34,949	13,433	15,524	14,934	7,075	741	40,343	220,955
Tennessee	19,227	7,194	8,282	8,352	4,125	18,450	7,042	8,554	6,992	3,491	309	13,584	105,602
Ohio	9,362	3,647	4,636	4,833	1,955	8,644	3,353	3,861	3,342	1,395	337	......	45,365
Indiana	854	347	466	645	262	791	280	424	393	115	163	135	4,875
Mississippi	1,009	356	482	780	290	953	376	352	416	165	182	3,489	8,850
	764,118	343,071	393,156	431,589	262,487	725,197	323,648	401,499	411,694	248,030	108,395	893,041	5,305,925

It must be recollected that the white population was increased by immigration, and the free coloured by emancipation. The increase from the first source was estimated by Dr. Seybert, on such imperfect data as he possessed, at 60,000 in the ten years from 1790 to 1800. But since an account has been taken of the foreign emigrants who arrive in our sea-ports, as well as from the intrinsic evidence afforded by the enumerations themselves, we must regard his estimate as much too low. The number of refugees from St. Domingo was known to make a considerable addition, at that period, to the steady stream of European emigration. The accession to our numbers from this source, instead of about $1\frac{1}{2}$ per cent, as Dr. Seybert supposed, was probably not short of 3 per cent.

The distribution of the three classes of our population, compared with that of the preceding census, may be seen in the following table:

	By the Census of 1790.	By the Census of 1800.
The proportion of the white population	80.73 per cent.	81.12 per cent.
" " free coloured	1.51 "	2.05 "
" " slaves	17.56 "	16.83 "
	100.	100.
Consequently, the proportion of the whole free population was	82.24	83.17
" " whole coloured	19.27	18.88

The age of sixteen divided the white population, as at the preceding census, into two nearly equal parts, and the excess of those under sixteen was yet less than in 1790. Thus,

The number of white males under sixteen was	1,117,169	
" " females "	1,038,845	
		2,156,014
The number of white males over sixteen	1,087,252	
" " females "	1,038,845	
		2,126,097

The white population is thus distributed according to ages, viz:

Those under the age of ten	34.6	per cent.
" between ten and sixteen . . .	15.5	"
" between sixteen and twenty-six . .	18.4	"
" between twenty-six and forty-five .	19.6	"
" forty-five and upwards . . .	11.9	"

which shows the numbers under and above sixteen to be yet nearer than 50.1 to 49.9.

The males of the whole white population exceeded the females in the proportion of 100 to 95.3, but there is great diversity in the proportion between the sexes at different ages. Thus,

Of those under ten years of age,* the proportion of males to females was as		100 to 94.9
" between ten and sixteen	"	94.3
" between sixteen and twenty-six	"	102.1
" between twenty-six and forty-five . .	"	95.4
" over forty-five	"	94.5

It appears from the preceding statement, that, notwithstanding the greater number of males born, yet from the greater number also who go abroad as travellers or seafaring men, or who die from casualties, the females between sixteen and twenty-six exceed the males between the same ages; and it may be presumed that they would maintain the excess in the after periods of life, but for the foreign emigrants, who consisted, at that time, far more of males than females. The small gain of the males on the females between ten and sixteen is probably to be referred to the same cause; though a part may be ascribed perhaps to the greater mortality of females at that period of life.

Although in every State of the Union the males under ten, and between that age and sixteen, exceed the females, yet in the subsequent ages there is a great diversity among the States. In all the New England States, except Vermont, the excess of females over sixteen is great as to outweigh the excess of males under sixteen, whereby the whole number of females exceeds that of males, thus:

In Maine the white males were		74,069,	the females	76,832
New Hampshire,	"	91,158	"	91,740
Massachusetts,	"	205,494	"	211,299
Rhode Island,	"	31,858	"	33,581
Connecticut,	"	121,193	"	123,528

In Vermont, however, the males of every age exceed the females. This diversity is doubtless owing principally to the seafaring habits of the people in the five first-mentioned States, and partly to the great number of emigrants which they send forth to the States south and west of them, who are or were mostly males. Vermont,

* Dr. Seybert, in his Statistics, p. 44, states, that of the persons under ten, the females exceeded the males. It is due however to him to remark, that while his computations appear to be accurate, according to the data he possessed, he has often been misled by the errors in the first publications of the first and second census, which a more careful revision of their returns has subsequently shown.

on the other hand, must have gained greatly by immigration, as its population nearly doubled in ten years, and thus its males, even between sixteen and twenty-six, somewhat exceeded its females.

The number of white females between sixteen and forty-five was 813,193, equal to 18.9 per cent of the whole white population; and this may be regarded as the ordinary proportion which the married and marriageable women in this country bear to the whole population, though it will of course be somewhat affected by a change in the rate of increase.

The increase of the whole coloured population, which neither gains nor loses much by migration, gives us very nearly the ratio of increase by natural multiplication. Supposing this ratio to be the same with the two races, then the further gain of the white population must be referred to immigration. By this rule, the accession to our numbers by foreign emigrants would be in ten years 3.45 per cent, equal to the difference between 35.68 and 32.23 per cent.

The second census showed a very great difference in the rate of increase among the different States. Thus, while the population of Georgia and Vermont nearly doubled, and that of Kentucky and Tennessee trebled in the ten years, that of Connecticut, of Delaware, of Maryland and Rhode Island increased less than 10 per cent. The difference was caused almost wholly by the flow of the population from the States where it was most dense to those where it was least so.

Table showing the number and proportions of Whites, Free Coloured, and Slaves, in the slaveholding States, on the 1st *of August,* 1800.

States and Territories.	Whole population.	Whites.	Free coloured.	Slaves.	Per centage of		
					Whites.	F. Col'd.	Slaves.
Delaware,	64,273	49,852	8,268	6,153	77.5	12.9	9.6
Maryland,	341,548	216,326	19,587	105,635	63.3	5.7	30.9
District of Columbia,	14,093	10,066	783	3,244	71.6	5.4	23.
Virginia,	880,200	514,280	20,124	345,796	58.4	2.3	39.3
North Carolina,	478,103	337,764	7,043	133,296	70.7	2.4	27.9
South Carolina,	345,591	196,255	3,185	146,151	57.7	.9	42.3
Georgia,	162,101	101,678	1,019	59,404	62.7	.7	36.6
Kentucky,	220,955	179,871	741	40,343	80.5	1.2	18.3
Tennessee,	105,602	91,709	309	13,584	86.8	.3	12.9
Mississippi,	8,850	5,179	182	3,489	57.9	2.7	39.4
Total,	2,621,316	1,702,980	61,241	857,095	65.	2.3	32.7

It thus appears that, in the slaveholding States, the white population had gained a little on the whole coloured, and yet more on the slaves, who, from being somewhat more than a third of the whole population, were now somewhat less.

CHAPTER III.

THE CENSUS OF 1810, BEING THE THIRD ENUMERATION UNDER THE CONSTITUTION.

The population was distributed under the same heads by this census, as by the census of 1800 ; but in addition to the population in the former territory of the United States, it comprehends that which was contained in the settled parts of Louisiana, which was purchased from France in 1803. The accession to our numbers from this source was about 77,000.

The distribution between the white and coloured races was as follows:

White males, . . .	2,987,571	
" females, . . .	2,874,433	
		5,862,004
Free coloured, . . .	186,446	
Slaves, ...	1,191,364	
		1,377,810
Total,		7,239 814

The decennial increase from all sources, compared with that of 1800, was

	1810.	1800.
Of the whole population .	36.45 per cent. .	. 35.02 per cent.
Of the whites	36.18 "	. . 35.68 "
Of the free coloured . .	72. "	. . 82.28 "
Of the slaves	33.40 "	. . 27.86 "
Of the whole coloured, bond and free	37.58 "	. . 32.23 "

The following table shows the whole population of the United States on the 1st of August, 1810:

POPULATION OF THE UNITED STATES ON THE 1st OF JUNE, 1810.

STATES AND TERRITORIES.	WHITE MALES.					WHITE FEMALES.							
	Under 10.	10 *and under* 16.	16 *and under* 26.	26 *and under* 45.	*Over* 45.	*under* 10.	10 *and under* 16.	16 *and under* 26.	26 *and under* 45.	*Over* 45.	*Free col'd persons.*	*Slaves.*	TOTAL.
Maine,..........	41,273	18,463	20,403	22,079	13,291	39,131	17,827	21,290	21,464	12,515	969	...	228,705
New Hampshire,	34,084	17,840	18,865	20,531	14,462	32,313	17,259	20,792	22,040	15,204	970	...	214,360
Vermont,........	38,062	18,347	19,678	20,441	13,053	36,613	17,339	21,181	20,792	11,457	750	...	217,713
Massachusetts,...	68,930	34,964	45,018	45,854	34,976	66,881	33,191	46,366	49,229	39,894	6,737	...	472,040
Rhode Island,...	10,735	5,554	7,250	6,765	5,539	10,555	5,389	7,520	7,635	6,372	3,609	108	77,031
Connecticut,.....	37,812	20,498	23,880	23,699	20,484	35,913	18,931	25,073	26,293	22,696	6,453	310	262,042
New York,......	165,933	73,702	85,779	94,882	53,985	157,945	68,811	85,139	85,805	46,718	25,333	15,017	959,049
New Jersey,......	37,814	18,914	21,231	21,394	16,004	36,065	17,787	21,184	21,359	15,109	7,843	10,851	245,555
Pennsylvania,....	138,464	62,506	74,203	74,193	52,100	131,769	60,943	75,960	70,826	45,840	22,492	795	810,091
Dalaware,........	9,632	4,480	5,150	5,866	2,878	9,041	4,370	5,541	5,527	2,876	13,136	4,177	72,674
Maryland,........	38,613	18,489	22,688	25,255	15,165	36,137	17,833	23,875	22,908	14,154	33,927	111,502	380,546
D. of Columbia,.	2,479	1,158	1,520	2,107	866	2,538	1,192	1,653	1,734	832	2,549	5,395	24,023
Virginia,..........	97,777	42,919	51,473	52,567	35,302	90,715	42,207	54,899	51,163	32,512	30,570	392,518	974,622
North Carolina,	68,036	30,321	34,630	34,456	21,189	65,421	30,053	37,933	33,944	20,427	10,266	168,824	555,500
South Carolina,..	39,669	17,193	20,933	20,488	11,304	37,497	16,629	20,583	18,974	10,926	4,554	196,365	415,115
Georgia,..........	28,002	11,951	14,085	14,372	7,435	26,283	11,237	13,461	12,350	6,238	1,801	105,218	252,433
Kentucky,........	65,134	26,804	29,772	29,553	17,542	60,776	25,743	29,511	25,920	13,482	1,713	80,561	406,511
Tennessee,......	44,494	17,170	19,486	19,957	10,656	41,810	16,329	19,864	17,624	8,485	1,317	44,535	261,727
Ohio,............	46,623	18,119	20,189	22,761	11,965	44,192	16,869	19,990	19,436	8,717	1,899	...	230,760
Indiana,..........	4,923	1,922	2,284	2,316	1,125	4,555	1,863	2,228	1,880	794	393	237	24,520
Mississippi,.......	4,217	1,637	2,692	3,160	1,444	4,015	1,544	2,187	1,753	675	240	17,088	40,352
Illinois,...........	2,266	945	1,274	1,339	556	2,019	791	1,053	894	364	613	168	12,282
Louisiana,........	5,848	2,491	2,963	5,130	2,508	5,384	2,588	2,874	3,026	1,499	7,585	34,660	76,566
Missouri,.........	3,438	1,345	1,568	2,069	967	3,213	1,265	1,431	1,369	562	607	3,011	20,845
Michigan,........	800	351	583	763	340	640	332	368	311	130	120	24	4,762
TOTAL,...	1,035,058	468,083	547,597	571,997	364,836	981,421	448,322	561,956	544,256	338,478	186,446	1,191,364	7,239,814

The greater rate of increase of the whole population, exhibited in the preceding comparison, is to be ascribed principally to the acquisition of Louisiana, and, in a small degree, to an increased importation of slaves before 1808, when it was known that Congress would avail itself of the power it would then possess, of prohibiting their further importation. These two circumstances are sufficient to account for the excess of increase under the census of 1810, which excess did not exceed 77,000 persons; and, indeed, as the slaves imported and acquired with Louisiana, probably amounted to more than half this number,* the remainder is not equal to the white inhabitants which Louisiana contained, and consequently we are justified in inferring, notwithstanding the augmented ratio of actual increase, a small diminution in the rate of gain from immigration or natural multiplication, or both united.

The three classes of the population were distributed in the following proportions in 1790, 1800, and 1810:

	1790.		1800.		1810.	
The white population	80.73	per cent,	81.12	per cent,	80.97	per cent.
Free coloured	1.51	"	2.05	"	2.57	"
Slaves	17.56	"	16.83	"	16.46	"
	100.		100.		100.	
Of the whole free pop.	82.24	"	83.17	"	83.54	"
Whole coloured	19.07	"	18.88	"	19.03	"

It thus appears that the free coloured population had a greater proportional increase than either of the other two classes; and that, while the whole free population gained on the servile, the whole coloured gained a little on the white.

The age of sixteen continued to divide the white population into two nearly equal parts, but the small excess of those under that age continued to diminish, thus:

Whites under sixteen, males . . .	1,503,141	
" " females . .	1,429,743	
		2,932,884

* Supposing the natural increase of the coloured population to be the same from 1800 to 1810, as from 1790 to 1800, and there is no reason for supposing it to be different, then the difference of the decennial gain in this class, shown by the two enumerations, shows the accessions to this class from the purchase of Louisiana and from importation. That difference is 5.35 per cent on the whole coloured population, which is equal to 53,576.

Whites over sixteen, males . . .	1,484,430
" " females . .	1,444,690
	——— 2,929,120

which shows the proportion under sixteen to be 50.03 per cent. But as the proportion of the females under that age was greater than that of males, the former being 50.26 and the latter 49.69, we may infer that, if there were no migration to the United States, which consists more of adults and of males than of children and females, an age somewhat below sixteen would constitute the point of equal division.

The distribution of the white population, according to age, differs little from that shown by the preceding census, viz :—

Those under ten were	34.4 per cent.
" between ten and sixteen . . .	15.6 "
" between sixteen and twenty-six .	18.9 "
" between twenty-six and forty-five .	19. "
" of forty-five and upwards . .	12. "

The increase in twenty years was as follows, viz:

Of the whole population	84.2 "
Whites	84.8 "
Free coloured	213.5 "
Slaves	70.7 "
Whole coloured	81.9 "

The proportion of males to females in the white population was as 100 to 96.2, showing an increase of females of 1.1 per cent since the census of 1800.

At the different ages specified in the census, the proportions of the sexes were as follows, viz:

Under ten, the males to the females were as 100 to	94.8
Between ten and sixteen . . . . "	95.7
Between sixteen and twenty-six . . "	102.7
Between twenty-six and forty-five . . "	97.3
Forty-five and upwards . . . . "	92.7

which proportions exhibit the same features of irregularity as those of the preceding census.

The number of white females between the ages of sixteen and forty-five was 1,106,212, which is 18.87 per cent of the whole white population, showing a very small variation from the proportion exhibited by the preceding census.

The following table shows the number of whites, free coloured, and slaves, in the slaveholding States and Territories, on the 1st of August, 1810, with the relative proportions of each:

States and Territories.	Whole population.	Whites.	Free coloured.	Slaves.	Per centage of		
					Whites.	F. Col'd.	Slaves.
Delaware,...............	72,674	55,361	13,136	4,177	76.2	18.1	5.7
Maryland,...............	380,546	235,117	33,927	111,502	61.8	8.9	29.3
District of Columbia,...	24,023	16,079	2,549	5,395	66.9	10.6	22.5
Virginia,...............	974,622	551,534	30,570	392,518	56.6	3.1	40.3
North Carolina,.........	550,500	376,410	10,266	168,824	67.8	1.8	30.4
South Carolina,.........	415,115	214,196	4,554	196,365	51.6	1.1	47.3
Georgia,................	252,433	145,414	1,801	105,218	57.6	1.7	41.7
Kentucky,...............	406,511	324,237	1,713	80,561	79.8	.4	19.8
Tennessee,..............	261,727	215,875	1,317	44,535	82.5	.5	17.
Mississippi,............	40,352	23,024	240	17,088	57.	.3	42.7
Louisiana,..	76,556	34,311	7,585	34,660	44.8	9.9	45.3
Missouri,...............	20,845	17,227	607	3,011	82.6	2.9	14.4
Total,...........	3,480,904	2,208,785	108,265	1,163,854	63.5	3.1	33.4

It appears from the preceding table that both descriptions of the coloured population in these States had gained on the whites in the preceding ten years, and that the slaves, which in 1800 had constituted a little less than a third of their aggregate number, now amounted to a little more than a third.

CHAPTER IV.

THE CENSUS OF 1820, BEING THE FOURTH DECENNIAL ENUMERATION UNDER THE CONSTITUTION.

THIS census was the first which made any discrimination in the coloured part of the population, either as to sex or age. It distributed the males and females, both of the free coloured persons and slaves, under the four following divisions, viz: those who were under fourteen; who were fourteen and under twenty-six; who were twenty-six and under forty-five; and who were forty-five and upwards.

It made no change in the distribution of the whites, except to add a column for those males who were between the ages of sixteen and eighteen.

The decennial increase, shown by this census, compared with that of 1810, was as follows:

	1820.	1810.
Of the whole population, .	33.35 per cent, .	36.45 per cent.
Of the white, ...	34.3 " . .	36.18 "
Of the free coloured, . .	27.75 " . .	72. "
Of the slave, ...	29.57 " . .	33.40 "
Of the whole coloured,. .	29.33 " . .	37.58 "

It thus appears that the increase of the whole population was 3.10 per cent more in the last ten years than in the ten preceding. But if we make a deduction from the increase shown by the census of 1810, for the extra gain by the purchase of Louisiana, and which may be estimated at 1½ per cent, the difference will be reduced to 1.6 per cent—equivalent to 115,837 persons. This falling off is to be attributed partly to the suspension of immigration during the war, partly to the slaves who fled to the enemy during the same period, and lastly to that gradual diminution of natural increase, of which the several enumerations furnish evidences, and which probably the war slightly increased.

The result of the census may be seen in the four following tables:

TABLE I.—SHOWING THE WHITE POPULATION OF THE UNITED STALES ON THE 1ST OF AUGUST, 1820.

STATES AND TERRITORIES.	MALES.							FEMALES.					
	Under 10.	10 *and under* 16.	*Between* 16 *and* 18	16 *and under* 26	26 *and under* 45.	45 *and upwards.*	TOTAL.	*Under* 10.	10 *and under* 16.	16 *and under* 26.	26 *and under* 45.	45 *and upwards.*	TOTAL.
Maine	49,217	24,528	7,146	28,530	27,742	19,178	149,195	46,565	23,982	30,823	28,248	18,527	148,145
New Hampshire	35,466	19,672	5,529	22,703	22,956	18,413	119,210	34,599	18,899	24,806	25,797	19,925	124,026
Vermont	35,708	19,241	5,860	24,137	22,035	16,189	117,310	35,327	18,577	24,713	23,683	15,236	117,536
Massachusetts	70,993	38,573	10,912	49,506	54,414	38,668	252,154	69,260	38,308	52,805	57,721	46,171	264,265
Rhode Island	11,530	5,860	1,767	7,596	7,618	5,888	38,492	10,917	5,769	8,407	8,671	7,157	40,921
Connecticut	36,848	20,682	6,284	25,731	25,632	21,814	130,707	35,289	19,833	27,205	29,069	25,078	136,454
New York	222,608	104,297	29,598	132,733	138,634	81,259	679,551	216,513	101,904	132,492	129,899	72,385	653,193
New Jersey	42,055	19,970	5,956	24,639	24,418	18,537	129,619	39,921	19,504	25,637	24,693	18,035	137,790
Pennsylvania	175,381	77,050	25,901	102,550	97,144	64,493	516,618	166,710	78,425	101,404	94,345	59,592	500,476
Delaware	9,071	4,448	1,719	5,516	5,607	3,263	27,905	8,657	4,311	5,573	5,537	3,299	27,377
Maryland	41,511	18,952	6,261	26,404	27,916	16,960	131,743	39,454	19,578	27,293	26,347	15,807	128,479
Dis't of Columbia	3,276	1,540	550	2,171	2,893	1,291	11,171	3,319	1,640	2,518	2,615	1,351	11,443
Virginia	103,963	45,762	13,148	58,863	57,898	38,245	304,731	98,485	45,766	62,411	55,995	35,686	298,343
North Carolina	75,488	32,912	9,748	39,527	36,264	25,453	209,644	70,998	33,101	42,253	38,069	25,135	209,556
South Carolina	42,658	18,258	5,877	23,984	22,115	13,919	120,934	39,891	18,741	23,662	20,939	13,273	116,506
Georgia	35,444	14,743	4,215	19,483	17,874	10,869	98,404	33,177	14,937	18,642	15,365	9,041	91,162
Kentucky	83,050	36,004	10,383	41,328	38,178	25,136	223,696	77,641	35,120	41,905	35,483	20,799	210,948
Tennessee	67,746	28,497	7,472	31,028	27,549	18,780	173,600	63,419	27,770	31,569	27,931	15,638	166,327
Ohio	111,683	45,858	12,607	57,008	54,432	31,626	300,607	106,036	44,106	53,337	48,797	23,689	275,965
Indiana	29,629	11,454	3,270	14,428	14,072	7,066	76,649	27,684	10,707	13,635	12,009	5,074	69,109
Mississippi	8,104	3,216	1,052	4,560	5,110	2,296	23,286	7,220	3,176	3,791	3,107	1,596	18,890
Illinois	10,554	4,227	1,313	6,224	5,755	2,641	29,401	9,558	4,018	4,842	4,166	1,803	24,987
Louisiana	11,817	4,710	2,105	8,747	11,236	4,822	41,332	11,062	5,484	6,708	5,695	3,102	32,051
Missouri	10,677	4,256	1,301	6,537	6,622	2,909	31,001	9,766	3,978	5,076	4,265	1,902	24,987
Alabama *	17,103	6,281	1,750	9,336	9,055	4,064	51,750	15,810	6,289	7,993	6,625	2,895	44,495
Michigan	1,220	559	152	1,334	1,661	609	5,383	1,130	525	692	595	266	3,208
Arkansas	2,420	985	329	1,427	1,453	686	6,971	2,142	927	1,179	934	426	5,608
TOTAL	1,345,220	612,535	182,205	776,030	766,283	495,065	4,001,064	1,280,570	605,375	781,371	736,600	462,888	3,871,647

* See note to table IV.

TABLE II.—SHOWING THE FREE COLORED POPULATION OF THE UNITED STATES ON THE 1ST OF AUGUST, 1820

STATES AND TERRITORIES	MALES.					FEMALES.				
	Under 14	14 *and under* 26.	26 *and under* 45.	45 *and upwards.*	TOTAL.	*Under* 14.	14 *and under* 26.	26 *and under* 45.	45 *and upwards.*	TOTAL.
Maine	170	86	91	90	437	168	115	126	83	492
New Hampshire	97	101	85	89	372	109	99	106	100	414
Vermont	152	113	93	80	438	170	125	97	73	465
Massachusetts	1,085	680	836	647	3,308	969	778	904	781	3,432
Rhode Island	577	388	343	279	1,587	550	523	465	429	1,967
Connecticut	1,432	911	865	629	3,837	1,421	961	950	675	4,007
New York	5,197	3,011	3,347	1,903	13,458	5,342	4,195	4,126	2,158	15,821
New Jersey	3,328	1,116	1,090	882	6,416	3,093	1,198	987	766	6,044
Pennsylvania	5,666	3,348	3,890	1,900	14,804	5,465	4,063	4,073	1,797	15,398
Delaware	2,812	1,317	1,207	1,143	6,479	2,742	1,379	1,307	1,051	6,479
Maryland	7,829	3,593	3,756	3,568	18,746	7,857	4,461	4,752	3,914	20,984
District of Columbia	756	338	349	288	1,731	828	549	548	392	2,317
Virginia	8,145	3,884	3,135	2,685	17,849	7,640	4,545	3,772	3,083	19,040
North Carolina	3,415	1,728	1,109	1,143	7,395	3,129	1,737	1,345	1,006	7,217
South Carolina	1,376	732	647	541	3,296	1,223	836	800	671	3,530
Georgia	320	195	180	146	851	349	209	195	159	912
Kentucky	585	281	284	343	1,493	488	254	244	280	1,266
Tennessee	700	323	240	238	1,501	532	297	224	173	1,226
Ohio	1,057	544	538	315	2,454	994	549	466	260	2,269
Indiana	275	146	141	92	654	251	137	120	68	576
Mississippi	87	62	52	38	239	84	52	44	39	219
Illinois	86	71	55	25	237	104	50	44	22	220
Louisiana	2,248	876	915	470	4,509	2,209	1,557	1,377	824	5,967
Missouri	93	40	36	17	186	62	39	34	26	161
Alabama*	118	83	68	49	357	91	69	58	35	276
Michigan	35	32	27	11	105	20	20	16	13	69
Arkansas	18	13	11	2	44	8	3	1	3	15
TOTAL	47,659	24,012	23,450	17,613	112,783	45,898	28,850	27,181	18,861	120,783

* See note to table IV.

TABLE III.—SHOWING THE SLAVE POPULATION OF THE UNITED STATES ON THE 1ST OF AUGUST, 1820.

STATES AND TERRITORIES.	MALES.					FEMALES.				
	Under 14.	14 *and under* 26.	26 *and under* 45.	45 *and upwards.*	TOTAL.	*Under* 14.	14 *and under* 26.	26 *and under* 45.	45 *and upwards.*	TOTAL.
Maine	......	......	......	......	......	......	......	......	......	......
New Hampshire	......	......	......	......	......	......	......	......	......	......
Vermont	......	......	......	......	......	......	......	......	......	......
Massachusetts	......	......	......	......	......	......	......	......	......	......
Rhode Island	2	1	1	14	18	2	3	3	22	30
Connecticut	......	......	13	24	37	......	......	13	47	60
New York	1,861	1,624	932	671	5,088	1,544	1,579	1,065	812	5,000
New Jersey	860	1,583	917	628	3,988	592	1,285	1,036	656	3,569
Pennsylvania	1	1	18	65	85	3	2	36	85	126
Delaware	1,244	839	337	135	2,555	979	611	233	131	1,954
Maryland	24,736	14,846	10,718	6,073	56,373	22,740	13,403	9,362	5,520	51,025
District of Columbia	1,245	775	671	316	3,007	1,311	990	696	373	3,370
Virginia	96,881	52,791	45,438	23,164	218,274	92,468	51,972	40,691	21,748	206,879
North Carolina	48,914	27,511	19,395	10,731	106,551	45,055	25,663	18,326	9,422	98,466
South Carolina	51,738	32,324	31,641	14,769	130,472	49,694	33,991	30,461	13,857	128,003
Georgia	33,204	19,541	16,249	6,922	75,916	32,141	19,879	15,631	6,089	73,740
Kentucky	31,469	17,132	10,944	4,369	63,914	29,231	17,407	11,801	4,379	62,818
Tennessee	20,314	10,078	6,529	2,826	39,747	19,251	11,153	7,192	2,764	40,360
Ohio	......	......	......	......	......	......	......	......	......	......
Indiana	43	37	11	7	98	40	21	21	10	92
Mississippi	7,016	4,600	4,061	1,173	16,850	6,677	4,807	3,506	974	15,964
Illinois	170	173	133	66	548	139	128	71	31	369
Louisiana	11,675	10,876	10,520	3,495	36,566	10,763	11,672	7,758	2,305	32,498
Missouri	2,491	1,511	852	487	5,341	2,281	1,461	855	284	4,881
Alabama*	9,665	6,563	4,200	1,352	24,717	9,140	6,141	3,779	1,039	22,722
Michigan	......	......	......	......	......	......	......	......	......	......
Arkansas	323	276	143	78	820	293	268	157	79	797
TOTAL	343,852	203,088	163,723	77,365	790,965	324,344	202,336	152,693	70,637	752,723

* See note to table IV.

TABLE IV.—SHOWING THE AGGREGATE NUMBER OF WHITES, FREE COLORED PERSONS, AND SLAVES, OF EACH SEX, IN THE SEVERAL STATES ON THE 1ST OF AUGUST, 1820.

STATES AND TERRITORIES.	WHITES.			FREE COLORED.			SLAVES.			TOTAL.
	Males.	*Females.*	*Total.*	*Males.*	*Females.*	*Total.*	*Males.*	*Females.*	*Total.*	
Maine	149,195	148,145	297,340	437	492	*995	......	......	......	298,335
New Hampshire	119,210	124,026	242,236	372	414	*925	......	......	......	244,161
Vermont	117,310	117,536	234,846	438	465	*918	......	......	......	235,764
Massachusetts	252,154	264,265	516,419	3,308	3,432	*6,868	......	......	......	523,287
Rhode Island	38,492	40,921	79,413	1,587	1,967	*3,598	18	30	48	83,059
Connecticut	130,707	136,454	267,161	3,837	4,007	*7,944	37	60	97	275,202
New York	679,551	653,193	1,332,744	13,458	15,821	*29,980	5,088	5,000	10,088	1,372,812
New Jersey	129,619	127,790	257,409	6,416	6,044	*12,609	3,988	3,569	7,557	277,575
Pennsylvania	516,618	500,476	1,017,094	14,804	15,398	*32,153	85	126	211	1,049,458
Delaware	27,905	27,377	55,282	6,479	6,479	12,958	2,555	1,954	4,509	72,749
Maryland	131,743	128,479	260,222	18,746	20,984	39,730	56,373	51,025	107,398	407,350
Dis't of Columbia	11,171	11,443	22,614	1,731	2,317	4,048	3,007	3,370	6,377	33,039
Virginia	304,731	298,343	603,074	17,849	19,040	*37,139	218,274	206,879	425,153	1,065,366
North Carolina	209,644	209,556	419,200	7,395	7,217	14,612	106,561	98,466	205,017	638,829
South Carolina	120,934	116,506	237,440	3,296	3,530	6,826	130,472	128,003	258,475	502,741
Georgia	98,404	91,162	189,566	851	912	*1,767	75,916	73,740	149,656	340,989
Kentucky	223,696	210,948	434,644	1,493	1,266	*2,941	63,914	62,818	126,732	564,317
Tennessee	173,600	166,327	339,927	1,501	1,226	*2,779	39,747	40,360	80,107	422,813
Ohio	300,607	275,965	576,572	2,454	2,269	*4,862	......	......	......	581,434
Indiana	76,649	69,109	145,758	654	576	1,230	98	92	190	147,178
Mississippi	23,286	18,890	42,176	239	219	458	16,850	15,964	32,814	75,448
Illinois	29,401	24,387	53,788	237	220	*506	548	369	917	55,211
Louisiana	41,332	32,051	73,383	4,509	5,967	*10,960	36,566	32,498	69,064	153,407
Missouri	31,001	24,987	55,988	186	161	*376	5,341	4,881	10,222	66,586
Alabama †	51,750	44,495	96,245	357	276	633	24,717	22,722	47,439	144,317
Michigan	5,383	3,208	8,591	105	69	*305	......	......	......	8,896
Arkansas	6,971	5,608	12,579	44	15	*77	820	797	1,617	14,273
TOTAL	4,001,064	3,871,647	7,872,711	112,783	120,783	238,197	790,965	752,723	1,543,688	9,654,596

* The numbers thus marked comprehend people of color who were designated in the census, in some of the returns, as "other free persons, except Indians, not taxed," without discrimination of sex. The whole number thus returned was 4,631.

† The population of this state was stated in the census published by the state department, in 1832, to be 127,901; but in the "statistical view," published by the same department three years afterwards, pursuant to resolutions of the Senate in 1833 and 1834, at was set down at 144,317—showing a difference of 16,416. The last of these official statements being believed to be correct, it has been here followed as to the aggregates of the whole population of the states, and of its three several classes; but as it omits the details, the distribution according to age, in the statement of 1832, remains uncorrected. There will therefore be found, between the aggregates and the details of the population of this state, a discrepancy of 16,416.

While there was so sensible a difference in the increase of the population shown by the two last enumerations, its distribution among the several classes continued in nearly the same proportions, viz:

	Census of 1820.		*Census of* 1810.
The whites amount to .	81.55	per cent. . . .	80.97
The free coloured. . .	2.46	"	2.57
The slaves	15.99	"	16.46
The whole free population,	84.01	"	83.54
The whole coloured,. .	18.45	"	19.03

It thus appeared that the white population had gained on both descriptions of the coloured.

The proportion between the sexes in the three classes was as follows:

In the white population the males exceed the females, as 100 to 96.77.

In the free coloured population the females exceed the males, as 107.09 to 100.

In the slave population the males exceed the females, as 100 to 95.16.

This excess of females in the free coloured class is to be ascribed principally to the seafaring and roaming habits of many of the males, and probably in a small degree to the greater number of females who are emancipated. The disproportion is therefore greatest between the ages of 14 and 45.

In five of the New England States, from the like prevalence of seafaring and migratory habits, the females exceed the males. In Maine, however, there is a small majority of males—the gain from immigration in that thinly settled State more than counterbalancing the loss by the pursuits of fishing and navigation. In the other States of the Union the males, both of the white and coloured population, exceed the females; and of the whites under ten years of age, the males are most numerous even in the New England States.

The excess of males exhibited by the census has doubtless been somewhat enhanced by foreign emigrants, of whom a majority are males, but it is to be referred principally to that curious and admirable provision of nature, by which the greater number of males born is sufficient, under ordinary circumstances, to compensate the peculiar casualties to which that sex is exposed. Even in the free coloured population, of which the females have a preponderance of 7 per cent, *the males under* fourteen exceed the females about 3 per cent.

The numbers of the three classes, male and female, within the several ages mentioned in the census, are respectively in the following proportions to the whole of each class, viz:

1st. *Of the whites,*

The males under 10 are	17.1	per cent.	The females,	16.3	per cent.
10 and under 16	7.8	"	"	7.7	"
16 and under 26	9.9	"	"	9.9	"
26 and under 45	9.7	"	"	9.4	"
45 and upwards	6.3	"	"	5.9	"
	50.8			49.2	

2d. *Of the free coloured,*

The males under 14 are	20.4	per cent.	The females,	19.7	per cent.
14 and under 26	10.3	"	"	12.4	"
26 and under 45	10.	"	"	11.6	"
45 and upwards,	7.5	"	"	8.1	"
	48.2			51.8	

3d. *Of the slaves,*

The males under 14 are	22.4	per cent.	The females,	21.1	per cent.
14 and under 26	13.2	"	"	13.2	"
26 and under 45	10.6	"	"	9.9	"
45 and upwards,	5.	"	"	4.6	"
	51.2			48.8	"

It thus appears that one-third of the white population was under ten years of age, and not quite half (48.9 per cent) under sixteen. This age does not so equally divide this part of the population as it did in the previous enumerations, since the same causes which occasioned the small decline in the rate of natural increase before adverted to, lessened the proportion of those who were under that age, and consequently placed the point of equal division at a somewhat greater age.

Of the free coloured population less than two-thirds, (62.8 per cent,) and of the slaves more than two-thirds, (69.9) are under twenty-six years of age.

The relative numbers of the white and coloured population in the slaveholding States, is exhibited in the following table:

States and Territories.	Whole population.	Whites.	Free coloured.	Slaves.	Per centage of		
					Whites.	F. col'd.	Slaves.
Delaware,..............	72,749	55,282	12,958	4,509	76.	17.8	6.2
Maryland,..............	407,350	260,222	39,730	107,398	63.9	9.7	26.4
District of Columbia, .	33,039	22,614	4,048	6,377	68.5	12.2	19.3
Virginia, ...	1,065,366	603,074	37,139	425,153	56.6	3.5	39.9
North Carolina,........	638,829	419,200	14,612	205,017	65.6	2.3	32.1
South Carolina,........	502,741	237,440	6,826	258,475	47.2	1.4	51.4
Georgia, ...	340,989	189,566	1,767	149,656	55.6	.5	43.9
Kentucky, ...	564,317	434,644	2,941	126,732	77.	.5	22.5
Tennessee,..............	422,813	339,927	2,779	80,107	80.4	.7	18.9
Mississippi,............	75,448	42,176	458	32,814	55.9	.6	43.5
Louisiana, ...	153,407	73,383	10,960	69,064	47.8	7.1	45.
Missouri, ...	66,586	55,988	376	10,222	84.1	.6	15.3
Alabama, ...	144,317	96,245	633	47,439	66.7	.4	32.9
Arkansas,..............	14,273	12,579	77	1,617	88.1	.5	11.3
Total,...........	4,502,224	2,842,340	135,304	1,524,580	63.13	3.01	33.86

It thus appears that in these States, since the preceding census, the white population lost, and the coloured portion gained nearly the half of one per cent.

CHAPTER V.

THE CENSUS OF 1830, BEING THE FIFTH DECENNIAL ENUMERATION UNDER THE CONSTITUTION.

In the act of Congress which directed the fifth census, some important deviations from the preceding acts were introduced. Thus it numbered the population as it was on the 1st day of *June*, instead of the 1st of *August*, as had been previously done, so that the increase shown, on a comparison with the preceding census, was not as heretofore, for ten years, but for nine years and ten months. There were also a greater number of divisions according to age, both in the white and coloured population.* The whites of each sex were arranged under thirteen heads, as follows:

Those under	5 years of age.
5 and under	10
10 "	15
15 "	20
20 "	30
30 "	40
40 "	50
50 "	60
60 "	70
70 "	80
80 "	90
90 "	100
100 and upwards.	

The coloured population of both descriptions, and of each sex, were arranged under the six following heads, viz:

Those under 10; 10 and under 24; 24 and under 36; 36 and under 55; 55 and under 100; 100 and upwards.

The result is exhibited in the five following tables:

---

* There were also columns for the deaf, and dumb, and blind, of different ages, which will be hereafter noticed.

TABLE I.—SHOWING THE NUMBER OF WHITE MALES IN THE UNITED STATES ON THE 1ST OF JUNE, 1830.

STATES AND TERRITORIES.	*Under* 5.	5 *to* 10.	10 *to* 15.	15 *to* 20.	20 *to* 30.	30 *to* 40.	40 *to* 50.	50 *to* 60.	60 *to* 70.	70 *to* 80.	80 *to* 90.	90 *to* 100.	100 & *upw'ds*	TOTAL.
Maine,	34,053	28,742	25,522	22,400	34,985	21,700	14,547	9,228	5,956	2,637	823	93	2	200,689
New Hampshire,	19,428	17,521	16,737	14,847	21,191	14,696	10,772	7,218	5,059	2,786	840	85	4	131,184
Vermont,	21,700	19,406	17,597	15,782	24,207	15,773	10,405	7,051	5,203	2,203	618	48	3	139,996
Massachusetts,	40,644	35,988	34,679	32,891	58,621	35,433	23,683	15,008	10,319	5,575	1,760	173	1	294,685
Rhode Island,	6,733	5,786	5,400	5,354	8,425	5,379	3,512	2,157	1,444	854	261	28	......	45,383
Connecticut,	19,033	17,891	17,788	16,509	26,166	16,608	11,595	7,851	5,495	3,154	871	81	5	143,047
New York,	158,077	137,071	118,523	101,712	176,754	113,136	68,871	40,503	23,909	10,034	2,561	255	35	951,441
New Jersey,	25,071	21,204	19,745	17,123	27,001	17,231	11,043	7,053	4,458	2,021	534	44	1	152,529
Pennsylvania,	117,853	96,199	82,375	73,113	121,359	75,172	46,600	28,032	16,085	6,979	1,775	228	42	665,812
Delaware,	4,744	4,099	3,919	3,184	5,508	3,206	2,036	1,286	609	202	43	9	......	28,845
Maryland,	23,737	19,438	17,886	15,778	29,397	18,215	11,072	6,565	3,462	1,375	355	53	7	147,340
D. of Columbia,	2,333	1,680	1,486	1,522	2,805	1,817	1,068	593	245	75	25	1	1	13,647
Virginia,	65,793	51,805	43,287	36,947	60,911	36,539	23,381	15,261	8,971	3,674	1,108	184	26	347,887
North Carolina,	46,749	35,950	30,527	25,452	39,428	23,042	14,998	10,536	5,968	2,489	649	138	28	235,954
South Carolina,	25,132	20,259	16,497	13,961	22,164	13,969	8,334	5,644	3,042	1,210	298	66	14	130,590
Georgia,	37,027	23,709	18,594	15,186	26,844	16,156	9,542	5,674	3,083	1,120	290	63	10	153,288
Alabama,	22,764	15,482	12,129	9,509	17,440	11,399	6,029	3,593	1,741	591	147	19	3	100,846
Mississippi,	7,918	5,572	4,591	3,623	7,237	4,632	2,419	1,595	632	189	47	11	......	38,456
Louisiana,	7,968	6,402	5,134	4,325	10,458	7,777	4,304	2,203	896	317	78	24	9	49,715
Tennessee,	59,576	45,366	36,044	29,247	44,982	25,111	15,108	11,188	5,543	2,107	657	105	32	275,066
Kentucky,	54,116	41,073	34,222	29,017	45,913	26,289	15,966	10,843	6,253	2,585	699	119	28	267,123
Ohio,	96,411	74,690	62,151	51,138	81,290	49,346	31,112	18,058	10,783	3.632	935	138	29	479,713
Indiana,	39,780	28,692	22,872	17,653	28,153	17,904	10,306	6,004	3,160	1,059	240	49	13	175,885
Illinois,	18,834	12,753	10,024	7,770	14,706	8,825	4,627	2,853	1,172	384	90	6	4	82,048
Missouri,	13,531	9,617	7,469	5,639	11,147	7,084	3,642	1,939	927	334	60	14	2	61,405
Michigan,	3,023	2,326	1,905	1,543	4,389	2,739	1,232	658	264	64	20	4	1	18,168
Arkansas,	3,020	2,021	1,626	1,272	2,835	1,820	876	834	209	69	12	1	......	14,195
Florida,	1,932	1,333	1,015	789	2,171	1,536	760	436	194	57	10	2	1	10,236
TOTAL,	972,980	782,075	669,734	573,196	956,487	592,535	367,840	229,284	135,082	57 772	15,806	2,041	301	5,355,133

Table II.—Showing the Number of White Females in the United States, on the 1st of June, 1830

States and Territories.	*Under* 5.	5 *to* 10.	10 *to* 15.	15 *to* 20.	20 *to* 30.	30 *to* 40.	40 *to* 50.	50 *to* 60.	60 *to* 70.	70 *to* 80.	80 *to* 90.	90 *to* 100.	100 & *upw'ds*	Total.
Maine,...............	32,471	27,676	24,067	22,348	35,596	22,259	14,183	9,330	5,904	2,688	911	138	3	197,574
New Hampshire,...	18,538	16,790	15,525	14,823	24,564	16,690	11,896	8,448	5,888	3,110	1,085	174	6	137,537
Vermont,............	21,334	18,632	16,575	15,978	26,540	17,937	13,214	9,245	6,707	3,760	1,228	156	3	139,775
Massachusetts,......	39,533	34,537	33,326	34,439	60,495	38,163	26,684	18,456	12,989	7,173	2,528	347	4	308,674
Rhode Island,......	6,623	5,642	5,213	5,584	9,203	5,756	4,024	2,826	1,939	1,058	376	44	......	48,288
Connecticut,........	18,270	16,943	16,575	15,978	26,540	17,937	13,214	9,245	6,707	3,760	1,228	156	3	146,556
New York,........	151,868	133,084	115,166	105,196	168,897	104,522	64,315	38,344	22,589	9,645	2,673	304	17	916,620
New Jersey,........	23,937	20,479	18,267	16,784	25,817	16,623	11,007	7,307	4,705	2,160	586	63	2	147,737
Pennsylvania,......	111,947	92,719	80,087	75,976	115,898	69,604	44,485	27,882	16,221	7,084	1,929	235	21	644,088
Delaware,..........	4,647	4,011	3,654	3,381	5,484	3,179	2.047	1,397	360	263	56	6	1	28,756
Maryland,..........	22,356	18,693	17,327	18,020	27,248	16,617	10,840	6,983	3,633	1,541	432	64	14	143,768
D. of Columbia,...	2,182	1,646	1,648	1,843	2,856	1,752	980	603	272	98	32	4	......	13,916
Virginia,............	62,411	49,964	41,936	40,479	62,044	36,456	23,750	15,447	8,765	3,847	1,098	188	28	346,413
North Carolina, ..	43,775	34,264	28,842	27,398	41,636	24,534	16,428	10,601	5,980	2,496	747	158	30	236,889
South Carolina,....	23,691	19,043	15,632	15,122	21,866	13,438	8,468	5,455	2,929	1,181	351	80	17	127,273
Georgia,............	30,958	22,590	17,988	16,452	24,036	13,974	8,427	5,089	2,664	987	268	65	20	143,518
Alabama,...........	21,340	14,801	11,092	9,951	14,457	8,559	4,695	2,731	1,319	432	144	29	10	89,560
Mississippi,.........	7,319	5,165	4,169	3,653	5,231	3,090	1,739	983	436	149	34	7	2	31,977
Louisiana,..........	7,890	6,193	5,140	4,709	6,930	4,204	2,310	1,257	660	222	73	17	1	39,516
Tennessee,.........	55,399	42,975	33,556	30,616	42,970	23,545	15,264	9,279	4,541	1,855	542	110	28	260,680
Kentucky,.....	50,835	39,439	32,197	29,623	41,936	23,463	15,476	9,499	5,315	2,195	575	97	14	250,664
Ohio,.................	89,873	71,851	59,306	52,635	75,574	43,894	27,546	15,898	8,293	2,915	736	89	6	448,616
Indiana,.............	37,505	27,313	21,072	18,087	26,702	15,703	9,028	4,808	2,275	780	212	25	4	163,514
Illinois,..............	17,429	12,000	9,246	8,053	12,461	6,850	3,750	2,047	812	273	77	14	1	73,013
Missouri,...........	12,561	9,077	6,794	5,765	8,791	5,121	2,718	1,499	766	227	60	9	2	53,390
Michigan,...........	2,743	2,066	1,686	1,438	2,540	1,399	726	390	140	35	10	5	......	13,178
Arkansas,,..........	2,782	1,897	1,494	1,225	2,012	1,087	528	301	107	31	9	3	......	11,476
Florida,..............	1,807	1,251	981	923	1,447	848	484	247	101	45	10	5	......	8,149
Total,......	921,934	750,741	638,856	596,254	918,411	555,531	356,046	223,504	131,307	58,336	17,434	2,523	238	5,171,115

TABLE III.—SHOWING THE NUMBER OF FREE COLORED PERSONS IN THE UNITED STATES, ON THE 1ST OF JUNE, 1830.

STATES AND TERRITORIES.	MALES.							FEMALES.						
	Under 10.	10 *to* 24.	24 *to* 36.	36 *to* 55.	55 *to* 100.	100 *and up'ds.*	*Total.*	*Under* 10.	10 *to* 24.	24 *to* 36.	36 *to* 55.	55 *to* 100.	100 *and up'ds.*	*Total.*
Maine,	163	172	111	108	54	2	610	143	175	117	93	52	....	580
New Hampshire,	67	78	53	44	32	1	275	68	97	54	63	45	2	329
Vermont,	121	116	78	60	48	3	426	121	131	73	71	57	2	4,555
Massachusetts,	806	887	718	629	314	4	3,350	812	967	815	661	396	39	3,699
Rhode Island,	337	501	317	238	152	3	1,548	355	597	443	350	265	3	2,013
Connecticut,	1,019	1,121	771	624	313	2	3,850	1,051	1,233	819	667	417	10	4,197
New York,	5,643	6,094	4,860	3,492	1,358	19	21,466	5,509	6,843	5,504	3,780	1,714	54	23,404
New Jersey,	3,033	3,234	1,458	1,196	573	7	9,501	2,811	2,890	1,428	1,113	554	6	8,802
Pennsylvania,	5,095	5,250	4,069	2,796	1,132	35	18,377	5,054	6,142	4,476	2,742	1,105	34	19,553
Delaware,	2,627	2,259	1,303	1,180	503	10	7,882	2,524	2,359	1,446	1,102	526	16	7,973
Maryland,	8,309	6,099	4,020	4,142	2,287	49	24,906	7,912	7,313	5,389	4,535	2,796	87	28,032
District of Columbia,	895	649	464	405	229	3	2,645	863	1,033	682	564	358	7	3,507
Virginia,	8,236	6,126	3,546	2,721	1,731	27	22,387	8,002	7,031	4,501	3,379	2,024	24	24,961
North Carolina,	3,438	2,955	1,400	1,062	685	21	9,561	3,287	3,118	1,649	1,179	720	29	9,982
South Carolina,	1,314	958	622	424	335	19	3,672	1,378	1,175	746	545	399	6	4,249
Georgia,	368	353	224	186	118	12	1,261	347	330	231	185	126	6	1,225
Alabama,	275	202	187	124	56	....	844	245	209	131	84	56	3	728
Mississippi,	81	82	59	43	22	1	288	72	51	45	49	14	....	231
Louisiana,	2,503	2,296	1,208	828	384	11	7,230	2,640	2,727	1,927	1,402	755	29	9,480
Tennessee,	842	583	361	321	216	7	2,330	772	616	359	285	187	6	2,225
Kentucky,	764	584	410	484	402	8	2,652	633	505	351	398	369	9	2,265
Ohio,	1,562	1,440	808	646	325	8	4,789	1,573	1,551	799	611	241	4	4,779
Indiana,	617	544	307	240	138	11	1,857	594	573	279	215	107	4	1,772
Illinois,	277	251	136	119	40	1	824	305	225	125	106	50	2	813
Missouri,	87	76	43	57	18	3	284	77	62	46	63	34	3	285
Michigan,	31	43	48	29	8	....	159	20	36	26	16	4	....	102
Arkansas,	27	17	23	17	3	1	88	17	13	10	7	6	....	53
Florida,	138	109	46	56	33	1	383	144	136	70	62	48	1	461
TOTAL	48,675	43,079	27,650	22,271	11,509	269	153,453	47 ,329	48,138	32,541	24,327	13,425	386	166,146

TABLE IV.—SHOWING THE NUMBER OF SLAVES IN THE UNITED STATES, ON THE 1ST OF JUNE, 1830.

STATES AND TERRITORIES.	MALES.							FEMALES.						
	Under 10.	10 to 24.	24 to 36.	36 to 55.	55 to 100.	100 and up'ds.	Total.	Under 10.	10 to 24.	24 to 36.	36 to 55.	55 to 100.	100 and up'ds.	Total.
Maine,	....	....	....	....	....	....	....	....	....	1	....	1	....	2
New Hampshire,	....	....	....	....	....	....	....	....	....	2	1	....	....	3
Vermont,	....	....	....	....	....	....	....	....	....	....	....	....	....	....
Massachusetts,	....	....	....	....	....	....	....	....	....	....	....	....	1	1
Rhode Island,	....	2	....	....	1	....	3	....	4	1	1	8	....	14
Connecticut,	1	2	....	1	4	....	8	1	3	....	4	9	....	17
New York,	5	6	....	1	....	1	13	23	12	17	3	6	1	62
New Jersey,	5	12	395	383	261	3	1,059	8	20	424	451	288	4	1,195
Pennsylvania,	23	102	25	11	10	1	172	32	106	22	25	42	4	231
Delaware,	580	853	245	83	42	3	1,806	508	617	230	80	49	2	1,486
Maryland,	17,880	17,759	8,846	6,135	2,772	50	53,442	17,002	16,236	8,331	5,329	2,601	53	49,552
District of Columbia,	794	1,024	542	375	114	3	2,852	816	1,270	612	391	176	2	3,267
Virginia,	84,000	68,917	43,189	30,683	12,155	133	239,077	83,207	66,921	40,927	27,206	12,275	144	230,680
North Carolina,	45,991	38,099	20,212	14,030	5,848	133	124,313	44,847	37,508	20,095	13,088	5,636	114	121,288
South Carolina,	51,820	44,600	29,710	21,674	7,567	98	155,469	51,524	45,517	32,689	22,006	8,112	84	159,932
Georgia,	38,367	34,253	19,440	12,818	3,847	92	108,817	38,102	33,917	20,527	12,325	3,765	78	108,714
Alabama,	21,837	19,553	11,100	5,158	1,495	27	59,170	21,386	19,669	11,088	4,898	1,312	26	58,379
Mississippi,	11,037	10,793	6,947	3,455	845	22	33,099	10,860	10,841	6,983	3,173	682	21	32,560
Louisiana,	13,627	17,926	15,784	8,443	2,089	42	57,911	13,687	16,613	13,534	6,249	1,552	42	51,677
Tennessee,	27,713	23,431	11,260	6,020	1,729	63	70,217	26,568	24,145	12,223	6,519	1,891	41	71,387
Kentucky,	31,500	27,449	13,520	7,499	2,280	61	82,309	30,975	27,346	13,854	8,107	2,572	50	82,904
Ohio,	....	1	....	....	....	....	1	....	2	3	....	....	....	5
Indiana,	....	....	....	....	....	....	....	....	2	....	1	....	....	3
Illinois,	98	118	76	47	6	2	347	144	128	61	52	12	3	400
Missouri,	4,872	4,364	2,058	923	208	14	12,439	4,611	4,605	2,199	1,014	219	4	12,652
Michigan,	2	7	11	1	1	....	22	1	3	3	3	....	....	10
Arkansas,	845	814	395	192	47	....	2,293	803	836	399	193	51	1	2,283
Florida,	2,501	2,482	1,830	948	224	....	7,985	2,560	2,449	1,561	768	177	1	7,516
	353,498	312,567	185,585	118,800	41,545	748	1,012,823	347,662	308,770	185,786	111,887	41,436	676	996,220

TABLE V.—SHOWING THE AGGREGATE NUMBER OF WHITES, FREE COLORED PERSONS, AND SLAVES,

OF EACH SEX, IN THE SEVERAL STATES, ON THE 1st OF JUNE, 1830.

STATES AND TERRITORIES.	WHITES.			FREE COLORED.			SLAVES.			GRAND TOTAL.
	Males.	*Females.*	*Total.*	*Males.*	*Females.*	*Total.*	*Males.*	*Females.*	*Total.*	
Maine,	200,689	197,574	398,263	610	580	1,190	....	2	2	399,455
New Hampshire,	131,184	137,537	268,721	275	329	604	....	3	3	269,328
Vermont,	139,996	139,775	279,771	426	455	881	....	....	....	280,652
Massachusetts,	294,685	308,674	603,359	3,358	3,690	7,048	....	....	....	610,408
Rhode Island,	45,383	45,288	93,621	1,548	2,013	3,561	3	14	17	97,199
Connecticut,	143,047	146,556	289,603	3,850	4,197	8,047	8	17	25	297,675
New York,	951,441	916,620	*1,873,663	21,466	23,404	44,870	13	62	75	1,918,608
New Jersey,	152,529	147,737	300,266	9,501	8,802	18,303	1,059	1,195	2,254	320,823
Pennsylvania,	665,812	644,088	1,309,900	18,377	19,553	37,930	172	231	403	1,348,233
Delaware,	28,845	28,756	57,601	7,882	7,973	15,855	1,806	1,486	3,292	76,748
Maryland,	147,340	143,768	291,108	24,906	28,032	52,938	53,442	49,552	102,994	447,040
D. of Columbia,	13,647	13,916	27,563	2,645	3,507	6,152	2,852	3,267	6,119	39,834
Virginia,	347,887	346,413	694,300	22,387	24,961	47,348	239,077	230,680	469,757	1,211,405
North Carolina,	235,954	236,889	472,843	9,561	9,982	19,543	124,313	121,288	245,601	737,987
South Carolina,	130,590	127,273	257,863	3,672	4,249	7,921	155,469	159,932	315,401	581,185
Georgia,	153,288	143,518	296,806	1,261	1,225	2,486	108,817	108,714	217,531	516,823
Alabama,	100,846	89,560	190,406	844	728	1,572	59,170	58,379	117,549	309,527
Mississippi,	38,456	31,977	70,443	288	231	519	33,099	32,560	65,659	136,621
Louisiana,	49,715	39,516	†89,441	7,230	9,480	16,710	57,911	51,677	109,588	215,739
Tennessee,	275,066	260,680	535,746	2,330	2,225	4,555	70,216	71,387	141,603	681,904
Kentucky,	267,123	250,664	517,787	2,652	2,265	4,917	82,309	82,904	165,213	687,917
Ohio,	479,713	448,616	928,329	4,789	4,779	9,568	1	5	6	937,903
Indiana,	175,885	163,514	339,399	1,857	1,772	3,629	....	3	3	343,031
Illinois,	82,048	73,013	155,061	824	813	1,637	347	400	747	157,445
Missouri,	61,405	53,390	114,795	284	285	569	12,439	12,652	25,091	140,455
Michigan,	18,168	13,178	31,346	159	102	261	22	10	32	31,639
Arkansas,	14,195	11,476	25,671	88	53	141	2,293	2,283	4,576	30,388
Florida,	10,236	8,149	18,385	383	461	844	7,985	7,516	15,011	34,730
TOTAL,	5,355,133	5,171,115	10,537,378	153,453	166,146	319,599	1,012,823	996,220	2,009,043	‡12,866,020

* This number comprehends 5,602 omitted in the marshal's return of the details.
† This number comprehends 210 omitted in the marshal's return of the details.
‡ This number comprehends the omissions in New York and Louisiana, and 5,318 persons on board the public ships.

The increase shown by this census, that is, for a period of nine years and ten months, is as follows:

The whole population, . . .	33.26 per cent.
Whites, ...	33.85 "
Free coloured, ...	34.17 "
Slaves, ...	30.15 "
The whole coloured, ...	30.7 "

If we add the increase for the two months required to make up the complete term of ten years, which is very nearly equal to the half of 1 per cent, the last decennial increase will thus compare with the preceding, viz:

	1830.	1820.
The whole population,	33.92 per cent.	33.35 per cent.
Whites, . .	34.52 "	34.3 "
Free coloured, .	34.85 "	27.75 "
Slaves, . .	30.75 "	29.57 "
The whole coloured, .	31.31 "	29.33 "

This comparative view shows that the rate of increase was somewhat greater in the last ten years than in the ten preceding, instead of being less, as would appear by the enumeration actually taken. The gain from a greater and more uninterrupted immigration, from 1820 to 1830, is more than equal to the additional increase here shown.

The increase of the three classes had been so nearly equal, that their relative proportions are nearly the same as in 1820. Thus:

In 1820,		In 1830,
The whites were	81.55 per cent.	81.90 per ct.
The free coloured,	2.46 "	2.48 "
The slaves,	15.99 "	15.62 "

Showing a small gain of the white population on the coloured, and of the free coloured on the slaves.

The males and females, in the three classes, were in the following proportions, viz:

In the white population the males exceed the females, as 100 to 96.56.
Free coloured " the females exceed the males, as 107.64 to100.
Slave " the males exceed the females, as 100 to 98.37.

The proportion between the sexes continued nearly the same as under the preceding census, with both descriptions of the free population; but with the slaves, the proportion of females was greater than under the preceding census by more than 3 per cent. This relative change in their numbers might have been caused by a greater mortality among the males; by an extraordinary number of runaways to foreign countries, who are chiefly males; or lastly, by a greater proportion of males of those who had been emancipated. As there seems to be no reason to suppose that more males than females were emancipated, the two first causes must be relied on to explain the difference in question; and neither of them is inconsistent with well-known facts. The instances of escape to Canada have greatly increased within the last twenty years; and of the slaves who are transported to the south, there is a greater proportion of males, and their lives are probably abridged by change of climate and habits.

The proportions of the males and females, at different ages, to the whole number of each sex in the several classes,* are as follows:

1st. *Of the whites,*

Males.				*Females.*	
Those under 5	years of age,	18.17	per cent.	17.83	per cent.
5 and under 10	"	14.60	"	14.52	"
10 and under 15	"	12.51	"	12.35	"
15 and under 20	"	10.70	"	11.53	"
20 and under 30	"	17.86	"	17.76	"
30 and under 40	"	11.09	"	10.74	"
40 and under 50	"	6.86	"	6.89	"
50 and under 60	"	4.28	"	4.32	"
60 and under 70	"	2.52	"	2.54	"
70 and under 80	"	1.08	"	1.13	"
80 and under 90	"	.29	"	.34	"
90 and under 100	"	.04	"	.05	"
		100.		100.	

2d. *Of the free coloured persons,*

Those under 10	"	31.72	per cent.	28.49	per cent.
10 and under 24	"	28.07	"	28.97	"
24 and under 36	"	18.02	"	19.59	"
36 and under 55	"	14.51	"	14.64	"

* It will be perceived that this comparative view differs from that given under the census of 1820. Here the number of males and females, at the different periods of life, are compared with the whole number *of the same sex*, in the respective classes; but there the same were compared with the whole number *of both sexes*. In that, the per centage of both sexes is found by adding the separate per centage of each; here, the same result is obtained by taking the medium per centage of both.

		Males.		*Females.*	
55 and under 100	years of age,	7.50	per cent.	8.08	per cent.
100 and upwards	"	.18	"	.23	"
		100.	"	100.	"
3d. *Of the slaves,*					
Those under 10	"	34.90	"	34.90	"
10 and under 24	"	30.86	"	30.99	"
24 and under 36	"	18.32	"	18.65	"
36 and under 55	"	11.74	"	11.23	"
55 and under 100	"	4.10	"	4.16	"
100 and upwards	"	.07	"	.07	"
		100.		100.	

The preceding tables show that, of the whole population, the number under ten years of age is exactly one third; but the slaves of the same age exceed that proportion, and both descriptions of the free population fall short of it.

If we compare the number of white children under 10, with the number of females between 16 and 45, whether of the same or the preceding census, we find the ratio continually diminishing. Thus:

1st. When compared with the females of the same census,

The children were to the females, in	1800,	as 183.1	to 100.
" " "	1810,	as 182.3	to 100.
" " "	1820,	as 173.0	to 100.

2d. When compared with the females of the succeeding census,

The children were to the females, in	1810,	as 248.	to 100.
" " "	1820,	as 237.4	to 100.
" " "	1830,	as 225.8	to 100.

For which diminution of ratio no satisfactory explanation can be given but a gradual decline in the rate of natural increase; of which fact we shall hereafter find satisfactory evidence.

The relative numbers of the three classes, in the slaveholding States, were thus distributed in 1830, viz:

States and Territories.	Whole population.	Whites.	Free coloured.	Slaves.	Percentage of		
					Whites.	F. col'd.	Slaves.
Delaware,	76,748	57,601	15,855	3,292	75.1	20.6	3.3
Maryland,	447,040	291,108	52,938	102,994	65.1	11.8	23.1
District of Columbia,	39,834	27,563	6,152	6,119	69.2	15.4	15.3
Virginia,	1,211,405	694,300	47,348	469,757	57.4	3.8	38.8
North Carolina,	737,987	472,843	19,543	245,601	64.1	1.6	33.3
South Carolina,	581,185	257,863	7,921	315,401	44.4	1.3	54.3
Georgia,	516,823	296,806	2,486	217,531	57.4	1.5	42.1
Alabama,	309,527	190,406	1,572	117,549	61.5	.5	38.
Mississippi,	136,621	70,443	519	65,659	51.5	.4	48.1
Louisiana,	215,739	89,441	16,710	109,588	41.5	7.7	50.8
Tennessee,	681,904	535,746	4,555	141,603	78.5	.7	20.8
Arkansas,	30,388	25,671	141	4,576	84.5	.5	15.
Kentucky,	687,917	517,787	4,917	165,213	75.3	1.3	23.5
Missouri,	140,455	114,795	569	25,091	81.7	.4	17.9
Florida,	34,730	18,385	844	15,501	53.1	2.3	44.6
Total,	5,848,303	3,660,758	182,070	2,005,475	62.60	3.11	34.29

By the preceding table both classes of the coloured population had gained a little on the whites in these States.

The numbers gained by the acquisition of Florida are included in the fifth enumeration, and the several estimates relative to it; but as its population at the time of its purchase (in 1821) probably did not exceed 10,000 persons, or the tenth of one per cent on the whole population, its disturbing influence has been disregarded in the preceding views.

CHAPTER VI.

THE CENSUS OF 1840, BEING THE SIXTH DECENNIAL ENUMERATION UNDER THE CONSTITUTION.

The population was distributed under the same heads by this census as by that of 1830. This, however, also exhibits copious details of every branch of productive industry in the United States, by which we are furnished with authentic data for estimating the revenue and wealth of the Union, and the several States. They will be used for this purpose after the subject of population is disposed of.

The decennial increase since the census of 1830, was

Of the whole population . .	32.67	per cent.
Of the whites	34.66	"
Of the free coloured . . .	20.88	"
Of the slaves	23.81	"
Of the whole coloured . . .	23.4	"

The distribution of the different classes under this census, compared with that of 1830, was as follows:

	1840.		1830.	
The whites amounted to	83.16	per cent. . .	81.90	per cent.
The free coloured . .	2.26	" . . .	2.48	"
The slaves	14.58	" . . .	15.62	"
	100.		100.	

The result of the census of 1840, as to population, may be seen in the five following tables, viz:

1.—*Number of Free White Males, of Different Ages, in each State and Territory of the United States, in* 1840.

STATES AND TERRITORIES.	FREE WHITE MALES.												
	Under 5.	5 *and under* 10.	10 *and under* 15.	15 *and under* 20.	20 *and under* 30.	30 *and under* 40.	40 *and under* 50.	50 *and under* 60.	60 *and under* 70.	70 *and und.* 80	80 *and und.* 90	90 & *under* 100.	100 & *up'ds.*	TOTAL.
Maine,..........	40,532	35,671	31,691	27,740	42,266	29,864	19,948	12,551	7,408	4,152	1,041	120	5	252,989
New Hamsphire,	18,435	17,300	16,929	15,663	22,170	16,781	12,915	8,690	5,485	3,447	1,084	103	2	139,004
Massachusetts,...	47,313	40,296	37,971	37,069	76,285	52,283	30,161	19,270	11,432	6,473	1,914	1[illegible]5	17	360,679
Rhode Island,...	7,121	5,947	5,969	5,659	9,878	6,798	4,452	2,799	1,570	862	287	20	.....	51,362
Connecticut,......	19,021	17,420	17,270	16,718	26,097	19,056	13,355	9,121	5,727	3,381	1,034	92	8	148,300
Vermont,.........	21,786	19,069	17,551	16,999	23,006	17,596	12,817	7,982	5,454	3,137	884	84	13	146,378
New York,......	187,730	158,107	139,752	130,094	230,981	158,194	97,542	54,975	30,869	14,694	3,984	379	56	1,207,357
New Jersey,.....	28,827	23,809	21,951	19,308	31,052	21,553	13,949	8,526	4,887	2,459	660	67	7	177,055
Pennsylvania,....	149,480	117,351	101,522	89,825	152,624	99,421	64,366	37,933	20,268	9,224	2,453	240	63	844,770
Delaware,........	4,939	3,957	3,581	3,104	5,722	3,549	2,117	1,270	682	268	61	5	4	29,259
Maryland,........	26,921	20,573	18,351	16,218	30,028	20,732	12,626	7,258	3,899	1,533	417	64	16	158,636
Virginia,..........	69,308	53,485	45,822	38,263	63,465	41,141	27,465	16,670	9,673	4,458	1,241	196	26	371,223
North Carolina,..	46,413	37,011	31,473	24,819	38,756	24,254	16,799	10,432	6,365	2,830	741	125	29	240,047
South Carolina,.	24,828	19,360	16,621	13,719	22,489	13,774	9,132	5,615	3,059	1,418	409	50	22	130,496
Georgia,..........	43,759	33,899	27,136	20,897	34,696	22,196	13,886	7,623	4,240	1,641	455	87	19	210,534
Alabama,.........	36,611	28,215	22,819	16,222	31,455	19,340	11,783	6,024	2,886	997	273	47	20	176,692
Mississippi,......	19,542	14,164	11,475	8,662	20,084	11,995	6,001	3,289	1,430	466	130	14	4	97,256
Louisiana,........	13,835	10,736	7,848	7,218	20,795	16,304	7,940	3,309	1,206	410	102	26	18	89,747
Tennessee,.......	67,182	53,821	44,489	34,218	51,112	31,323	19,369	12,755	7,140	3,039	855	109	22	325,434
Kentucky,........	59,290	46,242	39,190	32,611	53,265	32,206	19,958	11,809	6,639	3,092	860	130	31	305,323
Ohio,..............	144,582	115,832	96,697	81,431	138,755	85,944	54,992	30,298	18,182	6,778	1,617	200	52	775,360
Indiana,...........	70,468	57,457	46,129	36,599	60,002	37,565	21,678	13,789	6,195	2,258	551	68	14	352,773
Illinois,...........	48,363	37,278	31,062	24,876	52,580	31,428	15,809	8,755	3,660	1,119	257	35	13	255,235
Missouri,.........	34,597	26,054	21,222	16,784	33,772	20,568	11,384	5,620	2,439	814	183	28	5	173,470
Arkansas,.........	8,607	6,331	5,077	3,863	8,532	5,129	2,751	1,194	523	162	35	4	3	42,211
Michigan,.........	19,484	16,054	12,839	10,887	22,759	16,025	8,276	4,442	1,903	623	88	12	3	113,395
Florida,...........	2,455	1,947	1,520	1,305	4,388	2,801	1,193	530	220	73	20	3	1	16,456
Wiskonsin,.......	2,627	1,793	1,303	1,344	6,328	3,348	1,191	554	201	55	10	2	1	18,757
Iowa,..............	4,380	3,138	2,475	2,179	6,207	3,310	1,512	698	272	73	12	.....	.....	24,256
D. of Columbia,..	2,354	1,755	1,764	1,728	2,891	1,953	1,201	724	312	115	21	2	2	14,822
TOTAL,......	1,270,790	1,024,072	879,499	756,022	1,322,440	866,431	536,568	314,505	174,226	80,051	21,679	2,507	476	7,249,266

2.—*Number of Free White Females, of Different Ages, in each State and Territory of the United States, in 1840.*

STATES AND TERRITORIES.	FREE WHITE FEMALES.													
	Under 5.	5 and under 10.	10 and under 15.	15 and under 20.	20 and under 30.	30 and under 40.	40 and under 50.	50 and under 60.	60 and under 70.	70 and und. 80	80 and und. 90	90 & under 100.	100 & up'ds.	TOTAL.
Maine,	38,185	34,458	30,044	27,940	42,165	29,046	20,024	12,304	7,703	4,122	1,274	174	10	247,449
New Hamsphire,	17,959	16,693	15,689	15,457	24,679	18,269	14,183	9,824	6,702	4,000	1,388	181	8	145,032
Massachusetts,	45,313	40,115	36,832	40,360	74,250	49,324	33,109	22,684	14,645	8,387	2,955	375	2	368,351
Rhode Island,	6,504	5,812	5,710	6,030	10,833	7,138	4,891	3,430	2,176	1,196	444	59	2	54,225
Connecticut,	18,253	16,889	15,964	16,478	27,120	20,110	14,863	10,792	7,220	4,274	1,436	153	4	153,556
Vermont,	20,379	18,877	16,677	15,744	24,225	18,163	12,807	8,612	5,423	2,875	951	100	7	144,840
New York,	180,769	154,525	134,977	137,414	227,137	143,882	90,163	53,496	30,190	14,281	4,152	522	25	1,171,533
New Jersey,	27,505	23,161	20,362	19,701	31,514	20,530	14,009	8,841	5,253	2,769	803	82	3	174,533
Pennsylvania,	141,786	115,570	97,972	96,692	153,803	92,864	60,838	37,965	21,007	9,783	2,725	316	24	831,345
Delaware,	4,751	3,859	3,404	3,337	5,707	3,469	2,173	1,341	837	320	92	9	3	29,302
Maryland,	25,680	19,978	17,560	18,349	31,021	19,343	12,477	7,859	4,376	1,801	534	95	8	159,081
Virginia,	65,286	52,264	43,996	42,475	65,797	40,082	26,928	16,865	9,986	4,468	1,256	202	40	369,745
North Carolina,	43,637	35,221	29,646	26,965	43,132	25,906	18,114	11,374	6,754	2,943	962	150	19	244,823
South Carolina,	23,639	18,741	15,822	14,691	22,392	13,471	9,145	5,551	3,168	1,443	430	74	21	128,588
Georgia,	40,579	32,080	25,993	22,395	31,705	19,603	12,300	6,795	3,679	1,485	443	79	25	197,161
Alabama,	33,917	26,804	21,786	17,911	25,574	15,152	9,184	4,647	2,407	847	205	45	14	158,493
Mississippi,	18,235	13,328	10,919	8,911	14,464	7,847	4,284	2,250	1,075	381	96	22	6	81,818
Louisiana,	13,718	10,395	7,760	7,947	13,602	7,907	4,099	1,967	891	323	81	19	1	68,710
Tennessee,	62,684	51,013	42,327	35,965	51,907	30.597	19,198	11,535	6,465	2,617	732	126	27	315,193
Kentucky,	55,419	44,022	37,298	33,207	47,970	28,608	18,050	10,907	6,029	2,525	735	137	23	284,930
Ohio,	137,725	110,949	91,294	84,872	127,730	75,799	48,588	28,037	14,636	5,592	1,345	173	22	726,762
Indiana,	66,397	53,805	42,890	36,904	55,176	32,708	19,967	10,759	5,035	1,780	436	59	9	325,925
Illinois,	44,775	34,913	28,496	24,078	38,823	22,676	12,712	6,514	2,941	866	184	39	2	217,019
Missouri,	32,600	24,321	19,679	16,952	26,330	14,889	8,580	4,259	2,019	634	131	21	3	150,418
Arkansas,	8,108	5,853	4,869	3,911	5,881	3,317	1,715	805	357	113	30	3	1	34,963
Michigan,	18,401	15,089	11,798	10,819	18,706	11,864	6,109	3,394	1,441	451	80	11	2	98,165
Florida,	2,241	1,761	1,448	1,322	2,220	1,219	704	354	156	49	10	2	1	11,487
Wiskonsin,	2,528	1,692	1,289	1,200	2,713	1,423	612	360	128	37	7	2	1	11,992
Iowa,	4,082	2,962	2,188	2,064	3,789	1,865	979	494	187	51	6	....	1	18,668
D. of Columbia,	2,294	1,771	1,899	2,077	3,030	2,026	1,338	795	413	149	41	1	1	15,835
TOTAL,	1,203,349	986,921	836,588	792,168	1,253,395	779,097	502,143	304,810	173,299	80,562	23,964	3,231	315	6,939,842

3.—*Number of Free Colored Persons, Male and Female, in each State and Territory of the United States, in 1840.*

STATES AND TERRITORIES.	FREE COLORED MALES.							FREE COLORED FEMALES.						
	Under 10.	10 *and under* 24.	24 *and under* 36.	36 *and under* 55.	55 & *under* 100.	100 & *up'ds.*	TOTAL.	*Under* 10.	10 *and under* 24.	24 *and under* 36.	36 *and under* 55.	55 & *under* 100.	100 & *up'ds.*	TOTAL.
Maine,	149	231	135	137	67	1	720	147	195	128	109	54	2	635
New Hampshire,	57	68	42	48	33	......	248	50	66	54	61	56	2	289
Massachusetts,	908	1,119	1,444	871	306	6	4,654	899	1,058	868	771	417	2	4,014
Rhode Island,	355	388	319	242	109	......	1,413	318	489	425	360	232	1	1,825
Connecticut,	935	1,165	710	746	331	4	3,891	967	1,238	860	715	433	1	4,214
Vermont,	91	99	74	60	38	2	364	76	106	65	76	43	......	366
New York,	6,008	6,370	5,711	4,221	1,476	23	23,809	6,032	6,951	6,809	4,454	1,928	44	26,218
New Jersey,	3,019	3,429	1,978	1,639	711	4	10,780	2,834	3,106	2,079	1,485	748	12	10,264
Pennsylvania,	6,245	6,192	5,182	3,697	1,400	36	22,752	6,264	7,426	6,071	3,806	1,505	30	25,102
Delaware,	2,740	2,679	1,392	1,163	645	7	8,626	2,618	2,457	1,415	1,127	662	14	8,293
Maryland,	9,460	7,727	4,772	4,670	2,494	50	29,173	9,134	8,626	6,686	5,423	2,902	76	32,847
Virginia,	7,958	7,165	3,898	3,135	1,652	20	20,094	7,899	7,616	4,871	3,556	2,046	36	26,024
North Carolina,	3,962	3,593	1,665	1,255	734	18	11,227	3,704	3,475	2,043	1,454	801	28	11,505
South Carolina,	1,403	1,105	677	405	262	12	3,864	1,392	1,272	858	545	338	7	4,412
Georgia,	427	375	232	195	137	8	1,374	375	381	229	192	178	24	1,379
Alabama,	301	296	170	152	107	4	1,030	271	313	188	124	104	9	1,009
Mississippi,	228	168	125	114	76	4	718	181	151	133	122	59	5	651
Louisiana,	4,015	3,207	2,014	1,581	683	26	11,526	4,163	3,679	2,971	2,164	986	13	13,976
Tennessee,	973	772	372	379	294	6	2,796	881	742	445	367	285	8	2,728
Kentucky,	1,048	786	534	754	629	10	3,761	936	800	536	680	593	11	3,556
Ohio,	2,560	2,688	1,719	1,175	579	19	8,740	2,630	2,784	1,640	1,053	487	8	8,602
Indiana,	1,258	1,119	620	497	229	8	3,731	1,112	1,100	592	413	215	2	3,434
Illinois,	548	568	377	265	117	1	1,876	536	570	311	201	102	2	1,722
Missouri,	193	195	266	154	74	1	883	152	159	152	133	89	6	691
Arkansas,	77	56	62	34	16	3	248	67	60	35	32	21	2	217
Michigan,	93	103	119	62	16	......	393	80	98	76	46	13	1	314
Florida,	108	125	87	49	29	......	398	108	123	78	75	35	......	419
Wiskonsin,	16	32	28	19	6	......	101	21	27	20	12	4	......	84
Iowa,	20	31	22	14	6	......	93	14	39	8	16	2	......	79
Dist. of Columbia,	1,168	948	562	525	237	13	3,453	1,208	1,455	1,027	813	390	15	4,908
TOTAL,	56,323	52,799	35,308	28,258	13,493	286	186,467	55,069	56,562	41,673	30,385	15,728	361	199,778

4.—*Number of Colored Male and Female Slaves in each State and Territory of the United States, in* 1840.

STATES AND TERRITORIES.	MALE SLAVES.							FEMALE SLAVES.						
	Under 10.	10 *and under* 24.	24 *and under* 36.	36 *and under* 55.	55 *and und.* 100.	100 & *up'ds.*	TOTAL.	*Under* 10.	10 *and under* 24.	24 *and under* 36.	36 *and under* 55.	55 *and und.* 100.	100 & *up'ds.*	TOTAL.
Maine,														
N. Hampshire,									1					1
Massachus'tts,														
Rhode Island,					1		1				1	3		4
Connecticut,				5	3		8				1	8		9
Vermont,														
New York,								1	2			1		4
New Jersey,	1	1	7	137	157		303		4	7	168	190	2	371
Pennsylvania,	12	20			3		35	8	8		1	11	1	29
Delaware,	442	676	170	53	30		1,371	375	551	194	76	37	1	1,234
Maryland,	14,996	15,440	7,725	5,218	2,522	58	45,959	14,551	14,383	7,537	4,732	2,297	36	43,536
Virginia,	76,847	68,751	40,194	30,380	12,398	91	228,861	75,703	65,814	38,372	27,781	12,636	120	220,326
N. Carolina,	44,854	38,419	19,636	14,053	6,512	72	123,546	44,190	37,910	20,292	13,374	6,421	84	122,271
S. Carolina,	52,642	46,137	30,373	20,751	8,650	125	158,678	54,527	48,251	34,589	22,403	8,506	84	168,360
Georgia,	48,933	43,630	24,953	16,319	5,374	126	139,335	48,445	44,348	27,557	16,265	4,922	72	141,609
Alabama,	43,767	41,293	25,812	12,802	3,626	60	127,360	43,663	40,818	26,491	12,023	3,130	47	126,172
Mississippi,	31,736	31,564	22,008	10,120	2,537	38	98,003	31,972	32,358	21,670	9,019	2,162	27	97,208
Louisiana,	22,703	23,572	24,717	12,699	2,769	69	86,529	23,158	24,804	22,373	9,441	2,114	33	81,923
Tennessee,	34,115	30,883	15,068	8,665	2,717	29	91,477	33,705	30,356	15,635	9,021	2,832	33	91,582
Kentucky,	32,531	31,627	15,095	9,054	2,657	40	91,004	32,713	30,818	15,058	9,645	2,998	22	91,254
Ohio,			1	1			2		1					1
Indiana,				1			1		2					2
Illinois,	53	63	30	15	6	1	168	53	59	20	24	7		163
Missouri,	10,873	10,718	4,269	2,329	536	17	28,742	10,479	10,926	4,887	2,558	644	4	29,498
Arkansas,	3,450	3,514	2,069	890	182	14	10,119	3,302	3,558	1,930	849	174	3	9,816
Michigan,														
Florida,	4,044	4,070	2,907	1,496	512	9	13,038	3,992	4,120	2,673	1,446	440	8	12,679
Wiskonsin,	1	3					4	2	1	1	2	1		7
Iowa,	1	3	1	1			6	1	5	3	1			10
Dis. of Colum.	598	747	338	275	96	4	2,058	630	977	498	370	158	3	2,636
TOTAL,	422,599	391,131	235,373	145,264	51,288	753	1,246,408	421,470	390,075	239,787	139,201	49,692	580	1,240,805

TABLE V.—SHOWING THE AGGREGATE NUMBER OF WHITES, FREE COLORED PERSONS, AND SLAVES, OF EACH SEX, IN THE SEVERAL STATES ON THE 1ST OF JUNE, 1840.

STATES AND TERRITORIES.	WHITES.			FREE COLORED.			SLAVES.			GRAND TOTAL.
	Males.	*Females.*	*Total.*	*Males.*	*Females.*	*Total*	*Males.*	*Females.*	*Total.*	
Maine,..................	252,989	247,449	500,438	720	635	1,355	....	....	....	501,793
New Hampshire,......	139,004	145,032	284,036	248	289	537	....	1	1	284,574
Vermont,...............	146,378	144,840	291,218	364	366	730	....	....	....	291,948
Massachusetts,.........	360,679	368,351	729,030	4,654	4,014	8,668	....	....	....	737,699
Rhode Island,.........	51,362	54,225	105,587	1,413	1,825	3,238	1	4	5	108,830
Connecticut,...........	148,300	153,556	301,856	3,891	4,214	8,105	8	9	17	309,978
New York,.............	1,207,357	1,171,533	2,378,890	23,809	26,218	50,027	....	4	4	2,428,921
New Jersey,...........	177,055	174,533	351,588	10,780	10,264	21,044	303	371	674	373,306
Pennsylvania,.........	844,770	831,345	1,676,115	22,752	25,102	47,854	35	29	64	1,724,033
Delaware,..............	25,259	29,302	58,559	8,626	8,293	16,919	1,371	1,234	2,605	78,085
Maryland,..............	158,804	159,400	318,204	29,187	32,891	62,078	46,068	43,669	89,737	470,019
District of Columbia,.	14,822	15,835	30,657	3,453	4,908	8,361	2,058	2,636	4,694	43,712
Virginia,................	371,223	369,745	740,968	20,094	26,024	49,842	228,861	220,326	448,987	1,239,797
North Carolina,.......	240,047	244,823	484,870	11,227	11,505	22,732	123,546	122,271	245,817	753,419
South Carolina,.......	130,496	128,588	259,084	3,864	4,412	8,276	158,678	168,360	327,038	594,398
Georgia,................	210,534	197,161	407,695	1,374	1,379	2,753	139,335	141,609	280,944	691,392
Florida,.................	16,456	11,487	27,943	398	419	817	13,038	12,679	25,717	54,477
Alabama,...............	176,692	158,493	335,185	1,030	1,009	2,039	127,360	126,172	253,532	590,756
Mississippi,............	97,256	81,818	179,074	718	651	1,369	98,003	97,208	195,211	375,654
Louisiana,..............	89,747	68,710	158,457	11,526	13,976	25,502	86,529	81,923	168,452	352,411
Arkansas,..............	42,211	34,363	76,574	248	217	465	10,119	9,816	19,935	97,574
Tennessee,.............	325,434	315,193	640,627	2,796	2,728	5,524	91,477	91,582	183,059	829,210
Kentucky,..............	305,323	284,930	590,253	3,761	3,556	7,317	91,004	91,254	182,258	779,828
Missouri,...............	173,470	150,418	323,888	883	691	1,574	28,742	29,498	58,240	383,702
Ohio,.....................	775,360	726,762	1,502,122	8,740	8,602	17,342	2	1	3	1,519,467
Indiana,.................	352,773	325,925	678,698	3,731	3,434	7,165	1	2	3	685,866
Illinois,..................	255,235	217,019	472,254	1,876	1,722	3,598	168	163	331	476,183
Michigan,..............	113,395	98,165	211,560	393	314	707	....	....	....	212,267
Wisconsin,............	18,757	11,992	30,749	101	84	185	4	7	11	43,112
Iowa,.....................	24,256	18,668	42,924	93	79	172	6	10	16	30,945
TOTAL......	7,249,266	6,939,842	14,189,555	192,550	199,821	386,348	1,240,408	1,240,805	2,487,355	*17,063,353

* Add Seamen in United States service 6,100—grand total, 17,069,453.

If we compare the increase of numbers shown by this census with that shown by the census of 1830, by adding to the last the proportional increase for two months, we find that the ratio of increase had diminished in the last ten years from 33.92 to 32.67= 1.25 per cent. But as the ratio of increase in the largest class (the whites) had, at the same time, experienced an increase, (equal to 0.14 per cent,) the diminution was proportionally enhanced in the two smaller classes, constituting the coloured part of the population. Thus the increase of the free coloured persons had fallen off from 34.85 to 20.88, or 13.97 per cent, and the slaves from 30.75 to 23.81, or 6.94 per cent.

These differences are so great, compared with any before experienced, as to cast a shade of suspicion over the accuracy of the last enumeration, if they were not capable of explanation.

First, As to the greater rate of increase of the whites. This class has experienced a small advance in its decennial increase since 1820, as, by the census of that year, it was 34.30 per cent, by the fifth census 34.52 per cent, and by the sixth 34.66 per cent. The progressive increase of ratio thus shown is to be ascribed to the known increase of immigration, which, as will be subsequently shown, has augmented at a rate beyond our indigenous multiplication, and which would have manifested itself much more sensibly in the two last enumerations, if there had not been a decline of the natural increase in the old settled States, and if the settlement of Texas had not furnished, for the first time, an instance of emigration of whites from the United States. We have no data for estimating the number of whites who have thus emigrated, but they probably have not been short of 50,000 since 1830, and may have reached to double that number; that is, the loss from this source may be from one half to one per cent of the white population in 1830.

Secondly, The smaller rate of increase of the coloured population. This race has also lost by emigration. Slaves have been carried to Texas; some have escaped to the British dominions on this continent; and many free negroes are known to have migrated thither. This class has probably also received fewer accessions than formerly by emancipation. The zeal of abolitionists, by a natural reaction, has had the effect not only of making the holders of slaves less disposed to liberate them, but has also influenced the policy of some of the State legislatures, and created new difficulties in the way of manumission. These circumstances have had the greater comparative effect, because before the last ten years, and since 1810, the coloured race had received no accessions from abroad, and had sustained little loss from emigration.

We have no means of estimating these separate influences, but we learn how great must have been their united effect when we find that if the increase of the free coloured class had been as great in the last ten years as in the ten preceding, their numbers would have been 44,650 more than it was at the late census; and that if the increase of the slaves had also continued the same, their number would have been 128,000 more than it seems to be at present. A diminution in the rate of decennial increase of the coloured race so considerable as to be equivalent to 172,000 persons, may seem to some yet greater than can be reasonably ascribed to the conjoint effects of emigrations to Texas and to British America, and to the extraordinary mortality which was experienced by the slaves transported to the southwestern States during a part of the last decennial term; in which case, there seems to be no alternative but to question the accuracy of this part of the census.

The proportions between the sexes, in the several classes, were as follows:

In the white population, the males exceed the females as 100 to 95.73.

In the free coloured population, the females exceed the males as 107.14 to 100.

In the slave population, the males exceed the females as 100 to 99.55.

The proportion of white males was greater than it was in 1830, but that of the coloured males was less. The first difference was probably produced by the increased immigration of the whites, and the last by the greater emigration of the coloured race—a greater proportion of those who migrate being commonly males.

The males and females of each class were thus distributed, according to age, viz:

1st. *Of the white population,*

	Males.	*Females.*
Those under 5	17.53 per cent.	17.34 per cent.
5 and under 10	14.13 "	14.22 "
10 and under 15	12.13 "	12.06 "
15 and under 20	10.43 "	11.41 "
20 and under 30	18.24 "	18.06 "
30 and under 40	11.95 "	11.23 "

	Males.		*Females.*	
40 and under 50	7.40	per cent. . . .	7.23	per cent.
50 and under 60	4.34	"	4.39	"
60 and under 70	2.40	"	2.50	"
70 and under 80	1.11	"	1.16	"
80 and under 90	.30	"	.35	"
90 and under 100	.04	"	.05	"
	100.		100.	

2d. *Of the free coloured class,*

Those under 10	30.21	per cent. . . .	27.57	per cent.
10 and under 24	28.32	"	28.31	"
24 and under 36	18.93	"	20.86	"
36 and under 55	15.16	"	15.21	"
55 and under 100	7.23	"	7.87	"
100 and upwards	.15	"	.18	"
	100.		100.	

3d. *Of the slaves,*

Those under 10	33.91	per cent. . .	33.97	per cent.
10 and under 24	31.39	" . . .	31.44	"
24 and under 36	18.89	" . . .	19.32	"
36 and under 55	11.65	" . . .	11.22	"
55 and under 100	4.11	" . . .	4.	"
100 and upwards	.06	" . . .	.05	"
	100.		100.	

The above proportions do not materially vary from those of the preceding census. The chief difference is, that in all the classes the proportion of those under ten years of age was less in 1840 than in 1830, as may be thus seen, viz:

The number of

whites	under 10	was, in 1830,	32.53	p. cent—1840,	31.63	p. cent.
free col'd	" 10	" "	30.11	" "	28.88	"
slaves,	" 10	" "	34.09	" "	33.93	"

Table showing the Population in the slaveholding States, and how it was distributed among the three classes on the 1st of June, 1840.

States and Territories.	Whole population.	Whites.	Free coloured.	Slaves.	Percentage of		
					Whites.	F. col'd.	Slaves.
Delaware,	78,085	58,561	16,919	2,605	74.9	21.7	3.4
Maryland,	470,019	318,204	62,078	89,737	67.7	13.2	19.1
District of Columbia,	43,712	30,657	8,361	4,694	70.1	10.7	19.1
Virginia,	1,239,797	740,968	49,842	448,987	59.8	4.	36.2
North Carolina,	753,419	484,870	22,732	245,817	64.4	3.	32.6
South Carolina,	594,398	259,084	8,276	327,038	43.6	1.4	55.
Georgia,	691,392	407,695	2,753	280,944	59.	.4	40.6
Florida,	54,477	27,943	817	25,717	51.3	1.5	47.2
Alabama,	590,756	335,185	2,039	253,532	56.7	.3	42.9
Mississippi,	375,654	179,074	1,369	195,211	47.6	.4	52.
Louisiana,	352,411	158,457	25,502	168,452	44.9	7.2	47.8
Arkansas,	97,574	77,174	465	19,935	78.5	1.1	20.4
Tennessee,	829,210	640,627	5,524	183,059	77.2	.7	22.1
Kentucky,	779,828	590,253	7,317	182,258	75.7	.9	23.4
Missouri,	383,702	323,888	1,574	58,240	84.4	.4	15.2
Total,	7,334,434	4,632,640	215,568	2,486,226	63.41	2.92	33.67

It appears from the preceding table, that the whites, in the slaveholding States, have in the last ten years gained on both classes of the coloured population; but that in Mississippi, as well as South Carolina and Louisiana, the number of slaves exceeds that of the white population.

CHAPTER VII.

THE AGGREGATE INCREASE OF THE POPULATION IN FIFTY YEARS, AND OF THE DIFFERENT RACES WHICH COMPOSE IT.

Having exhibited in succession the six enumerations which have been taken of the population of the United States, and noticed the more striking and important facts to be inferred from each, it will now be our purpose to examine them in the aggregate, together with such general results as may be deduced from them.

We therefore propose to take a comparative view of the progress of population during the half century that has elapsed since the first census was taken, in the several States and Territories, in the larger geographical divisions, and in the different races and classes;

To investigate the subject of the proportion between the sexes, and inquire into the causes of the diversities among different classes, and of the variations in the same class;

To compare the sexes and the different races as to longevity, and the maladies of deafness and blindness;

To inquire into the natural increase, in the United States generally, in the old and the new States, and of the different races; the past and future increase, and the future progress of population;

To inquire into the future progress of domestic slavery, and some of its remote effects;

To notice the distribution of political power so far as it depends upon numbers; of that of the population into town and country, also among the different classes of industry;

And lastly, we shall estimate the annual income of the several States, and of the Union, from all sources, and compare the increase of wealth with that of the population.

By the following table we may compare

The Population of each State and Territory, as exhibited by six enumerations in fifty years, with its Decennial Rate of Increase during the same period.

	POPULATION.						DECENNIAL INCREASE.				
	1790.	1800.	1810.	1820.	1830.	1840.	1800.	1810.	1820.	1830.	1840.
Maine, .	96,540	151,719	228,705	298,335	399,455	501,793	57.1	50.7	30.4	33.9	26.2
N. Ham.	141,899	183,762	214,360	244,161	269,328	284,574	57.1	50.7	30.4	33.9	25.6
Verm., .	85,416	154,465	217,713	235,764	280,652	291,948	80.8	41.	8.2	19.	4.
Mass., ..	378,717	423,245	472,040	523,287	610,408	737,699	11.7	11.5	10.9	16.6	20.8
R. Isl'd,	69,110	69,122	77,031	83,059	97,199	108,830	0.	11.4	7.8	17.	11.9
Conn., ...	238,141	251,002	262,042	275,202	297,675	309,978	5.4	4.3	5.	8.1	4.1
	1,009,823	1,233,315	1,471,891	1,659,808	1,954,717	2,234,822	21.1	19.3	12.8	17.7	14.3
N. York	340,120	586,756	959,049	1,372,812	1,918,608	2,428,921	72.5	63.4	43.1	39.7	26.6
N. Jer., .	184,139	211,949	245,555	277,575	320,823	373,306	15.1	15.9	13.	15.5	16.3
Penn., ..	434,373	602,365	810,091	1,049,458	1,348,233	1,724,033	38.6	34.4	29.5	28.5	27.9
Delaw'e	59,096	64,273	72,674	72,749	76,748	78,085	8.7	13.	0.1	5.5	1.7
Maryl'd	319,728	341,548	380.546	407,350	447,040	470,019	6.8	11.4	7.	9.7	5.1
D. of C.,	....	14,093	24,023	33,039	39,834	43,712	......	36.8	28.9	29.2	23.3
	1,337,456	1,820,984	2,491,938	3,212,983	4,151,286	5,118,076	36.3	10.7	9.3	13.7	2.3
Virgin'a	748,308	880,200	974,622	1,065,379	1,211,405	1,239,797	17.6	10.7	9.3	13.7	2.3
N. Car.,	393,751	478,103	555,500	638,829	737,987	753,419	21.3	16.2	15.	15.5	2.1
S. Car., .	249,073	345,591	415,115	502,741	581,185	594,398	38.7	20.1	18.1	15.6	2.3
Georgia,	82,548	162,110	252,433	340,987	516,823	691,392	96.4	55.1	35.1	51.2	33.8
Florida,	....	....	....	....	34,730	54,477	......	......	......	......	56.8
	1,473,680	1,865,995	2,197,670	2,547,936	3,082,130	3,333,483	26.6	17.8	15.9	21.	8.2
Alab'a, .	....	....	....	144,317	309,527	590,756	......	......	......	142.	90.8
Missis., .	....	8,850	40,352	75,448	136,621	375,651	......	356.	87.	81.	175.
Louisi'a	....	....	76,556	153,407	215,739	352,411	......	......	100.4	40.6	63.3
Arkan., .	....	....	....	14,273	30,388	97,574	......	......	......	112.9	221.1
Tennes.	35,791	105,602	261,727	422,813	681,904	829,210	200.	147.8	61.5	61.3	21.6
	35,791	114,452	378,635	810,258	1,374,179	2,245,602	219.8	230.8	114.	69.6	63.4
Miss'uri	....	....	20,845	66,586	140,455	383,702	......	......	219.5	110.9	173.2
Kent'y, .	73,077	220,955	406,511	564,317	687,917	779,828	200.	83.1	38.8	21.9	13.3
Ohio, ...	....	45,365	230,760	581,434	937,903	1,519,467	......	408.7	152.	61.3	62.
Indiana,	....	4,875	24,520	147,178	343,031	685,866	......	403.	500.2	133.	99.9
Illinois, .	....	....	12,282	55,211	157,445	476,183	......	......	349.5	185.2	202.4
Mich., ..	....	....	4,762	8,896	31,639	212,267	......	......	86.8	255.6	570.9
Wiscon.	....	....	....	....	....	30,945	......	......	......	......	......
Iowa, ..	....	....	....	....	....	43,112	......	......	......	......	......
	73,077	271,195	699,680	1,423,622	2,298,390	4,131,370	271.1	158.	103.5	61.4	79.7
	3,929,827	5,305,925	7,239,814	9,654,596	12,866,020	17,069,453	35.01	36.45	33.35	33.26	32.67

As the States and Territories naturally arrange themselves into five divisions, which are separated not only by their geographical position, but also, with few exceptions, in their modes of industry and commercial interest, it is thought proper to compare the progress of population in these divisions, as may be seeen in the following table:

Divisions.	Increased population from August 1, 1790, in				
	10 years.	20 years.	30 years.	40 years.*	50 years.*
1. The New England States,.........	122.4	145.8	164.4	193.6	221.3
2. The Middle States, with Dist. of Columbia,....................	136.2	186.3	240.2	310.4	382.7
3. The Southern States, with the Territory of Florida,..........	126.6	149.1	172.9	209.1	226.1
4. The Southwestern States,.........	319.8	1,058.	2,264.	3,839.	6,174.
5. The Northwestern States, with the Territories of Wisconsin and Iowa,........................	371.6	857.5	1,948.	3,145.	5,654.
Total of the United States,........	135.	184.2	245.3	327.4	434.5

* It will be recollected that by the change of the day of taking the census from the 1st of August to the 1st of June, the periods referred to in the two last columns want two months of the terms mentioned.

The very great disparity exhibited by the preceding table between the rate of increase in the three first divisions, which comprise the thirteen original States, and that of the two western divisions, is to be referred almost entirely to migration, the Atlantic States losing yet more than they gain by emigrants, whilst the Western States gain largely and steadily both from foreign and domestic emigration. There is, moreover, a small difference in their natural increase, as we shall see in a subsequent part of this memoir.

The distribution of the population into the three classes of whites, free persons of colour, and slaves, at each census, with the decennial increase of each class, are presented in the following table:

Classes	1790.	1800.	1810.	1820.	1830.	1840.	Decennial increase per cent in				
							1800.	1810.	1820.	1830.	1840.
Whites,.	3,172,464	4,304,489	5,862,004	7,872,711	10,537,373	14,189,555	35.7	36.2	34.3	33.8	34.7
Free col.	59,466	108,395	186,446	238,197	319,599	386,348	32.3	72.2	27.7	34.2	20.9
Slaves,..	697,897	893,041	1,191,364	1,543,688	2,099,043	2,487,355	27.9	83.4	29.6	30.1	23.8
Tot. free,	2,231,930	4,412,884	6,048,450	8,110,908	10,866,972	14,575,903	36.4	37.	34.1	33.7	34.1
Tot. col.,	757,363	1,001,436	1,377,810	1,781,885	2,328,642	2,873,703	32.2	37.6	29.3	30.6	23.4

The total increase of the three classes in fifty years, has been,

of whites, as 100 to 447.3
" " " of free coloured, . 649.7
" " " of slaves, ... 356.4
" " " of the whole coloured, 379.4

The relative proportions of the three classes, at each census, is as follows:

	1790.	1800.	1810.	1820.	1830.	1840.
Whites, ...	80.7	81.1	81.	81.5	81.9	83.1
Free coloured,................	1.5	2.1	2.1	2.5	2.5	2.3
Slaves, ...	17.8	16.4	16.4	16.	15.6	14.6

It appears from the preceding comparison, that in half a century the whites have gained, and the coloured persons have lost 2.4 per cent of the whole population; and that the free persons have gained, and the slaves have lost 3.2 per cent.

CHAPTER VIII.

THE PROPORTION BETWEEN THE SEXES.

It seems to be a general law of the human species, that the number of males born exceeds that of females in a small proportion; and a disparity continues through the subsequent periods of life, until we reach that stage when the greater casualties, to which males are exposed, have counterbalanced the original excess. Is this an ultimate fact which we must refer to a final cause, or is its proximate cause the greater strength and vigour of the male sex, by reason of which fewer of that sex are still-born, or perish by abortion, or other casualties before birth?

The numbers of the two sexes, and the proportion between them, as exhibited by each census, were as follows:

	1790.		1800.		1810.		1820.		1830.		1840.	
WHITES, Males,....	1,615,625	*As* 100. *to*	2,204,421	*As* 100. *to*	2,987,571	*As* 100. *to*	4,001,064	*As* 100. *to*	5,355,133	*As* 100. *to*	7,249,266	*As* 100. *to*
Females, .	1,556,839	96.3	2,100,068	95.3	2,874,433	96.2	3,871,647	96.8	5,171,115	96.6	6,940,161	95.7
FREE COL. Males,....	....						112,734		153,453		186,467	
Females, .	No discrimination of the sexes in the coloured population at these enumerations.						125,463	111.3	166,146	108.3	199,778	107.1
SLAVES, Males,....	....						788,028		1,012,323		1,246,517	
Females, .	....						755,660	95.9	996,220	98.4	1,240,938	99.5

It appears, by the preceding table, that, while both in the white and the slave population, the males always exceed the females, commonly between three and four per cent in the free coloured portion, the females exceed the males from seven to eleven per cent. This diversity is to be ascribed principally to the roving habits of the men of this class, many of whom take to a seafaring life, and some travel and even settle abroad. Perhaps, too, there are in some of the States a greater proportion of females emancipated. The census furnishes us with no data for verifying this conjecture, as the excess of females is by far the greatest at that period of life when either cause would be most operative; that is, between the ages of ten and thirty-six. By the fifth census, the males of this class between ten and twenty-four, were 43,079, and females 47,329; and of those between twenty-four and thirty-six, the males were 27,650, and the females 32,541. In like manner, by the sixth census, the males between ten and twenty-four were 52,805, and the females 56,592; and between twenty-four and thirty-six, the males were 35,321, and the females 41,682; so that of the whole excess of females by the fifth census, amounting to 12,693, nearly three-fourths (9,141) were between the ages of ten and thirty-six; and of the excess by the sixth census, 13,341 more than three-fourths (10,148) were between the same ages. Nor can any argument against the supposed greater emancipation of females be drawn from the fact, that there is no correspondent deficiency of female slaves between the ages of ten and thirty-six, since such emancipation may be counterbalanced, and more than counterbalanced, by the runaway slaves, who are mostly males.

It will be also perceived, that there was, both in 1830 and 1840, a greater preponderance of males on the part of the whites than of the slaves, owing partly to the excess of males of the white emigrants from Europe, and partly to the diminution of male slaves by running away.

Of the whites, the excess of males was the greatest in 1800; being to the females as 100 to 95.3. This was probably owing to the great number of French emigrants who thronged to the United States about the close of the last century. A similar flow of emigrants from Europe, between 1830 and 1840, has caused the like excess of white males, which is shown by the last census.

To free the comparison between the sexes from the influence of immigration as far as practicable, let us take the males and females under ten years of age. Their numbers were first taken in 1800:

By the second census the white males were to females as 100 to	93.6
By the third census " " " " "	94.8
By the fourth census " " " " "	95.2
By the fifth census " " " " "	95.3
By the sixth census " " " " "	95.4

By this, it appears that there has been a steady increase in the proportion of females during the last forty years. But the greater disproportion between the sexes, which is shown by the two first enumerations, than that which appears in the three last, seems to require explanation. Perhaps it is to be found in the interruption given to navigation from 1806 to 1815, by which the number of boys formerly going to sea, or on board fishing-vessels and coasters being diminished, augmented the proportion of males.

Let us now compare the proportion of males to females in the different races, which we can do only under the two last enumerations:

	In 1830.	*In* 1840.
The white males under ten were to the females as 100 to	95.3	95.4
The free coloured males " " "	97.2	97.4
The slaves " " " " "	98.4	99.7

For the greater excess of males at this early age, in the white population, than in the coloured race, I am able to assign no reason, unless it be that there is a disproportion of boys, as well as men, among the European emigrants, or that slave boys, near the age of ten, being put to work out of doors, are more exposed than girls to accidents and diseases, whereby their original excess is more diminished than with the whites.

But why is it that the proportional excess of males in all the classes has been progressively diminishing? If we suppose that the excess of boys over girls, among the emigrants from Europe, is gradually decreasing in its relative influence, that would apply only to the whites, and leaves the difficulty as to the coloured race unsolved. The only solution that occurs to me, as applicable to both races is, that those occupations by which the lives and health of boys are more exposed than are those of girls, have been slightly but gradually increasing; and it may be remarked, that the excess of males under ten is less, in the New England States, which are most maritime, than in the southern and western States, which are least so.

It deserves notice, that in the slave population, although the females between fourteen and twenty-six, in the fourth census, approach to or exceed the males, yet after twenty-four, the preponderance of the males is restored. In the fifth census, too, of the slaves between twenty-four and thirty-six, the females slightly exceed the males, but both with all those at both the earlier and later periods of life, the males exceed the females; from which it would appear, that the diversity in their respective employments, which takes place in the vigour of manhood, abridges life with males more than with females; but that in subsequent periods, the chance of life is in favour of the male sex. According to the sixth census, the two sexes approach to equality in the slaves between ten and twenty-four, but at all other ages the males exceed the females.

CHAPTER IX.

THE PROBABILITIES OF LIFE.—THE DEAF AND DUMB, THE BLIND, AND THE INSANE.

ON these interesting topics our information is far more meagre than could be wished, but it has been gradually enlarging since 1790. The census of that year, indeed, afforded none, except the single fact of the number of white males above and below sixteen. The enumerations of 1800 and 1810 gave the numbers both of white males and females at five periods of life; but, like the first, made no discrimination of the sex or age of the coloured race. That of 1820 gave the numbers both of the free coloured and slaves, of both sexes, at four periods of life; and those of 1830 and 1840 have extended the discriminations of the whites to thirteen periods, and those of the coloured race to six periods. The two last have also numbered the deaf and dumb at three periods of life, and the blind of both races; but the census of 1840 has added the number of insane, and has confined the discriminations of the deaf and dumb, according to age, to the whites.

The following tables show, as far as materials thus scanty and irregular permit, the comparative probabilities of life, between the sexes of each race, at different ages, saving the slight disturbances from migration, by which the white males gain, and the coloured males lose:

I.—*The proportion of white Males and Females at different ages, according to the enumerations of* 1800, 1810, *and* 1820.

AGES.	1800.		1810.		1820.		1800.	1810.	1820.
	Males, p. cent.	Females p. cent.	Males, p. cent.	Females p. cent.	Males, p. cent.	Females p. cent.	Proportion of Males to Females as 100 to		
1. Whites under 10,	34.66	34.37	34.64	34.14	33.67	33.12	94.9	94.8	95.3
2. 10 and under 16,	16.01	15.34	15.67	15.60	15.33	15.65	94.3	95.8	98.9
3. 16 " 26,	17.84	19.03	18.33	19.55	19.43	20.21	102.1	102.6	100.7
4. 26 " 45,	19.58	19.51	19.15	18.93	19.18	19.05	95.5	95.1	96.1
5. 45 and upwards,	11.91	11.75	12.21	11.78	12.39	11.97	94.5	92.8	93.5
	100.	100.	100.	100.	100.	100.			

II.—*The proportion of white Males and Females, of different ages, according to the enumerations of* 1830 *and* 1840.

Ages.	1830.		1840.		1830.	1840.
	Males, per cent.	Females, per cent.	Males, per cent.	Females, per cent.	Proportion of Males to Females as 100 to	
1. Whites under 5,....	18.17	17.83	17.53	17.34	94.7	94.7
2. 5 and under 10,....	14.60	14.53	14.13	14.22	96.	96.4
3. 10 " 15,....	12.51	12.35	12.13	12.06	95.4	95.1
4. 15 " 20,....	10.70	11.53	10.43	11.41	104.	104.8
5. 20 " 30,....	17.86	17.76	18.24	18.06	96.	94.8
6. 30 " 40,....	11.09	10.74	11.95	11.23	93.7	89.8
7. 40 " 50,....	6.86	6.89	7.40	7.23	96.8	93.6
8. 50 " 60,....	4.28	4.32	4.34	4.39	97.5	96.9
9. 60 " 70,....	2.52	2.54	2.40	2.50	97.2	99.5
10. 70 " 80,....	1.08	1.13	1.11	1.16	109.5	100.1
11. 80 " 90,....	.29	.34	.30	.35	110.3	110.
12. 90 " 100,....	.04	.05	.04	.05	112.2	128.9
13. 100 and upwards,....	......	......	......	......	79.1	66.2
	100.	100.	100.	100.		

Whilst, of the children born alive, the males commonly exceed the females by about the twentieth part, the preceding tables show that the mortality of the males somewhat exceeds that of females in the middle periods of life, so as to more than counterbalance the original preponderance. This is owing, no doubt, to the greater casualties to which the male sex is exposed, and, probably, somewhat more to their frequent use of spirituous liquors in excess.

At the two last periods of life in the three first enumerations, viz, from twenty-six to forty five, the males gain upon the females until they pass beyond their original excess. This is the effect, not of a greater mortality of the females, but of a greater accession of males by immigration, as will more clearly appear by the fuller details of the two last enumerations.

According to these, the males gain upon the females from the age of twenty to forty, after which the proportion of females gradually increases until the period from seventy to eighty, when it preponderates, and the excess still increases until the age of one hundred, after which the number of males is greatest. In these enumerations, it will be seen that the proportion of males was smaller in the first class, (those under five,) than at any of the twelve succeeding periods, except the class between thirty and forty in the fifth census, that between thirty and fifty in the sixth census, and the class over one hundred in both. Now, as most of those who have migrated to this country within ten years preceding a census would be above thirty at the time it was taken, and a majority are also known to be males, this partial and small increase in the proportion of males may be attributed, in part, to immigration, and in part, perhaps, to the greater mortality of women at this period of life. But to whatever cause we ascribe it, the census conclusively shows in the subsequent periods a diminished mortality of females, with the single exception of the small number who live above a century.

From this exception, conflicting as it does with the excess and increasing excess of females shown in the periods of life immediately preceding, we are not warranted in deducing any general rule on the comparative probabilities of life between the sexes, unless we knew the circumstances, or, at least, the place of birth, of these rare instances of longevity; for if the greater part, or even a considerable part of them were of foreign birth, and from countries of greater average salubrity than the United States, that fact, from the known disproportion of male immigrants, would tend to increase the proportion of males in the advanced stages of life; and whilst such increase would not be manifested in classes that consisted of thousands, (as do all those under 100,) it might have so much effect in the few hundreds above that age as to produce the excess of males that we see, and thus explain the seeming anomaly.

In comparing the chances of longevity in this country with those of other countries, we must take into account our more rapid increase of numbers. Thus, to ascertain what proportion of our population attain the age of 100, we must compare the number of those who have attained it, not with the present population, but with that which existed 100 years since; and this, at a moderate estimate of the intermediate increase, was less than one-sixteenth of our present numbers; whereas, in most densely peopled countries, the increase, in the same period, may not have been from one-eighth to one-fourth as great.* To make, then, the comparison fairly, we must multiply the number of persons in this country of the age supposed in the same proportion. In like manner, to compute the chances of here attaining the age of fifty, we must compare the number who have now reached that age with the population at the first census, when it was less than one-fourth of its present amount.

As the census has, since 1830, made quinquennial classes of the

* In England, the population in 1730 was 5,687,993, and in 1831 was 14,174,204, less than 2½ times as great; and from 1700 to 1800 the numbers had not even doubled. In every other part of Europe, except Russia, the increase is yet more slow.

whites of both sexes under twenty, and decennial for all above that age and under 100, it had afforded the means of estimating, with great accuracy, the probability of life of each sex at different periods by comparing the numbers of the several classes in the preceding census, with those of the classes ten years older in the succeeding census, if it were not for the interference of two causes, whose quantities we have no means of precisely ascertaining. These are, the diminution of males from boyhood to middle age, by roaming and going to sea, and the increase of both males and females, but in unequal quantities, by immigration; of which disturbing influences the census affords us the most satisfactory evidence. Thus, the class of females between fifteen and twenty, in the census of 1840, which corresponds to the class between five and ten, in the census of 1830, instead of exhibiting a decrease, by reason of the deaths in the intervening period of ten years, shows an increase of 41,427, equivalent to 5½ per cent; which effect must necessarily have been produced by accessions from abroad, supposing the ages of the females to be accurately noted.* Thus, too, whilst the females of this class show an increase of 5½ per cent, a similar comparison of the males between five and ten, in 1830, with those between fifteen and twenty, in 1840, exhibits a decrease of 3⅓ per cent; which seems to indicate that, although immigration has considerably swelled their numbers in ten years, it has done so to a less extent than with females, principally by the number of boys who have gone abroad, and in some degree by the greater mortality of males, which is manifested by the general tenor of the census.

It is proper to add that the same sources of error which have been mentioned, must affect any estimates that can be made of the probabilities of life in the United States, and that, therefore, the tables that have been given must be regarded as only approximating to the truth.

Let us now advert to the coloured race in reference to this subject.

The following tables compare the decrease of life between the

---

* As it seems scarcely credible that the number, at any period of life, should have gained by immigration in any given time equal to the loss sustained in the same time by death, it is rational to suppose that some error has crept into this part of the census. Can it be that many of this class of females, who work from home, are counted twice? or must we suppose that many, who have passed twenty, have reduced their age within more desirable limits?

free and slave portions of the coloured population, and between the males and females of each, according to the three last enumerations, when the discriminations were first made:

I.—*The proportion of coloured Males and Females, according to the census of* 1820.

AGES.	FREE COLOURED.		SLAVES.		FREE COL.	SLAVES.
	Males, per cent.	Females, per cent.	Males, per cent.	Females, per cent.	Proportion of Males to Females as 100 to	
Under..........14,..........	42.27	38.	43.63	43.24	96.3	94.3
14 and under 26,..........	21.30	23.89	25.77	26.98	120.1	99.6
26 " 45,..........	20.80	22.50	20.78	20.36	115.9	95.4
45 and upwards,..........	15.63	15.61	9.82	9.42	107.1	91.3
	100.	100.	100.	100.	107.2	95.1

II.—*The proportion of coloured Males and Females, according to the census of* 1830.

AGES.	FREE COLOURED.		SLAVES.		FREE COL.	SLAVES.
	Males, per cent.	Females, per cent.	Males, per cent.	Females, per cent.	Proportion of Males to Females as 100 to	
Under..........10,..........	31.72	28.49	34.90	34.90	97.4	98.3
10 and under 24,..........	28.07	28.97	30.86	30.99	111.7	98.8
24 " 36,..........	18.02	19.59	18.32	18.65	117.7	100.1
36 " 55,..........	14.51	14.64	11.74	11.23	109.3	94.1
55 " 100,..........	•7.50	8.08	4.10	4.16	115.6	99.7
100 and upwards,..........	.18	.23	.07	.07	143.5	90.4
	100.	100.	100.	100.	108.3	98.4

III.—*The proportion of coloured Males and Females, according to the census of* 1840.

AGES.	FREE COLOURED.		SLAVES.		FREE COL.	SLAVES.
	Males, per cent.	Females, per cent.	Males, per cent.	Females, per cent.	Proportion of Males to Females as 100 to	
Under..........10,..........	30.20	27.57	33.91	33.97	97.8	99.7
10 and under 24,..........	28.32	28.31	31.38	31.44	107.2	99.7
24 " 36,..........	18.93	20.86	18.88	19.32	118.	101.9
36 " 55,..........	15.16	15.21	11.66	11.22	107.5	95.8
55 " 100,..........	7.24	7.87	4.11	4.	116.5	96.9
100 and upwards,..........	.15	.18	.06	.05	126.2	77.
	100.	100.	100.	100.	107.2	99.3

These tables seem to indicate a much greater mortality among the males than the females of the free coloured population; as though, in the class under the age of puberty, the males exceed the females about 2 or 3 per cent, yet, in all the subsequent periods of life, the females have the preponderance, and after the age of fifty-five the disproportion greatly increases. Part of this excess, indeed, is to be ascribed to the roving habits of the males; yet, as this cause operates chiefly with the young and middle aged, the increasing excess of females after fifty-five can be attributed only to their greater longevity.

The period between thirty-six and fifty-five, in the two last enumerations, presents an exception to the supposed greater mortality, as the excess of females, which, between the ages of twenty-four and thirty-six, had been as much as eighteen per cent, had, in the period from thirty-six to fifty-five, declined from eight to ten per cent.

This single instance of a decrease in the proportion of females might be caused either, 1st. by a greater number of males emancipated than of females between thirty-six and fifty-five; 2d. by the return of a part of those males who had gone abroad before the age of thirty-six; or, lastly, by a greater mortality of females at this period of life. There seems to be no ground for presuming the existence of the first cause; but the census, both in 1830 and 1840, affords some evidence of both the others. Thus, if the free coloured males between thirty-six and fifty-five be compared with those between twenty-four and thirty-six, the former will be found to be only twenty per cent less; whereas, if the male slaves at the same periods of life be compared, the diminution is from thirty-five to forty per cent. This difference between the two portions of the coloured race, so greatly exceeding any supposable difference of mortality, must be referred to a return of a part of the free coloured who had roamed abroad. We are also warranted in attributing a part of the difference to the greater mortality of women about this period of life, because we perceive the same falling off in the proportion of females between the ages of thirty-six and fifty-five in the class of slaves, in which none of the males who leave the country ever return to it; and because, also, we have some evidence of a falling off in the proportion of white females about the same time of life.

In the slave portion of the coloured population, there seems to be but little difference in the chances of life between the sexes. From the age of ten to twenty-four, the males retain the small excess of from one to two per cent, which they had under ten years of age; from twenty-four to thirty-six, the number of females slightly preponderates; from thirty-six to fifty-five, the males gain on the females; from fifty-five to one hundred, the females gain on the males; and after one hundred, the males regain, and exceed their original preponderance.

We are the more warranted in referring these alterations to general causes, as they are found in both the last enumerations. The gain of the females between the ages of twenty-four and thirty-six, may be referred to the greater casualties to which the male sex is exposed, and to the greater number of runaways of that sex. The loss of the females from thirty-six to fifty-five, is probably to be ascribed to that greater mortality of the sex which has been observed in the other classes at this period of life. The gain of the females from fifty-five to one hundred may be confidently attributed to their greater longevity, after they have passed the age of fifty; and if the excess of males above one hundred, which is shown by the census, may seem to contradict this supposition, the fact admits of a similar explanation to that given for the excess of white males of this extreme age. Most of the male slaves over one hundred may have been Africans by birth, and have thus had constitutions more favourable to long life than the average of the native slaves, much the largest part of whom live in the least healthy parts of the United States. This supposition derives some probability from the fact that in the free coloured class, which is known to consist almost entirely of natives, the females above one hundred exhibit a continuance of the same progressive excess which they had exhibited in the periods of life immediately preceding.

There is a manifest difference in mortality and longevity between the two portions of the coloured race, in favour of the free coloured class. By the census of 1820, of those under thirty-six, the proportional numbers of the two classes are nearly the same; but of those over that age, the free coloured are fifteen per cent of the whole number, while the slaves are but ten per cent. By the two last enumerations, the centesimal proportions of each class from twenty-four to thirty-six are nearly equal; but after thirty-six, the proportion of the free coloured increase in an augmented ratio.

A part of this excess is attributable to emancipation, which commonly takes place in middle life, whether it be effected by the favour of the master, or by the purchase of his freedom by the slave himself; but the change in the relative numbers of the two portions in after life, shows that those who are free are more long-lived than the slaves.

The causes of this difference may arise from several circumstances. Of the coloured population, a much larger proportion of the free than of the slaves is probably descended from the white, as well as the African race ; and it is possible that this mixed breed may possess some advantages of temperament, as they certainly do of appearance, which is favourable to longevity. Or it may be, that the small number who attain old age may have been better provided with the comforts of life, and have taken better care of their health than the slaves are able to do. Or lastly, since many of the free coloured consist of those who have been emancipated for their merits or services, or have purchased their freedom by the earnings of a long course of industry, sobriety, and frugality, it may happen that the excess of the long-lived is derived from this description of persons, who would, from the regularity and good conduct implied by their change of condition, be most likely to attain long life.

As the enumerations, both of 1830 and 1840, have adopted different discriminations of age for the whites and the coloured race between the ages of ten and one hundred, we cannot accurately compare the chances of life between the two races for the intermediate periods. But by the census of 1820, the discriminations of the coloured classes coincided with those of the whites in that census, as well as the two preceding enumerations, in two particulars, to wit: as to those who were between the ages of twenty-six and forty-five, and those who were above forty-five. Let us, then, compare the two races at these periods of life.

By the enumerations of 1800, 1810, and 1820, the white males between twenty-six and forty-five were 19.58, 19.15, and 19.18 per cent of the whole number, making an average of 19.30 per cent ; and the white females were 19.51, 18.93, and 19.05, making an average of 19.16 per cent.

By the census of 1820, the males of the free coloured class were 20.80 per cent, those of the slaves were 20.78, and both together, equal to 20.79 per cent of the whole coloured population ;* and the females of the free coloured were 22.50, those of the slaves, 20.36, and both together, equal to 20.40 per cent of the whole. At this period of life, then, the centesimal proportion of the whites of each sex was about one and a half per cent less than that of the coloured race.

---

* By uniting the two classes of the coloured race, the comparison is not disturbed by emancipation, by which the numbers of one class is increased and the other diminished, to the same absolute extent, indeed, but in very different proportions.

If those over forty-five be similarly compared, the centesimal proportion will be as follows:

1st. *Of the Males,*		Per cent.
Whites, in 1800, 1810, and 1820, 11.91, 12.21, 12.39,	average	12.17
Free coloured and slaves, in 1820	"	10.55
	Difference,	1.62
2nd. *Of the Females,*		
Whites, in 1800, 1810, and 1820, 11.75, 11.78, 11.97,	average	11.83
Free coloured and slaves, in 1820	"	10.30
	Difference,	1.53

This relative gain of the whites after forty-five may seem at first to indicate greater mortality in the coloured race in the later periods of life. But when it is recollected that the whites gain largely by those who migrate to this country, (sometimes, as we shall see, more than ten per cent,) and that the coloured race, on the contrary, lose somewhat by emigration, the influence of these two causes might be expected to make a greater difference than has been mentioned, if they were not counteracted by the greater tenacity of life of persons of the coloured race when they have passed middle age.

Such a comparison, between the two races at a later period of life, as we are able to make under the enumerations of 1830 and 1840, affords evidence of the same fact. Thus, by taking the proportional mean between the whites over fifty and those over sixty, we obtain the probable number over fifty-five, which we may then compare with the numbers of the coloured race of that age, according to actual enumeration. The number of white males over fifty-five, by computation, was, in 1830, 568 per cent of the whole number; and in 1840, 5.62 per cent. The number of white females in 1830, 5.84 per cent; and in 1840, 5.86 per cent. The comparison, therefore, between the whites and the coloured race past forty-five, will be as follows:

Males,		Per cent.
Whites, 5.68, 5.62 per cent. . . .	average, .	5.65
Free coloured and slaves, 5.72, 4.59 . .	" .	4.65
Difference,		1.

Females,		*Per cent.*
Whites, 5.84, 5.86 per cent. . . .	average, .	5.85
Free coloured and slaves, 4.81, 4.61 . .	" .	4.71
	Difference,	1.14

By which it appears, that the small proportionate excess of the whites over forty-five, was, at a period of life ten years later, diminished about one half of one per cent. We unfortunately have no means of comparing the two races at any intermediate period between fifty-five and one hundred, by which we should be able to see whether, as the influence of immigration declined, (but a very small number of European emigrants to this country being past middle age,) the proportion of the coloured race continued to increase. But a comparison of their respective numbers under fifty-five and upwards of one hundred, would lead us to expect that result. Thus:

In 1830,

The whites over 100 were,	males 301			
" " "	females 238			
		539,	equal to 1 in	19,529
" free coloured,*	males 269			
" " "	females 386			
		655,	" 1 in	487
" slaves, "	males 748			
" " "	females 676			
		1,424,	" 1 in	1,410

According to which, the chances of attaining this extraordinary longevity were more than thirteen times as great with the slaves, and forty times as great with the free coloured as the whites.

In 1840,

The whites over 100 were,	males 476			
" " "	females 315			
		791,	equal to 1 in	17,938
" free coloured, "	males 286			
" " "	females 361			
		647,	" 1 in	597
" slaves, "	males 753			
" " "	females 580			
		1,333,	" 1 in	1,866

* The free coloured and the slaves are here separated, as emancipation scarcely ever takes place at this advanced age.

Which shows a less, but still extraordinary disproportion in favour of the coloured race; the proportionate number of the slaves to that of the whites being more than as nine to one, and of the free coloured to the whites as thirty to one.

It is proper to remark, that the ages of the coloured part of the population are, for the most part, conjectural, their births being rarely recorded even in family registers; and consequently, that the uncertainty is greatest in the most advanced stages of life. There is, moreover, a very prevalent disposition among the slaves who are past middle age to over-state their ages, either by way of furnishing an excuse for a relaxation of labour, or of presenting stronger claims to kindness and charity.

On the other hand, the temperate mode of living, the steady but moderate labour to which most of the slaves are habituated; their freedom from cares about the future, and, as a consequence of these incidents to their condition, their comparative exemption from some of the maladies which greatly abridge life with the whites, as diseases of the stomach, of the liver, and the lungs, obviously tend to increase the proportion of those who attain extraordinary longevity. It has also been supposed by some that more than a fair quota of the superannuated few are native Africans, who would thus seem to have better constitutions than the average of their race born in the United States. And lastly, it is possible that an undue proportion of the long-lived may be of the mixed breed, and that such may be more tenacious of life than either the white or the negro race. Should this prove to be the fact, it may aid us, as has been already mentioned, in accounting for the greater longevity of the free coloured than of the slaves. It is only by a careful attention to the individual cases of longevity, that these questions in the statistics of life can be solved.

The following diagram presents to the eye the proportions in which the whites, free coloured persons, and slaves, are respectively distributed, according to age; and it would accurately show the mortality of each class save for emigration, by which the number of whites is increased and that of the coloured classes is diminished; and also for emancipation, by which one of these classes gains and the other loses. The horizontal lines indicate the number of persons living at and above the ages annexed to them; the outer curve marking the numbers of the free coloured, the middle line those of the whites, and the inner line those of the slaves:

The comparative decrease of life of the White, Free Coloured, and Slave population in the United States: the black horizontal lines showing the proportion of persons living at and above the ages respectively annexed. The outer curve marks the lines of the Free Colored, the middle, that of the Whites, and the inner, that of the Slaves.

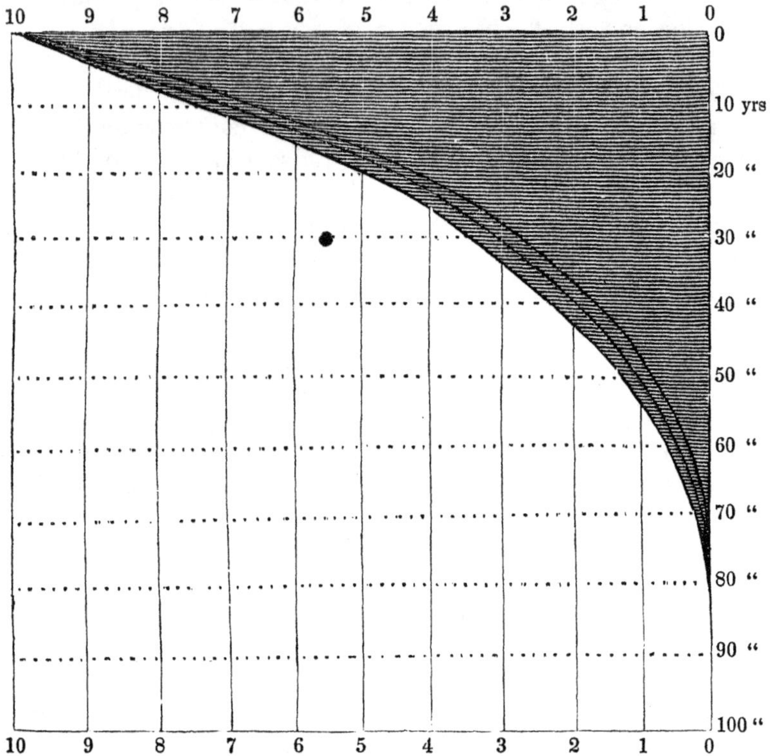

The diagram following shows the proportion of living males, at different ages, in England and Connecticut,* in conformity with the following comparison of the distribution of life in the two countries, as exhibited by the census of Great Britain, in 1821, and by that of the United States, in 1840. According to these, of every 10,000 males there are living

	In England.		*In Connecticut.*	
Under 10 years of age,		2,881		2,458
10 to 20	2,157		2,292	
20 to 30	1,990		1,760	
30 to 40	1,156		1,285	
	——	4,783	——	5,337

* This State is selected because it is one of the few which do not gain by immigration.

	In England.		*In Connecticut.*	
40 to 50 . .	940		900	
50 to 60 . .	666		615	
60 to 70 . .	448		386	
	——	2,054	——	1,901
70 to 80 . .	222		228	
80 to 90 . .	56		69	
90 to 100, &c. .	4		7	
	——	282	——	304
		10,000		10,000

The comparative decrease of life in England and Connecticut: the black lines show the proportion of 10,000 *persons living at and above the ages respectively annexed. Those of England are bounded by the inner curved line, and those of Connecticut by the outer.*

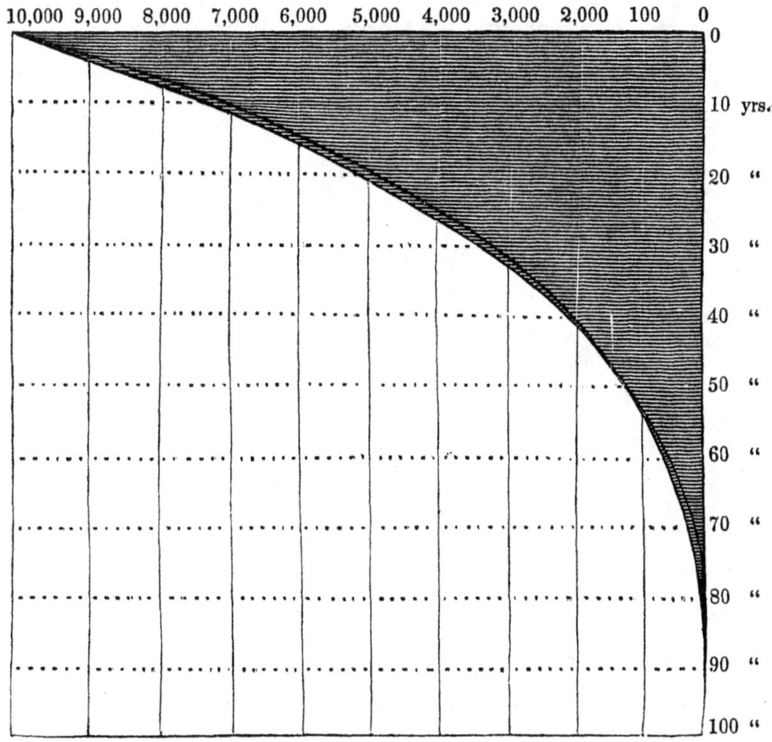

By which we perceive that under ten years of age, the number in England is greatest by about fourteen per cent; from ten to forty, the number in Connecticut exceeds about twelve per cent; from forty to seventy, the excess is again in favour of England by five per cent; and after seventy, Connecticut again exceeds by about seven per cent. It is not easy to say in what degrees these diversities, thus varying and alternating, are influenced by a difference of natural increase, of emigration, and of mortality in the two countries. It must be admitted that there are few parts of the United States which would compare as advantageously with England in the probabilities of life as Connecticut.

The number of Deaf, and Dumb, and Blind, in the white and coloured population of the United States, on the 1st of August, 1830.

States and Territories.	Whites.					Coloured Persons.				
	Deaf and Dumb.				Blind.	Deaf and Dumb.				Blind.
	Under 14.	14 to 25.	25 and upw'ds.	Total.		Under 14.	14 to 25.	25 and upw.	Total.	
Maine, ...	64	60	56	180	159	4	......	1	5	1
New Hampshire,.	32	55	48	135	105	5	1	3	9	....
Vermont,..........	39	59	55	153	51	3	......	2	5	....
Massachusetts, ...	56	62	138	256	218	2	3	4	9	5
Rhode Island,.....	6	22	28	56	56	2	2	......	4	8
Connecticut,.......	43	152	99	294	188	4	2	......	6	7
New York,........	277	310	255	842	642	17	14	12	43	82
New Jersey,.......	64	71	72	207	205	5	2	8	15	22
Pennsylvania,.....	222	279	255	758	475	12	12	15	39	28
Delaware,..........	6	15	14	35	18	......	5	4	9	11
Maryland,..........	50	31	54	135	147	40	30	26	96	124
Dist. of Columbia,.	4	5	3	12	11	1	2	3	6	16
Virginia, ...	132	118	169	419	356	51	41	38	130	438
North Carolina,....	70	81	79	230	223	31	27	25	83	161
South Carolina,....	60	52	62	174	102	9	27	33	69	136
Georgia,............	50	51	44	145	150	26	21	12	59	123
Florida,............	2	......	3	5	3	1	2	3	6	16
Alabama, ...	45	25	19	89	68	9	7	7	23	48
Mississippi,........	12	10	7	29	25	2	8	2	12	31
Louisiana,..........	15	15	19	49	36	7	5	9	21	77
Tennessee,........	59	59	54	172	176	13	9	6	28	37
Arkansas,..........	6	2	2	10	8	4	......	......	4	2
Kentucky, ...	100	113	90	303	169	16	25	5	46	83
Missouri,..........	12	5	10	27	27	2	1	5	8	10
Ohio,...............	148	160	118	426	232	5	......	4	......	6
Indiana,............	49	59	33	141	85	1	2	......	3	2
Illinois, ...	23	27	16	66	35	......	......	......	......	4
Michigan,..........	4	7	4	15	5	......	......	......	......	....
Total,.........	1,652	1,905	1,806	5,363	3,974	272	246	224	743	1,470

The white population at that time being 10,537,373, and the coloured 2,328,642, the number of whites, deaf and dumb, according to the preceding table (5,363) was equivalent to 1 in 1,964, and of coloured persons (743) was 1 in 3,134. Of the blind, the number of whites (3,974) was 1 in 2,651, and of coloured persons, 1 in 1,584. This shows an excess of whites, deaf and dumb, in a somewhat greater proportion than three to two, and an excess of blind in the coloured race in about the same ratio.

The number of Deaf and Dumb, Blind, and Insane, of the white and coloured population of the United States, on the 1st of August, 1840.

STATES AND TERRITORIES.	WHITES.						COLOURED PERSONS.		
	DEAF AND DUMB.				BLIND.	INSANE AND IDIOTS.	DEAF AND DUMB.	BLIND.	INSANE AND IDIOTS.
	Under 14.	14 to 25.	25 and upw'ds.	Total.					
Maine, ...	47	13	102	222	180	537	13	10	94
New Hampshire,.	43	41	97	181	153	486	9	3	19
Vermont, ...	27	19	89	135	101	398	2	2	13
Massachusetts,...	56	63	164	283	308	1,071	17	22	200
Rhode Island,....	15	25	34	74	63	203	3	1	13
Connecticut,......	60	141	108	309	143	498	8	13	44
New York,.......	269	362	408	1,039	875	2,146	68	91	194
New Jersey,......	33	29	102	164	126	369	15	26	73
Pennsylvania,....	225	225	331	781	540	1,946	51	96	187
Delaware,.........	18	15	12	45	15	52	8	18	28
Maryland, ...	43	59	79	181	171	400	68	101	150
Dist. of Columbia,	1	5	2	8	6	14	4	9	7
Virginia, ...	133	111	209	453	426	1,048	150	466	384
North Carolina,.	82	80	118	280	223	580	74	167	221
South Carolina,..	40	41	59	140	133	376	78	156	137
Georgia, ...	78	62	53	193	136	294	64	151	134
Florida,............	6	4	4	14	9	10	2	10	12
Alabama,..........	72	53	48	173	113	232	53	96	125
Mississippi,.......	25	16	23	64	43	116	28	69	82
Louisiana,........	14	17	11	42	37	55	17	36	45
Arkansas, ...	18	11	11	40	26	45	2	8	21
Tennessee,.......	102	93	96	291	255	699	67	99	152
Kentucky,........	120	128	152	400	236	795	77	141	180
Missouri,..........	48	32	46	126	82	202	27	42	68
Ohio,...............	167	198	194	559	372	1,195	33	33	165
Indiana,...........	112	91	94	297	135	487	15	19	75
Illinois,............	54	48	53	155	86	213	24	10	79
Michigan,.........	7	9	15	31	25	39	2	4	26
Wisconsin, ...	1	4	....	5	9	8	....	....	3
Iowa,..............	3	2	5	10	3	7	4	3	4
Total,.......	1,919	2,057	2,709	6,685	5,030	14,521	979	1,902	2,935

According to the preceding table,

The deaf and dumb of the whites was . . 1 in 2,123
" " of the coloured . . 1 in 2,933

The number of the blind was,
" of the whites . . . . . 1 in 2,821
" of the coloured . . . . 1 in 1,509

The number of the insane was,
" of the whites . . . . . 1 in 977
" of the coloured . . . . 1 in 978

This census, like the preceding, shows a greater proportion of whites among the deaf and dumb, and of the coloured race among the blind; but in both descriptions, their relative proportions were changed in favour of the whites. Thus, in the deaf and dumb, the ratio of the whites had diminished from $\frac{1}{1964}$ to $\frac{1}{2123}$, whilst that of the coloured population had increased from $\frac{1}{3134}$ to $\frac{1}{2933}$; and in the blind, the ratio of the whites had decreased from $\frac{1}{2651}$ to $\frac{1}{2821}$, but that of the coloured classes had slightly increased, that is, from $\frac{1}{1584}$ to $\frac{1}{1509}$. These opposite changes in the two races are probably not greater than can be accounted for by the extraordinary loss which the coloured population has sustained from emigration in the last ten years, (as is shown by the census,) and also by the unusual influx of Europeans in the same time, since persons falling under either class of disability would be rarely found among emigrants.

It deserves to be remarked, as favouring some of the conjectural views that have been hazarded in comparing the two races, that of the three privations here considered, the only one that is always congenital is far less frequent with the coloured than the white population; whereas, the greater proportionate number of blind in the former class may be reasonably referred to the severer labour and greater exposure to which they are occasionally subject, to their greater improvidence, and greater want of medical assistance.

Of the insane and idiotic, the proportions in the two races would seem to be identical; somewhat more than one in a thousand in both being visited by this greatest of all human maladies. The census distinguishes between those patients of this description who were at public and at private charge, as follows:

At public charge, whites . . .	4,333	
" " coloured . . .	833	
	——	5,166
At private charge, whites . . .	10,188	
" " coloured . . .	2,102	
	——	12,290

Showing, that in both classes of the population, the proportion at public charge is the same, and that it is about forty per cent of the number at private charge.

The diversities among the several States, as to the proportion of insane of their white population, is not greater than may be referred to emigration; for, as insane persons are seldom or never seen among emigrants, we ought to find the proportion of this class greater in those States that lose by emigration, as the New England

States, and least in those which gain from that source, as the western States. If, then, we make fair allowance for this influence, we shall find that the difference among the different States, as to this afflicting visitation, is insignificant; and that in all of them, as to the white population, if we deduct the foreign emigrants, the proportion of the insane will be very nearly as 1 to 1,000.

But as to the coloured population, it appears to be far otherwise. We find an extraordinary difference among the States, in the proportion of the insane of the coloured race. The proportions in the several States appear to be as follows:

States and Territories.	Coloured population.	No. of Insane.	Ratio as 1 to	States and Territories.	Coloured population.	No. of Insane.	Ratio as 1 to
Maine,........	1,355	94	14.4	Georgia,.......	283,697	134	2117.
New Hamp..	537	19	28.2	Florida,.......	26,534	12	2211.
Vermont,.....	730	13	56.1	Alabama,....	255,571	125	2044.
Massachus., .	8,668	200	43.3	Mississippi,...	196,580	82	2397.
R. Island,....	3,238	13	249.	Louisiana,....	193,954	45	4310.
Connecticut,.	8,105	44	184.	Arkansas,....	20,400	21	971.
New York,..	50,031	194	257.	Tennessee,...	188,583	152	1240.
New Jersey,.	21,718	73	297.	Kentucky,....	189,575	180	1053.
Pennsylvania	47,918	187	256.	Missouri,.....	59,814	68	879.
Delaware,....	19,524	28	697.	Ohio,........ .	17,345	165	105.
Maryland,....	151,815	151	1005.	Indiana,.......	7,168	75	95.5
Dist. of Col.,.	13,055	7	1865.	Illinois,.......	3,929	79	49.7
Virginia,......	495,105	384	1289.	Michigan,....	707	26	27.2
N. Carolina,.	268,549	221	1215.	Wisconsin,...	196	3	65.3
S. Carolina, .	335,314	137	2447.	Iowa,..........	188	4	47.
Total,........					2,873,945	2,936	978.8

It thus appears, that the proportion of insane is greatest among the coloured population of the northern States, and that it considerably decreases as we proceed south; from which we may infer that the rigours of a northern winter, which have no influence on the temperament of the whites, affect the cerebral organs of the African race. There are, however, two other circumstances, which operate to produce the great diversity we see; and these are, emigration and slavery—the slave population seeming to be less liable to this malady than the free coloured population, and the insane very rarely migrating. By a due regard to these three circumstances, of coldness of climate, migration, and the proportion of slaves in the coloured population of a State, we may probably go far to reconcile most of the diversities which are exhibited in the above table. But perhaps it is premature to theorize on this subject; for when we see in some of the States so large a proportion of the coloured population as 1 in 43, and in Maine nearly 1 in 14, so anomalous a fact throws a doubt over the correctness of this part of the census, and at least inclines us to suspend our opinion, until we have further evidence or explanation.

CHAPTER X.

EMIGRATION.

That emigration from the old world to the new, from which the whole present population of the United States is directly or remotely derived, still continues to make large annual additions to our numbers. After the political connexion with the parent country was severed, foreign emigration, which had been suspended during the war of independence, returned with unabated force; and, what was still less to have been expected, its subsequent increase has been yet greater than that of the whole population which it helped to swell.

This tide of European emigration ceases to be an object of wonder, when it is recollected that labour and skill are more than twice as well rewarded in the United States as in Europe; that capital receives nearly twice the profits; and, above all, that land can be here purchased in absolute property at a smaller cost than would there be its annual rent. In addition to these strong inducements, which apply to nearly all Europeans, the British and Irish emigrants find here the language, laws, usages, and manners to which they have been accustomed. They, therefore, constitute the larger part of the emigrants from Europe to the United States. Next to these, the Germans are the most numerous; for they, too, with the recommendations of cheap land and high-priced labour, meet, in many of the States, thousands whose language* and manners are the same as those they have left behind. From the time that the first German settlers came to this country, in 1682, under the auspices of William Penn, there has been a steady influx of emigrants from Germany, principally to the middle States, and, of late years, to the west.

---

* As early as 1793, a journal, in the German language, was established at Germantown, in Pennsylvania. From that time to the present, the number of German newspapers has continued to increase in that State.

The coloured part of the population, which also owes its origin exclusively* to the old continent, has, since 1808, received no accessions from abroad; but is, on the contrary, constantly losing, by emigration, a part of what it gains by natural increase.

It is obvious, that if the number of persons thus migrating to and from the United States could be ascertained, the census, periodically taken, would enable us to determine the precise rate of our natural multiplication. But such certainty is, as yet, unattainable. Of the coloured race, we have no means of knowing the loss sustained, either from the free portion who settle abroad, or from runaway slaves; and our estimates of the whites who migrated hither before 1819, were purely conjectural. In that year, indeed, an act of Congress required accounts to be taken by the collectors at the seaports of all passengers who arrived from abroad, distinguishing foreigners from citizens, and to be returned to the office of the Secretary of State. But even this regulation has not afforded the desired certainty, for, besides that the returns are defective, a part of the British emigrants who arrive at New York, take that route to Canada, in preference to a voyage up the St. Lawrence; whilst, on the other hand, a part of those who pass directly from Great Britain or Ireland into Canada, migrate thence by land into the United States; and the numbers of neither portion have we any means of ascertaining. With these sources of uncertainty, our estimates of the amount of emigration to and from the United States, with all the collateral aid to be derived from the census, can be considered only as approximations to the truth.

Let us first estimate, from such data as we possess, the number of white persons who have migrated to the United States from 1790 to 1840.

In the twenty years between the census of 1790 and that of 1810, Dr. Seybert supposes the number of foreign emigrants to the United States to be 120,000, averaging 6,000 per annum. From 1810 to 1820, I have been able to procure no data, except Dr. Seybert's estimate for the year 1817, founded on the records of the custom-houses at the principal seaports; according to which estimate, the number of passengers who arrived in the United States that year,

* The number of Indians, or descendants of Indians, comprehended in the decennial enumerations of the people of the United States, is too small to deserve to be regarded as an exception. It certainly would not amount to a thousandth, perhaps not to a ten-thousandth part of the whole population.

was 22,840. He supposes that the number, in any preceding year, did not amount to 10,000, except, perhaps, in 1794. In three of the years of this decennial term, that is, during the war with Great Britain, migration to this country was almost totally suspended. If, then, we suppose, that in the three years from 1818 to 1820, both inclusive, the number of passengers was the same as in 1817, and if we deduct from the whole number 2,840, (1,840 for the American citizens, that being about the proportion at that time,) we shall have 84,000 for the number of foreign emigrants to the United States for those four years. If we further suppose, that in the remaining six years the number was 30,000,* we shall have 114,000 for the whole number of white immigrants from 1810 to 1820.

From 1820 to 1830, when the collectors of the customs were required to report to the State department the number of foreigners who had arrived in their respective ports by sea, we might have expected entire accuracy; but these reports are so much at variance with other documents, entitled to respect, and are confessedly so defective, that they cannot be relied on. Thus, to give an example, the number of emigrants who left the United Kingdom in 1829 for the United States, was, according to British official returns, 15,678; yet the whole number of foreign emigrants from all parts of the world, reported to the State department in the same year, was but 15,285, there being, besides less important omissions, that of New York for the third quarter. Again, the number of foreign emigrants returned to the State department for 1830, is but 9,466, though 30,224 landed in New York alone in that year, for the whole of which the proper officers had failed to make any return. In consequence of these, and like instances of failure of duty, the number of foreign emigrants returned to the State department for the six years from 1825 to 1830, both inclusive, was only 87,140;† whilst the number who emigrated from the United King-

---

* That is, 10,000 per annum for three years, excluding the three years of war. I have not ventured to go beyond 10,000 a year, from respect to Dr. Seybert's opinion; and I could not take a less number, from a regard to the progressive increase of immigration both before and after this period.

† This number is obtained partly by computation, that is, by adding to the official number returned for five and a quarter years, (from the 30th Sept., 1825, to the 31st Dec., 1830,) three-fourths of the number returned for the year 1825. This was necessary, as the annual returns to the State department were, before 1828, closed on the 30th September, and subsequently, at the end of the year.

dom to the United States for the same six years, according to the official accounts in that country, was 80,522, which allows but 6,618 for the number of emigrants to the United States from all the other parts of theworld, though it is known that these (including the emigrants from the rest of the British dominions) are nearly equal to the number from the United Kingdom.

The more accurate returns, subsequently made to the State department, furnish us with some data for correcting these errors. By the official returns of British consuls residing in America, the number of emigrants from Great Britain and Ireland to the United States for the five years from 1833 to 1837, was 163,447; but, according to the reports of the collectors here to the State department, the whole number of foreigners who came to the United States, in the same period, was 324,750, which is very nearly double the number of those who were from Great Britain and Ireland.

If, then, we suppose that the British accounts were not less accurate in the last period of five years than in the first period of six, (and they were probably more so,) and that the emigrants from other countries to the United States bore as large a proportion to those from Great Britain and Ireland in the first period as the last, (which there is no reason to question,) then the British returns of emigrants to the United States would be to the whole number from all parts of the world in the ratio of 163,447 to 324,750, unless it were proper to make a deduction from the last number for those British emigrants who took their route to Upper Canada by way of New York.

To some, this deduction may not seem to be necessary, because they would consider that the number of those who came to the United States from Canada was likely to equal those who went to Canada by the route of New York, and especially during the civil commotions that broke out within the five years in question. Yet as, since 1834, the proportion* of British emigrants who take the New York route is said to be "considerable," let us assume, in the absence of all precise data, that as many as one-third of those emigrants who land in New York afterwards proceed to Canada, and see how far the above-mentioned ratio is affected by that proportion.

The number of British and Irish emigrants who arrived at New York from 1833 to 1837, inclusive, was 152,164; and the number

---

* Porter's Progress of the Nation.

of those who left Canada for the United States, in the years 1834, 1835, 1836, and 1837, was 10,256. Supposing the number, in 1833, to have been in the same proportion, the whole number for five years would be 12,820. With these facts, the whole number of emigrants to the United States would be thus reduced, viz :

The total number who arrived in the United States,		324,750
British emigrants who left New York for Canada, one-third of 152,164, ...	50,821	
Deduct for those who left Canada for the United States, ...	12,820	
		38,001
		286,749

On this liberal estimate, then, of the number of British emigrants from New York to Canada, the proportion which the number from the United Kingdom to the United States bears to the whole number from all countries, is as 163,447 to 286,749, or nearly as 4 to 7. Applying, then, this rule to the 80,522 who emigrated from the United Kingdom to the United States from 1825 to 1830, we have 141,300 for the whole number of immigrants for the same six years. In the remaining four years, from 1821 to 1824, the number of foreign emigrants returned to the State department was 31,158, which, we may presume, bore the same proportion to the actual number as 87,140 to 141,300, and consequently would be 50,500. This number for the four years, added to 141,300 for the six years, would give us 191,800 for the whole number of immigrants from 1820 to 1830. If we make a lower estimate of the number who proceed from New York to Canada, as probably we ought, and allow something for deficient returns to the State department, we cannot suppose the whole number to be short of 200,000, and I shall accordingly so consider it.

From 1830 to 1840, we have better materials than in any preceding decennial term, for estimating the number of foreign emigrants to this country. The following is a summary of the returns that have been made to the State department of the number of passengers who arrived in the United States in that period :

Years.	*Americans.*	*Foreigners.*
1831	1,256	15,713
1832	1,155	34,970
1833	1,251	58,262
1834	2,114	64,916

Years.	Americans.	Foreigners.
1835	3,320	45,444
1836	4,029	76,923
1837	3,813	79,205
1838	3,964	42,731
1839	4,171	70,494
1840	5,810	86,338
Total . . .	30,883	574,996

It appears, however, that this account, though far more accurate than any preceding it, is not free from errors, some of which are considerable. Thus, the numbers of foreigners in the preceding statement for 1831 and 1832, are set down at 15,713 and 34,970, making together 50,683 ; whereas the number who arrived in New York alone in those years, was 80,328. If to this number we add one-fourth for the ordinary proportion arriving at other ports, we shall have 107,104, thus showing omissions in those two years amounting to 56,421. The omissions in the subsequent years are believed to be comparatively small. Correcting, then, these errors, the whole number of emigrants who arrived at all the ports in the United States from all parts of the world, between 1830 and 1840, would be 631,417. Allowing the number of those who left New York for Canada to be in the same proportion as before, that is, as 38,000 to 324,750, we have 58,690 for the number of persons thus migrating in the whole ten years. Deducting this number, and 100,000 for the emigration of American citizens to Texas and Canada, from 631,417, we have 472,727 for the whole gain to the white population by immigration in the same period.

To the number of foreign emigrants in the several decennial terms, should be added their probable natural increase during each term. If the number was the same every year of a decennial term, and if the number of females was in the same proportion as in the rest of the population, we might estimate the increase at half its ordinary amount in ten years, or at about 16 per cent. But as neither of these suppositions is true, let us adapt our estimate to the varying circumstances.

In the first place, as the number of foreign emigrants to the United States progressively increases, and consequently is greater in the last years of a decennial term than in the first, our estimate of the increase of each term should be computed on a mean between the number of emigrants of that term and of the preceding term.

Secondly, as to the proportion of females. This is known to be much less in the class of emigrants than it is in the whole population, of which the following table affords illustrations:

Emigrants from the United Kingdom to Quebec in 1834 *and* 1837.

Years.	*Males.*	*Females.*	*Children, under* 14.	*Total.*
1834 . .	13,565	9,687	7,681	30,933
1837 . .	11,740	6,079	4,082	21,901
Total . .	25,305	15,766	11,763	52,834

Thus showing, that the females over fourteen were about 30 per cent of the whole number. But inasmuch as the females between sixteen and forty-five constitute but about 19 per cent of the whole population, and as a very small proportion of the female immigrants are over forty-five, if we make a deduction for the excess, and also for the number between fourteen and sixteen years of age, (which does not exceed 2½ per cent of the whole number,) we shall find the proportion of women within the child-bearing ages greater with the emigrant class than with the whole population. Thus:

The proportion of women over 14, was .		29.8	per cent.
Deduct the proportion over 45, suppose .	2.		
That between 14 and 16 . . .	2.5	4.5	"
The proportion between 16 and 45 . .		35.3	"

After making some deduction for the decrease of this proportion, the number of females under sixteen not being sufficient to keep up the number of marriageable women, we should be justified in estimating the average increase of the emigrants for the ten years at 20, instead of 16 per cent.

Applying these principles, and dividing the supposed number of emigrants in the two first decennial terms (120,000) into 50,000 for the first term, and 70,000 for the second, the number, with their increase at each term, would be as follows:

From 1790 to 1800—number of emigrants .	50,000	
Increase, 20 per cent on 40,000 .	8,000	
		58,000
From 1800 to 1810—number of emigrants .	70,000	
Increase, 20 per cent on 60,000 .	12,000	
		82,000

From 1810 to 1820—number of emigrants	.	114,000	
Increase, 20 per cent on 97,000	.	19,400	
			133,400
From 1820 to 1830—number of emigrants	.	200,000	
Increase, 20 per cent on 157,000	.	31,400	
			231,400
From 1830 to 1840—number of emigrants	.	472,727	
Increase, 20 per cent on 336,363	.	67,273	
			540,000

Thus, while the whole population had, in fifty years, increased about fourfold, the average annual immigration had increased more than ninefold in the same time. So great and so disproportionate an increase may seem to some improbable, but the deductions have been made on so liberal a scale, that the preceding estimate, I am persuaded, rather falls short of the truth than exceeds it. In truth, the steady extension of our settlements into the western wilderness continues to multiply the opportunities of buying land at prices as low as ever, without being placed more beyond the benefits of civilization and commerce; and the rapid growth of our cities and manufacturing industry is constantly enlarging the field of employment for tradesmen and artizans. Whilst these circumstances present to the indigent and enterprising foreigner more and more points of attraction, the long peace in Europe seems to have given a proportionate increase to the repellent force that is there felt. Whether both these facts are likely long to continue, and though they should, whether considerations political, moral, or economical, may not induce the national legislature to check this tide of foreign emigration, are among the uncertain problems of the future.

Of that part of the coloured race who emigrate from the United States, we have no means of estimating the number, except by comparing the rate of increase in the last decennial terms with that of the first term, when there were few emigrants of this description, and when they were probably balanced by the Africans then imported. In making this comparison, it is assumed that the rate of natural increase has continued unchanged, which fact there seems no reason to doubt, at least as to the six-sevenths who are slaves.

From 1790 to 1800, the increase of the coloured population was 32.2 per cent, which, for the reasons mentioned, we consider to indicate the rate of its natural increase in the United States. In the next ten years, from 1800 to 1810, the increase was 37.6 per cent; but in that time the increase was enhanced by the acquisition of Louisiana and by the increased importation of slaves, both on account of the increased demand for them for the cultivation of cotton and sugar, and because it was known that the further importation of them would cease after 1807. The accessions from these combined causes, beyond what was lost by emigration, was 5.4 per cent on 1,001,436 persons, equal to 54,000. In the following term, from 1810 to 1820, the increase declined to 29.6 per cent, owing principally to the slaves who escaped to the British during the war. From 1820 to 1830, it was 30.7 per cent; and from 1830 to 1840, it sunk to the unprecedented rate of 23.4 per cent.

These rates of decennial increase since 1810, compared with that between 1790 to 1800, show the loss by emigration, exclusive of their probable increase at each term, as follows:

				Emigrants.
From 1810 to 1820,	decrease	(32.2—29.3) is 2.9	per cent	= 29,300
" 1820 to 1830,	"	(32.2—30.7) is 1.5	"	= 20,600
" 1830 to 1840,	"	(32.2—23.4) is 8.8	"	=204,900

From the number in the last decennial term, a considerable deduction should be made for the extraordinary mortality of the slaves sent to Alabama, Mississippi, and Louisiana, during a part of the term, and perhaps, their slower rate of increase. The census shows an increase of the slaves in those three States, between 1830 and 1840, of 324,399 on a population of 292,796, which is 230,000 more than the probable natural increase; and it is known that, during a part of the term, disease, especially the cholera, made frighful ravages among the negroes brought from other States. The remainder of the 204,900 is to be referred to emigrations to Texas, and to the unusual number both of the free coloured, and slaves, who betook themselves to Canada in the ten years preceding 1840.

In conclusion, we may say that, without attempting a computation in which we must yet further rely on conjecture, the facts here stated are sufficient to satisfy us that, after deducting what the country has lost by emigration, the foreign emigrants and their descendants in fifty years, now add above a million to its population.

CHAPTER XI.

THE PAST NATURAL INCREASE OF THE POPULATION, WHITE AND COLOURED.

LET us now direct our inquiries to the natural increase of our numbers, independent of all accessions from abroad. No fact disclosed by the census is of equal importance to this in the eyes of the statesman and political economist; since, in an underpeopled country like the United States, such increase is the surest index of the nation's present abundance and comfort, as well as of its future strength and resources.

I. The natural increase of the white population.

If we deduct, from the whole increase of this class at each census, the number gained by immigration beyond the number of our own emigrants, the result would of course give us the precise amount of increase from natural multiplication. The following statement shows the result of such deduction, according to the estimates of immigration made in the preceding chapter:

From 1790 to 1800, the increase of the whites was 35.7 per cent.
Deduct the number immigrating, 58,000, equal to 1.8 "
——33.9 per c't.

From 1800 to 1810, the increase was . . 36.2
Deduct, 1. The whites acquired with Louisiana, 51,000,* equal to . . 1.2
2. The number immigrating, equal to 1.9
—— 3.1
—— 33.1 "

* I have ventured to put down the whole number of whites returned in 1810 for Louisiana and Missouri, (then called the territories of New Orleans and Louisiana,) as an accession to the population since 1800, though doubtless a part of them had migrated from other States. No deduction was made on this account, partly because other citizens were acquired by the purchase, who were not comprehended in the returns for those territories, and partly because the estimate of the immigration between 1800 and

From 1810 to 1820, the increase was . .	34.3	per cent.
Deduct the number immigrating, 132,400, equal to	2.2	
	——	32.1 "
From 1820 to 1830, the increase was . .	33.8	
Deduct the number immigrating, 231,000, equal to	2.9	
	——	30.9 "
From 1830 to 1840, the increase was . .	34.7	
Deduct the number immigrating, 540,000, equal to	5.1	
	——	29.6 "

According to which computation the actual and natural increase, in each decennial term, may be thus compared:

	Per cent.	*Per cent.*	*Per cent.*	*Per cent.*	*Per cent.*
Actual increase,	35.7	36.2	34.3	33.8	34.7
Natural increase,	33.9	33.1	32.1	30.9	29.6

Thus showing, in the rate of decennial natural increase, a diminution of 4.3 per cent during forty years, or an average of about 1 per cent for each term of ten years.

It will be perceived that this diminution of ratio is not uniform, but that it increases progressively, and with a regularity which is remarkable, and which gives some assurance that the estimates made of the numbers acquired by immigration are not wide of the truth. The differences of ratio are in the following series: 8, 10, 12, 13.

Let us now see how far this decline in the rate of natural increase derives confirmation from the census itself. If there be such a diminution of ratio, it will be manifested by the decreasing proportion of children under ten years of age, since, at each census, they constitute all of the population who have been born since the preceding census.

From 1800 to 1840, the number of white females and of children under ten, and their proportions to each other, were as follows:

	1800.	1810.	1820.	1830.	1840.
No. of females,..................	2,100,068	2,874,433	3,871,647	5,171,115	6,939,842
No. of children under 10,......	1,489,315	2,016,479	2,625,790	3,427,730	4,485,130
Prop. of children, per cent,...	70.92	70.15	67.82	66.20	64.63

1810 is probably too low. Dr. Seybert, on whose authority I have stated the immigration from 1790 to 1810 at only 120,000, estimates the whole gain from immigrants and their increase at 180,000; whereas, the estimate made in the preceding chapter would not reckon it at more than 160,000, viz.: 58,000+82,000+the increase of 58,000 for 10 years, which could not exceed 20,000. He has thus, probably, more than corrected the error of underrating the number of immigrants by too high an estimate of their increase.

Thus showing a gradual decrease in the proportion of children during forty years of 6.29 per cent; which, allowing for the ordinary difference between the number of males and females, is equivalent to something more than 3 per cent of the whole population. So, if the children under ten, be compared with the females of the preceding census, we see a correspondent diminution of ratio, viz:

	1790.	1800.	1810.	1820.	1830.
No. of females,..................	1,556,839	2,100,068	2,874,433	3,871,647	5,171,115
No. of children at the succeeding census,.....................	1,489,315	2,016,479	2,625,790	3,427,730	4,485,130
Prop. of children, per cent,....	95.66	96.02	91.35	88.53	86.73

But these proportions are also affected by immigration. In the first case, in which the comparison is made between the children and the females of the same census, the proportion of children is lessened by reason of the greater proportion of adults in the immigrating class than in the whole population. But in the last case, in which the children of the succeeding census are compared with the females of the preceding, the proportion of children is increased by immigration.

The first source of error is, however, inconsiderable. The increase of immigrants in ten years, we have seen, may be estimated at 20 per cent of the whole number; and to such increase we must add the portion of immigrant children under ten at the time the census is taken. Now, if we suppose the females to constitute one-third of those who migrate hither, and the children one-sixth, (as seemed to be the proportion in Canada,) and if we further suppose that, one-tenth of those children who arrive in the first year of the decennial term would be under ten years of age at the succeeding census, two-tenths of those who arrive in the second year, three in the third, and so on throughout the term, we shall find, after making a fair deduction for the intervening deaths, that the proportion of children to females in such immigrants will be little inferior to the proportion in the indigenous population. Let us, however, assume it to be 3 per cent less, or 30 per cent on the whole number of immigrants and their increase, and to adapt our estimates to this supposition, we must in the first comparison add 3 per cent of the whole number of immigrants to compensate for the excess of adults, and in the second comparison deduct 30 per cent to correct the excess of children gained by immigration. With these corrections the proportion of children will be as follows:

First, when the children are compared with the females of the same census.

	1800.	1810.	1820.	1830.	1840.
No. of children under 10,.....	1,490,315	2,016,479	2,625,790	3,427,730	4,485,130
Add 3 per cent on the number of immigrants in each decennial term,.............	1,640	2,460	3,972	6,930	16,200
Total,.......................	1,490,955	2,018,939	2,629,762	3,427,730	4,323,200
Prop. of children, per cent,...	71	70.23	67.92	66.55	64,87

Secondly, when the children are compared with the females of the preceding census.

No. of children under 10,.....	1,489,315	2,016,479	2,625,790	3,427,730	4,485,200
Deduct 30 per ct. of the immigrants in each term,.....	16,400	42,483	39,720	69,300	162,000
Total,...................	1,472,915	1,973,996	2,586,070	3,358,430	4,323,200
Prop. of children, per cent,..	94.61	94	89.97	86.75	83.60

It thus appears that the addition of 3 per cent on the number of immigrants in the first comparison, reduces the decrease in forty years only from 6.29 to 6.13 per cent of the females, though the addition of 30 per cent in the second, augments the decrease from 8.93 to 11.01 per cent of the females at the preceding census; which corresponds more nearly with the estimate first made.

We arrive at a similar result if we make the more limited, but perhaps more satisfactory comparison of the children under ten with the females between the child-bearing ages of sixteen and forty-five, in 1800, 1810, and 1820, when their number was ascertained by the census. That class of females amounted in those years, respectively, to 813,193, 1,106,212, and 1,517,971. When compared with the children under ten in the same year.

The proportion of children in 1800, is 183.1 per cent.
" " " " 1810, is 182.3 "
" " " " 1820, is 173.2 "

Showing a decrease in the proportion of children, of nearly 10 per cent of this class of females in twenty years; and thus, by whatever test we compare the rate of natural increase, as exhibited by the different enumerations, we have the same evidence of a continual diminution of such increase.

Let us now compare the rates of diminution of decennial increase which these tests severally indicate, estimating the females at 49 per cent of the whole population; those of the preceding census, at one-third less, or 32 per cent; and those between sixteen and forty-five, at 19 per cent. When reduced to the same standard, the foregoing comparative estimates exhibit the following rates of diminution of increase in the whole population from 1800 to 1840:

	Decrease of ratio in 40 years.	*Decrease of ratio in 10 years.*
1. Where the whole population at each census is compared, after deducting for immigration,......	4.3 per cent=1	per cent.
2. Where the children under 10 are compared with the females of the same census,..............	6.13=3. "	=0.75 "
3. Where the children under 10 are compared with the females of the preceding census,.......	11.02=3 5 "	=0.89 "
	Decrease in 20 *years.*	
4. Where the children under 10 are compared with the females between 16 and 45,............	9. 9=1.88 "	=0.94 "

The average of these rates of diminution is very nearly nine-tenths of 1 per cent for ten years, and this is probably somewhat beyond the truth; first, because in the second comparison, which makes the lowest estimate, there seems to be fewer sources of error than in the rest; and secondly, because a moderate addition to the supposed number of emigrants in the first decennial term would approximate the first comparison, which makes the highest estimate, to the other three; and there is more than one reason for believing that Dr. Seybert's estimate of the immigration, which has been here adopted, is too low. We may, then, on the whole, conclude that the rate of increase of the white population has diminished, on an average, between 1, and ¾ of 1 per cent, in ten years; and that the diminution has been in a slightly increasing ratio.

II. The natural increase of the coloured population.

In the preceding chapter it was assumed that the natural increase of the coloured race in the United States was uniform, and that it was 32.2 per cent in ten years, which was their rate of increase between 1790 and 1800, when it was supposed the number brought into the country equalled those who went out of it. But we have no proof that the slaves imported into South Carolina and Georgia, (the only States which then received them from abroad,) were equal to those who escaped to other countries, together with the free coloured persons who emigrated; and if they were inferior in number, the supposed rate of increase would be too low. It certainly seems improbable, at the first view, that the natural increase of the whites should have exceeded that of the coloured race 1.7 per cent in ten years, as has been supposed in the preceding estimates; and it is very possible that the one is somewhat too high, and the other too low.

The uniformity of increase in this part of our population was presumed, because the same circumstances which tend to check multiplication with the whites have no existence with the coloured race ; certainly not with the slaves, who now constitute more than six-sevenths of the whole, and, in 1790, constituted more than eleven-twelfths. Nor are they likely to exist to the same extent in the free coloured class as with the whites, since the diminution of increase with these may be occasioned principally by the delay of marriage in the richer classes of society, which cause might not extend to the poorer, who now find it as easy to obtain the necessaries of life, and even its substantial comforts, as ever. No deduction was therefore made on account of the free coloured class.

The census, unfortunately, affords us not the same means of ascertaining the natural increase of the coloured population as of that of the whites ; it not having distinguished the ages of coloured persons before 1820, and having adopted a different distribution then, from that made in the two subsequent enumerations. To these last, therefore, our inquiries will be limited.

As emancipation seeems not to have varied much in the two last decennial terms, we will investigate the natural increase of the two classes of the coloured race separately, beginning with the slaves.

If the increase of slaves, from 1830 to 1840, had been proportionally as great as it was from 1820 to 1830, the number at the last census would have been 2,615,000, instead of 2,487,000 ; thus showing a deficiency of 128,000. How is so great a deficiency to be explained, without supposing a decline in the rate of increase? The following circumstances obviously contributed to lessen the number of slaves in 1840.

1. The emigration to Texas, which may account, perhaps, for a third of the deficiency or more.

2. The increase of runaway slaves. It is a fact of general notoriety, that the number of those who have taken refuge in Canada or the northern States, has greatly increased within the last two years.

3. The extraordinary mortality which prevailed in Mississippi, Louisiana, and South Alabama, in the first year of the term, among the slaves, and especially that large portion of them who had been transported from the more northern slave-holding States. The census shows the unwonted extent of such transportation. In the three States of Alabama, Mississippi, and Louisiana, the slaves, which in 1830 were 292,796, in 1840 amounted to 617,195, thus

showing an excess of 230,000, after allowing for the decennial increase 32.2 per cent; whilst, on the other hand, Maryland, Virginia, and the Carolinas, had a smaller number of slaves in 1830 than in 1840, by 21,000, though their natural increase, at the same rate of 32.2 per cent, would have amounted to 334,000. So great a number as these facts imply, transported from a more, to a less salubrious climate, and often subjected to new habits of life and new modes of treatment, necessarily supposes a great increase of mortality, without the aid of cholera, and other epidemics, which, however, did their part also in the waste of life.

4. The slower rate of natural increase in most of the southwestern States. Although the slaves may have, as we have supposed, the same ratio of increase in the same State, they may have very different ratios in different States, according to diversities of climate, occupation, and treatment; and the census shows that the States to which so many slaves were carried between 1830 and 1840, for the culture of cotton, are much less favourable to the natural multiplication of that class, or, at least, have hitherto been so, than are the States, from which they were transported, as may be thus seen:

In 1840, the total number of slaves, and that of the slave children under ten, were respectively as follows:

In Alabama, whole number of slaves,			253,532—number of children under 10,				87,430
In Mississippi,	"	"	195,211	"	"	"	63,708
In Louisiana,	"	"	168,452	"	"	"	45,861
In Florida,	"	"	25,717	"	"	"	8,036
Total,			642,912				205,035

If, on the whole number of slaves, 642,912, we take 34.9 per cent as the proportion of children under ten, (which was the proportion throughout the Union in 1830,) it will give 224,376 for the number of children in 1840, which is 19,341 more than the number returned by the census. It may be supposed by some that, inasmuch as the States in question received large importations of slaves from other States, of whom there was an over proportion of adults, a part, if not the whole of the deficiency here mentioned, may be referred to such importations, and that it would be compensated by an excess of children in the slave-exporting States. But we perceive no such disproportion of adults in the case of slaves transferred from State to State, as exists in the case of emigrants from foreign countries. When the slave-holder migrates to the south, none of his slaves are too young to be taken with him, and it is the aged only, who are left behind. Even the slave-dealers, although they confine their odious traffic chiefly to adults, confine it also to those who are young and healthy, and whose increase, consequently, or the loss of it, in a few years corrects, and more than corrects, the slight temporary change in the proportion between children and females, which their removal occasioned both in the State they had left and in the State they were carried to. We accordingly find, that Virginia exhibits no excess of slave children, in consequence of the 180,000 slaves which the census shows she had lost between 1830 and 1840. On the contrary, the number had undergone a sensible decrease (from 35.6 to 33.9) in that time; and North Carolina, which had parted with a smaller proportion of slaves in the same time, (about 80,000,) exhibits also, a correspondent decrease in the proportion of children, that is, from 37. to 36.2 per cent. These facts seem to show that the transportation of slaves from State to State, by settlers and slavedealers, tends rather to raise than to lower the proportion of children in the importing State.

Though we have no data for estimating the other causes of diminution with even an approach to accuracy, we must admit that their combined force does not seem insufficient to account for the large deficiency (128,000) shown by the census of 1840; and no one well acquainted with the condition of slavery in the United States, will admit, without the most indubitable evidence, a falling off in the natural increase of the slaves, farther than to the qualified extent that has been mentioned. This natural increase probobly exceeded 32 per cent in ten years, during the three first terms, and was certainly below 33 per cent. The subsequent diminution, in consequence of the great movement of the slave population to the south, when cotton bore a high price and money was redundant, has scarcely been more than from 1 to 2 per cent of the whole slave population, so as to make the average decennial increase in fifty years not widely different from the 32.2 per cent supposed,

The natural increase of the free coloured population is the more difficult to estimate on account of emancipation, which we have no means of ascertaining, and which, while it but slightly diminishes the rate of increase of slaves, greatly augments that of the free coloured class. Thus, the decennial increase of this class has varied from 82.3 to 20.9 per cent, though that of the slaves has ranged only from 33.4 to 23.8 per cent. The census, nevertheless, affords persuasive evidence that the natural increase of the free portion of the coloured population is less than that of the slaves. The number of the former in 1820, was 238,197, and in 1840, 386,348, showing an increase in 20 years, of 62.2 per cent; and the slaves in the same time, showed an increase of 61.1, although the number of slaves emancipated in New York and New Jersey,* was probably more than 15,000; and which, consequently, made an accession of near six per cent to the free coloured in 1820. Making, then, but a moderate allowance for their gain from this source, the increase of the slaves shown by the census will considerably exceed that of the free coloured. It is true, that whilst this class gained largely by emancipation, it is known also to have lost largely by emigration, especially in the last decennial term; but such emigration is not likely to have much exceeded the diminution of slaves from a similar cause, and certainly not enough to balance the gain from emancipation.

But further: the proportion of children under 10 in this class, thus compares with that of the other two classes in 1830 and 1840, viz:

		Per cent.		*Per cent.*		*Per cent.*
Whites, . .	in 1830,	32.54—	In 1840,	31.61—	Difference,	0.93
Slaves, . .	"	34.90	"	33.94	"	0.96
Free coloured	"	30.04	"	28.88	"	1.12

By which it appears that the proportion of free coloured children under ten was, at both enumerations, more than two per cent less than that of the whites, and more than four per cent less than that of the slaves. Now we cannot refer this inferiority to emigration, which, so far as it has any effect, tends to increase the proportion of children; and whether we refer the whole or part of it to emancipation, (which, by adding only adults to the class, unquestionably diminishes the proportion of children,) an inferiority in the rate of increase is the necessary result. If we refer the whole, then we suppose such an accession from this source that, when deducted from the total number of the class, the remainder would prove a slower rate of increase than the census exhibits in the slaves, and, perhaps in the whites; and if we refer only a part of the difference

* In 1820, the number of slaves in those States was 17,645, and in 1830, it was reduced to 2,329. It may be presumed that the whole, or nearly the whole of the difference, was the effect of emancipation in the intervening ten years.

of proportion to emancipation, then the other part of it directly indicates a smaller decennial increase.

In the cities and towns, to which most of the free persons of colour resort, we find much reason for believing that their natural increase is slower than that of the slaves or the whites. They are, taken as a class, poor, improvident, immoral, and consequently, little likely to rear large families. The licentiousness, too, which characterizes many of the young females of this class, consigns a large portion of them either to unfruitfulness or a premature grave. In New York, Philadelphia, and Baltimore, they occupy much more than their proportion of the pauper list. These facts are not inconsistent with the supposed greater longevity of this class; for the rate of its natural increase depends upon the greater number, and its character for longevity, on a few.

In comparing the proportion of children under ten, in 1830 and 1840, we find the falling off to be greater in this class than the other classes; and if we cannot refer it to an increase of emancipation in last decennial term, of which we have no evidence, it seems to indicate a small diminution in the rate of increase.

Let us now compare the increase of the white and coloured population, in fifty years, supposing the former not to have gained, and the latter not to have lost by migration.

In 1790, the white population was	3,172,464
Increase in 10 years, exclusive of immigration, 33.9 per cent	1,075,465
In 1800	4,247,929
Increase in 10 years, 33.1 per cent . . .	1,406,064
In 1810, ...	5,653,993
Increase in 10 years, 32.1 per cent . . .	1,814,932
In 1820, ...	7,468,925
Increase in 10 years, 30.9 per cent . . .	2,307,897
In 1830, ...	9,776,822
Increase in 10 years, 29.6 per cent . . .	2,929,136
In 1840, ...	12,705,958

Which shows an increase in fifty years, or rather in forty-nine years and ten months, in the proportion of 100 to 400.4

In 1790, the whole coloured population was . .	757,363
Increase in 10 years, 32.2 per cent . . .	244,073
In 1800, ...	1,001,436
Increase in 10 years, 32.2 per cent . . .	322,462
In 1810, ...	1,323,898
Increase in 10 years, 32.2 per cent . . .	426,295
In 1820, ...	1,750,193
Increase in 10 years, 32.2 per cent . . .	563,562
In 1830, ...	2,313,755
Increase in 10 years, 32.2 per cent . . .	745,029
In 1840, ...	3,058,784

Which shows an increase, in the same period, in the proportion of 100 to 403.9 per cent, or three and a half per cent more than that of the white population.

It may seem improbable, at the first view, that the natural increase of the white population was greater than that of the coloured in the two first decennial terms, as we have supposed it; and altogether inconsistent with that greater exemption from all the ordinary restraints on marriage, which keeps the increase of this race nearly uniform. It has been already stated, that the difference between them in 1800 and 1810, may have been overrated, and that we should, perhaps, be nearer the truth, to lower the increase of the whites by a higher estimate of the immigration, and to make a small addition to the increase of the coloured population in the first decennial terms. But we must not allow too much to the considerations that have been mentioned; for it must be remembered that, in the first decennial terms, most of the slaves lived in the more insalubrious portions of the southern States, whilst most of the whites occupied much more healthy regions. Besides, if a greater proportion of the coloured females are mothers, and mothers at an earlier age, they probably do not rear such large families, and a greater number of their offspring die from disease and neglect. It is known that, while the slaves have a greater proportion of children under ten than the whites,* they are also subject to greater mortality in after life, and, perhaps, the last circumstance may balance or nearly balance the first. These, and other questions connected with the progress of our population, can be accurately solved only after fuller and more frequent statistical details than we now possess.

---

* It must, however, be remembered, that a part of the excess must be referred to emancipation, which, by being confined to adults, enhances the proportion of children. But the precise extent of this disturbing influence we have no means of ascertaining.

CHAPTER XII.

THE FUTURE INCREASE OF THE POPULATION.

Having ascertained the actual increase of our population during half a century, and estimated its natural increase, unaffected by adventitious circumstances, let us now inquire whether the past increase affords us a rule for calculating its future progress; and since, as we have seen, the ratio of its increase has been diminishing, whether it will continue to diminish at the same rate.

The ratios of decennial increase, we have estimated as follows:

	1800.	1810.	1820.	1830.	1840.
Natural increase of the white population, per cent, . .	33.9	33.1	32.1	30.9	29.6
Of the coloured, " . .	32.2	32.2	32.2	32.2	32.2
Actual increase of the whole population, per cent, . .	35.02	36.45	33.35	33.26	32.67

In the last series there are two irregularities, which deserve notice. One was occasioned by the acquisition of Louisiana; the other was, that but nine years and ten months intervened between the census of 1820 and that of 1830, instead of ten years, which was the interval between the other enumerations. The first augmented the ratio of increase between 1800 and 1810, about one and a half per cent; the last underrated it between 1820 and 1830, about two-thirds of one per cent.

When these irregularities are corrected, the series of rates of increase, per cent, will stand thus:

35.02 34.95 33.45 33.92 32.67

And this would probably exhibit that diminishing series in the ratios of increase, which would take place if the gain to the whites and loss to the coloured population by migration, were to continue to increase in the same proportion that they have heretofore done.

9*

This, however, is not to be expected. European emigration would be immediately affected by a European war, which would at once check natural increase, and give new employment to a great number; so that, instead of emigrants from that source increasing, as they have done for the last thirty years, they would be considerably diminished. Besides, though peace should continue, it is not probable that those emigrants will increase in proportion to our increasing numbers, and still less, in the same ratio as heretofore. The increase of their number depends upon the condition of both countries; and although, when the United States contain one hundred millions of people, they may present six times as many points of attraction as at present, yet it does not follow that Europe will then be able to spare inhabitants to the same extent. So far as England is concerned, Canada, New Holland, and New Zealand may draw off the largest portion of her redundant numbers; nor can it be foreseen how much our own policy may change in encouraging immigration, when the Western States have attained a density equal to that of the Middle States.

But will the diminution in the rate of natural increase continue unchanged; and will it not even augment as the density of population increases?

On this subject, very contrary opinions have prevailed. Whilst some have calculated upon an undeviating rule of multiplication until we have reached 200,000,000 or more, others have maintained that, although our population might continue its past rate of increase until it had reached 60,000,000, a change in that rate would certainly then take place; as such a population supposes the whole territory of the Union occupied, and all the fertile lands under cultivation. These opinions seem equally removed from probability. The first is satisfactorily disproved by the diminution in the ratio of increase which has already been shown, and which diminution we may rationally expect to increase with the increasing density of numbers. The other hypothesis would arrest the present progress of our population when it has reached 60,000,000, which would not be equal to 64 persons to a square mile on the country now occupied by the people of the United States. But when it is recollected that the unoccupied country west of the Mississipi is yet larger than that now settled, we may presume that, when the population has reached 60,000,000, the whole of the western territory to the Pacific will be more or less settled, and consequently, that the population will then average less than 33 to a square mile; a degree of density which supposes indeed a progressive abatement in the rate of increase, such as we are now witnessing, but certainly none arising from the difficulty of obtaining subsistence. That is not likely to be an efficient check on the progress of our population until it has reached an average density of from 60 to 80 to the square mile.

Without doubt, other checks to natural multiplication, those arising from prudence or pride, will continue to operate with increased force as our cities multiply in number and increase in magnitude, and as the wealthy class enlarges. These circumstances will have the effect of retarding marriage ; and in the most densely peopled States, the fall in the price of labour, and consequently, the increased difficulty of providing for a family, may operate also on the poorer classes. It is even probable, that these checks operate sooner in this country than they have operated in other countries, by reason of the higher standard of comfort with which the American people start, and of that pride of personal independence which our political institutions so strongly cherish. The census shows that their influence has been felt ever since the first enumeration ; but we have no reason to believe that they will operate with a more accelerated force than they have done, until the lapse of near a centnry.

We find that each of the States exhibits a similar diminution in the ratio of increase to that which we have seen in the whole Union, and that it is equaily manifest whether population is dense or thin—is rapidly or slowly advancing—is sending forth emigrants, or receiving them from other States. This fact, which seems hitherto not to have been suspected, will clearly appear in the following tables, in which the progress of population from 1800 to 1840, is shown in all the States whose numbers at the former period have been ascertained :

Table showing the Number of White Females, of White Children under 10 *years of age, and of Persons to a Square Mile, in twenty States, in* 1800 *and* 1840*; the Proportion of Children to Females, at the same periods; the Increase in the number of persons, and the Decrease in the proportion of children during the* 40 *years; and the average Decrease in* 10 *years.*

States.	Years.	Females.	Children under 10.	Persons to a sq. mile.	Increase of persons.	Proportion of childr'n.	Decrea'e of proportion.	Decrea'e in 10 years.
Maine, ...	1800	74,069	54,869	5.	11.7	74.*	13.9	3.4
	1840	247,449	148,846	16.7		60.1		
New Hampshire,.	1800	91,740	60,465	19.9	11.	65.9	17.4	4.3
	1840	145,032	70,387	30.9		48.5		
Vermont, ...	1800	74,580	57,692	15.7	14.	77.3	22.	5.5
	1840	144,840	80,111	29.7		55.3		
Massachusetts,....	1800	211,299	124,566	48.3	36.	58.9	12.	3.
	1840	368,351	173,037	84.3		46.9		
Rhode Island,....	1800	33,579	19,466	53.1	30.6	57.9	11.1	2.8
	1840	54,225	25,384	83.7		46.8		
Connecticut,.......	1800	123,528	73,682	49.2	11.5	59.6	12.9	3.2
	1840	153,556	71,783	60.7		46.7		
New York,.......	1800	258,587	195,840	11.9	25.7	75.7	17.6	4.4
	1840	1,171,533	681,091	47.6		58.1		
New Jersey,.......	1800	95,600	67,402	28.2	21.	70.5	11.4	2.8
	1840	174,533	103,302	49.2		59.1		
Pennsylvania, ...	1800	284,627	270,233	12.6	23.9	71.2	8.2	2.
	1840	831,345	524,189	36.5		63.		
Delaware,..........	1800	24,819	15,878	29.2	6.2	63.9	4.5	1.1
	1840	29,302	17,406	35.4		59.4		
Maryland,.........	1800	105,676	69,648	30.6	11.5	65.9	7.5	1.9
	1840	159,400	93,072	42.1		58.4		
Virginia,...........	1800	252,151	179,761	11.7	6.9	71.3	6.3	1.6
	1840	369,745	240,343	18.6		65.		
North Carolina,...	1800	166,116	122,191	9.6	5.6	73.5	7.3	1.8
	1840	244,833	162,282	15.2		66.2		
South Carolina,...	1800	95,339	72,075	10.8	7.9	75.6	8.3	2.
	1840	128,588	86,566	18.7		67.3		
Georgia,...........	1800	48,298	38,248	2.6	8.6	81.1	4.9	1.2
	1840	197,161	150,317	11.2		76.2		
Mississippi,........	1800	2,262	1,962	.18	5.9	86.7	7.	1.7
	1840	81,818	65,269	6.1		79.7		
Tennessee,........	1800	44,529	37,677	2.6	18.	84.6	10.2	2.5
	1840	315,193	234,700	20.6		74.4		
Kentucky,.........	1800	85,915	72,234	5.4	13.8	83.9	12.	3.
	1840	250,664	204,978	19.2		71.9		
Ohio,................	1800	20,595	18,276	1.1	37.1	88.7	15.4	3.8
	1840	726,762	509,088	38.2		73.3		
Indiana,............	1800	2,003	1,645	.13	17.7	82.1	6.	1.5
	1840	325,925	248,127	18.8		76.1		

The following table gives the same comparative view of the preceding twenty States when comprehended under five divisions, viz :

* As the number of females is very nearly one-half of the population, one-half the numbers in this column may be taken as the several proportions of the children to the whole population in each State.

Local divisions.	Years.	Females.	Children under 10.	Persons to a sq. mile.	Increase of persons.	Proportion of childr'n.	Decrea'e of proportion.	Decrea'e in 10 years.
N. England States,	1800	608,795	386,723	19.2	15.6	63.5	12.4	3.1
	1840	1,113,453	569,348	34.8		51.1		
Middle States,....	1800	784,068	554,783	15.3	28.3	70.7	15.	3.75
	1840	2,381,948	1,327,362	43.6		55.7		
Southern States,..	1800	561,904	412,276	8.9	7.	73.	6.4	1.6
	1840	940,317	637,510	15.9		67.8		
Southw'n States of Mississippi and Tennessee,.....	1800	46,791	38,639	1.3	12.4	77.6	2.1	.5
	1840	397,011	299,969	13.7		75.5		
Northw'n States of Kentucky, Ohio and Indiana,....	1800	108,513	92,155	2.3	23.2	84.9	11.1	3.8
	1840	1,303,351	962,193	25.5		73.8		

We see by the preceding tables that the natural increase of the population is inversely as its density; and this is apparent, whether we compare the increase of the same State at different periods, or the increase of one State or one division with another. Thus, in New England, where, with the exception of Maine, which is comparatively a newly settled State, the population is most dense, averaging 50 to a square mile, the proportion of children is the smallest, that is, 48.8 per cent of the females; in the Middle States, the population is 43.6 to a square mile, and the proportion of children, 55.7 per cent; in the Southern States, the population is 15.7 persons to the square mile, and the proportion of children, 67.8 per cent; in the South-western States, the population is 13.7 persons to the square mile, and the proportion of children 75.5 per cent; and if the Northwestern States seems to be an exception to the rule, in having a greater proportion of children than the Southern States, while they have also a denser population by 9.6 persons to the square mile, it is owing to the extraordinary fertility of those States, whereby 25 persons to the square mile does not indicate so great a relative density as 16 to the square mile in the Southern States.

This rule of the rate of natural increase acts so uniformly, that we may perceive the falling off in the rate, not only in 40 years, as we have seen, but also in each decennial term, of which the largest States in the five great divisions may serve as examples, viz:

	1800.	1810.	1820.	1830.	1840.
Massachusetts, *prop. of children under* 10,.........	58.9	57.6	53.	48.	46.9
New York,...	75.7	72.8	67.2	63.2	58.1
Virginia,...	71.2	69.6	68.	66.4	65.
Tennessee,..	84.6	82.9	78.8	78.	74.4
Ohio,..	88.7	83.1	79.	74.2	73.3

What is true in these States will be found true in the others; and there are not more than two or three cases, out of near a hundred, in which the comparison can be made, that the proportion of children, and consequently the rate of increase, is not less at each census then at the census preceding.

When we perceive the causes of the diminution of increase operating so steadily, and so independently of the greater or less facility of procuring subsistence, we are warranted in assuming that the diminution will continue to advance at the same moderate rate it has hitherto done, until all the vacant territory of the United States is settled, after which, another law of diminution and an accelerated rate may be expected to take place.

In conformity with the preceding views, we may conclude that the future increase of the population of the United States will not greatly differ from the following series during the next half century, if immigration continues to advance as it has done, viz:

1850.	1860.	1870.	1880.	1890.	1900.
32 p. cent.	31.3 p. cent.	30.5 p. cent.	29.6 p. cent.	28.6 p. cent.	27.5 p. cent.
22,400,000	29,400,000	38,300,000	49,600,000	63,000,000	80,000,000

If, however, immigration were to continue as it is, or have but a moderate increase, the ratios of increase might be thus reduced:

1850.	1860.	1870.	1880.	1890.	1900.
31.8 p. cent.	30.9 p. cent.	30 p. cent.	29 p. cent.	27.9 p. cent.	26.8 p. cent.
22,000	28,800,000	36,500,000	46,500,000	59,800,000	74,000,000

At which time, the population will not exceed the average density of from 35 to 40 persons to the square mile, after making ample allowance for the Rocky mountains and the tract of desert lying at their eastern base.

The preceding estimates suppose a slower rate of increase than has been commonly assumed in our political arithmetic, and, for a part of the time, even by those who have set the lowest limit to our future numbers; but this rate cannot be much augmented without overlooking some of the facts or laws deducible from our past progress, or gratuitously assuming some new and more favourable circumstances in our future progress. The lowest estimate, however, ought to satisfy those whose pride of country most looks to its physical power, for, at the reduced rate of increase supposed, our population would, in a century from this time, or a little more, amount to 200,000,000, and then scarcely exceed the present density of Massachusetts, which is still in a course of vigorous increase. In these estimates, the increase of the coloured population is supposed likely to continue as it has been, or with such small changes as will not materially vary the result. But the future condition of that part of our population will be separately considered in the next chapter.

Some of our readers, who may wish to make calculations concerning the past or future increase of the population, may find a convenience in the following

Table showing, in different rates of Decennial Increase, the corresponding rates for the intermediate years, and the number of years necessary for the Population to double, at different rates of Increase.

INCREASE IN TEN YEARS.	INCREASE, PER CENT, IN—									No. of years required to double.
	1 year.	2 years.	3 years.	4 years.	5 years.	6 years.	7 years.	8 years.	9 years.	
20 p. cent,	1.84	3.71	5.62	7.56	9.54	11.56	13.61	15.70	17.83	38.017
21 "	1.92	3.89	5.88	7.92	10.	12.12	14.27	16.87	18.72	36.362
22 "	2.01	4.06	6.15	8.28	10.45	12.67	14.93	17.24	19.60	34.837
23 "	2.09	4.23	6.41	8.63	10.90	13.22	15.19	18.01	20.48	33.483
24 "	2.17	4.40	6.66	8.98	11.36	13.76	16.25	18.78	21.36	32.222
25 "	2.25	4.56	6.92	9.33	11.80	14.33	16.91	19.54	22.24	31.062
26 "	2.33	4.73	7.18	9.68	12.25	14.87	17.56	20.31	23.12	29.991
27 "	2.42	4.90	7.43	10.03	12.69	15.42	18.21	21.07	24.	28.999
28 "	2.50	5.06	7.66	10.38	13.14	15.96	18.86	21.83	24.88	28.078
29 "	2.58	5.22	7.94	10.78	13.58	16.51	19.51	22.59	25.76	27.220
30 "	2.65	5.37	8.19	11.06	14.02	17.05	20.16	23.35	26.68	26.419
31 "	2.73	5.54	8.44	11.40	14.45	17.59	20.81	24.11	27.51	25.669
32 "	2.81	5.71	8.68	11.74	14.89	18.12	21.45	24.87	28.38	24.966
33 "	2.89	5.87	8.93	12.08	15.32	18.66	22.09	35.62	29.26	24.305
34 "	2.97	6.03	9.18	12.42	15.76	19.20	22.73	26.38	30.13	23.683
35 "	3.04	6.18	9.42	12.75	16.19	19.73	23.35	27.13	31.01	23.097
36 "	3.12	6.34	9.66	13.09	16.62	20.26	24.01	27.88	31.88	22.542
37 "	3.19	6.50	9.90	13.42	17.05	20.79	24.66	28.64	32.75	22.018
38 "	3.27	6.65	10.14	13.75	17.47	21.32	25.29	29.29	33.93	21.520
39 "	3.34	6.81	10.38	14.08	17.90	21.84	26.92	30.14	34.50	21.049
40 "	3.42	6.96	10.62	14.41	18.32	22.37	26.56	30.89	35.36	20.600

According to the preceding table, the population on the 1st of the present year, or three years after the census was last taken, is as follows:

The increase on the last decennial term was 32.67 per cent, and the rate of increase for three years, in the table, being 8.68 per cent, where the decennial increase is 32 per cent, and 8.93 per cent where the decennial increase is 33 per cent, the intermediate rate of incfrease or three years, now, is 8.85 per cent. This gives an increase of 1,510,646, which, added to 17,069,453, shows the whole population of the United States to have been, on the 1st of June last, 18,580,000. In the latter year of the current decennial term, a small deduction must be made for the gradual diminution in the rate of increase.

CHAPTER XIII.

THE FUTURE PROGRESS OF SLAVERY.

So far as can now be seen, the progress of the slave population in the United States is likely to undergo but little change for several decennial terms, and to be no more affected by schemes of emancipation or colonization, or even by individual cases of manumission, than it has been.

This is not the place for assailing or defending slavery; but it may be confidently asserted, that the efforts of abolitionists have hitherto made the people in the slaveholding States cling to it more tenaciously. Those efforts are viewed by them as an intermeddling in their domestic concerns that is equally unwarranted by the comity due to sister States, and to the solemn pledges of the federal compact. In the general indignation which is thus excited, the arguments in favour of negro emancipation, once open and urgent, have been completely silenced, and its advocates among the slaveholders, who have not changed their sentiments, find it prudent to conceal them. Philosophy no longer ventures to teach that this institution is yet more injurious to the master than the slave; religion has ceased to refuse it her sanction; and even the love of liberty, which once pleaded for emancipation, is now enlisted against it. Statesmen and scholars have tasked their ingenuity to show that slavery is not only legitimate and moral, but expedient and wise. The scheme of Las Casas, which, to relieve Indians from the prospective yoke of bondage, actually placed it on the necks of Africans, is no longer deemed a paralogism in morals, and the slavery of a part of the community is gravely maintained to be essential to a high State of civil freedom in the rest.

Such have been the fruits of the zeal of northern abolitionists in those States in which slavery prevails; and the fable of the Wind and the Sun never more forcibly illustrated the difference between gentle and violent means in influencing men's wills. Nor is the effect a temporary one. All the prejudices of education and habit in favour of slavery, have struck their roots the deeper for the rudeness with which they have been assailed. The slave himself, too, has suffered by the change. The progressive amelioration of his condition has been arrested; and in the precautions which the schemes of abolitionists (whose numbers have been as much overrated by the slave-owners as their power has been by themselves,) have suggested, his condition has, in some instances, become positively worse. Even where this has not been the case the "bliss of ignorance" has been converted by his misguided friends into a sullen and hopeless discontent. The irritating conflicts and recriminations to which the subject has given occasion between different parts of the Union, have afforded new means of gaining popular favour, which crafty politicians on both sides have gladly seized; and the dissensions thus inflamed, induce those who look with evil eyes on the future strength and greatness of this republican confederacy, to indulge in vain hopes of its dissolution.

The causes of this strife of feeling and opinion are too deeply seated in the human heart not to be supposed to continue for the period that has been mentioned; and, accordingly, the State of domestic slavery, and the progress of the slave population, will probably experience no material change for forty or fifty years, or even a yet longer term, in any of the slaveholding States, except Delaware, and perhaps Maryland.

But if we carry our views to a yet more distant future, we shall find causes at work whose effects on this institution neither the miscalculating sympathies of fanaticism or philanthropy, nor their re-action on the slave owners, can avert or long delay. The population of the slaveholding States, at its present rate of increase, and even at a reduced rate, will, in no long time, have reached that moderate degree of density which supposes all their most productive lands taken into cultivation. As soon as that point is reached, the price of labour, compared with the means of subsistence, will begin to fall, according to the great law of human destiny, so ably developed by Malthus, and which is the inevitable result of man's tendency to increase and multiply; of his dependence on the soil for his subsistence; and of the limited extent of that soil. Labour, then, as it increases in quantity, must exchange either for less or for cheaper food; and such reduction is altogether independent of a gradation of soils. It must take place if every rood of earth was of equal fertility with the American Bottom in Illinois, since every succeeding generation being more numerous than the preceding, the products of but a smaller portion of the earth's surface can fall to the share of one individual. In this progressive declension of its value, labour will finally attain a price so low, that the earnings of a slave will not repay the cost of rearing him, when, of course, his master will consider him as a burdensome charge rather than a source of profit; and as the same decline in the value of labour once liberated the villeins or slaves of western Europe, and will liberate the serfs of Russia, so must it put an end to slavery in the United States, should it be terminated in no other way.

This may be called the euthanasia of the institution, as it will be abolished with the consent of the master no less than the wishes of the slave; and the period of termination will be sooner reached because the labour of slaves, by reason of the inferiority in industry, economy, and skill, inseparable from their condition, is less productive than that of freemen.

But this depression in the value of labour will reach the different States at different periods of time, and it will advance more slowly as we proceed south. Yet the facility with which slaves can be transported from one State to another, will countervail much of this difference; and slave labour, in the more northern of the slaveholding States, will not greatly decline in price so long as it is very profitable in the more southern. If Maryland, Virginia, and North Carolina were insulated from the rest, then, at no very distant day, slave labour in those States, with its inherent disadvantages, would not more than defray the cost of its maintenance; but so long as their slaves can be readily transferred to other States, they will retain a value in every State proportionate and approaching to their value in other States. This would, moreover, be the case, if the trade in slaves, now carried on, were interdicted, and their importation were permitted only in those cases in which they migrate with the families of proprietors, so many of whom are ever seeking to improve their condition in the south and the west. We must, therefore, in our estimates of the future progress and duration of slavery, regard all the slaveholding States as one community for a considerable time to come; and expect that, if the institution remains undisturbed by State legislation, (for that of the United States is not only unwarranted by the constitution, but is inconsistent with a continuance of the Union,) they will all approach to the same density of slave population, except so far as it may be affected by diversities of soil and other local circumstances.

The slaveholding States and territories had, in 1840, a population of 7,534,431, on an area of 629,500 square miles; and their comparative density, both as to the whole number and the slave portion, may be seen in the following

Table, showing the Density of Population in the Slaveholding States.

STATES AND TERRITORIES.	Area—miles.	Whole Population.	Slaves.	NO. TO THE SQ. MILE.	
				Whole pop.	Slaves.
Delaware,	2,200	78,085	2,605	35.5	1.2
Maryland,	11,150	470,017	89,737	42.1	8.
District of Columbia,	100	43,712	4,694	43.7	4.7
Virginia,	66,620	1,239,797	448,987	18.6	6.7
North Carolina,	49,500	753,419	245,817	15.2	5.
South Carolina,	31,750	594,398	327,038	18.7	10.
Georgia,	61,500	691,392	280,944	11.2	4.5
Florida,	55,680	54,477	25,717	.9	.5
Louisiana,	49,300	352,411	168,452	7.1	3.4
Alabama,	52,900	590,756	253,532	11.2	4.8
Mississippi,	47,680	375,651	195,211	8.3	4.
Arkansas,	55,000	97,574	19,535	1.7	.3
Tennessee,	40,200	829,210	183,059	20.5	4.5
Kentucky,	40,500	779,828	182,258	19.2	4.5
Missouri,	65,500	383,702	58,240	5.8	.9
Total,	629,580	7,334,431	2,486,226	11.6	4.1

The slaveholding States and Territories, then, taken together, have an average population of not quite twelve to the square mile, of which somewhat more than one-third are slaves; and they, as well as the free portion, are very unequally distributed over these States.

To ascertain when the population of those States will attain a density which will make slave labour unprofitable, let us inquire, first, into that precise degree of density which reduces the price of labour to the cost of its maintenance; and secondly, into the future rate of increase of those States.

I. To answer our first inquiry, we have but scanty materials. In those countries of Europe in which slavery has been abolished, history seems to be entirely unacquainted with the motives of the abolition, and it is left only to conjecture to infer that it was because it was no longer gainful to the master. Supposing this fact established, we have no authentic data for determining the density of population, and still less for estimating the state of husbandry, which must be taken into the account; since a population of 50 to the square mile in the 12th and 13th centuries, when slavery was abolished in England, might be equal to twice or thrice as many at the present day, by reason of the increased productiveness of the soil. It is, however, clear, that slavery is still profitable in Russia, and that it would be unprofitable in every part of western

Europe. As there, a large part even of the free labour can barely earn a subsistence, and a portion cannot always do that, it follows that slaves, whose labour is inherently less profitable, could not earn enough for their snpport. We may, therefore, infer that a far less dense population than now exists in the western part of Europe would be inconsistent with slavery: and that the degree of density which would render it productive of more profit than expense, would be some intermediate point between that of Russia and that of the other States of Europe. But the population of those States is about 110 to the square mile, whilst that of Russia is but 25; and though the degree of density when slavery first ceases to be profitable is somewhere between the two, yet, between such wide extremes, we have no means of ascertaining that intermediate point, or of even approximating to it. Nor could any rule, drawn from countries differing so widely in soil, climate, goodness of tillage, and mode of living, be of easy application to the United States.

But we may make a nearer approach to the truth if we confine our speculations to the abolition of slavery in England, though that part of her history is involved in no little darkness and contradiction. In the fourteenth century, when the emancipation of villeins had made considerable progress, the population in England and Wales was computed, from the returns of a poll-tax, to be 2,350,000, which is 40 persons to the square mile. About the end of the seventeenth century (in 1690,) when no vestige of villeinage remained, from the number of houses returned under the hearth-tax, the population was estimated at 5,318,100, which is 92 to the square mile. The medium point of density is 66, which we may assume to be inconsistent with any profit from domestic slavery.

But in applying this fact to the slaveholding States, there are several points of diversity between them and England to be taken into consideration. 1. The difference of fertility. Though three of the slaveholding States, Kentucky, Tennessee, and Missouri, constituting less than one-fourth of the whole, are naturally more fertile than England, and are capable of supporting a denser population than she was at the period supposed, the other three-fourths are yet more inferior to England in fertility.

2. The standard of comfort for the labouring class is much higher here than it is in England, so far as it concerns the consumption of animal food, in consequence of the peculiar circumstances of this country, where the husbandry and useful arts of a cultivated people are conjoined with the thin population of a rude one. In every

part of Europe, population and the arts have advanced at the same rate; and the ascertained slowness of the rate supposes straitened means of subsistence in every stage of the progress. This is conclusively proved, as to England, by the fact that her population, which, in 1377, had been 2,350,000, had increased in 1800, that is, in 423 years, only to 8,872,980; since nothing but great difficulty in obtaining the means of subsistence, and extreme discomfort with the great mass of the people, could have retarded the period of duplication with our progenitors to upwards of two hundred years! Now, although the standard of comfort for the free labourer is not necessarily that for the slave, yet, in the same country and at the same time, the last will approximate to the first—at least, that has hitherto been the case in the United States, where animal food always constitutes a part of the daily aliment of the slave.

3. The difference of husbandry. Agriculture is doubtless much less skilful and productive in the United States than it is in England at the present day; but it is probably much more so than it was in that country at the period to which we refer. Of all, or nearly all, the improvements in husbandry, whether taught by experience or science, our agriculturists readily avail themselves; and the chief difference between the two countries is, that the labour which there neatly tills a small surface, here slovenly tills a large one.

Of these diversities, the effect of the last is to make the rate of density that is inconsistent with slavery greater here than it was in England, and that of the second is to make it smaller. Let us suppose that the two neutralize each other; and that the more liberal consumption of the slave in the United States is compensated by the superiority of their tillage to that which prevailed in England at the supposed era. If, then, we make a deduction from the assumed density of 66 to the square mile, for the greater natural fertility of England, which we will suppose to be greater than that of the slaveholding States by one-fourth, that is, as 100 to 75, then the density, which in those States will be found inconsistent with profit from domestic slavery, will be reduced to about 50 persons to the square mile.

Should this moderate degree of density be considered inadequate to the effect here ascribed to it, it must be recollected that *adult* slave labour may still be profitable, though it may not be sufficiently so to defray the expense of rearing it from infancy; and that the payment of this expense is assumed to be an indispensable condition to the continuance of the institution. In any country less populous than China, the labour of grown slaves would generally be profitable; and the barbarous policy of making slaves of prisoners of war may continue slavery in some countries, as it does in Africa, in which its profits could not keep up its own stock. But in the United States, those who would appropriate to themselves the labour of the adult slave, must consent to incur the previous charge of his childhood.

We must also bear in mind that the slaveholding States are almost exclusively agricultural, and, consequently, that their population is principally rural. Not over one-thirtieth of their population, if we take away Baltimore and New Orleans, live in towns, and with the inhabitants of those cities, not one-sixteenth part. In densely peopled countries, however, from one-half to two-thirds live in cities and towns; thus showing that from a third to a half of their whole population is sufficient for their culture; of course, were the density as much as 120 to the square mile, from 40 to 60 persons would be as many as could be advantageously employed on the soil; and thus the value of labour would decline as much and as fast in a country that was purely agricultural, as it would in another of twice its population that was also manufacturing. Should, then, agriculture continue to be the principal occupation of the slaveholding States, and they not betake themselves more extensively to manufactures, the population, when it amounts to 50 persons to the square mile, will have reached that point when every addition to it will rapidly depreciate the value of labour. We may, therefore, reasonably infer that, if its value in the slaveholding States should not have attained the supposed point of depression when they have a population of 50 to the square mile, they will attain it in no long time afterwards.

It affords some confirmation of these views, that when emancipation took place in New Jersey, which probably has the average fertility of the present slaveholding States, the population was something less than 40 to the square mile, and that, even then, the labour of slaves was thought not much to exceed the cost of their subsistence; and that many judicious slave-owners in Maryland and eastern Virginia, where the population, exclusive of Baltimore, scarcely exceeds 35 to the square mile, believe that the labour of their slaves yields but a small net profit.

Supposing, then, a density of 50 persons to the square mile to be incompatible with the longer continuance of slavery in the States now permitting it, their aggregate population would then amount to

31,479,000. When are they likely to attain this number? Their past progress, from 1790 to 1840, has been as follows:

	1790.	1800.	1810.	1820.	1830.	1840.
Total population,......	1,961,372	2,621,316	3,480,904	4,502,235	5,848,303	7,334,431
Increase in each decennial term, per cent,.	....	33.7	32.8	29.3	30.2	25.4

The whole increase in fifty years has been as 100 to 383.7. The rate of increase, it will be perceived, has declined in the four decennial terms between 1800 and 1840, from 33.7 per cent to 25.4 per cent, showing a falling off in that time of 8.3 per cent in the ratio of increase for ten years. But more than half of this decline took place between 1830 and 1840, in consequence of the emigration to Texas, which was principally from the slaveholding States. As much of that emigration was the consequence of an ardent desire to aid the Texians in their struggle for independence, as well as of the great and sudden reverse of prosperity experienced by some of those States, and as motives equally strong are not likely to recur, we, perhaps, ought to regard this unwonted reduction of increase as temporary, and to consider the previous rate as affording the just rule for our estimates. Between 1800 and 1830, the falling off in the decennial increase was only 3½ per cent; but between 1800 and 1810, it was augmented 3 per cent by the acquisition of Louisiana. Let us, then, take a medium course, and suppose a rate of diminution greater than that shown by the four first enumerations, but smaller than that shown by the last. Let us suppose that, in the future progress of the slaveholding States, the increase in each decennial term will be one-fifteenth part less than the increase of the preceding term, and see when, from that increase, the population will attain a density of 50 to the square mile.

The rate of increase thus diminishing, will be 23.3 per cent in 1850; 21.7 per cent in 1860; and so on, in a descending series, by which, in a little upwards of eighty years, the population would reach the required density, and amount to 31,000,000. But inasmuch as the other States increase in a much greater ratio, as experience has shown, this circumstance is likely, after a time, to accelerate the rate of increase in the slaveholding States. In fifty years, when, on the supposed rate of increase, the latter would not exceed 30 to the square mile, many, perhaps most of the free States, will have attained a density of upwards of 100 on the same area. The difference in the price of land which these different densities imply, cannot but induce an increase of emigration from the free States to the slaveholding States. The swarms from the New England hive prefer, at present, migrating to States where there are no slaves ; but as soon as the northwestern States are settled throughout, and before they are densely peopled, the cheaper lands of the slaveholding States will hold out inducements to the settler too strong to be resisted. These States, instead of sending out emigrants, as at present, will then receive them ; and thus the rate of their increase, instead of continuing in a descending ratio, will be a while stationary, and then moderately increase. The effect of this change, depending upon so many contingencies, it is impossible to calculate ; but it might hasten the period in question some twenty years or more.

The period, too, when slavery will be likely to expire of itself, will reach the different States at different times. So long as the labour of slaves is very profitable in any of the States, their value, as we have seen, is enhanced in all the others ; but when that labour has greatly declined in value, as it will do when greatly augmented, the influence of one State on another will have proportionally diminished, and not be sufficient to overcome other obstacles to the removal of slaves. The diversities of the States, physical and moral, will then have an unchecked operation, and they are considerable. Some States and parts of States raise grain and cattle, which occupations require but little labour, and, of course, can support but few slaves ; whilst others, cultivating cotton, sugar, tobacco, and rice, which, requiring much labour and manipulation, cannot be grown without a much larger number. In the former, then, emancipation will be at once easier and sooner ; and thus after Delaware, in which it will first, and in no long time take place, the States of Maryland, Virginia, North Carolina, Tennessee, Kentucky, and Missouri, may be expected to abolish slavery some considerable time before slave labour has ceased to be profitable in the States south of them. The climate, too, may have the effect of prolonging slavery in the last mentioned States, both because it indisposes men to field labour, and because it is less suited to the white than the negro temperament.

Such appears to be the result of general visible causes, whose operation is beyond human controul. It may, however, be hastened or retarded by contingent events, the influence of which, as well as their occurrence, time alone can determine. The following circumstances would tend to delay the termination of slavery : Further emigrations to Texas ; the formation of new slaveholding States, which, though it would accelerate the increase of the slaveholding population, would lessen its density; or, should slave labour be more extensively applied to manufactures, which does not seem impossible, as they would incur no greater charge for superintendence than is now incurred by agriculture; or, should the cultivation of the sugar-cane be extended to meet the growing demands of our increasing population, and that commodity should maintain its monopoly price; or, lastly, should new articles of culture requiring much labour, such as silk and wine, be introduced in the slaveholding States.

But, on the other hand, should none of these events take place, and should the sympathies now felt for the slave subside, or find sufficient employment at home, the same liberal sentiments which once prevailed in most of the slaveholding States may revive, and decide on the gradual abolition of slavery, or lessen its amount by colonization and private manumission. The natural multiplication of the slaves, too, may be affected by a less careful and kind treatment of them, as their value declines. Or, popular enthusiasm may be excited by religion or otherwise in favour of emancipating them; or the same popular feeling, in a frenzy of fear or resentment, may aim to destroy or expel them. These and other causes, not now foreseen, may prolong or abridge the existence of this institution in the United States, but none of them seem capable of averting its ultimate destiny. We may say of it, as of man: the doom of its death, though we know not the time or the mode, is certain and irrevocable.

To conclude this subject, so pregnant with matter of serious reflection to all: the citizens of the slaveholding States are persuaded that emancipation will necessarily lead, first, to political equality, and finally, to an amalgamation of the two races. Believing, as they really do, that the negroes are physically, as well as morally and intellectually, their inferiors, they regard this intermixture as a contamination of their own race; and these supposed consequences constitute their most invincible objections to the liberation of their slaves. Those who entertain these opinions, and who also believe that the result here inferred is inevitable, or even probable, have it now in their power to make some preparation for an issue so fraught with mischief, and so abhorrent to their feelings. If they think the number of their slaves is too great for them quietly to remain, when the period of natural liberation arrives, as an inferior caste, or with a qualified freedom, they ought to lessen the number by all allowable means—as by colonization ; and, since the emancipated class are found to increase more slowly than either the slaves or the whites, they ought to encourage, rather than check, private manumission. Even as a measure of precaution, the policy of prohibiting the liberation of slaves is very questionable ; and if so, the States which have adopted it, have not only yielded to the common temptation of avoiding a present danger by incurring a greater one hereafter, but, perverting a wise maxim, have incurred a certain evil to avoid one that is doubtful.

Though the natural increase of the free coloured class is less than that of the slaves or the whites, yet by its accessions from emancipation, its actual increase is far greater than that of either of the other two classes, as may be thus seen in the following

Table, showing the Increase of the White and the Coloured Population in the Slave-holding States.

	1790.	1800.	1810.	1820.	1830.	1840.	DECENNIAL INCREASE PER CENT IN				
							1800.	1810.	1820.	1830.	1840.
Whites,...	1,271,692	1,702,980	2,208,785	2,842,341	3,660,758	4,631,998	33.9	29.7	28.7	28.8	26.5
Free col...	32,635	61,241	88,678	135,294	182,070	211,889	87.7	44.8	52.6	37.7	16.4
Slaves,....	657.047	1,857,095	1,163,754	1,524,220	1,996,758	2,486,226	30.4	35.8	31.0	31.6	24.5

The increase in the whole 50 years has been as follows:

Whites,	as 100 to	364.2
Free coloured,	"	649.3
Slaves,	"	378.4
Total coloured	"	391.2

It is thus seen that, in these States, the whites have increased a little less than the whole population, (383.7 per cent,) and the slaves a little more ; but that the free coloured have increased almost twice as fast as the whites. The table further shows that, but for emancipation, the slaveholding States would, at this time, have contained from 200,000 to 300,000, perhaps over 300,000 slaves more than they now contain ; and that the reduction would have been still greater than it now is, if none of them had prohibited or impeded manumission.

CHAPTER XIV.

THE INCREASE OF THE ATLANTIC AND WESTERN, SLAVEHOLDING AND NON-SLAVEHOLDING STATES, COMPARED.

THE several States and Territories have been differently divided, according to circumstances. Sometimes they are classed, as we have seen, under five divisions, as they severally agree in climate, products, and in the prevailing habits and pursuits of their people. Sometimes, again, they are divided into Atlantic and Western States; and lastly, according to the fact of their permitting slavery or not. By combining the last twofold divisions, they admit of a fourfold division, as the Atlantic slaveholding and non-slaveholding States, and the Western slaveholding and non-slaveholding States. These four divisions will now be compared as to their present numbers, density of population, and rate of increase.

The following tables show the population, area, number of persons to the square mile, and increase at each enumeration since 1810, of the four divisions, composed of the Atlantic and Western States, slaveholding and non-slaveholding:

ATLANTIC STATES.

LOCAL DIVISIONS.	POPULATION IN—				Area—Square Miles.	No. to a sq. mile.	*Increase, p. cent, in—*		
	1810.	1820.	1830.	1840.			10 yrs.	20 yrs.	30 yrs.
I. Non-slavehold'g States.									
Maine, ...	228,705	298,335	399,455	501,793	32,000	15.6	......	......	......
New Hampshire,..	214,360	244,161	269,328	284,574	9,200	30.9	......	......	......
Vermont, ...	217,713	235,764	280,652	291,948	9,800	29.8	......	......	......
Massachusetts,....	472,040	523,287	610,408	737,699	8,750	86.5	......	......	......
Rhode Island,.....	77,031	83,059	97,199	108,830	1,300	83.7	......	......	......
Connecticut, ...	262,042	275,202	297,675	309,978	5,100	60.8	......	......	......
New York,.......	959,049	1,372,812	1,918,606	2,428,921	49,000	49.5	......	......	......
New Jersey,......	245,555	277,575	320,823	373,306	7,500	49.7	......	......	......
Pennsylvania,.....	810,091	1,049,458	1,348,233	1,724,033	47,500	36.6	......	......	......
Total, ...	3,486,586	4,359,653	5,542,381	6,761,082	170,150	39.4	22.	55.	94.
II. Slaveh'g St'tes.									
Delaware,........	72,674	72,749	76,748	78,085	2,200	35.5	......	......	......
Maryland,........	380,546	407,350	447,040	470,019	11,150	42.	......	......	......
Dist. of Columbia,.	24,023	33,039	39,834	43,712	100	43.7	......	......	......
Virginia, ...	974,622	1,065,379	1,211,405	1,239,797	66,620	18.6	......	......	......
North Carolina,...	555,500	638,829	737,987	753,419	49,500	15.2	......	......	......
South Carolina,...	415,115	502,741	581,185	594,398	31,750	18.7	......	......	......
Georgia,..........	252,433	340,987	516,823	691,392	61,500	11.2	......	......	......
Florida, ...	....	....	34,730	54,477	55,680	.9	......	......	......
Total, ...	2,674,913	3,061,074	3,645,752	3,925,299	278,500	14.1	5.3	25.3	43.5

WESTERN STATES.

LOCAL DIVISIONS.	POPULATION IN—				Area—Square miles.	No. to a sq. mile.	*Increase, p. cent, in—*		
	1810.	1820.	1830.	1840.			10 yrs.	20 yrs.	30 yrs.
III. Slavehold'g S.									
Louisiana,........	76,566	153,407	215,739	352,411	49,300	7.1	......	......	......
Mississippi,.......	40,352	75,448	136,621	375,651	47,680	7.8	......	......	......
Alabama, ...	....——..	144,317	309,527	590,756	52,900	11.1	......	......	......
Arkansas, ...	....	14,273	30,388	97,574	55,000	1.7	......	......	......
Tennessee,........	261,727	422,813	681,904	829,210	40,200	20.6	......	......	......
Missouri, ...	20,845	66,586	140,455	383,702	65,500	5.8	......	......	......
Kentucky,........	406,511	564,317	687,917	779,828	40,500	19.2	......	......	......
Total,........	805,991	1.441,161	2,202,551	3,409,132	351,080	9.4	54.8	136.	323.
IV. Non-slaveholding States.									
Ohio,.............	230,760	581,434	937,903	1,519,467	39,750	38.2	......	......	......
Indiana, ...	24,520	147,178	343,031	685,866	36,500	18.8	......	......	......
Illinois,...........	12,282	55,211	157,445	476,183	57,900	8.2	......	......	......
Michigan, ...	4,762	8,896	31,639	212,267	59,700	3.5	......	......	......
Wisconsin, ...	....	....	....	30,945	95,000	.3	......	......	......
Iowa, ...	....	....	....	43,112	200,000	.2	......	......	......
Total,........	272,324	802,719	1,470,018	2,967,840	488,850	6.	102.	269.	1090.

ATLANTIC AND WESTERN STATES—SLAVEHOLDING AND NON-SLAVEHOLDING STATES.

							Decennial incr. in—		
							1820.	1830.	1840.
Atlantic States,...	6,161,499	7,420,727	9,188,133	10,686,381	448,650	23.8	20.4	23.8	16.3
Western States,...	1,078,315	2,243,880	3,672,569	6,376,972	839,930	7.6	108.1	63.7	73.6
Non-slavehold'g S.	3,758,910	5,162,372	7,012,399	9,728,922	659,000	14.7	37.3	35.8	38.7
Slavehold'g States,	3,480,904	4,502,235	5,848,303	7,334,431	629,580	11.6	29.3	29.9	25.4

It will be seen by the preceding tables that the four divisions differ considerably in numbers, but far more in density of population; that the Atlantic non-slaveholding division has the greatest number and density, and the Western non-slaveholding division has the least. If, however, the vast Territories of Wisconsin and Iowa, which are comparatively unsettled, be deducted, this fourth division would rank second in density of numbers; its four States containing, in 1840, nearly 15 persons to the square mile.

It will also be seen that the slaveholding States have increased more slowly than the States without slaves, though they are less densely peopled, which fact is owing principally to the difference of their accessions from immigration. In the thirty years from 1810 to 1840,

The increase of the States without slaves has been as 100 to 258.8
That of the slaveholding States has been as . . 100 to 210.7

The disparity of increase between the Atlantic and Western States, has been far greater; for, whilst the former have not doubled in thirty years, the latter have, in the same time, augmented nearly sixfold. Thus,

Increase of Atlantic States from 1830 to 1840, was as			100 to 173.4
That of the Western States	"	"	100 to 591.4

Should their respective rates of increase in the current decennial term be the same as it was in the last, the numbers in the Atlantic States would, in 1850, be 12,428,000, and those in the Western States, 11,170,000. It, therefore, will not be before the next succeeding census, in 1860, that those States will have preponderance in numbers and political power, unless there should be, in the present decennial term, a further disparity in their rate of increase.

On this subject it may be remarked, that most of the Western States, which are as yet but thinly settled compared with their extraordinary capabilities, have increased faster in the last ten years than in the ten years preceding, and that the same causes may continue to operate until the next census ; whereas, in the Atlantic States, the cases of such increasing ratio are only two, and those to a small extent. They are Massachusetts, whose decennial increase has augmented from 16.6 per cent in 1830, to 20.9 in 1840, —the great extension of her manufactures having checked her wonted emigration—and New Jersy, whose increase has, in like manner, augmented from 15.5 per cent to 16.4 per cent, in consequence of her sympathetic growth with the cities of New York and Philadelphia. In every other Atlantic state, the ratio of decennial increase has diminished, so as to make the diminution in the New England States from 17.8 to 14.3 per cent ; in the Middle States, from 29.2 to 23.3. per cent ; and in the Southern States, from 21. to 8.2. per cent.

But of the Western States, Mississippi augmented its ratio of increase, in the same time, from 81. to 175. per cent ; Louisiana, from 40.6 to 61.6 ; Arkansas, from 112.8 to 221.1 ; Missouri, from 140.4 to 173.2 ; Illinois, from 185.1 to 202.4 ; Michigan, from 255.6 to 555.6 ; and even Ohio, the third State in the Union, from 61.3 to 62. per cent. And in most of these States, the next decennial increase may possibly be yet greater than the last. In the Atlantic States, on the other hand, the diminution may continue, though probably at a less rate, since the emigration from the more northern slaveholding States to the cotton-growing States may be much less in the present term of ten years than it was in the last. On the whole, should the decennial increase of the Atlantic States continue to decline as it has done, which is not probable, and should the Western States continue to increase in the same accelerated ratio, which also seems improbable, and unwarranted by the history of other States similarly circumstanced, these two great divisions of the Union will, in 1850, be nearly equal in population and political power.

CHAPTER XV.

DISTRIBUTION OF POLITICAL POWER.

As, by the federal constitution, political power, in some of its highest functions, is distributed among the several States according to their respective numbers, their relative weight in the government, besides being very unequal, has greatly varied after every census, in consequence of their very different rates of increase.

The following table shows the number of representatives in congress assigned to each State under the several apportionments:

Apport'nment before the Census.		Apportionments according to the Census.											
		1790.		1800.		1810.		1820.		1830.		1840.	
States.	No. of Reps.	States.	No. of Reps.	States.	No. of Reps.	States.	No. of Reps.	States.	No. of Reps.	States.	No. of Reps.	States.	No. of Reps.
Virgin'a	10	Virgin'a	19	Virgin'a	22	N. York,	27	N. York,	34	N. York,	40	N. York	34
Mass.,...	8	Mass.,..	14	Penn.,..	18	Penn.,..	23	Penn.,..	26	Penn.,..	28	Penn.,...	24
Penn.,...	8	Penn.,.	13	N. York,	17	Virgin'a	23	Virgin'a	22	Virgin'a	21	Ohio,...	21
N. York,	6	N. York,	10	Mass.,..	17	Mass.,..	20	Ohio,...	14	Ohio,...	19	Virgin'a	15
Maryl'd,	6	N. Car.,	10	N. Car.,.	12	N. Car.,.	13	Mass.,..	13	N. Car.,	13	Tenn.,..	11
Conn.,..	5	Maryl'd,	8	Maryl'd,	9	Kent'y,.	10	N. Car.,.	13	Kent'y,.	13	Mass.,..	10
N. Car.,.	5	Conn,..	7	S. Car.,.	8	Maryl'd,	9	Kent'y,.	12	Tenn.,..	13	Kent'y,.	10
S. Car.,.	5	S. Car.,.	6	Conn.,..	7	S. Car.,.	9	Maryl'd,	9	Mass.,..	12	Indiana,	10
N. Jer.,.	4	N. Jer.,.	5	N. Jer.,.	6	Conn.,..	7	S. Car.,.	9	S. Car.,.	9	N. Car.,.	9
N. Ham.	3	N. Ham.	4	Kent'y,.	6	N. Ham.	6	Tenn.,..	9	Georgia,	9	Georgia,	8
Georgia,	3	R. Isl'd,.	2	N. Ham.	5	Verm't,.	6	Georgia,	7	Maine,..	8	Maine, .	7
R. Isl'd,.	1	Verm't,.	2	Verm't,.	4	N. Jer.,.	6	Maine, .	7	Maryl'd,	8	S. Car.,.	7
Delaw'e	1	Georgia,	2	Georgia,	4	Georgia,	6	N. Ham.	6	Indiana,	7	Alaba'a,	7
13 States,	65	Kent'y,.	2	Tenn.,..	3	Tenn.,...	6	Conn.,..	6	Conn.,..	6	Illinois,.	7
		Delaw'e	1	R. Isl'd,.	2	Ohio,...	6	N. Jer.,.	6	N. Jer.,.	6	Maryl'd,	6
		Tenn.,*	1	Delaw'e	1	R. Isl'd,.	2	Verm't,.	5	N. Ham.	5	N. Jer.,.	5
16 States under 1st app.,			106	Ohio,*...	1	Delaw'e	2	Louis., .	3	Verm't,.	5	Misso'ri,	5
17 States under 2d app., ...					142	Louis.,*	1	Indiana,	3	Alaba'a,	5	N. Ham.	4
						Indi'a,.*	1	Alaba'a,	3	Louis., .	3	Conn.,..	4
19 States under 3d app., ...							183	R. Isl'd,.	2	Illinois,.	3	Verm't,.	4
								Delaw'e	1	R. Isl'd,.	2	Louis.,..	4
								Miss.,* .	1	Miss.,...	2	Miss.,...	4
								Illin'is,*	1	Misso'ri,	2	Mich.,..	3
								Miss'ri,*	1	Delaw'e	1	R. Isl'd,.	2
24 States under 4th app., ...									213	Mich.,* .	1	Delaw'e	1
										Ark.,*..	1	Ark.,...	1
26 States under 5th and 6th app., ...											242	....	223

NOTE.—The States marked thus * were admitted into the Union after the apportionment under which they are here arranged was made, but before the succeeding census.

It will be seen, by the preceding table, that the largest State, New York, has thirty-four times as much weight in the house of representatives as either Delaware or Arkansas; and that the six largest States are entitled to more votes than the remaining twenty, so great is their disparity. So great, too, have been their relative changes, that Tennessee, which, in 1790, was at the bottom of the list of sixteen States, is now the fifth of twenty-six; that Ohio, which was the lowest in 1800, is now the third in rank; and that Virginia, which was first, and New York, which was the fourth, in 1790, have now changed places.

But the dangers threatened by this gross inequality of power, and the changes which its distribution is ever undergoing, are effectually guarded against by the senate, a co-ordinate branch of the legislature, in which every State has two members. By this provision, the smaller States are protected from the possible abuse of the power possessed by the larger; and the community from those sudden changes of public policy, which might be apprehended from the changes in the relative weight of the States after every census.

In the election of president and vice president, the votes of the States also vary according to their several numbers; but as each State has as many votes as it has members in both houses of congress, the inequality is here much less than it is in the house of representatives, and the relative weight of the smaller States receives a great proportionate increase. Thus, New York, which has thirty-four times as much weight in the house of representatives as Delaware or Arkansas, has but twelve times as much in the presidential election, that is, as 36 to 3. Rhode Island, which is but one-seventeenth of New York in the house, is one-ninth in the election; and New Hampshire, and the other States entitled to four votes, have their relative weight increased, on a like comparison, from less than an eighth ($\frac{4}{34}$) to a sixth ($\frac{6}{36}$.) New York herself, which has more than a seventh of the whole number of representatives, has less than a seventh of the presidential electors, or, more accurately, her relative weight is reduced from 15.2 per cent to 13.1 per cent. The States of a medium population have nearly the same relative weight in both cases.

Time, which will augment the inequality among the States in some respects, will diminish it in others. When they shall have attained a dense population, the disproportion between the largest and the smallest States will probably be greater than that which now exists between New York and Delaware, and certainly greater than that which is between New York and the next smallest States; but there will then, also, be a greater number of States which will approach equality than at present. Of the twenty-six States, while eight* of them have, together, an extent of but 54,000 square miles, the smallest of the other eighteen has an area of upwards of 31,000 miles, about that of Ireland, and the area of the largest does not much exceed that of England and Wales. Nor is it probable, that any State hereafter admitted into the Union will contain less, or much less, than 50,000 square miles.

It must also be recollected that, even at this time, with those great divisions of the Union, composed of States which are similar in modes of industry and local interests, the disparity is far less than it is with the individual States, as may be seen by the following statement:

New England States............	31	*Representatives*	=13.9	per cent—	43	*Electors*	=15.6
Middle States......................	70	"	=31.4	"	80	"	=29.1
Southern States....................	39	"	=17.5	"	47	"	=17.1
Southwestern States..............	27	"	=12.1	"	37	"	=13.5
Northwestern States..............	56	"	=25.1	"	68	"	=24.7
Total,..........................	223		100.		275		100.

The subjoined diagrams show to the eye the inequality of the States in population and political power; their different rates of increase, and the comparative areas of the five great local divisions. The lines opposite to each State represent its population at each successive census:

* These are New Hampshire, Vermont, Massachusetts, Rhode Island, Connecticut, New Jersey, Delaware, and Maryland.

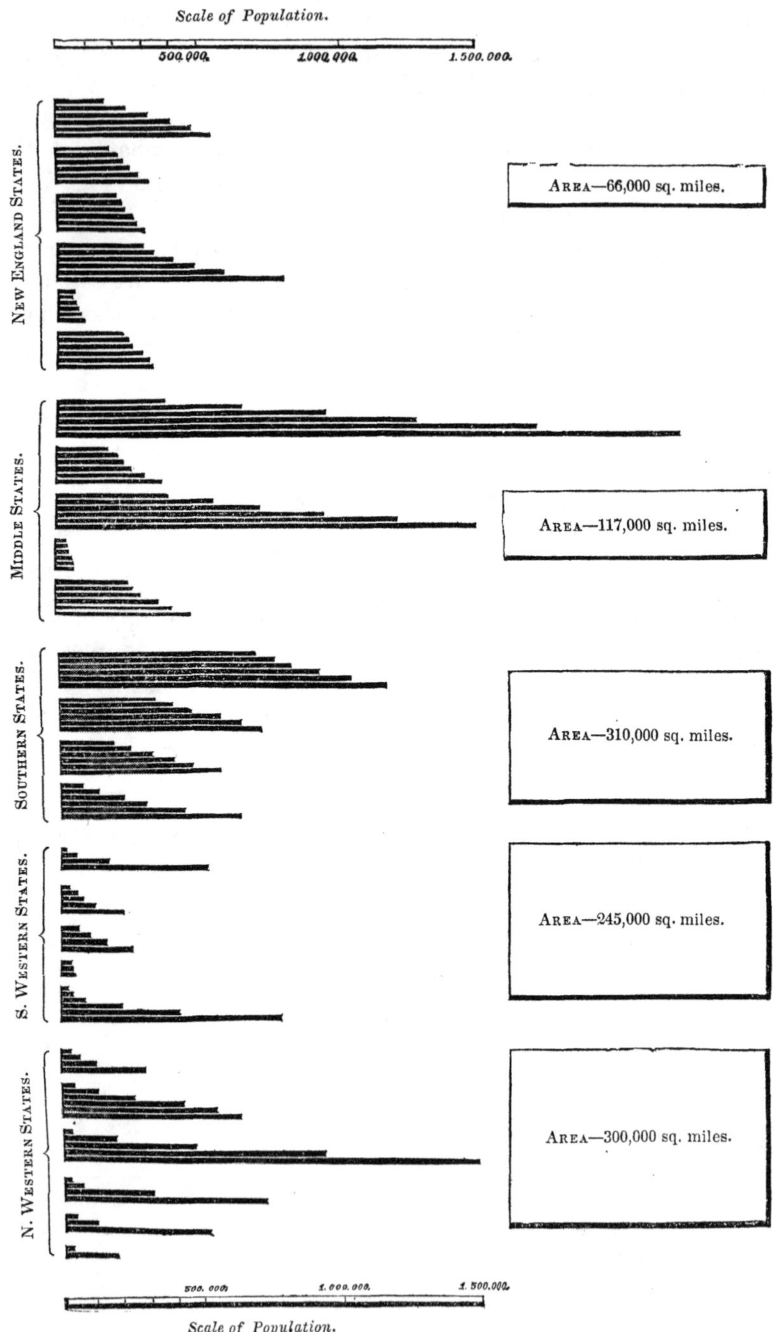
Scale of Population.
500.000
1000.000
1.500.000
NEW ENGLAND STATES.
AREA—66,000 sq. miles.
MIDDLE STATES.
AREA—117,000 sq. miles.
SOUTHERN STATES.
AREA—310,000 sq. miles.
S. WESTERN STATES.
AREA—245,000 sq. miles.
N. WESTERN STATES.
AREA—300,000 sq. miles.
500.000
1.000.000
1.500.000
Scale of Population.

CHAPTER XVI.

CITIES AND TOWNS.

The proportion between the rural and town population of a country is an important fact in its interior economy and condition. It determines, in a great degree, its capacity for manufactures, the extent of its commerce, and the amount of its wealth. The growth of cities commonly marks the progress of intelligence and the arts, measures the sum of social enjoyment, and always implies increased mental activity, which is sometimes healthy and useful, sometimes distempered and pernicious. If these congregations of men diminish some of the comforts of life, they augment others: if they are less favourable to health than the country, they also provide better defences against disease, and better means of cure. From causes both physical and moral, they are less favourable to the multiplication of the species. In the eyes of the moralist, cities afford a wider field both for virtue and vice; and they are more prone to innovation, whether for good or evil. The love of civil liberty is, perhaps, both stronger and more constant in the country than the town; and if it is guarded in the cities by a keener vigilance and a more farsighted jealousy, yet law, order, and security, are also, in them, more exposed to danger, from the greater facility with which intrigue and ambition can there operate on ignorance and want. Whatever may be the good or evil tendencies of populous cities, they are the result to which all countries, that are at once fertile, free, and intelligent, inevitably tend.

The following table shows the population of the towns in the United States, of 10,000 inhabitants and upwards, in 1820, 1830, and 1840; their decennial increase, and the present ratio of the town population, in each State, to its whole population:

Towns.	States.	Population of Towns in				Decennial Increase.		Ratio of Town populat. per cent.
		1820.	1830.	1840.		1830.	1840.	
Portland,.....	Maine,.........	8,581	12,601	....	15,218	63.9	20.8	3.
Boston,.......	Massachusetts	43,298	61,392	93,383		41.8	52.1	....
Lowell,*......	"	....	6,474	20,796		....	221.2	....
Salem,........	"	11,346	13,836	15,082		21.9	9.1	....
New Bedford,	"	3,947	7,592	12,087		92.3	59.2	....
Charlestown,.	"	6,591	8,783	11,484		33.3	30.7	....
Springfield,..	"	3,914	6,784	10,985		73.3	61.9	22.2
				———	163,817			
Providence,..	Rhode Island,.	11,767	16,833	....	23,171	43.1	37.7	21.3
New Haven,.	Connecticut,..	7,147	10,180	....	12,960	42.4	27.3	4.18
New York,...	New York,....	123,706	202,589	312,710		63.8	44.7	....
Brooklyn,....	"	7,175	15,396	36,233		114.6	135.3	....
Albany,.......	"	12,630	24,238	33,721		91.9	39.1	....
Rochester,....	"	1,767	9,207	20,191		421.	119.	....
Troy,..........	"	5,264	11,405	19,334		116.6	69.6	....
Buffalo,.......	"	2,095	8,668	18,213		313.7	110.	....
Utica,..........	"	2,972	10,183	12,782		242.6	25.5	18.6
				———	453,184			
Newark,......	New Jersey,..	6,507	10,953	....	17,290	68.3	57.8	4.6
Philadelphia,.	Pennsylvania,.	119,325	161,427	205,580		36.1	25.6	....
Pittsburg & Alleghany,	"	10,000	18,000	31,204		80.	73.3	13.7
				———	237,054			
Baltimore,....	Maryland,.....	62,738	80,625	....	102,313	28.5	26.8	21.7
Richmond,...	Virginia,.......	12,067	16,060	20,153		33.1	25.5	....
Petersburg,...	"	6,690	8,322	11,136		20.6	33.8	....
Norfolk,.......	"	8,478	9,816	10,920		18.4	11.2	3.4
				———	42,209			
Charleston,...	S. Carolina,...	24,780	†30,289	....	29,261	22.2	....	4.9
Savannah,....	Georgia,.......	7,523	†7,423	....	11,214	....	51.	1.8
Mobile,.......	Alabama,......	1,500	3,914	....	12,672	112.9	296.7	2.1
New Orleans,	Louisiana,....	27,178	46,082	....	102,193	68.6	121.7	29.
Louisville,....	Kentucky, ...	4,012	10,196	....	21,210	154.	108.	2.7
St. Louis,....	Missouri,......	4,123	6,694	....	16,469	62.4	146.	4.3
Cincinnati,...	Ohio,..........	9,642	24,831	....	46,338	157.5	86.6	3.
Washington,.	Dist. of Col.,.	13,247	18,227	....	23,364	40.8	28.2	....
31 Towns.	16 States.	570,010	878,300	....	1,329,937	54.	51.3	7.79

It appears, from the preceding table, that the population in all the towns of the United States, containing 10,000 inhabitants and upwards, is something more than one-thirteenth ($\frac{10}{128}$) of the whole number; that ten of the States, whose united population exceeds 4,000,000, have, as yet, no town of that rank; and that, in the other sixteen States, the ratio of their town population to their whole population, varies from something less than one-third, to less than a sixteenth part. It further appears, that the increase of those towns has been nearly the same, from 1830 to 1840, as from 1820

* Lowell had no existence before 1822.

† The decline of population here indicated, was the effect of very destructive fire.

to 1830; and that, in both decennial periods, it exceeds that of the whole population, nearly as 50 to 32.

By extending our estimate of this description of the population to towns of a lower rank, we may not only better compare the different States in this particular, but, perhaps, also better draw the line between the town and country population. Congregations of a much smaller number than 10,000, whether their dwelling-place be called a city, town, or village, have the chief characteristics which distinguish the main part of the inhabitants of cities, as to their habits, manners, and character. Though these characteristics are but partially found in towns and villages of not more than 2,000 inhabitants, yet, as the census has, in many of the States, numbered these among the "principal towns," we will extend our estimate to them, and endeavour to supply its omissions, in other States, by a reference to the best geographical authorities:

Table of all Towns in the United States containing between 10,000 *and* 2,000 *Inhabitants, according to the Census of* 1840.

States.	*Towns.*	*Pop.*	*Towns.*	*Pop.*	*Total.*
Maine,	Bangor,	8,627	Bucksport,	3,015	
	Thomaston,	6,227	Camden,	3,005	
	Augusta,	5,314	Gorham,	3,001	
	Bath,	5,141	Waterville,	2,971	
	Gardenier,	5,042	Vassalborough,	2,952	
	Hallowell,	4,654	Calais,	2,934	
	Saco,	4,408	Eastport,	2,876	
	Brunswick,	4,259	North Yarmouth,	2,824	
	Belfast,	4,186	Kennebunk,	2,768	
	Westbrook,	4,116	Buxton,	2,688	
	Frankfort,	3,603	Freeport,	2,662	
	Minot,	3,550	Biddeford,	2,574	
	Prospect,	3,492	South Berwick,	2,314	
	Poland,	3,360	Ellsworth,	2,263	
	York,	3,111		——	107,937
N. Hampshire,	Portsmouth,	7,887	Haverhill,	2,784	
	Dover,	6,458	Hanover,	2,613	
	Nashua,	6,054	Keene,	2,610	
	Concord,	4,897	Hopkinton,	2,455	
	Somersworth,	3,283	Rochester,	2,431	
	Meredith,	3,351	Goffstown,	2,376	
	Manchester,	3,235	Peterborough,	2,163	
	Exeter,	2,925		——	55,459
Vermont,	Burlington,	4,271	Windsor,	2,744	
	Montpelier,	3,725	Rutland,	2,708	
	Bennington,	3,429	St. Albans,	2,702	
	Woodstock,	3,315	Brattleboro',	2,624	
	Middlebury,	3,162	Rockingham,	2,330	
				——	31,010
Massachusetts,	Lynn,	9,367	Cambridge,	8,409	
	Roxbury,	9,089	Taunton,	7,645	
	Nantucket,	9,012	Worcester,	7,497	
	Newburyport,	7,161	Mendon,	3,524	
	Fall River,	6,738	Quincy,	3,486	
	Gloucester,	6,350	Newton,	3,351	
	Marblehead,	5,575	Dedham,	3,290	

Table of all the Towns in the United States, etc.—Continued.

States.	*Towns.*	*Pop.*	*Towns.*	*Pop.*	*Total.*
Massachusetts, .	Plymouth, ...	5,281	Abingdon, ...	3,214	
	Andover, ...	5,207	Randolph, ...	3,213	
	Middleborough, ...	5,085	Farmingham, ...	3,030	
	Danvers, ...	5,020	Ipswich, ...	3,000	
	Dorchester, ...	4,875	Woburn, ...	2,993	
	Beverley, ...	4,689	Salisbury, ...	2,739	
	Haverhill, ...	4,336	Falmouth, ...	2,589	
	Barnstable, ...	4,301	Yarmouth, ...	2,554	
	Dartmouth, ...	4,135	Amherst, ...	2,550	
	Fairhaven, ...	3,951	Malden, ...	2,514	
	Scituate, ...	3,886	Waltham, ...	2,504	
	Rochester, ...	3,864	Medford, ...	2,478	
	Northampton, ...	3,750	Amesbury, ...	2,471	
	Weymouth, ...	3,738	Chelsea, ...	2,390	
	Sandwich, ...	3,719	Methuen, ...	2,251	
	Adams, ...	3,703	Bradford, ...	2,222	
	West Springfield, .	3,626	Braintree, ...	2,168	
	Attleborough, ...	3,585	Stoughton, ...	2,142	
	Hingham, ...	3,564	Provincetown, ...	2,122	
	Westfield, ...	3,526	Easton, ...	2,074	
				——	225,553
Rhode Island, . .	Smithfield, ...	9,534	Scituate, ...	4,090	
	Newport, ...	8,333	Bristol, ...	3,490	
	Warwick, ...	6,726	Tiverton, ...	3,183	
	North Providence,	4,207	Warren, ...	2,437	
				——	42,000
Connecticut, ...	Hartford, ...	9,468	Stamford, ...	3,516	
	New London, ...	5,519	Saybrook, ...	3,417	
	Danbury, ...	4,504	Berlin, ...	3,411	
	Norwich, ...	4,200	Windham, ...	3,382	
	Litchfield, ...	4,038	Bridgeport, ...	3,294	
	New Milford, ...	3,974	Newton, ...	3,189	
	Greenwich, ...	3,921	Glastonbury, ...	3,077	
	Stonington, ...	3,898	Woodstock, ...	3,053	
	Norwalk, ...	3,863	Groton, ...	2,963	
	Wethersfield, ...	3,824	Derby, ...	2,851	
	Killingly, ...	3,685	Ridgefield, ...	2,474	
	Waterbury, ...	3,668	Milford, ...	2,455	
	Fairfield, ...	3,654	Plainfield, ...	2,383	
	East Windsor, ...	3,600	Mansfield, ...	2,276	
	Thompson, ...	3,535	Plymouth, ...	2,205	
	Middleton, ...	3,511		——	112,808
New York, ...	Poughkeepsie, ...	8,000	Waterloo, ...	2,600	
	Schenectady, ...	6,748	Ogdensburg, ...	2,600	
	Syracuse, ...	6,500	Salina, ...	2,600	
	Lockport, ...	6,500	Plattsburg, ...	2,600	
	Newburgh, ...	6,000	Little Falls, ...	2,500	
	Hudson, ...	5,672	Saratoga Springs, ...	2,500	
	Auburn, ...	5,626	Sing Sing, ...	2,500	
	West Troy, ...	5,000	Rome, ...	2,500	
	Williamsburg, ...	5,000	Elmira, ...	2,300	
	Oswego, ...	4,500	Kingston, ...	2,300	
	Ithaca, ...	4,000	Ulster, ...	2,300	
	Watertown, ...	4,000	Batavia, ...	2,000	
	Geneva, ...	3,600	Flushing, ...	2,000	
	Lansingburg, ...	3,000	Palmyra, ...	2,000	
	Seneca Falls, ...	3,000	Peekskill, ...	2,000	
	Binghampton, ...	2,800	Sackett's Harbour, ...	2,000	
	Catskill, ...	2,800	Keeseville, ...	2,000	
	Canandaigua, ...	2,600		——	124,646

Table of all the Towns in the United States, etc.—Continued.

States.	*Towns.*	*Pop.*	*Towns.*	*Pop.*	*Total.*
New Jersey,....	Paterson,...........	7,596	Orange,...................	3,264	
	Elizabeth Boro',...	4,184	Jersey City,............	3,072	
	Trenton,...........	4,035	Princeton,...............	3,055	
	Burlington,.........	3,434	Belville,................	2,466	
	Camden,...........	3,371		——	34,477
Pennsylvania,..	Lancaster,..........	8,417	Erie,.....................	3,412	
	Reading,............	8,410	Chambersburg,........	3,229	
	Harrisburg,.........	5,980	Norristown,............	2,939	
	Easton,............	4,865	West Chester,..........	2,152	
	York,...............	4,779	Washington,...........	2,062	
	Carlisle,............	4,351	Lewistown,............	2,058	
	Pottsville,..........	4,345		——	56,999
Delaware,......	Wilmington,.......	8,367	Newcastle, ...	2,737	
	Dover,..............	3,790		——	14,894
Maryland,......	Fredericktown, ...	7,179	Annapolis,..............	2,792	
	Hagerstown,.......	5,132	Cumberland,...........	2,428	
				——	17,531
Dist. of Colum.,	Alexandria,.........	8,459	Georgetown,...........	7,312	
				——	15,771
Virginia,........	Wheeling, ...	7,885	Fredericksburg,........	3,974	
	Portsmouth,.......	6,477	Winchester,............	3,454	
	Lynchburg,........	6,395		——	28,185
North Carolina,	Wilmington,.......	4,744	Newbern,...............	3,690	
	Fayetteville,.......	4,285	Raleigh,.................	2,444	
				——	15,163
South Carolina,	Columbia,...			4,340	
				——	4,340
Georgia,........	Augusta,...........	6,403	Columbus,..............	3,114	
	Macon,.............	3,927	Milledgeville,..........	2,095	
				——	15,539
Alabama,........	Montgomery,......	2,179	Tuscaloosa,*...........	2,000	
				——	4,179
Mississippi,......	Natchez,............	4,800	Vicksburg, ...	3,104	
				——	7,904
Louisiana,......	Lafayette,..........	3,207	Baton Rouge,...........	2,269	
				——	5,476
Tennessee,......	Nashville, ...	6,929	Knoxville,†............	3,500	
				——	10,429
Kentucky,......	Lexington,.........	6,997	Covington,..............	2,026	
	Maysville,..........	2,741	Frankfort,‡............	2,000	
				——	13,764
Ohio,............	Cleveland, ...	6,071	Lancaster,..............	3,272	
	Dayton,.............	6,067	Newark, ...	2,705	
	Columbus,..........	6,048	Mount Vernon,........	2,362	
	Zanesville,..........	4,766	Circleville,..............	2,329	
	Steubenville, ...	4,247	Springfield,............	2,062	
	Chillicothe,........	3,977		——	43,906
Indiana,........	New Albany,......	4,226	Indianapolis,...........	2,692	
	Madison,..........	3,798	Richmond,..............	2,070	
				——	12,786

* This town, the seat of government in Alabama, had a population of but 1,949 when the census was taken.

† The population of this town is not given in the census.

‡ This town, the seat of government in Kentucky, had a population of but 1,917 when the census was taken.

Table of all the Towns in the United States, etc.—Continued.

States.	*Towns.*	*Pop.*	*Towns.*	*Pop.*	*Total.*
Illinois,..........	Chicago,.............	4,470	Alton, ...	2,340	
	Springfield,.........	2,579	Quincy,..................	2,319	
					11,708
Michigan,.......	Detroit, ...			9,102	
					9,102
Florida,..........	St. Augustine, ...			2,453	
					2,453

Total of towns of between 10,000 and 2,000 inhabitants each,.......... 991,590

Table of the aggregate Town Population in each State, and of its ratio to the whole Population of the State.

STATES, &c.	POPULATION OF TOWNS— Of 10,000 inhabitants and upw.	POPULATION OF TOWNS— Between 10,000 and 2,000 inhab.	TOTAL.	Ratio to whole Population.
Maine,..............................	15,218	107,937	123,155	24.5
New Hampshire,.....................	....	55,459	55,459	19.4
Vermont, ...	....	31,010	31,010	10.6
Massachusetts,......................	163,817	225,553	389,370	52.7
Rhode Island,.......................	23,171	42,000	65,171	60.4
Connecticut,.........................	12,960	112,808	125,768	37.9
New England States,..........	215,166	574,767	789,933	35.3
New York,...........................	453,184	92,217	545,401	22.4
New Jersey,..........................	17,290	34,477	51,767	13.8
Pennsylvania,........................	237,054	56,999	294,053	17.3
Delaware,............................	....	14,894	14,894	19.
Maryland,............................	102,313	17,531	119,844	25.5
District of Columbia,..............	23,364	15,771	39,135	....
Middle States,....................	833,205	231,889	1,065,094	20.8
Virginia, ...	42,209	28,185	70,394	5.6
North Carolina,......................	....	15,163	15,163	2.
South Carolina,......................	29,261	4,340	33,601	5.6
Georgia,..............................	11,214	15,539	26,753	3.8
Florida,..............................	....	2,453	2,453	4.5
Southern States,.................	82,684	65,680	148,364	4.4
Alabama,.............................	12,672	4,179	16,851	2.8
Mississippi,..........................	....	7,904	7,904	2.1
Louisiana, ...	102,193	5,476	107,669	30.5
Arkansas, ...	....	....	....	....
Tennessee,...........................	....	10,429	10,429	1.2
Southwestern States,..........	114,865	27,988	142,853	6.6
Missouri, ...	16,469	....	16,469	4.3
Kentucky, ...	21,210	13,764	34,974	4.5
Ohio,.................................	46,338	43,906	90,244	5.9
Indiana,..............................	....	12,786	12,786	1.8
Illinois, ...	....	11,708	11,708	2.4
Michigan,............................	....	9,102	9,102	4.3
Northwestern States,..........	84,017	91,266	175,283	4.2
Total, ...	1,329,937	991,590	2,321,527	13.6

By thus extending our estimate to all the "principal towns" mentioned in the census, we find that the number is increased from thirty-one towns to two hundred and fifty, and that the proportion of town population is augmented from about a thirteenth to near a seventh, with a yet greater disparity among the States than was shown as to the towns of more than 10,000 inhabitants. But this state of facts is, in part, fallacious. It involves an important error, resulting from the application of the term "towns," in New England, to those subdivisions of a country, which are generally called "townships" or "parishes;" and whose whole population in New England, though the greater part is essentially rural, has, by reason of this inconvenient provincialism, been returned by the census as town population. For the want of adequate means of separating the inhabitants of the town or village from those of the township, (which, moreover, would, from the irregular dispersion of the buildings, be not always easy even to those on the spot,) the census has been implicitly followed as to these "principal towns" in New England; though, from the proportion of their inhabitants who are agricultural, it seems probable that more than half their population should be deducted from the town population here estimated.

In New York, where the same provincialism extensively prevails, the census has erred in an opposite way, by noticing in the northern part of the State none but incorporated cities; and thus busy and compactly built towns, here called "villages," of 5,000 inhabitants and upwards, have been omitted in one-half the State, while, in the other, much smaller towns. and even townships, have been occasionally noticed; though in neither district has it descended to towns of but 2,000 inhabitants. To supply these omissions, the estimate made of the town population of New York, in "Holley's State Register," for 1843, has been adopted.

Similar omissions of small towns may also have occurred in other States, which we have not the same means of correcting. They, altogether, cannot equal the omissions in New York.

But were these errors corrected, the three more southern New England States would still have the largest proportion of town population of any of the States. The circumstances which determine this proportion, in a State, are the density of its population, the extent of its commerce, and that of its manufactures. It is mainly owing to the first cause, that all the New England and the Middle States have a greater town population than the other divisions. It is from their extensive commerce, that Maryland and Louisiana exceed the neighbouring States in the same way, and that Massachusetts exceeds the rest of New England. It is to the want both of commerce and manufactures, that Indiana, Tennessee, and North Carolina, have so few and such small towns. It is, indeed, from their exclusive pursuit of agriculture, in the slaveholding States, as well as their difference in density, that the number of their town inhabitants, with the exception of Delaware, Maryland, and Louisiana, rarely exceeds a twentieth, and will not average more than a thirtieth of their whole population. If the proportion in the whole United States could be correctly ascertained, by the correction of the errors adverted to, it would probably be found that those who live in towns and villages containing at least 2,000 inhabitants, are not much more nor much less than one-eighth of the entire number.

The effect of railroads, and of transportation by steam generally, is to stimulate the growth of towns, and especially of large towns. It is, therefore, likely that our principal cities will, at the next census, show as large a proportional increase as they have experienced in the last decennial period.

CHAPTER XVII.

DISTRIBUTION OF THE INDUSTRIOUS CLASSES.

In 1820, for the first time, the census took an account of the number of persons who were severally employed in agriculture, commerce, and manufactures. In the succeeding census, no notice was taken of the occupations of the people; but that of 1840 gave a fuller enumeration of the industrious classes, distinguishing them under the several heads of mining, agriculture, commerce, manufactures, navigating the ocean, internal navigation, and the learned professions. The result of each census may be seen in the following tables:

Table I.—*Showing the number of persons engaged in Agriculture, Commerce, and Manufactures in the several States, according to the census of* 1820.

States and Territories.	Agriculture.	Commerce.	Manufactures.	States and Territories.	Agriculture.	Commerce.	Manufactures.
Maine,	55,031	4,297	7,643	South Carolina,	166,707	2,684	6,747
New Hampshire,	52,384	1,068	8,699	Georgia,	101,185	2,139	3,557
Vermont,	50,951	776	8,484				
Massachusetts,	63,460	13,301	33,464	Southern States,	718,510	11,883	54,484
Rhode Island,	12,559	1,162	6,091				
Connecticut,	50,518	3,581	17,541	Alabama,	30,642	452	1,412
				Mississippi,	22,033	294	650
New England S.,	284,903	24,185	81,922	Louisiana,	53,941	6,251	6,041
				Tennessee,	101,919	882	7,860
New York,	247,648	9,113	60,038	Arkansas,	3,613	79	179
New Jersey,	40,812	1,830	15,941				
Pennsylvania,	140,801	7,083	60,215	Southwestern S.	212,148	7,958	16,142
Delaware,	13,259	533	2,821				
Maryland,	79,135	4,771	18,640	Kentucky,	132,161	1,617	11,779
Dist. of Columbia,	853	312	2,184	Ohio,	110,991	1,459	18,956
				Indiana,	61,315	429	3,229
Middle States,	522,508	23,842	159,839	Illinois,	12,395	233	1,007
				Missouri,	14,247	495	1,952
Virginia,	276,422	4,509	32,336	Michigan,	1,468	392	196
North Carolina,	174,196	2,551	11,844				
				Northwestern S.	332,577	4,625	37,110
Total of United States,					2,070,646	72,493	349,506

TABLE II.—*Showing the number of persons engaged in Mining, Agriculture, Commerce, Manufactures, Navigating the Ocean, Internal Navigation, and the Learned Professions, according to the census of* 1840.

STATES AND TERRITORIES.	Mining.	Agriculture.	Commerce.	Manufactures.	Navigating the Ocean.	Internal navigation.	Learned professions.	TOTAL.
Maine,.............	36	101,630	2,921	21,879	10,091	539	1,889	
New Hampshire,..	13	77,949	1,379	17,826	452	198	1,640	
Vermont,..........	77	73,150	1,303	13,174	41	146	1,563	
Massachusetts,....	499	87,837	8,063	85,176	27,153	372	3,804	
Rhode Island,......	35	16,617	1,348	21,271	1,717	228	457	
Connecticut,.......	151	56,955	2,743	27,932	2,700	431	1,697	
New England S.,.	811	414,138	17,757	187,258	42,154	1,914	11,050	675,082
New York,.........	1,898	455,954	28,468	173,193	5,511	10,167	14,111	
New Jersey,.......	266	56,701	2,283	27,004	1,143	1,625	1,627	
Pennsylvania,.....	4,603	207,533	15,338	105,883	1,815	3,951	6,706	
Delaware,..........	5	16,015	467	4,060	401	235	199	
Maryland,..........	320	72,046	3,281	21,529	717	1,528	1,666	
Dist. of Columbia,.	....	384	240	2,278	126	80	203	
Middle States,.....	7,092	808,633	50,077	333,947	9,713	17,586	24,512	1,251,580
Virginia,............	1,995	318,771	6,361	54,147	582	2,952	3,866	
North Carolina,....	589	217,095	1,734	14,322	327	379	1,086	
South Carolina,....	51	198,363	1,958	10,325	381	348	1,481	
Georgia,............	574	209,383	2,428	7,984	262	352	1,250	
Florida,.............	1	12,117	481	1,177	435	118	204	
Southern States,..	3,210	955,729	12,962	87,955	1,987	4,149	7,887	1,073,879
Alabama,..........	96	177,439	2,212	7,195	256	758	1,514	
Mississippi,........	14	139,724	1,303	4,151	33	100	1,506	
Louisiana,..........	1	79,289	8,549	7,565	1,322	662	1,018	
Arkansas,..........	41	26,355	215	1,173	3	39	301	
Tennessee,.........	103	227,739	2,217	17,815	55	302	2,042	
Southwestern S.,.	255	650,546	14,496	37,899	1,669	1,861	6,381	713,107
Missouri,...........	742	92,408	2,522	11,100	39	1,885	1,469	
Kentucky,..........	331	197,738	3,448	23,217	44	968	2,487	
Ohio,................	704	272,579	9,201	66,265	212	3,323	5,663	
Indiana,.............	233	148,806	3,076	20,590	89	627	2,257	
Illinois,.............	782	105,337	2,506	13,185	63	310	2,021	
Michigan,..........	40	56,521	728	6,890	24	166	904	
Wisconsin,........	794	7,047	479	1,814	14	209	259	
Iowa,................	217	10,469	355	1,629	13	78	365	
Northwestern S.,.	3,843	890,905	22,315	144,690	498	7,566	15,425	1,085,242
Total,.........	15,211	3,719,951	117,607	791,749	56,021	33,076	65,255	4,798,870

TABLE III.—*Comparative View of the number of persons employed in Agriculture, Commerce, and Manufactures, in the five great divisions of the United States, in* 1820 *and* 1840, *and the relative proportions of each class.*

Geographical Divisions.		Number of persons employed in			Total.	Centesimal proportions.		
		Agriculture.	Commerce.	Manufactures.		Agriculture.	Commerce.	Manufactures.
New England S.,	1820	283,903	24,184	81,922	391,010	72.8	6.2	21.
	1840	414,138	17,757	187,258	619,153	66.7	2.9	30.2
Middle States,	1820	522,508	23,842	159,839	706,189	74.	3.4	22.6
	1840	808,633	50,077	333,947	1,192,657	67.8	4.2	28.
Southern States,	1820	718,510	11,883	54,484	784,877	91.6	1.5	6.9
	1840	955,729	12,962	87,955	1,056,646	90.5	1.2	8.3
Southwestern S.,	1820	212,148	7,958	16,142	236,248	89.8	3.4	6.8
	1840	650,546	14,496	37,899	702,941	92.5	2.1	5.4
Northwestern S.,	1820	332,577	4,625	37,119	364,321	88.5	1.3	10.2
	1840	890,905	22,315	144,690	1,057,910	84.2	2.2	13.6
Total U. States,	1820	2,070,646	72,493	349,506	2,483,645	83.4	2.9	13.7
	1840	3,719,951	117,607	791,749	4,629,307	80.4	2.5	17.1

TABLE IV.—*Showing the proportions in which the several industrious classes of the Union, according to the census of* 1840, *are distributed among its great geographical divisions.*

Geographical Divisions.	Per centage of persons employed in—							Total.
	Mining.	Agriculture.	Commerce.	Manufactures.	Navigating the Ocean.	Internal navigation.	Learned professions.	
New England States,	5.3	11.1	15.1	23.6	75.3	5.8	16.9	14.1
Middle States,	46.7	21.7	42.6	42.2	17.3	53.2	37.6	26.1
Southern States,	21.1	24.8	11.	11.1	3.5	5.6	12.1	22.3
Southwestern States,	1.6	18.5	12.3	4.8	3.	12 5	9.8	14.9
Northwestern States,	25.3	23.9	19.	18 3	.9	22.9	23.6	22.6
	100.	100.	00.	100.	100.	100.	100.	100.

TABLE V.—*Showing the ratio which the number of persons in the several industrious classes of each great geographical division of the States bears to the whole population of such division, according to the census of* 1840.

Geographical Divisions.	Number of persons employed in—							Whole laboring class, as 1 to
	Mining, as 1 to	Agriculture, as 1 to	Commerce, as 1 to	Manufactures, as 1 to	Navigating the Ocean, as 1 to	Internal navigation, as 1 to	Learned professions, as 1 to	
New England States,	2755	5.4	126	12.	53	1161	202	3 31
Middle States,	723	6.3	102	15.3	528	291	209	4.08
Southern States,	1038	3.5	257	37.9	1677	802	422	3.01
Southwestern States,	8806	3.4	155	56.6	1345	1206	351	3.14
Northwestern States,	1075	4.6	185	28.5	8336	546	267	3.8
	1122	4.58	145	21.5	304	516	261	3.55

It seems, by the preceding tables, that the whole number of persons employed in agriculture, commerce, and manufactures, bears nearly the same proportion to the whole population in both enumerations. In 1820, these classes, amounting to 2,483,645 persons, in a population of 9,638,131, were 25.7 per cent of the whole number; and, in 1840, the same classes amounted to 4,629,307 persons in a population of 17,069,453, which is 27.1 per cent. If the four classes, then added, be taken into the estimate, the proportion will be 28 per cent. This proportion must be regarded as a very large one, when it is recollected that the three classes in question comprehend a very small number of females, and that one-half, or very nearly one-half of the males, are under seventeen years of age.

The proportion of adult males, in the industrious classes of Great Britain, seems to be nearly the same as in the United States, so far as we can compare them by means of the very different plans adopted in the two countries of enumerating those classes by the census. There, only the males of twenty years of age and upwards are reckoned; whilst here, all persons employed in the several branches of industry are counted, without distinction of age, sex, or condition.

In 1831, the whole number of males in Great Britain, twenty years of age and upwards, was 3,944,511, who were thus distributed, according to the census:

Employed in agriculture, as occupiers or labourers,...	1,243,057	—equal to 31.5 p. cent.
" manufactures,...	404,317	" 39.7 "
" retail trade or handicraft,...	1,159,867	
Labourers, employed in labour not agricultural,...	608,712	" 28.8 "
Servants,...	78,699	
Capitalists, professional and other educated men,...	214,390	
Other males,...	235,499	
Total,...	3,944,511	100.

From this enumeration, it appears that, exclusive of the two last mentioned classes, amounting to 449,889 persons, there were 3,494,622 males, above the age of twenty, who were engaged in profitable, and, for the most part, manual occupations; and, consequently, according to Mr. G. R. Porter, one of the most accurate statistical writers of that country, the residue, who were not thus engaged, constitute 114 out of every 1,000 males of twenty years of age; and if the males included in the army and navy, and as seamen in registered vessels, be added to the whole population, the number will be reduced to 106 of every 1,000, or 10.6 per cent.

To ascertain the number of the industrious class in the United

States, correspondent to that in the British enumeration, we must deduct, from the whole number returned by the census of 1840, the slaves comprehended under that class, the free coloured persons, the white females, the white males under twenty years of age, and the professional men, for none of which deductions, except the last, have we any data at once precise and authentic. The following conjectural estimate, however, is probably not wide of the truth. 1. *The slaves.* As, in this part of the population, both women and children are employed in field labour, especially in the cotton-growing States, we are led to assign to the labouring class a far greater proportion of the whole number than is usual; but, on the other hand, that proportion must be greatly reduced when we recollect that nearly 34 per cent of the whole number are under ten years of age; and that much the larger part of the females, as well as a considerable number of the males, both adults and boys, are employed as household servants, who were not reckoned in this part of the census. When, to these deductions, we make a fair allowance for the infirm and superannuated, two-fifths of the whole number would seem to be a liberal estimate for the slave labour comprehended in the census; and this rough estimate receives confirmation from a careful inspection of the returns, and a comparison between the number of productive labourers in the slaveholding and other States. 2. *The free coloured.* The occupations of persons of this class being nearly the same as those of the slaves, we will also deduct two-fifths of their whole number. 3. *The white females.* These are not employed in great numbers in any branch of industry noted in the census, except in the manufactories of cotton, and other woven fabrics. The whole number thus employed, in doors and out of doors, was, according to the census of 1840, 109,612. If, in some of these establishments, the females are most numerous, in others, there are few or none. We will, therefore, suppose one-half of the whole number to be females. 4. *The white males under twenty years of age.* In the absence of all other data, let us suppose that the number of this description is equal to the whole number of white males between fifteen and twenty years of age, (756,022,) after deducting the scholars attending the colleges and grammar schools, (180,503.) This would make the boys, comprehended in the industrious classes, 575,519.

If the several deductions be made, in conformity with the preceding views, the result will be as follows:

In all the departments of industry,............................persons		4,798,870
Deduct, for two-fifths of the coloured population,....................	1,149,598	
" the white females employed in manufactures,..........	54,806	
" white males under 20 years of age,......................	575,519	
" professional men,..	65,255	
		1,845,178
The whole number of white males above 20 years of age employed in trade and manual labour,..		2,953,692

Now, the whole number of free white males over twenty years of age was, by the census of 1840, 3,318,837; from which, if the above number of 2,953,692 be deducted, the difference, which is 365,145, and which comprehends the professional, the superannuated, and the idle classes, is equivalent to 110 adult males out of 1,000, or 11 per cent. If, however, two-fifths be too large a proportion for the working slaves reckoned in the census, as many will think, a reduction of their number will, to the same extent, increase the number of white male labourers, and diminish the number of the professional and unproductive class. But the proportion of this class is not likely to differ much in the two countries; for, in truth, nineteen-twentieths of the men in every country are compelled to work by their hands or their wits for the means of subsistence, suited to their habits and tastes, and the difference between different countries is not so much in the quantity of the labour performed, as in its quality and efficiency.

Whilst all civilized countries are so much alike as to the amount of labour put in requisition to satisfy human wants, they differ very greatly as to the distribution of that labour among the three principal branches of industry; and the difference is very great in this respect, not only between the several States, but in the whole United States, in 1820 and 1840. It is seen by Table III. that the proportion of labour employed in agriculture and commerce had diminished; while that employed in manufactures had, in twenty years, increased from 13.7 per cent to 17.1 per cent of the whole. The positive increase in that time was from 349,506 persons employed in 1820, to 791,749 employed in 1840.

This increase was greatest in the New England States, whose manufacturing population had enlarged from 21 per cent, in 1820, to 30.2 per cent in 1840; in which time the same class of population had nearly trebled in Massachusetts, and more than trebled in Rhode Island. In the Southwestern States, alone, the proportion of the agricultural class had increased; in all the others it had diminished. In the Middle and Northwestern States, the proportion employed in commerce experienced a small increase. In several of the States, not only was the proportion less in 1840 than it had been in 1820, but the number of persons actually employed in commerce was less. This was the case in Maine, Massachusetts, Connecticut, Maryland, and to a smaller extent, in Delaware, North Carolina, and South Carolina. Is this falling off to be attributed solely to the loss of our legitimate share of the West India trade since 1830, or, in part, also, to some difference in the mode of taking the census, by which a portion of the seamen, who, in 1840, were separately numbered, were, in 1820, reckoned among the persons employed in commerce? The first cause seems quite adequate to the effect produced.

If we suppose that the whole labour of Great Britain is distributed among the several departments of industry in the same proportions as the labour of the males above twenty years of age, the difference of distribution in that country and this is very striking. In that country, agricultural labour is but 31.5 cent of the whole; here, it is 77.5 per cent. In that country, manufactures and trade employ 28.8 per cent of the whole labour; here, they employ but 18.9 per cent. Each country employs its industry in that way which is most profitable, and best suited to its circumstances.

Table IV. shows how the different departments of productive industry are distributed among the five great divisions of the States, in centesimal proportions. Two-thirds of the mining labour is in the Middle and Southern States. The Southern States stand foremost in agricultural labour, though they hold but the third rank in population. The Middle States employ the least labour in agriculture, in proportion to their numbers. In commerce, however, they employ the most, and next to them, the New England States. The same two divisions take the lead in manufactures, they contributing nearly two-thirds of the labour employed in this branch of industry. Three-fourths of the seamen are furnished by New England, of which nine-tenths belong to Massachusetts and Maine. More than half the labour employed in inland navigation is in the Middle States, and, next to them, are the Northwestern States.

Of that department of industry which comprehend the learned professions, and which is at once the best fruit of civilization, and the most powerful agent of its further advancement, the New England and Middle States have the largest proportion, though there is less diversity in this than in any other class of industry.

Of the individual States, New York, Pennsylvania, and Virginia employ the greatest number in mining; in agriculture, New York,

Virginia, and Ohio ; in commerce, New York, Pennsylvania, Louisiana, and Massachusetts ; in ocean navigation, next to Massachusetts and Maine, but far behind, is New York ; in internal navigation, New York, Pennsylvania, Ohio, and Virginia furnish 20,000 out of the 30,000 employed.

In Table V. we see the various ratios which the persons employed in the several branches of industry bear to the whole population in the several divisions of the States. According to this table, without regarding local diversities, and taking the whole United States together, the great classes of occupation range themselves in the following order, viz :

The number of persons	employed in	agriculture,	1	out of	4½
"	"	"	manufactures,	"	21½
"	"	"	commerce,	"	145
"	"	"	the learned professions,	"	261
"	"	"	navigating the ocean,	"	304
"	"	"	internal navigation,	"	516
"	"	"	mining,	"	1122

Taking all the employments together, the number engaged is 355 out of every 1,000 of the whole population ; which implies, on the grounds already stated, that there can be but a very small proportion of males who are not occupied in some mode of profitable industry.

CHAPTER XVIII.

EDUCATION.

In addition to the new subjects already mentioned, the census of 1840, also, for the first time, embraced the statistics of education. For this purpose, all schools for the instruction of youth were divided into three classes, viz: 1. Universities or colleges. 2. Academies and grammar schools. 3. Primary schools; and the number of each description, together with the number of scholars attending each, in the several States, were given. It also enumerated the scholars educated at the public charge in each State, and the number of white persons over twenty years of age who could not read and write.

Of the many substantial benefits of educating the people, it is scarcely necessary now to speak; since, wherever the experiment has been made, it has been found to favour industry, prudence, temperance, and honesty, and thus eminently conduce to the respectability and happiness of a people. But the motives for giving knowledge a wide diffusion are peculiarly strong in this country, where the people being the sole source of political power, all legislation and measures of public policy must, in a greater or less degree, reflect the opinions and feelings of the great mass of the community, and be wise and liberal, or weak and narrow-minded, according to the character of those by whose suffrages authority is given and is taken away. If the body of the people be not instructed and intelligent, how can they understand their true interests—how distinguish the honest purposes of the patriot from the smooth pretences of the hypocrite—how feel the paramount obligations of law, order, justice, and public faith?

Table showing the number of Universities or Colleges, of Academies and Grammar Schools, of Primary and Common Schools, in the United States, with the number of Scholars of each description, the number of Scholars at public charge, and the number of White Persons over 20 *years of age who cannot read and write, according to the census of* 1840.

STATES AND TERRITORIES.	Universities and colleges.	Students.	Academies & Gram'ar Schools.	Scholars.	Primary Schools.	Scholars.	Scholars at public charge.	Illiterate.
Maine,..............	4	266	86	8,477	3,385	164,477	60,212	3,241
New Hampshire,..	2	433	68	5,799	2,127	83,632	7,715	942
Vermont,...........	3	233	46	4,113	2,402	82,817	14,701	2,276
Massachusetts, ...	4	769	251	16,746	3,362	160,257	158,351	4,448
Rhode Island,......	2	324	52	3,664	434	17,355	10,749	1,614
Connecticut, ...	4	832	127	4,865	1,619	65,739	10,912	526
N. England States,	19	2,857	630	43,664	13,329	574,277	262,640	13,041
New York,.........	12	1,285	505	34,715	10,593	502,367	27,075	44,452
New Jersey,.......	3	443	66	3,027	1,207	52,583	7,128	6,385
Pennsylvania,......	20	2,034	290	15,970	4,978	179,989	73,908	33,940
Delaware, ...	1	23	20	764	152	6,924	1,571	4,832
Maryland, ...	12	813	133	4,289	565	16,851	6,624	11,817
Dist. of Columbia,.	2	224	26	1,389	29	851	482	1,033
Middle States,.....	50	4,822	1,040	60,154	17,514	741,565	116,788	102,459
Virginia,............	13	1,097	382	11,083	1,561	35,331	9,791	58,787
North Carolina,....	2	158	141	4,398	632	14,937	124	56,609
South Carolina,....	1	168	117	4,326	566	12,520	3,524	20,615
Georgia, ...	11	622	176	7,878	601	15,561	1,333	30,717
Florida, ...	....	....	18	732	51	925	14	1,303
Southern States,...	27	2,045	834	28,417	3,411	79,274	14,786	168,031
Alabama,...........	2	152	114	5,018	639	16,243	3,213	22,592
Mississippi,.........	7	454	71	2,553	382	8,236	107	8,360
Louisiana, ...	12	989	52	1,995	179	3,573	1,190	4,861
Arkansas,..........	....	....	8	300	113	2,614	....	6,567
Tennessee, ...	8	492	152	5,539	983	25,090	6,907	58,531
Southw'rn States,.	29	2,087	397	15,405	2,296	55,756	11,417	100,911
Missouri,............	6	495	47	1,926	642	16,788	526	19,457
Kentucky, ...	10	1,419	116	4,906	952	24,641	429	40,018
Ohio, ...	18	1,717	73	4,310	5,186	218,609	51,812	35,394
Indiana, ...	4	322	54	2,946	1,521	48,189	6,929	38,100
Illinois,.............	5	311	42	1,967	1,241	34,876	1,683	27,502
Michigan, ...	5	158	12	485	975	29,701	998	2,173
Wisconsin,.........	....	....	2	65	77	1,937	315	1,701
Iowa,...............	....	....	1	25	63	1,500	....	1,118
Northw'rn States,.	48	4,222	347	16,630	10,657	376,241	62,692	165,463
Total,.........	173	16,233	3,248	164,270	47,207	1,845,113	468,323	549,905

Table showing the Ratio which the number of College Students, of Students in the Grammar Schools and in the Primary Schools, and the number of the Illiterate in each State, bear to the white population of such State.

STATES AND TERRIT'RIES.	Rat. to white pop. of sch. in			Ratio to Illiter'e.
	Col-leges.	Gram. Schools.	Primary Schools.	
	As 1 to	As 1 to	As 1 to	As 1 to
Maine, ...	1833	59.	3.	154.
N. Hamp.,.	656	48 8	3.4	300.
Vermont,...	1250	70.8	3 5	128.
Massachus.,	948	43.5	4.5	164.
R. Island,...	326	28 8	6.	65.4
Connectic't,	362	62 6	4.6	574.
N. Engl'd S.	774	50.6	3.8	169.6
New York,.	1851	68.5	4.7	53.5
N. Jersey,..	793	116.	6.7	55.
Pennsylvan.	825	105.	9.3	49.4
Delaware,..	2546	76.6	8.4	12.1
Maryland, .	391	74.3	16.9	26 9
Dist. of Col.,	136	2.2	36.6	29.6
Middle S.,..	998	80.	6.5	47.
Virginia,....	678	60.9	20.9	12.6
N. Carolina,	3662	110.	32.4	8 5
S. Carolina,	1542	59 9	20.7	12 5
Georgia,....	655	51.7	26.2	13.2

STATES AND TERRIT'RIES.	Rat. to white pop. of sch. in			Ratio to Illiter'e.
	Col-leges.	Gram. Schools.	Primary Schools.	
	As 1 to	As 1 to	As 1 to	As 1 to
Florida,.....	....	38.1	30.2	21.4
Southern S.,	939	67.5	24.2	11.4
Alabama,...	2205	66.8	20.6	14.8
Mississippi,.	394	70.1	21.7	21.4
Louisiana, .	160	79.4	44.3	32.6
Arkansas, .	....	258.	29.6	11.8
Tennessee,.	1302	115.	25.5	10.9
S'west'rn S.	666	90.2	24.9	13.7
Missouri, ...	654	168.	19.3	16.6
Kentucky, .	416	120.	23.9	14.7
Ohio,........	874	348.	6.8	42.4
Indiana, ...	2107	233.	14.	17.8
Illinois,.....	1518	240.	13.5	17.1
Michigan, .	1382	436.	7.1	97.3
Wisconsin,.	....	473.	15 9	18.
Iowa, ...	....	1717.	28.6	38.4
N'west'n S.,	912	231.	10.2	23.3
Total,....	874	86.37	7.69	25 27

The preceding table shows, that the number of college students amounts to somewhat more than a nine-hundredth part of the white population; that the scholars of the academies and grammar schools are ten times as numerous as the college students; that the scholars of the primary schools are near twelve times as numerous as the last; and that the scholars of every description are equal to just one-seventh of the white population. The relative numbers, distributed in centesimal proportions, would be as follows:

College students,..	0.8	per cent.
Scholars in grammar schools,..	8.1	"
" primary schools,..	91.1	"
	100.	

If the free coloured be added to the white population, in consideration of that class furnishing a proportion of the scholars in the primary schools, the proportion which each description of scholars bears to the free population would be thus reduced, viz: college students, as 1 to 8.90; scholars in grammar schools, as 1 to

13

$88.\frac{7}{10}$; scholars in primary schools, as 1 to $7.\frac{9}{10}$; and the scholars of every description, as 1 to 7^{19} .

The diversity among the States, as to the proportion of scholars, is principally in those of the primary schools. In the number of college students, no division of the States has greatly above or below the average of 1 to 874 of the white population ; and in the scholars of the grammar schools, the Northwestern States differ widely from the other divisions. But in the primary, or elementary schools, the proportion in New England is nearly double that of the Middle States, nearly three times that of the Northwestern States, and between six and seven times as great as those of the Southern, and Southwestern States. The difference, as to the number of illiterate, is yet greater. If the other divisions be compared with New England, the number who cannot read and write is, in the last, three and a half times as great in the Middle States ; seven times as great in the Northwestern States ; twelve times in the Southwestern States ; and nearly fifteen times in the Southern States.

These diversities are attributable to several causes, but principally to the difference in density of numbers. and in the proportion of town population. In a thinly-peopled country, it is very difficult for a poor man to obtain schooling for his children, either by his own means, or by any means that the State is likely to provide but where the population is dense, and especially in towns, it is quite practicable to give to every child the rudiments of education, without onerously taxing the community. This is almost literally true in all the New England States and New York, and is said to be the case in the kingdom of Prussia. It is true that, in the Northwestern States, and particularly those which are exempt from slaves, the number of their elementary schools is much greater than that of the Southern or Southwestern States, although their population is not much more dense ; but, besides that, the settlers of those States, who were mostly from New England or New York, brought with them a deep sense of the value and importance of the schools for the people, they were better able to provide such schools, in consequence of their making their settlements, as had been done in their parent States, in townships and villages. We thus see that Michigan, which has but a thin population even in the settled parts of the State, has schools for nearly one-seventh of its population. The wise policy pursued, first in New England, and since by the States settled principally by their emigrants, of laying off their territory into townships, and of selling all the lands of a portion before those of other townships are brought into market, has afforded their first settlers the benefits of social intercourse and of co-operation. In this way, they were at once provided with places of worship and with schools adapted to their circumstances.

The census also shows a great difference among the States, as to the number of scholars at public charge; but this difference is owing principally to the different modes in which they have severally provided for popular instruction. In some, the primary schools are supported by a tax, as Massachusetts, Maine, New Hampshire, and Vermont; in others, by a large public fund, as in Connecticut, Virginia, and some others; and others, again, partly by the public treasury and partly by private contribution, as in New York. In both the last cases, the children are not considered as educated at the public expense, though the difference between them and the first class of cases is essentially the same, so far as regards the public bounty.

Of the three descriptions of schools, the elementary, by their great number, seem to be far the most deserving of consideration, if we look merely to their direct influence on individuals; but if we regard the political and general effects of each, it is not easy to say which contributes most to the well-being of the community. The primary schools give instruction and improvement to the bulk of the voters, the great reservoir of political power. The grammar schools educate that class whose views and feelings mainly constitute public opinion on all questions of national policy, legislation, and morals, and who thus give political power its particular directions. It is from the least numerous class—the collegiate—that the most efficient legislators, statesmen, and other public functionaries are drawn, as well as those professional men who take care of the health, the rights, and the consciences of men.

There is another important class of instructors of which the census takes no separate notice, that is, the ministers of religion, who, once a week or oftener, besides performing the rites of worship, each according to the modes of his sect, indoctrinate large congregations in articles of faith, and inculcate man's religious and moral duties. The number of ministers of every denomination, at the taking of the last census, was computed to exceed 20,000, and the deeply interesting character of the topics on which they treat, gives to this class of teachers a most powerful influence over the minds of men; but, fortunately, it is so divided by the mutual counteractions of rival sects, that it can no longer upheave the foundations of civil society, or seriously affect the public peace. Yet the influence of the ministers over their respective followers is rather enhanced than diminished by the rivalry of different sects, and the more, as they are all improving in information and oratorical talent. They occasionally bear away the palm of eloquence both from the bar and the deliberative assemblies. If this vast moral power spends its force yet oftener on speculative subtleties than on awakening emotion or influencing conduct; if it aims more to teach men what to think, than how to feel or to act, this circumstance affords, perhaps, as much matter of congratulation as regret, when we recollect how easy the pure, mild, and healthy influence which religion might exert, and which we sometimes see it exert, could be converted into bitter intolerance and the excesses of wild fanaticism.

There is yet another source of popular instruction—the periodical press—which is noticed by the census as a branch of manufacturing industry, and which is exclusiuely occupied, not merely with worldly affairs, but with the events of the passing hour. It keeps every part of the country informed of all that has occurred in every other which is likely to touch men's interests or their sympathies. Nor, in attending to the vast, does it overlook the minute. Every discovery in science or art, every improvement in husbandry or household economy, in medicine or cosmetics, real or supposed, is immediately proclaimed. Scarcely can an overgrown ox or hog make its appearance on a farm, or even an extraordinary apple or turnip, but their fame is heralded through the land. Here we learn every legislative measure, from that which establishes a tariff to that which gives a pension; every election or appointment, from a president to a postmaster; the state of the market, the crops, and the weather. Not a snow is suffered to fall, or a very hot or very cold day to appear, without being recorded. We may here learn what every man in every city pays for his loaf or his beefsteak, and what he gives, in fact, for almost all he eats, drinks, and wears. Here deaths and marriages, crimes and benefactions, the pursuits of business and amusement, exhibit the varied, ever-changing drama of human life. Here, too, we meet with the speculations of wisdom and science, the effusions of sentiment, and the sallies of wit; and it is not too much to say, that the jest that has been uttered in Boston or Louisville is, in little more than a week, repeated in every town in the United States, or that the wisdom or the pleasantry, the ribaldry or the coarseness exhibited in one of the Halls of

Congress, is made as promptly, by the periodical press, to give pleasure or distaste to one hundred thousand readers.

Nor is its agency limited to our own concerns. It has eyes to see and ears to hear all that is said and done in every part of the globe; and the most secluded hermit, if he only takes a newspaper, sees, as in a telescope, and often as in a mirror, everything that is transacted in the most distant regions; nor can anything memorable befall any considerable part of our species, that it is not forthwith communicated with the speed of steam to the whole civilized world.

The newspaper press is thus a most potent engine, both for good and evil. It too often ministers to some of our worst passions, and lends new force to party intolerance and party injustice.

"Incenditque animum dictis, atque aggerat iras."

But its benefits are incalculably greater. By communicating all that is passing in the bustling world around us, whether it be little or great, useful or pernicious, pleasurable or painful, without those exaggerations and forced congruities which we meet with in other forms of literature, it imparts much of the same knowledge of men and things as experience and observation. Its novelties gives zest to life. It affords occupation to the idle, and recreation for the industrious. It saves one man from torpor, and relieves another from care. Even in its errors, it unconsciously renders a homage to virtue, by imputing guilt to those it attacks, and praising none to whom it does not impute merit and moral excellence. Let us hope that it will in time, without losing any of its usefulness, less often offend against good taste and good breeding, and show more fairness in political controversy.

According to the census of 1840, there were then in the United States 130 daily newspapers, 1,142 issued weekly, and 125 twice or thrice a week, besides 237 other periodical publications. Such a diffusion of intelligence and information has never existed in any other country or age.

CHAPTER XIX.

THE PRODUCTS OF INDUSTRY.

HAVING traced the progress of the population of the United States from 1790 to 1840; shown its distribution according to age, sex, race, condition, and pursuit; and deduced the laws of its increase, let us now turn our attention to that part of the census of 1840 which estimated the annual products of industry. These were arranged under the six heads of Mines, Agriculture, Commerce, Fisheries, the Forest, and Manufactures; each of which was subdivided into specific commodities and sources of profit, as follows:

MINES.

1. Cast iron.	4. Gold.	7. Anthracite coal.
2. Bar iron.	5. Other metals.	8. Bituminous coal.
3. Lead.	6. Salt.*	9. Granite, marble, &c.

AGRICULTURE.

1. Horses and mules.	11. Indian corn.	21. Silk cocoons.
2. Neat cattle.	12. Wool.	22. Sugar.
3. Sheep.	13. Hops.	23. Firewood.
4. Swine.	14. Wax.	24. Products of the dairy.
5. Poultry.	15. Potatoes.	25. " " orchard.
6. Wheat.	16. Hay.	26. Wine.
7. Barley.	17. Hemp and flax.	27. Produce of market gardens.
8. Oats.	18. Tobacco.	28. Produce of nurseries, &c.
9. Rye.	19. Rice.	29. Domestic goods.
10. Buckwheat.	20. Cotton.	

COMMERCE.

1. Capital in foreign trade.	4. Capital in internal transportation.
2. " retail trade.	5. " the business of butchers, packers, &c.
3. " lumber trade.	

FISHERIES.

1. Smoked and dried fish.	3. Spermaceti oil.	5. Whalebone, and other products of the fisheries.
2. Pickled fish.	4. Other fish oil.	

THE FOREST.

1. Lumber.	3. Pot and pearl ashes.	5. Ginseng, and other products of the forest.
2. Tar, pitch, &c.	4. Skins and furs.	

MANUFACTURES.

1. Machinery.	7. Manuf. of granite, marble, &c.	12. Manuf. of flax.
2. Hardware, cutlery, &c.	8. Bricks and lime.	13. Mixed manufactures.
3. Cannon.	9. Manuf. of wool.	14. Manuf. of tobacco.
4. Small arms.	10. Manuf. of cotton.	15. Hats and caps.
5. Manuf. of prec. metals.	11. " of silk.	16. Straw bonnets.
6. Manuf. of various metals.		17. Sole leather.

* This comprehends salt manufactured from sea-water as well as mineral salt.

MANUFACTURES—Continued.

18. Upper leather.
19. Manuf. of leather.
20. Soap.
21. Tallow candles.
22. Spermaceti & wax candles.
23. Distilled spirits.
24. Brewed liquors.
25. Gunpowder.
26. Drugs, paints, dyes, &c.
27. Turpentine and varnish.
28. Glass.
29. Pottery.
30. Refined sugar.
31. Chocolate.
32. Paper.
33. Manuf. of paper.
34. Bookbinding.
35. Printing.
36. Cordage.
37. Musical instruments.
38. Carriages.
39. Flour mills.
40. Grist mills.
41. Saw mills.
42. Oil mills.
43. Ships.
44. Furniture.
45. Houses.
46. Other manufactures.

In about half of the preceding articles, the number or quantity is given by the census; in the rest, only the value annually produced. To all, except the products of agriculture, the number of men employed, and the amount of capital invested in each occupation, are severally annexed. Some further details are added to a few branches of business, as may be seen in the following compendium of this part of the census of 1840.

MINES.—IRON.

STATES AND TERRITORIES.	CAST IRON.		BAR IRON.		*Tons of Fuel Consumed.*	*Men Empl'd, including mining operations.*	*Capital Invested.*
	Number of Furnaces.	*Tons Produced.*	*Bloom'ies, Forges, & Roll. Mills*	*Tons Produced.*			
Maine,	16	6,122	1	......	285	48	$185,950
New Hampshire,	15	1,320	2	125	2,104	121	98,200
Massachusetts,	48	9,332	67	6,004	199,252	1,097	1,232,875
Rhode Island,	5	4,126	......	......	227	29	22,250
Connecticut,	28	6,495	44	3,623	16,933	895	577,300
Vermont,	26	6,743	14	655	388,407	788	664,150
New York,	186	29,088	120	53,693	123,677	3,456	2,103,418
New Jersey,	26	11,114	80	7,171	27,425	2,056	1,721,820
Pennsylvania,	213	98,395	169	87,244	355,903	11,522	7,781,471
Delaware,	2	17	5	449	971	28	36,200
Maryland,	12	8,876	17	7,900	24,422	1,782	795,650
Virginia,	42	18,810½	52	5,886	36,588	1,742	1,246,650
North Carolina,	8	968	43	963	11,598	468	94,961
South Carolina,	4	1,250	9	1,165	6,334	248	113,300
Georgia,	14	494	29	......	630	41	24,000
Alabama,	1	30	5	75	157	30	9,500
Mississippi,	......	......	......	......	......	......	......
Louisiana,	6	1,400	2	1,366	4,152	145	357,000
Tennessee,	34	16,128½	99	9,673	187,453	2,266	1,514,736
Kentucky,	17	29,206	13	3,637	35,501	1,108	449,000
Ohio,	72	35,236	19	7,466	104,312	2,268	1,161,900
Indiana,	7	810	1	20	787	103	57,700
Illinois,	4	158	......	......	240	74	40,300
Missouri,	2	180	4	118	300	80	79,000
Arkansas,	......	......	......	......	......	......	......
Michigan,	15	601	......	......	451	99	60,800
Florida,	......	......	......	......	......	......	......
Wiskonsin,	1	3	......	......	1	3	4,000
Iowa,	......	......	......	......	......	......	......
District of Columbia,	......	......	......	......	......	......	......
TOTAL,	804	286,903	795	197,233	1,528,110	30,497	20,432,131

MINES.—LEAD—GOLD—OTHER METALS.

STATES AND TERRITORIES.	LEAD.				GOLD.			
	Smelting Houses, or Fires.	*Pounds Produced.*	*Men Employed.*	*Capital Invested.*	*Smelting Houses.*	*Value Produced.*	*Men Employed.*	*Capital Invested.*
Maine,........	....	....	....	....	....	....	....	....
New Hampshire,.	1	1,000	2	$500	....	....	....	....
Massachusetts,....	....	....	....	....	....	....	....	....
Rhode Island,.....	....	....	....	....	....	....	....	....
Connecticut,.	....	....	....	....	....	....	....	....
Vermont,........	....	....	....	....	....	....	....	....
New York,........	9	670,000	333	221,000	....	....	....	....
New Jersey,.......	....	....	....	....	....	....	....	....
Pennsylvania,......	....	....	....	....	....	....	....	....
Delaware,.........	....	....	....	....	....	....	....	....
Maryland, ...	....	....	....	....	....	....	....	....
Virginia,..........	5	878,648	73	21,500	11	$51,758	131	$103,650
North Carolina,...	2	10,000	30	50,000	10	255,618	389	9,832
South Carolina,...	....	....	....	....	5	37,418	69	40,000
Georgia, ...	....	....	....	....	130	121,881	405	79,343
Alabama, ...	....	....	....	....	....	61,230	47	1,000
Mississippi,.......	....	....	....	....	....	....	....	....
Louisiana, ...	....	....	....	....	....	....	....	....
Tennessee,........	2	....	4	350	....	1,500	4	400
Kentucky, ...	....	....	....	....	....	....	....	....
Ohio, ...	....	....	....	....	....	....	....	....
Indiana,..........	....	....	....	....	....	....	....	....
Illinois,...........	20	8,755,000	73	114,500	1	200	1	100
Missouri,..........	21	5,295,455	252	235,806	....	....	....	....
Arkansas,.........	....	....	....	....	....	....	....	....
Michigan,.........	....	....	....	....	....	....	....	....
Florida,..........	....	....	....	....	....	....	....	....
Wiskonsin,.......	49	15,129,350	220	664,600	....	....	....	....
Iowa,.............	11	500,000	30	38,500	....	....	....	....
Dist. of Columbia,	....	....	....	....	....	....	....	....
TOTAL,......	120	31,239,453	1,017	1,346,756	157	$529,605	1,046	$234,325

MINES, ETC.—*Continued.*

STATES AND TERRIT'RIES.	OTHER METALS.			STATES AND TERRIT'RIES.	OTHER METALS.		
	Val. Produced.	*Men Employed.*	*Capital Invested.*		*Val. Produced.*	*Men Employed.*	*Capital Invested.*
Maine,......	$1,600	4	$1,000	Mississippi,.	....	....	....
N. Hampsh.	10,300	11	9,500	Louisiana,..	....	....	....
Massachu's,	2,500	14	1,200	Tennessee,.	....	....	....
Rhode Isl'd,	....	....	....	Kentucky,..	....	....	....
Connectic't,	....	....	....	Ohio,........	16,000	1	$500
Vermont,...	70,500	156	92,500	Indiana,.....	....	....	....
New York,.	84,564	119	42,930	Illinois,......	....	2	....
New Jers'y,	39,550	33	15,000	Missouri,...	15,600	25	9,150
Pennsylv'a,.	100,200	285	62,200	Arkansas,...	....	....	....
Delaware,...	....	....	....	Michigan,...	....	....	....
Maryland,...	28,800	73	5,000	Florida,......	....	....	....
Virginia,....	....	....	....	Wiskonsin,.	....	....	....
N. Carolina,	1,000	5	....	Iowa,.......	....	....	....
S. Carolina,	....	....	....	Dist. of Col.	....	....	....
Georgia,....	....	....	....				
Alabama,...	....	....	....	TOTAL,...	$370,614	728	$238,980

MINES.—COAL—SALT—GRANITE, MARBLE, AND OTHER STONE.

STATES AND TERRITORIES.	ANTHRACITE COAL.			BITUMINOUS COAL.			DOMESTIC SALT.			GRANITE, MARBLE, ETC.		
	Tons (28 bush. each) Raised.	*Men Employed.*	*Capital Invested.*	*Bushels Raised.*	*Men Employed.*	*Capital Invested.*	*Bushels Produced.*	*Men Employed.*	*Capital Invested.*	*Value Produced.*	*Men Employed.*	*Capital Invested.*
Maine,							50,000	15	$25,000	$107,506	305	$160,360
New Hampshire,				29,920			1,200	1	2,500	16,038	43	5,714
Massachusetts,							376,596	463	502,980	790,855	970	608,130
Rhode Island,	1,000	27	$6,000							17,800	29	7,500
Connecticut,				38,000	6		1,500	2	3,000	313,469	692	332,275
Vermont,										33,855	104	18,270
New York,							2,867,884	332	5,601,000	1,541,480	3,649	1,002,555
New Jersey,							500	1	1,500	35,721	118	10,600
Pennsylvania,	859,686	2,977	4,334,102	11,620,654	1,798	$300,416	549,478	255	191,435	238,831	540	172,272
Delaware,							1,160	17	200	16,000	46	5,000
Maryland,				222,000	23	4,470	1,200	3	100	22,750	61	17,200
Virginia,	200	2	100	10,622,345	995	1,301,855	1,745 618	624	300,560	84,489	233	49,290
North Carolina,	50	4		75	1		4,493	8	7,090	3,350	14	930
South Carolina,							2,250	7	1,500	3,000	4	500
Georgia,										51,990	199	36,300
Alabama,				23,650						13,700	22	10,000
Mississippi,												
Louisiana,												
Tennessee,				13,942	21					30,100	73	15,860
Kentucky,	2,125	27	14,150	588,167	213	76,627	219,695	291	163,585	19,592	100	6,212
Ohio,	296	4	1,250	3,513,409	434	45,525	297,350	240	113,195	195,831	296	27,496
Indiana,				242,040	47	9,300	6,400	19	20,050	35,021	105	6,750
Illinois,	132	2		424,187	152	120,076	20,000	22	10,000	74,228	142	14,020
Missouri,				249,302	69	9,488	13,150	36	3,550	28,110	33	15,025
Arkansas,				5,500	7	605	8,700	25	20,800	15,500	30	
Michigan,										2,700	4	3,000
Florida,							12,000	4	30,000	2,650	30	14,500
Wiskonsin,										968	17	400
Iowa,				10,000	2	500				350		
Dist. of Columbia,												
TOTAL,	863,489	3,043	4,355,602	27,603,191	3,768	1,868,862	6,179,174	2,365	6,998,045	3,695,884	7,859	2,540,159

AGRICULTURE.—LIVE STOCK—CEREAL GRAINS.

STATES AND TERRITORIES.	LIVE STOCK.					CEREAL GRAINS.					
	Horses & Mules.	*Neat Cattle.*	*Sheep.*	*Swine.*	*Estim. Val. of Poultry.*	*Bushels of Wheat.*	*Bush. of Barley.*	*Bushels of Oats.*	*Bushels of Rye.*	*Bush. of Buckw't.*	*Bushels o Ind'n Corn*
Maine,..................	59,208	327,255	649,264	117,386	$123,171	848,166	355,161	1,076,409	137,941	51,543	950,528
New Hampshire,.......	43,892	275,562	617,390	121,671	107,092	422,124	121,899	1,296,114	308,148	105,103	1,162,572
Massachusetts,.........	61,484	282,574	378,226	143,221	178,157	157,923	165,319	1,319,680	536,014	87,000	1,809,192
Rhode Island,..........	8,024	36,891	90,146	30,659	61,702	3,098	66,490	171,517	34,521	2,979	450,498
Connecticut, ...	34,650	238,650	403,462	131,961	176,629	87,009	33,759	1,453,262	737,424	303,043	1,500,441
Vermont,................	62,402	384,341	1,681,819	203,800	131,578	495,800	54,781	2,222,584	230,993	228,416	1,119,678
New York,..............	474,543	1,911,244	5,118,777	1,900,065	1,153,413	12,286,418	2,520,068	20,675,847	2,979,323	2,287,885	10,972,286
New Jersey,............	70,502	220,202	219,285	261,443	336,953	774,203	12,501	3,083,524	1,665,820	856,117	4,361,975
Pennsylvania,..........	365,129	1,172,665	1,767,620	1,503,964	685,801	13,213,077	209,893	20,641,819	6,613,873	2,113,742	14,240,022
Delaware, ...	14,421	53,883	39,247	74,228	47,265	315,165	5,260	927,405	33,546	11,299	2,099,359
Maryland,..............	92,220	225,714	257,922	416,943	218,765	3,345,783	3,594	3,534,211	723,577	73,606	8,233,086
Virginia,................	326,438	1,024,148	1,293,772	1,992,155	754,698	10,109,716	87,430	13,451,062	1,482,799	243,822	34,577,591
North Carolina,........	166,608	617,371	538,279	1,649,716	544,125	1,960,855	3,574	3,193,941	213,971	15,391	23,893,763
South Carolina,.........	129,921	572,608	232,981	878,532	396,364	968,354	3,967	1,486,208	44,738	72	14,722,805
Georgia,.................	157,540	884,414	267,107	1,457,755	449,623	1,801,830	12,979	1,610,030	60,693	141	20,905,122
Alabama, ...	143,147	668,018	163,243	1,423,873	404,994	828,052	7,692	1,406,353	51,008	58	20,947,004
Mississippi, ...	109,227	623,197	128,367	1,001,209	369,482	196,626	1,654	668,624	11,444	61	13,161,237
Louisiana, ...	99,888	381,248	98,072	323,220	283,559	60	....	107,353	1,812	....	5,952,912
Tennessee,...............	341,409	822,851	741,593	2,926,607	606,969	4,569,692	4,809	7,035,678	304,320	17,118	44,986,188
Kentucky,...............	395,853	787,098	1,008,240	2,310,533	536,439	4,803,152	17,491	7,155,974	1,321,373	8,169	39,847,120
Ohio, ...	430,527	1,217,874	2,028,401	2,099,746	551,193	16,571,661	212,440	14,393,103	814,205	633,139	33,668,144
Indiana,.................	241,036	619,980	675,982	1,623,608	357,594	4,049,375	28,015	5,981,605	129,621	49,019	28,155,887
Illinois,.................	199,235	626,274	395,672	1,495,254	309,204	3,335,393	82,251	4,988,008	88,197	57,884	22,634,211
Missouri,...............	196,032	433,875	348,018	1,271,161	270,647	1,037,386	9,801	2,234,947	68,608	15,318	17,332,524
Arkansas,...............	51,472	188,786	42,151	393 058	109,468	105,878	760	189,553	6,219	88	4,846,632
Michigan,...............	30,144	185,190	99,618	295,890	82,730	2,157,108	127,802	2,114,051	34,236	113,592	2,277.039
Florida, ...	12,043	118,081	7,198	92,680	61,007	412	30	13,829	305	....	898,974
Wiskonsin, ...	5,735	30,269	3,462	51.383	16,167	212,116	11,062	406,514	1,965	10,654	379,359
Iowa,....................	10,794	38,049	15,354	104,899	16,529	154,693	728	216,385	3,792	6,212	1,406,241
District of Columbia,..	2,145	3,274	706	4,673	3,092	12,147	294	15,751	5,081	272	39,485
TOTAL,..........	4,335,669	14,971,586	19,311,374	26,301,293	9,344,410	84,823,272	4,161,504	123,071,341	18,645,567	7,291,743	377,531,875

AGRICULTURE.—VARIOUS CROPS.

WOOL—HOPS—WAX—POTATOES—HAY—HEMP AND FLAX.

STATES AND TERRITORIES.	*Wool. Pounds.*	*Hops. Pounds.*	*Wax. Pounds.*	*Potatoes. Bushels.*	*Hay. Tons.*	*Hemp & Flax.*
Maine,	1,465,551	36,940	3,723½	10,392,280	691,358	Tons 38
New Hampshire,	1,260,517	243,425	1,345	6,206,606	496,107	26½
Massachusetts,	941,906	254,795	1,196	5,385,652	569,395	2¼
Rhode Island,	183,830	113	165	911,973	63,449	¼
Connecticut,	889,870	4,573	3,897	3,414,238	426,704	41¾
Vermont,	3,699,235	48,137	4,660	8,869,751	836,739	29½
New York,	9,845,295	447,250	52,795	30,123,614	3,127,047	1,130⅝
New Jersey,	397,207	4,531	10,061	2,072,069	334,861	2,165¾
Pennsylvania,	3,048,564	49,481	33,107	9,535,663	1,311,643	2,649¾
Delaware,	64,404	746	1,088	200,712	22,483	52¾
Maryland,	488,201	2,357	3,674	1,036,433	106,687½	488
Virginia,	2,538,374	10,597	65,020	2,944,660	364,708½	25,594¼
North Carolina,	625,044	1,063	118,923	2,609,239	101,369	9,879⅓
South Carolina,	299,170	93	15,857	2,698,313	24,618	....
Georgia,	371,303	773	19,799	1,291,366	16,969¾	10¾
Alabama,	220,353	825	25,226	1,708,356	12,718	5
Mississippi,	175,196	154	6,835	1,630,100	171	16
Louisiana,	49,283	115	1,012	834,341	24,651	....
Tennessee,	1,060,332	850	50,907	1,904,370	31,233	3,344½
Kentucky,	1,786,847	742	38,445	1,055,085	88,306	9,992¼
Ohio,	3,685,315	62,195	38,950	5,805,021	1,022,037	9,080¼
Indiana,	1,237,919	38,591	30,647	1,525,794	178,029	8,605½
Illinois,	650,007	17,742	29,173	2,025,520	164,932	1,976¼
Missouri,	562,265	789	56,461	783,768	49,083	18,010¾
Arkansas,	64,943	....	7,079	293,608	586	1,039½
Michigan,	153,375	11,381	4,533	2,109,205	130,805	755¼
Florida,	7,285	....	75	264,617	1,197	2
Wiskonsin,	6,777	133	1,474	419,608	30,938	2
Iowa,	23,039	83	2,132	234,063	17,953	313¼
District of Columbia,	707	28	44	12,035	1,331	....
TOTAL,	35,802,114	1,238,502	628,303½	108,298,060	10,248,108¾	95,251¾

AGRICULTURE.—VARIOUS CROPS, ETC.—*Continued.*

TOBACCO—RICE—COTTON.

STATES, ETC.	*Tobacco Gathered. Pounds.*	*Rice. Pounds.*	*Cotton Gathered. Pounds.*	STATES, ETC.	*Tobacco Gathered. Pounds.*	*Rice. Pounds.*	*Cotton Gathered. Pounds.*
Me...	30	....	....	Miss...	83,471	777,195	193,401,577
N. H.	115	....	....	La......	119,824	3,604,534	152,555,368
Mass.	64,955	....	....	Tenn...	29,550,432	7,977	27,701,277
R. I...	317	....	....	Ky......	53,436,909	16,376	691,456
Conn.	471,657	....	....	Ohio,...	5,942,275	....	....
Verm.	585	....	....	Ind.....	1,820,306	....	180
N. Y.	744	....	....	Illin....	564,326	460	200,947
N. J...	1,922	....	....	Mo.....	9,067,913	50	121,122
Penn.	325,018	....	....	Ark....	148,439	5,454	6,028,642
Del...	272	....	334	Mich...	1,602	....	....
Md...	24,816,012	....	5,673	Fa......	75,274	481,420	12,110,533
Va....	75,347,106	2,956	3,494,483	Wisk...	115	....	....
N. C..	16,772,359	2,820,388	51,926,190	Iowa,..	8,076	....	....
S. C...	51,519	60,590,861	61,710,274	D. of C.	55,550	....	....
Geo...	162,894	12,384,732	163,392,396				
Ala...	273,302	149,019	117,138,823	TOTAL,	219,163,319	80,841,422	790,479,275

AGRICULTURE.—SILK—SUGAR—WOOD—DAIRIES—ORCHARDS—WINE—FAMILY GOODS, ETC.

STATES AND TERRITORIES.	*Silk Cocoons. Pounds.*	*Sugar Made. Pounds.*	*Wood Sold. Cords.*	*Dairy Products. Value.*	*Orchard Products. Value.*	*Wine Made. Gallons.*	*Family Goods. Value.*
Maine,.......	211	257,464	205,011	$1,496,902	$149,384	2,236	$804,397
N. Hampshi.	419⅞	1,162,368	116,266	1,638,543	239,979	94	538,303
Massachus's,	1,741	579,227	278,069	2,373,299	389,177	193	231,942
Rhode Isl'nd,	458	50	48,666	223,229	32,098	803	51,180
Connecticut,.	17,538	51,764	159,062	1,376,534	296,232	2,666	226,162
Vermont,.....	4,286	4,647,934	96,399	2,008,737	213,944	94	674,548
New York,...	1,735¾	10,048,109	1,058,923	10,496,021	1,701,935	6,799	4,636,547
New Jersey,.	1,966	56	340,602	1,328,032	464,006	9,416	201,625
Pennsylv'nia,	7,262½	2,265,755	269,516	3,187,292	618,179	14,328	1,303,093
Delaware,....	1,458¾	....	67,864	113,828	28,211	322	62,116
Maryland,...	2,290½	36,266	178,181	457,466	105,740	7,585	176,050
Virginia,......	3,191	1,541,833	403,590	1,480,488	705,765	13,911	2,441,672
Nr. Carolina,	3,014	7,163	40,034	674,349	386,006	28,752	1,413,242
Sh. Carolina,	2,080	30,000	171,451	577,810	52,275	643	930,703
Georgia,......	2,992¼	329,744	57,459	605,172	156,122	8,647	1,467,630
Alabama,....	1,592¼	10,143	60,955	265,200	55,240	177	1,656,119
Mississippi,...	91	77	118,423	359,585	14,458	12	682,945
Louisiana,...	317	119,947,720	202,867	153,069	11,769	2,884	65,190
Tennessee,...	1,217	258,073	104,014	472,141	367,105	653	2,886,661
Kentucky,...	737	1,377,835	264,222	931,363	434,935	2,209	2,622,462
Ohio,.........	4,317½	6,363,386	272,527	1,848,869	475,271	11,524	1,853,937
Indiana,......	379	3,727,795	183,712	742,269	110,055	10,265	1,289,802
Illinois,.......	1,150	399,813	134,549	428,175	126,756	474	993,567
Missouri,.....	70	274,853	81,981	100,432	90,878	22	1,149,544
Arkansas,....	95	1,542	78,606	59,205	10,680	....	489,750
Michigan,....	266	1,329,784	54,498	301,052	16,075	....	113,955
Florida,.......	124¾	275,317	9,943	23,094	1,035	....	20,205
Wiskonsin,...	½	135,288	22,910	35,677	37	....	12,567
Iowa,.........	....	41,450	7,304	23,609	50	....	25,966
D. of Colum.	651	....	1,287	5,566	3,507	25	1,500
TOTAL,.....	61,552½	155,100,809	5,088,891	33,787,008	7,256,904	124,734	29,023,380

HORTICULTURE.—GARDENS—NURSERIES.

STATES AND TERRITORIES.	GARDENS.		NURSERIES.		STATES AND TERRITORIES.	GARDENS.		NURSERIES.	
	Market Produce. Value.	*Nursery Prod'ce. Value.*	*Men Emp'd.*	*Capital Invested.*		*Market Produce. Value.*	*Nursery Prod'ce. Value.*	*Men Emp'd.*	*Capital Invested.*
Me.....	$51,579	$460	689	$84,774	Miss...	$42,896	$499	66	$43,060
N. H...	18,085	35	21	1,460	La......	240,042	32,415	349	359,711
Mass...	283,904	111,814	292	43,170	Tenn..	19,812	71,100	34	10,760
R. I....	67,741	12,604	207	240,274	Ky.. ...	125,071	6,226	350	108,597
Conn...	61,936	18,114	202	126,346	Ohio,...	97,606	19,707	149	31,400
Ver....	16,276	5,600	48	6,677	Ind.....	61,212	17,231	309	73,628
N. Y...	499,126	75,980	525	258,558	Illin....	71,911	22,990	77	17,515
N. J...	249,613	26,167	1,233	125,116	Mo.....	37,181	6,205	97	37,075
Penn...	232,912	50,127	1,156	857,475	Ark....	2,736	415	8	6,036
Del.....	4,035	1,120	9	1,100	Mich...	4,051	6,307	37	24,273
Md.....	133,197	10,591	619	48,841	Fa......	11,758	10	60	6,500
Va.....	92,359	38,799	173	19,900	Wisk..	3,106	1,025	89	85,616
N. C....	28,475	48,581	20	4,663	Iowa,..	2,170	4,200	10	1,698
S. C....	38,187	2,139	1,058	210.980	D. of C.	52,895	850	163	42,933
Geo....	19,346	1,853	418	9,213					
Ala....	31,978	370	85	58,425	TOTAL,	2,601,196	593,534	8,553	2,945,774

COMMERCE.—WHOLESALE AND RETAIL HOUSES—LUMBER TRADE—INTERNAL TRANSPORTATION—BUTCHERS AND PACKERS, Etc.

STATES AND TERRITORIES.	*Commer'l Houses in Fo. Tr'de.*	*Commission Houses.*	*Capital Invested.*	*Ret'l Dryg'ds, Grocery, and other stores.*	*Capital Invested.*	*Lumber Trade. Yards.*	*Capital Invested.*	*Men Employed.*	*Internal Transp'n. Men Em.*	*Butchers, Pack's, &c. Employed.*	*Capital Invested.*
Maine,............	70	14	$1,646,926	2,220	$3,973,593	68	$305,850	2,068	123	56	$95,150
New Hampshire,.	18	6	1,330,600	1,075	2,602,422	9	29,000	626	117	38	54,120
Massachusetts,....	241	123	13,881,517	3,625	12,705,038	137	1,022,360	3,432	799	480	407,830
Rhode Island,.....	44	57	2,043,750	930	2,810,125	41	254,900	262	58	83	71,050
Connecticut,.......	10	13	565,000	1,630	6,687,636	57	438,425	582	293	76	162,065
Vermont,..........	....	....	....	747	2,964,060	14	45,506	321	183	11	26,090
New York,........	469	1,044	49,583,001	12,207	42,135,795	414	2,694,170	9,592	7,593	804	2,833,916
New Jersey,......	2	8	99,000	1,504	4,113,247	86	410,570	1,280	423	30	204,900
Pennsylvania,......	194	178	3,662,811	6,534	35,741,770	284	2,241,040	5,064	2,146	466	727,850
Delaware,..........	....	....	....	327	967,750	22	83,280	140	23	6	13,800
Maryland,..........	70	117	4,414,000	2,562	9,246,170	48	307,300	1,330	103	211	28,880
Virginia,...........	31	64	4,299,500	2,736	16,684,413	41	113,210	1,454	931	103	100,680
North Carolina,...	4	46	151,300	1,068	5,082,835	20	46,000	432	213	24	9,000
South Carolina,...	41	41	3,668,050	1,253	6,648,736	14	100,000	1,057	125	46	112,900
Georgia,...........	4	82	1,543,500	1,716	7,361,838	26	75,730	442	194	17	12,885
Alabama,..........	51	101	3,355,012	899	5,642,885	9	1,800	73	49	57	93,370
Mississippi,........	7	67	673,900	755	5,004,420	11	132,175	228	40	15	4,250
Louisiana,.........	24	381	16,770,000	2,465	14,301,024	121	260,045	597	3	291	144,523
Tennessee,........	13	52	1,495,100	1,032	7,357,300	9	6,700	1,126	31	5	98,811
Kentucky,.........	5	50	620,700	1,685	9,411,826	95	105,925	571	101	183	183,850
Ohio,...............	53	241	5,928,200	4,605	21,282,225	78	373,268	2,891	854	1,061	4,617,570
Indiana,...........	11	26	1,207,400	1,801	5,664,687	37	90,374	767	2,705	237	582,165
Illinois,............	2	51	333,800	1,348	4,904,125	39	93,350	405	117	268	642,425
Missouri,..........	3	39	746,500	1,107	8,158,802	45	318,029	345	79	128	173,650
Arkansas,..........	10	10	91,000	263	1,578,719	9	12,220	263	....	3	600
Michigan,..........	....	26	177,500	612	2,228,988	15	45,600	312	142	4	39,200
Florida,............	23	21	542,000	239	1,240,380	16	64,050	92	87	32	12,200
Wiskonsin,........	1	7	63,000	178	661,550	14	21,180	133	62	3	14,100
Iowa,..............	....	14	92,300	157	437,550	3	16,250	29	....	....	....
Dist. of Columbia,	7	2	310,000	285	2,701,890	11	140,000	49	....	70	59,100
TOTAL,.......	1,408	2,881	119,295,367	57,565	250,301,799	1,793	9,848,307	35,963	17,594	4,808	11,526,950

FISHERIES, AND PRODUCTS OF THE FOREST.

SMOKED AND PICKLED FISH—SPERM AND WHALE OIL—WHALEBONE, Etc.
LUMBER—NAVAL STORES—POT ASHES—FURS—GINSENG, Etc.

STATES AND TERRIT'RIES.	FISHERIES.							PRODUCTS OF THE FOREST.					
	Smoked or Dri'd Fish. Quintals.	*Pickled Fish. Barrels.*	*Spermaceti Oil. Gallons.*	*Whale, and oth. F. Oil. Gallons.*	*Whalebone, & oth. Prod. Value.*	*Men Empl'd.*	*Capital Invested.*	*Lumber Produced. Value.*	*Tar, Pitch, Turp., &c. Barrels.*	*Pot & Pearl Ashes. Tons.*	*Skins and Furs. Value.*	*Ginseng, & all oth. Products—Val.*	*Men Empl'd.*
Maine,	279,156	54,071	1,044	117,807	$2,351	3,610	$526,967	$1,808,683		260¾	$8,027	$32,271	2,892
N. Hampsh.	28,257	1,714½		15,234		399	59,680	433,217		113½	2,230	1,929	553
Massachu's,	389,715	124,755	3,630,972	3,364,725	442,974	16,000	11,725,850	344,845		6	60	31,669	174
Rhode Isl'd,	4,034	2,908	487,268	633,860	45,523	1,160	1,077,157	44,455				155	50
Connectic't,	1,384	6,598	183,207	1,909,047	157,572	2,215	1,301,640	147,841			19,760	13,974	120
Vermont,								346,939		718½	1,750	2,500	392
New York,	5	22,224	400,251	1,269,541	344,665	1,228	949,250	3,891,302	402	7,613¾	15,556	143,332	4,664
New Jers'y,		1,134	12,000	80,000	74,000	179	93,275	271,591	2,200	2	20,000	65,075	446
Pennsylv'a,		2,012			15,240	58	16,460	1,150,220	1,595	263	9,571	14,297	1,988
Delaware,		28,000	49,704	142,575	7,987	165	170,000	5,562				7,557	
Maryland,		71,292			12,167	7,814	88,947	226,977			2,527	11,690	115
Virginia,		30,315	262		4,150	556	28,383	538,092	5,809		23,214	49,654	2,218
N. Carolina,	2,385	73,350		2,387	23,800	1,784	213,502	506,766	593,451		3,126	46,040	2,694
S. Carolina,		425				53	1,617	537,684	735		1,225	9,247	508
Georgia,		14				6		114,050	153		2,928	155	221
Alabama,	2							169,008	197		3,585	4,281	84
Mississippi,	9							192,794	2,248		3,382	6,873	123
Louisiana,								66,106	2,233		1,179		54
Tennessee,		97				7	242	217,606	3,336	1	2,602	1,635	282
Kentucky,								130,329	700		17,860	34,510	508
Ohio,		3,506		14		165	12,210	262,821	5,631	6,809½	37,218	15,206	326
Indiana,		14			1,150			420,791		2	220,883	9,902	799
Illinois,		1		28				203,666		½	39,412	6,763	368
Missouri,								70,355	356		373,121	4,015	1,134
Arkansas,								176,617	34		37,047	3,805	343
Michigan,		16,535		60		453	28,640	392,325		145	54,232	6,483	320
Florida,	69,000	73			6,000	67	10,000	20,346			7,004		6
Wiskonsin,		9,021		1,500	155	138	61,300	202,239	1		124,776	3,562	593
Iowa,								50,280	25		33,594		67
Dist. of Col.		24,300			15,500	527	64,500						
TOTAL,	773,947	472,359½	4,764,708	7,536,778	1,153,234	36,584	16,429,620	12,943,507	619,106	15,935½	1,065,869	526,580	22,042

MANUFACTURES.—MACHINERY—HARDWARE—FIRE ARMS—METALS—GRANITE, MARBLE, Etc.

STATES AND TERRITORIES.	MACHINERY.		HARDWARE, ETC.		FIRE ARMS, ETC.			PREC'S METALS.		VARI'S METALS.		GRANITE, ETC.	
	Value.	*Men Employed.*	*Cutlery, &c. Value.*	*Men Employed.*	*Cannon.*	*Small Arms.*	*Men Emp'd.*	*Value.*	*Men Emp'd.*	*Value.*	*Men Emp'd.*	*Value.*	*Men Emp'd.*
Maine,	$69,752	339	$65,555	119	....	152	4	....	....	$56,512	51	$98,720	280
New Hampshire,	106,814	191	124,460	197	....	425	7	$8,040	11	136,334	224	21,918	55
Massachusetts,	926,975	913	1,881,163	1,109	50	22,652	397	92,045	61	1,773,758	1,042	217,180	274
Rhode Island,	437,100	534	138,720	164	....	....	....	283,500	179	147,550	138	36,202	43
Connecticut,	319,680	335	1,114,725	1,109	....	12,832	148	199,100	126	1,733,044	1,095	50,866	55
Vermont,	101,354	87	16,650	33	....	1,158	42	3,000	8	24,900	44	62,515	116
New York,	2,895,517	3,631	1,566,974	962	112	8,308	203	1,106,203	708	2,456,792	1,713	966,220	1,447
New Jersey,	755,050	932	83,575	123	....	2,010	71	159,302	7	405,955	130	10,000	16
Pennsylvania,	1,998,152	1,973	786,982	770	5	21,571	168	2,679,075	245	1,260,170	635	443,610	536
Delaware,	314,500	299	22,000	10	....	....	....	3,500	7	10,700	18	12,000	10
Maryland,	348,165	723	15,670	36	....	80	3	13,300	21	312,900	216	152,750	247
Virginia,	429,858	445	50,504	150	....	9,330	262	41,000	52	128,256	219	16,652	40
North Carolina,	43,285	89	1,200	43	....	1,085	40	875	1	16,050	24	1,083	15
South Carolina,	65,561	127	13,465	26	....	167	7	3,000	4	....	....	....	....
Georgia,	131,238	184	7,866	19	....	95	5	250	1	5,350	6	10,640	10
Alabama,	131,825	96	13,875	41	4	428	20	1,650	7	25,700	17	7,311	17
Mississippi,	242,225	274	....	....	....	90	7	6,425	3	36,900	20	....	....
Louisiana,	5,000	....	30,000	8	....	....	....	....	....	....	....	....	....
Tennessee,	257,704	266	57,170	142	....	564	34	28,460	11	100,870	100	5,400	10
Kentucky,	46,074	149	22,350	30	....	2,341	109	19,060	21	164,080	174	8,820	25
Ohio,	875,731	858	393,300	289	3	2,450	70	53,125	37	782,901	589	256,131	401
Indiana,	123,808	120	34,263	83	....	885	47	3,500	2	14,580	26	6,720	28
Illinois,	37,720	71	9,750	20	20	238	12	2,400	7	31,200	29	16,112	26
Missouri,	190,412	191	....	....	....	959	48	5,450	12	60,300	72	32,050	73
Arkansas,	14,065	51	....	....	....	6	1	....	....	1,240	5	50	....
Michigan,	47,000	67	1,250	7	....	195	6	5,000	1	57,900	45	7,000	6
Florida,	5,000	8	....	....	....	....	....	500	....	4,000	3	....	....
Wiskonsin,	716	6	....	....	....	12	1	....	....	3,500	5	....	....
Iowa,	....	....	....	....	....	40	2	....	....	....	....	....	....
District of Columbia,	60,300	42	500	2	80	....	30	17,200	24	28,000	37	3,000	4
TOTAL,	10,980,581	13,001	6,451,967	5,492	274	88,073	1,744	4,734,960	1,556	9,779,442	6,677	2,442,950	3,734

MANUFACTURES.—BRICKS AND LIME—WOOL—COTTON.

STATES AND TERRIT'RIES.	BRICKS & LIME.		Capital Invested in those already mentioned.	WOOL.					COTTON.					
	Value.	Men Emp'd.		F'lling Mills.	Factories.	Goods. Value.	P'rs'ns Emp'd.	Capital Invested.	Factories.	Spindles.	Dye and Print Wks.	Articles. Value.	P'rs'ns Emp'd.	Capital Invested.
Maine,......	$621,586	864	$300,822	151	24	$412,366	532	$316,105	6	29,736	3	$970,397	1,414	$1,398,000
N. Hampsh.	63,166	236	166,003	152	66	795,784	893	740,345	58	195,173	4	4,142,304	6,991	5,523,200
Massachu's,	310,796	758	3,081,985	207	144	7,082,898	5,076	4,179,850	278	665,095	22	16,553,423	20,928	17,414,099
Rhode Isl'd,	66,000	113	639,150	45	41	842,172	961	685,350	209	518,817	17	7,116,792	12,086	7,326,000
Connectic't,	151,446	307	2,294,810	157	119	2,494,313	2,356	1,931,335	116	181,319	6	2,715,964	5,153	3,152,000
Vermont,...	402,218	224	141,385	239	95	1,331,953	1,450	1,406,950	7	7,254		113,000	262	118,100
New York,.	1,198,527	3,160	4,563,188	890	323	3,537,337	4,636	3,469,349	117	211,659	12	3,640,237	7,407	4,900,772
New Jers'y,	376,805	572	1,312,510	49	31	440,710	427	314,650	43	63,744	13	2,086,104	2,408	1,722,810
Pennsylv'a,.	1,733,590	3,888	2,557,540	346	235	2,319,061	2,930	1,510,546	106	146,494	40	5,013,007	5,522	3,325,400
Delaware,...	56,536	116	92,500	3	2	104,700	83	107,000	11	24,492		332,272	566	330,500
Maryland,...	409,456	1,042	426,984	39	29	235,900	388	117,630	21	41,182	3	1,150,580	2,284	1,304,400
Virginia,....	393,253	1,004	164,041	47	41	147,792	222	112,350	22	42,262	1	446,063	1,816	1,299,020
N. Carolina,	58,336	276	17,165	1	3	3,900	4	9,800	25	47,934		438,900	1,219	995,300
S. Carolina,	193,408	1,281	72,445		3	1,000	6	4,300	15	16,355		359,000	570	617,450
Georgia,....	148,655	555	200,700		1	3,000	10	2,000	19	42,589	2	304,342	779	573,835
Alabama,...	91,326	264	95,370						14	1,502		17,547	82	35,575
Mississippi,.	273,870	693	222,745						53	318		1,744	81	6,420
Louisiana,..	861,655	1,467	2,432,600						2	706		18,900	23	22,000
Tennessee,.	119,371	417	166,728	4	26	14,290	45	25,600	38	16,813		325,719	1,542	463,240
Kentucky,..	240,919	657	148,191	5	40	151,246	200	138,000	58	12,358	5	329,380	523	316,113
Ohio,........	712,697	1,469	677,056	206	130	685,757	935	537,985	8	13,754		139,378	246	113,500
Indiana,.....	206,751	1,007	140,469	24	37	58,867	103	77,954	12	4,985	1	135,400	210	142,500
Illinois,......	263,398	995	104,648	4	16	9,540	34	26,205						
Missouri,...	185,234	671	256,484		9	13,750	13	5,100						
Arkansas,...	319,696	66	11,020		1	129	1	12,600	2	90			7	2,125
Michigan,...	68,913	298	77,075	16	4	9,734	37	34,120						
Florida,......	37,600	136	90,900											
Wiskonsin,.	6,527	43	4,355											
Iowa,........	13,710	39	8,200			800								
Dist. of Col.	151,500	189	153,800											
TOTAL,...	9,736,945	22,807	20,620,869	2,585	1,420	20,696,999	21,342	15,765,124	1,240	2,284,631	129	46,350,453	72,119	51,102,359

MANUFACTURES.—SILK—FLAX—MIXED—TOBACCO.

STATES AND TERRITORIES.	SILK.					FLAX.			MIXED.			TOBACCO.		
	Reeled, & other sorts.	*Value.*	*Males Emp'd.*	*Females & Chil'n Emp.*	*Capital Invested.*	*Value.*	*P'rs'ns Emp'd.*	*Capital Invested.*	*Val. Produced.*	*P'rs'ns Emp'd.*	*Capital Invested.*	*Articles. Value.*	*P'rs'ns Emp'd.*	*Capital Invested.*
Maine,	*Pounds* 9½	$91		1	$125	$4,000			$47,598	280	$7,640	$18,150	37	$6,050
N. Hampshi.	82⅞	924	5	26	865	50	1		46,800	34	40,750	10,500	17	2,100
Massachus's,	4,633½	38,079	30	116	68,719	75,100	41	$30,050	1,157,035	1,101	644,525	176,264	286	90,500
Rhode Isl'nd,	16	15							448,044	500	167,690	71,560	123	34,900
Connecticut,	6,901½	55,485	23	100	85,430	90	4	40	530,520	1,484	343,900	122,684	233	67,875
Vermont,	39	99	5	2	1,150	55			155,276	282	101,740			
New York,	377⅝	2,415	35	66	8,034	46,429	90	15,000	1,497,067	2,005	675,953	831,570	669	395,530
New Jersey,	158½	858	10	7	2,020	83,314	178	105,709	151,352	363	86,500	92,600	106	47,590
Pennsylv'nia,	2,350½	14,644	64	88	88,917	75,672	486	56,511	1,098,810	3,903	1,642,015	550,159	950	287,859
Delaware,	15	117		1								17,000	34	5,800
Maryland,	40		2	18	5,000				541,300	1,162	230,958	232,000	278	125,100
Virginia,	94¼	515	11	10	2,714	4,873			227,861	343	101,462	2,406,671	3,342	1,526,080
N. Carolina,	7	55		1		1,866	95					189,868	482	91,065
S. Carolina,	46	380	1	3	50				2,450	9		3,500	7	5,000
Georgia,	97	458	14	7	955				225	3	120	9,563	33	6,313
Alabama,	13	99			75				705			2,260	2	
Mississippi,												10		
Louisiana,	70	420		3								150,000	414	95,000
Tennessee,	19¾	218	14	31	2,500	3,139	142		9,542	24	537	89,462	259	247,475
Kentucky,	86	819	3	11	5,467	7,519	249	444	127,875	3,142	39,803	413,585	587	230,400
Ohio,	652	3,740	23	27	2,290	11,737	31	242	280,293	552	183,415	212,818	187	68,810
Indiana,	9	94	4	1	3	6,851	261	100	46,329	596	13,145	65,659	88	24,706
Illinois,	17	235		1	10	1,480	50		11,711	49	8,233	10,139	24	3,093
Missouri,									11,115	40	4,885	89,996	188	51,755
Arkansas,									585			750	3	250
Michigan,	8	34	2		50	30						5,000	12	1,750
Florida,	1½	15										10,480	21	5,240
Wiskonsin,	1	5		1					1,500	4	550			
Iowa,												40	2	
D. of Colum.									151,510	29	75,350	37,280		16,950
TOTAL,	15,745½	119,814	246	521	274,374	322,205	1,628	208,087	6,545,503	15,905	4,368,991	5,819,568	8 384	3 437,191

MANUFACTURES.—HATS, CAPS, BONNETS, Etc.—LEATHER, TANNERIES, SADDLERIES, Etc.

STATES AND TERRITORIES.	HATS, CAPS, BONNETS, ETC.				LEATHER, TANNERIES, SADDLERIES, ETC.							
	Hats and Caps, &c. (Value)	*Straw Bonnets.* (Value)	*P'rs'ns Emp'd.*	*Capital Invested.*	*Tanneries.*	*Sole. Tanned.* (Sides)	*Upper. Tanned.* (Sides)	*Men Emp'd.*	*Capital Invested.*	*All other Fact'ries.*	*Articles. Value.*	*Capital Invested.*
Maine,........	$74,174	$8,807	212	$28,050	395	123,747	85,856	754	$571,793	530	$443,846	$191,717
New Hampshire,........	190,526	9,379	2,048	48,852	251	42,396	122,514	776	386,402	2,131	712,151	230,649
Massachusetts,........	918,438	821,646	6,656	602,292	355	212,844	391,608	2,446	1,024,699	1,532	10,553,826	3,318,544
Rhode Island,........	92,465	86,106	411	66,427	27	1,534	50,860	89	72,000	44	182,110	70,675
Connecticut,........	649,580	236,730	1,814	350,823	197	33,081	126,867	1,359	494,477	408	2,017,931	829,267
Vermont,........	62,432	2,819	126	32,875	261	102,763	102,937	509	403,093	399	361,468	168,090
New York,........	2,914,117	160,248	3,880	1,676,559	1,216	1,252,890	827,993	5,579	3,907,348	2,849	6,232,924	2,743,765
New Jersey,........	1,181,562	23,220	957	332,029	159	57,590	86,764	1,090	415,728	478	1,582,746	637,621
Pennsylvania,........	820,331	80,512	1,470	449,407	1,170	415,655	405,933	3,445	2,783,636	2,223	3,482,793	1,255,738
Delaware,........	15,300	450	35	9,075	18	20,648	22,075	66	89,300	75	166,037	161,630
Maryland,........	153,456	13,200	205	76,620	161	190,065	191,867	1,035	713,655	408	1,050,275	434,127
Virginia,........	155,778	14,700	340	85,640	660	135,782	206,216	1,422	838,141	982	826,597	341,957
North Carolina,........	38,167	1,700	142	13,141	353	62,050	89,032	645	271,797	238	185,387	76,163
South Carolina,........	3,750	....	20	315	97	68,018	89,586	281	212,020	243	109,472	45,662
Georgia,........	22,761	....	55	7,950	132	55,066	71,280	437	127,739	102	123,701	60,932
Alabama,........	8,210	....	31	4,045	142	36,705	42,777	300	147,463	137	180,152	58,332
Mississippi,........	5,140	....	13	8,100	128	15,332	15,093	149	70,870	42	118,167	41,945
Louisiana,........	....	....	....	....	25	12,760	13,705	88	132,025	7	108,500	89,550
Tennessee,........	104,949	....	177	49,215	454	133,547	171,329	909	484,114	374	359,050	154,540
Kentucky,........	201,310	4,483	194	118,850	387	107,676	155,465	978	567,954	548	732,646	369,835
Ohio,........	728,513	3,028	963	369,637	812	161,630	234,037	1,790	957,383	1,160	1,986,146	917,245
Indiana,........	122,844	2,048	183	69,018	428	122,780	157,581	978	399,627	579	730,001	247,549
Illinois,........	28,395	1,570	68	12,918	155	28,383	34,654	305	155,679	626	247,217	98,503
Missouri,........	111,620	100	82	30,195	155	31,959	55,186	325	208,936	340	298,345	179,527
Arkansas,........	1,400	....	3	400	37	9,263	9,811	70	43,510	545	17,400	8,830
Michigan,........	30,463	659	42	20,007	38	7,017	9,832	99	70,240	101	192,190	69,2[illegible]2
Florida,........	1,500	....	....	750	3	5,250	1,250	15	14,500	10	6,200	4,250
Wiskonsin,........	61	....	1	10	1	150	150	3	2,000	13	11,800	7,002
Iowa,........	19,900	5,100	....	....	3	340	410	4	4,400	5	4,875	1,645
District of Columbia,	47,200	....	48	22,100	9	16,690	9,200	72	80,400	7	110,450	66,750
TOTAL,........	8,704,342	1,476,505	20,176	4,485,300	8,229	3,463,611	3,781,868	26,018	15,650,929	17,136	33,134,403	12,881,262

MANUFACTURES.—SOAP AND CANDLES—DISTILLED AND FERMENTED LIQUORS.

STATES AND TERRITORIES.	SOAP AND CANDLES.					DISTILLED AND FERMENTED LIQUORS.					
	Soap. Pounds.	*Tallow Candles.* (Pounds)	*Spermaceti & Wax Candles.* (Pounds)	*Men Employed.*	*Capital Invested.*	*Distilleries.*	*Gallons Produced.*	*Breweries.*	*Gallons Produced.*	*Men Emp'd.*	*Capital Invested.*
Maine,	85,455	213,898	3,023	23	$19,500	3	190,000			7	$29,000
New Hampshire,	10,900	28,845	50,000	20	13,550	5	51,244	1	3,000	7	15,998
Massachusetts,	12,560,400	1,257,465	2,162,710	403	873,956	37	5,177,910	7	429,800	154	963,100
Rhode Island,	1,237,050	157,250	264,500	57	252,628	4	855,000	3	89,600	42	139,000
Connecticut,	337,000	440,790	20,002	39	46,000	70	215,892			42	50,380
Vermont,	50,300	28,687		2		2	3,500	1	12,800	5	8,850
New York,	11,939,834	4,029,783	353,000	489	618,875	212	11,973,815	83	6,059,122	1,486	3,107,066
New Jersey,	483,229	372,546		27	38,400	219	334,017	6	206,375	394	230,870
Pennsylvania,	5,097,690	2,316,843	5,002	353	294,442	1,010	6,240,193	87	12,765,974	1,607	1,589,471
Delaware,	367,240	159,834		9	24,000			3	39,500	9	8,000
Maryland,	1,865,240	731,446	35,000	93	98,600	73	366,213	11	828,140	199	185,790
Virginia,	1,200,308	463,525	837	126	28,881	1,454	865,725	5	32,960	1,631	187,212
North Carolina,	1,612,825	148,546	335	367	4,754	2,802	1,051,979		17,431	1,422	180,200
South Carolina,	586,327	68,011		168	300	251	102,288			219	14,342
Georgia,	764,528	111,066	75	2,633	27,126	393	126,746	22		218	28,606
Alabama,	219,024	23,047	621	2	3,500	188	127,230	7	200	220	34,212
Mississippi,	312,084	31,957	97			14	3,150	2	132	12	910
Louisiana,	2,202,200	3,500,030	40,000	75	115,500	5	285,520	1	2,400	27	110,000
Tennessee,	594,289	65,388		2	6,000	1,426	1,109,107	6	1,835	1,341	218,182
Kentucky,	2,282,426	563,635	315	516	28,765	889	1,763,685	50	214,589	1,092	315,308
Ohio,	3,603,036	2,318,456	151	105	186,780	390	6,329,467	59	1,422,584	798	893,119
Indiana,	1,135,560	228,938	111	30	13,039	323	1,787,108	20	188,392	500	292,316
Illinois,	519,673	117,698	42	25	17,345	150	1,551,684	11	90,300	233	138,155
Missouri,	138,000	243,000		15	16,700	293	508,368	7	374,700	365	189,976
Arkansas,	142,775	16,541	632	32	200	53	26,415			38	10,205
Michigan,	78,100	57,975		6	6,000	34	337,761	10	308,696	116	124,200
Florida,	10,887	2,812	168								
Wiskonsin,	64,317	12,909	48	5	3,432	3	8,300	3	14,200	11	14,400
Iowa,	9,740	4,436	282	1		2	4,310			3	1,500
District of Columbia,	310,060	189,150		18	19,000	1	6,000	1	165,000	25	67,000
TOTAL,	49,820,497	17,904,507	2,936,951	5,641	2,757,273	10,306	41,402,627	406	23,267,730	12,223	9,147,368

MANUFACTURES.—GLASS, EARTHENWARE, Etc.—SUGAR REFINERIES, CHOCOLATE, Etc.

STATES AND TERRITORIES.	GLASS, EARTHENWARE, ETC.									SUGAR REFINERIES, CHOCOLATE, ETC.					
	Glass-houses.	*Cut'g Sh'ps.*	*Men Emp.*	*Articles, incl'd'g Mirrors. Value*	*Capital Invested.*	*Potteries.*	*Articles. Value.*	*Men Emp'd.*	*Capital Invested.*	*Refineries.*	*Value Produced.*	*Choc'late. Value.*	*Confect'ry. Value.*	*Men Emp'd.*	*Capital Invested.*
Me....						21	$20,850	31	$11,353				$16,900	18	$6,000
N. H...	3		85	$47,000	$44,000	14	19,100	29	6,840				11,200	10	3,100
Mass...	4	1	372	471,000	277,000	20	44,450	71	27,975	2	$1,025,000	$37,500	137,300	220	374,300
R. I....													14,500	15	4,500
Conn...	2		64	32,000	32,000	14	40,850	44	31,880				31,800	16	12,800
Ver. ...	2		70	55,000	35,000	8	23,000	30	10,350						
N. Y...	13	11	498	411,371	204,700	47	159,292	197	88,450	7	385,000	5,000	386,142	416	474,656
N. J...	23	4	1,075	904,700	589,800	22	256,807	122	135,850				1,000	2	500
Penn...	28	15	835	772,400	714,100	182	157,902	322	75,562	20	891,200	14,000	227,050	197	272,450
Del....						2	4,300	9	1,100				6,500	9	2,500
Md....	1		37	40,000	30,000	23	60,240	90	25,120	6	176,000	11,400	73,450	102	104,370
Va.....	4	2	164	146,500	132,000	33	31,380	64	10,225	1			43,850	15	16,200
N. C....						16	6,260	21	1,531				3,300	1	1,000
S. C....						8	19,300	49	12,950				29,333	112	87,200
Geo....						6	2,050	12	790	1	500	5,000	3,100	12	5,500
Ala....						7	8,300	13	11,250				13,800	15	6,120
Miss...						1	1,200	2	200				10,500	2	
La.....						1	1,000	18	3,000	5	770,000	7,000	20,000	101	351,000
Tenn..						29	51,600	50	7,300						
Ky.. ...		1	2	3,000	500	16	24,090	51	9,670				36,050	28	14,250
Ohio,...						99	89,754	199	43,450	1	3,000		60,450	43	26,800
Ind....						45	35,835	79	13,685				4,000	3	1,000
Illin....						23	26,740	56	10,225				2,240	3	825
Mo....						12	12,175	33	7,250				1,000	1	500
Ark....															
Mich...	1		34	7,322	25,000	3	1,100	4	625				3,000	3	1,200
Fa.....															
Wisk ..															
Iowa,..						4	1,050	7	350						
D. of C.						3	6,200	9	4,450				7,500	11	2,800
TOTAL,	81	34	3,236	2,890,293	2,084,100	659	1,104,825	1,612	551,431	43	3,250,700	79,900	1,143,965	1,355	1,769,571

MANUFACTURES.—PAPER—PRINTING AND BINDING.

STATES AND TERRITORIES.	PAPER.					PRINTING AND BINDING.							
	Factories.	*Value Produced.*	*All other fabrics of Paper—Cards, &c.*	*Men Emp'd.*	*Capital Invested.*	*Prin'g Offices.*	*Binderies.*	*Daily Papers*	*We'kly Papers*	*Semi and Tri-w'kly*	*Periodicals.*	*Men Emp'd.*	*Capital Invested.*
Maine,	6	$84,000	*Value*	89	$20,600	34	14	3	30	3	5	196	$68,200
New Hampshire,	13	150,600	$1,500	111	104,300	36	22		27		6	256	110,850
Massachusetts,	82	1,659,930	56,700	967	1,082,800	104	72	10	67	14	14	922	416,200
Rhode Island,	2	25,000	8,500	15	45,000	16	8	2	10	4	2	122	35,700
Connecticut,	36	596,500	64,000	454	653,800	36	17	2	27	4	11	368	217,075
Vermont,	17	179,720	35,000	195	216,500	29	14	2	26	2	3	156	194,200
New York,	77	673,121	89,637	749	703,550	321	107	34	198	13	57	3,231	1,876,540
New Jersey,	41	562,200	7,000	400	460,100	40	20	4	31	1	4	198	104,900
Pennsylvania,	87	792,335	95,500	794	581,800	224	46	12	165	10	42	1,709	681,740
Delaware,	1	20,800	1,500	15	16,200	6	2		3	3	2	33	11,450
Maryland,	17	195,100	3,000	171	95,400	48	15	7	28	7	7	376	159,100
Virginia,	12	216,245	1,260	181	287,750	50	13	4	35	12	5	310	168,850
North Carolina,	2	8,785		6	5,000	26	4		26	1	2	103	55,400
South Carolina,	1	20,000		30	30,000	16	7	3	12	2	4	164	131,300
Georgia,						24	5	5	24	5	6	157	134,400
Alabama,						22	1	3	24	1		105	98,100
Mississippi,						28	1	2	28	1		94	83,510
Louisiana,						35	5	11	21	2	3	392	193,700
Tennessee,	5	46,000	14,000	87	93,000	41	5	2	38	6	10	191	112,500
Kentucky,	7	44,000		47	47,500	34	3	5	26	7	8	226	86,325
Ohio,	14	270,202	80,000	305	208,200	159	41	9	107	7	20	1,175	446,720
Indiana,	3	86,457	54,000	100	68,739	69	6		69	4	3	211	58,505
Illinois,	1	2,000				45	5	3	38	2	9	175	71,300
Missouri,						40		6	24	5		143	79,350
Arkansas,						9	1		6	3		37	13,100
Michigan,	1	7,000		6	20,000	28	2	6	26		1	119	62,900
Florida,						10	1		10			39	35,200
Wiskonsin,						6			6			24	10,300
Iowa,						4			4			15	5,700
District of Columbia,	1	1,500		4	5,000	12	10	3	5	6	3	276	150,700
TOTAL,	426	5,641,495	511,597	4,726	4,745,239	1,552	447	138	1,141	227	227	11,523	5,873,815

MANUFACTURES.—POWDER MILLS—DRUGS AND MEDICINES, PAINTS AND DYES—CORDAGE.

STATES AND TERRITORIES.	POWDER MILLS.				DRUGS AND MEDICINES, PAINTS AND DYES.				CORDAGE.			
	Po'der Mills.	*Powder. Pounds.*	*Men Emp'd.*	*Capital Invested.*	*Medicinal Drugs, Paints, Dyes, &c.* (*Value*)	*Turpentine & Varnish.* (*Value*)	*Men Emp'd.*	*Capital Invested.*	*Rope-walks.*	*Value Produced.*	*Men Emp'd.*	*Capital Invested.*
Maine,	1	150,000	3	$7,500	$9,200	$700	12	$3,280	4	$32,660	34	$23,000
New Hampshire,	7	185,000	11	58,000	10,039	2,289	9	3,589	1	15,000	10	6,000
Massachusetts,	14	2,315,215	69	255,000	405,725	25,820	85	224,700	51	852,200	672	555,100
Rhode Island,	.....	.....	.....	.....	40,000	5,000	17	30,000	9	49,700	45	28,300
Connecticut,	8	662,500	26	77,000	55,400	19,000	22	67,300	16	150,775	107	85,700
Vermont,	.....	.....	.....	.....	38,475	.....	32	25,950	2	4,000	9	3,800
New York,	8	1,185,000	41	81,500	877,816	431,467	677	1,267,835	46	792,910	597	242,180
New Jersey,	.....	.....	.....	.....	127,400	43,000	70	140,800	8	93,075	60	37,305
Pennsylvania,	30	1,184,225	58	66,800	2,100,074	7,865	519	2,179,625	39	274,120	272	136,070
Delaware,	27	2,100,000	145	220,000	350	100	5	9,500	1	2,500	7	1,000
Maryland,	5	669,125	47	46,000	80,100	100	52	85,100	13	141,050	198	70,550
Virginia,	10	2,850	11	805	66,633	25	36	61,727	9	37,320	60	32,753
North Carolina,	1	200	.....	30	8,635	116,750	73	152,275	.....	.....	.....	.....
South Carolina,	.....	.....	.....	.....	4,100	.....	6	2,100	.....	.....	.....	.....
Georgia,	.....	.....	.....	.....	38,525	.....	28	35,885	.....	.....	.....	.....
Alabama,	.....	.....	.....	.....	16,600	.....	4	16,000	.....	.....	.....	.....
Mississippi,	.....	.....	.....	.....	3,125	.....	4	500	.....	.....	.....	.....
Louisiana,	.....	.....	.....	.....	42,000	.....	10	6,000	.....	.....	.....	.....
Tennessee,	10	10,333	11	1,490	3,337	1,485	15	3,360	28	132,630	258	84,230
Kentucky,	11	282,500	58	42,000	26,994	2,000	25	16,630	111	1,292,276	1,888	1,023,130
Ohio,	2	222,500	13	18,000	101,880	200	70	126,335	21	89,750	66	37,675
Indiana,	1	.....	1	.....	47,720	26	26	17,984	5	5,850	11	2,270
Illinois,	.....	.....	.....	.....	19,001	5,000	20	13,350	.....	.....	.....	.....
Missouri,	1	7,500	2	1,050	13,500	.....	8	7,000	21	98,490	139	71,589
Arkansas,	1	400	.....	700	400	.....	.....	.....	.....	.....	.....	.....
Michigan,	.....	.....	.....	.....	1,580	.....	3	650	.....	.....	.....	.....
Florida,	.....	.....	.....	.....	200	.....	1	500	.....	.....	.....	.....
Wiskonsin,	.....	.....	.....	.....	250	.....	.....	.....	.....	.....	.....	.....
Iowa,	.....	.....	.....	.....	2,340	.....	7	.....	.....	.....	.....	.....
District of Columbia,	.....	.....	.....	.....	10,500	.....	12	9,700	3	14,000	31	24,925
TOTAL,	137	8,977,348	496	875,875	4,151,899	660,827	1,848	4,507,675	388	4,078,306	4,464	2,465,577

MANUFACTURES.—CARRIAGES AND WAGONS—MILLS, AND THE ARTICLES PRODUCED.

STATES AND TERRITORIES.	CARRIAGES AND WAGONS.			MILLS, AND THE ARTICLES PRODUCED.							
	Value Produced.	*Men Employed.*	*Capital Invested.*	*Flouring Mills.*	*Flour Prod'd. Barrels.*	*Grist Mills.*	*Saw Mills.*	*Oil Mills.*	*Articles. Value.*	*Men Emp'd.*	*Capital Invested.*
Maine,	$174,310	779	$75,012	20	6,969	558	1,381	20	$3,161,592	3,630	$2,900,565
New Hampshire,	232,240	450	114,762	3	800	449	959	9	758,260	1,296	1,149,193
Massachusetts,	803,999	1,402	334,660	12	7,436	678	1,252	7	1,771,185	1,808	1,440,152
Rhode Island,	78,811	161	36,661			144	123		83,683	166	152,310
Connecticut,	929,301	1,289	513,411	7	15,500	384	673	57	543,509	895	727,440
Vermont,	162,097	437	101,570	7	4,495	312	1,081	20	1,083,124	1,374	999,750
New York,	2,364,461	4,710	1,485,023	338	1,861,385	1,750	6,356	63	16,953,280	10,807	14,648,814
New Jersey,	1,397,149	1,834	644,966	64	168,797	509	597	21	3,446,895	1,288	2,641,200
Pennsylvania,	1,207,252	2,783	560,681	736	1,193,405	2,554	5,389	166	9,424,955	7,990	7,869,034
Delaware,	49,417	143	25,150	21	76,194	104	123		737,971	288	294,150
Maryland,	357,622	690	154,955	189	466,708	478	430	9	3,267,250	898	1,069,671
Virginia,	647,815	1,592	311,625	764	1,041,526	2,714	1,987	61	7,855,499	3,964	5,184,669
North Carolina,	301,601	698	173,318	323	87,641	2,033	1,056	46	1,552,096	1,830	1,670,228
South Carolina,	189,270	420	132,690	164	58,458	1,016	746	19	1,201,678	2,122	1,668,804
Georgia,	249,065	461	93,820	114	55,158	1,051	677	6	1,268,715	1,581	1,491,973
Alabama,	88,891	235	49,074	51	23,664	797	524	16	1,225,425	1,386	1,413,107
Mississippi,	49,693	132	34,345	16	1,809	806	309	28	486,864	923	1,219,845
Louisiana,	23,350	51	15,780	3		276	139	50	706,785	972	1,870,795
Tennessee,	219,897	518	80,878	255	67,881	1,565	977	26	1,020,664	2,100	1,310,195
Kentucky,	168,724	533	79,378	258	273,088	1,515	718	23	2,437,937	2,067	1,650,689
Ohio,	701,228	1,490	290,540	536	1,311,954	1,325	2,883	112	8,868,213	4,661	4,931,024
Indiana,	163,135	481	78,116	204	224,624	846	1,248	54	2,329,134	2,224	2,077,018
Illinois,	144,362	307	59,263	98	172,657	640	785	18	2,417,826	2,204	2,147,618
Missouri,	97,112	201	45,074	64	49,363	636	393	9	960,058	1,326	1,266,019
Arkansas,	2,675	15	1,555	10	1,430	292	88	1	330,847	400	288,257
Michigan,	20,075	59	13,150	93	202,880	97	491		1,832,363	1,144	2,460,200
Florida,	11,000	15	5,900			62	65	2	189,650	410	488,950
Wiskonsin,	2,600	8	325	4	900	29	124		350,993	850	561,650
Iowa,	1,200	3	1,400	6	4,340	37	75		95,425	154	166,650
District of Columbia,	59,535	97	38,550	4	25,500	4	1		183,370	30	98,500
TOTAL,	10,897,887	21,994	5,551,632	4,364	7,404,562	23,661	31,650	843	76,545,246	60,788	65,858,470

MANUFACTURES.—SHIPS AND OTHER VESSELS—HOUSEHOLD FURNITURE—HOUSES.

STATES AND TERRITORIES.	SHIPS, ETC.	HOUSEHOLD FURNITURE.			HOUSES.			
	Ships and Vessels Built.	*Furniture. Value.*	*Men Employed.*	*Capital Invested.*	*Brick and Stone Houses Built.*	*Wooden Houses Built.*	*Men Employed.*	*Cost of Construction.*
Maine	*Value* $1,844,902	$204,875	1,435	$668,558	34	1,674	2,482	$733,067
New Hampshire	78,000	105,827	233	59,984	90	434	935	470,715
Massachusetts	1,349,994	1,090,008	2,424	962,494	324	1,249	2,947	2,767,134
Rhode Island	41,500	121,131	195	83,300	6	292	887	379,010
Connecticut	428,900	253,675	786	342,770	95	517	1,599	1,086,295
Vermont	72,000	83,275	190	49,850	72	468	912	344,896
New York	797,317	1,971,776	3,660	1,610,810	1,233	5,198	16,768	7,265,844
New Jersey	344,240	176,566	517	130,525	205	861	2,086	1,092,052
Pennsylvania	668,015	1,155,692	2,373	716,707	1,995	2,428	9,974	5,354,480
Delaware	35,400	16,300	130	34,800	47	104	299	145,850
Maryland	279,771	305,360	834	339,336	389	592	2,026	1,078,770
Virginia	136,807	289,391	675	143,320	402	2,604	4,694	1,367,393
North Carolina	62,800	35,002	223	57,980	38	1,822	1,707	410,264
South Carolina	60,000	28,155	241	133,600	111	1,594	2,398	1,527,576
Georgia	....	49,780	95	29,090	38	2,591	2,274	693,116
Alabama	....	41,671	53	18,430	67	472	882	739,871
Mississippi	13,925	34,450	41	28,610	144	2,247	2,487	1,175,513
Louisiana	80,500	2,300	129	576,050	248	619	1,484	2,736,944
Tennessee	229	79,580	203	30,650	193	1,098	1,467	427,402
Kentucky	....	273,350	453	139,295	485	1,757	2,883	1,039,172
Ohio	522,855	761,146	1,928	534,317	970	2,764	6,060	3,776,823
Indiana	107,223	211,481	564	91,022	346	4,270	5,519	1,241,312
Illinois	39,200	84,410	244	62,223	334	4,133	5,737	2,065,255
Missouri	....	....	....	....	413	2,202	1,966	1,441,573
Arkansas	500	20,293	45	7,810	21	1,083	1,251	1,141,174
Michigan	10,500	22,494	65	28,050	39	1,280	1,978	571,005
Florida	14,100	....	36	18,300	9	306	689	327,913
Wiskonsin	7,159	6,945	29	5,740	7	509	644	212,085
Iowa	....	4,600	12	1,350	14	483	324	135,987
District of Columbia	20,257	125,872	190	85,000	60	33	142	168,910
TOTAL	7,016,094	7,555,405	18,003	6,989,971	8,429	45,684	85,501	41,917,401

CHAPTER XX.

VALUE OF THE ANNUAL PRODUCTS OF INDUSTRY.

The census of 1840 has thus given us a mass of materials for estimating the annual income of the United States, which has been rarely if ever, afforded to seventeen millions of people. Yet, with all this valuable aid, precise accuracy is still unattainable; for those diversities and fluctuations of price, from which no country is exempt, are particularly great in this country. Articles of raw produce, which vary in price, from year to year, far more than manufactures, constitute here the unusually large proportion of more than two-thirds of the whole annual product. In a country, moreover, of such large extent as the United States, differing so widely in soil, climate, density of numbers, and easy access to market, the price of the same commodity varies considerably among the different States in the same year. Nay, more—with the larger States, the same local diversities apply to different parts of the same State, and often make the price of the more bulky commodities, at one place of production, more than twice as high as the price they bear at another. To make, then, a fair average, it is necessary to take into account the quantities produced in the several parts, as well as the difference of price. There are also sources of revenue, in which the census has not given the annual product, but the whole value of the capital invested, as in the case of live stock, and of the capitals employed in commerce; in which items, there being room for further difference of opinion, there is a further source of uncertainty. Even in those manufactures of which the census has determined their gross values, we may expect, in deducting the value of the raw materials which have been estimated under other heads, somewhat of the same difference of opinion, and the same uncertainty. The most careful estimate practicable must therefore rest, in part, on conjecture and probability. Yet, if the estimate be cautiously made, and be founded on the opinion of judicious persons, who look not beyond their own experience and observation, the unavoidable errors will probably so balance and compensate each other, that the result will afford an approximation to the truth, which is all that the subject admits of, and, indeed, all that it is important for us to know.

In making the subjoined estimate, the following course has been pursued :—Of those articles of which the census has given, only the quantities, the market price at the place produced, or where the producer transports it by his own labour, is considered the fair value. To ascertain this, local information, from persons competent to give it, has been procured, as far as practicable. The prices affixed ought, in strictness, perhaps, to have been those which prevailed in 1840, when the census was taken ; but, as the prices of most articles of commerce were not uninfluenced, even then, by the distention of the currency which succeeded the termination of the Bank of the United States, in 1836, it was thought that a medium between the prices of 1840 and those of the present year, 1843, when they are unusually depressed, would give a fair average.

In estimating the product of live stock, one-fourth of its gross value has been assumed to be its annual value. This may be somewhat too much for horses and mules, but it is far too little for sheep and hogs, and may not be quite enough for neat cattle. The products of this branch of husbandry is compounded in a small degree of rent, but principally of the wages of personal service and the profits of capital ; and, considering the high price which both labour and capital bear in this country, 25 per cent seems to be not too high. In England, it is supposed that one-fourth of the cattle is slaughtered in the year. As those fatted for the shambles are worth about double the general average, this rule would give twice the amount of the present estimate ; but then it would be necessary to deduct the value of the food consumed in the process of fattening, which would bring us to nearly the same result. From the gross value of *domestic* manufactures, included in the products of agriculture, one-half is deducted for the raw materials.

In estimating the products of commerce, as they also are compounded of the wages of industry and the profits of capital, they have, in like manner, been set down at 25 per cent on the capital employed. Without doubt, this greatly exceeds the rate of profits in the wholesale and foreign trade, but it is also far short of the retail trade, in which, for the most part, the capital is turned over several times in the year. The census shows, that upwards of

100,000 families are engaged in the employments comprehended under the head of commerce; and a less profit than the one supposed would not be adequate to the support of that number, in a style of living which far exceeds the average rate of that of the whole community.

From the gross value of manufactured products, one-third has been deducted for the value of the raw materials, leaving two-thirds for the wages of labour and the profits of capital. These are the average proportions in the official statements of the manufactures of New York. From this valuation, however, the articles manufactured by mills have been excepted. Three-fourths of the gross value of these articles have been deducted. Even this would not be enough, if the products of sawmills and oilmills, in which human labour bears a much larger proportional part, were not comprehended. A separate estimate is made of the products of printing and bookbinding, by allowing 25 per cent on the capital invested, and $200 for each man employed.

In estimating the annual products of the mines, the fisheries, and the forest, the whole value at the place of production, or of sale by the producer, has been the measure—that value being made up of the profits of land, of labour, and of capital.

In all cases, the prices at which the principal products of each State have been estimated, may be seen by comparing the values with the quantities, so that every one may correct the estimate wherever he deems it erroneous.

It is proper to remark, that the census omits several products of industry, whose aggregate value would make no insignificant addition to the total amount. Among these, are—1. The blades of Indian corn, an excellent fodder for horses and cattle; and which, estimating twenty pounds for every bushel of grain, amounts to 3,775,000 tons, worth $37,750,000. 2. Peas and beans. 3. Flax-seed. 4. Broom-corn. 5. Sumach. 6. Honey. 7. Feathers.

In the subjoined table, the values of the principal products of agriculture and of manufactures, and occasionally of other branches of industry, are specifically stated, while the rest are included under the general heads.

ANNUAL PRODUCTS OF INDUSTRY IN MAINE.

I. *Agriculture.*			
Horses and mules,............No.	59,208	$2,960,400	
Neat cattle,..........................	327,255	4,908,825	
Sheep,................................	649,264	973,896	
Hogs,..................................	117,386	352,158	
25 per cent of................................		$9,195,279	
is..		$2,298,819	
Poultry,..		123,171	
			$2,421,980
Wheat,.......................bush.	848,166	$1,061,207	
Oats,..................................	1,076,409	376,743	
Maize,................................	950,528	712,896	
Other grain,........................	544,645	435,716	
Potatoes,............................	10,392,280	2,078,556	
			4,665,118
Wool,..........................lbs.	1,465,551	$492,942	
Products of dairy,..................................		1,496,902	
" orchards,..................................		149,381	
Hay,...........................tons	691,358	5,530,864	
Other products,....................................		1,099,083	
			8,769,172
			$15,856,270
II. *Manufactures.*			
Metals and machinery,............	$194,099		
Lime, &c.,............................	621,583		
Woollen,..............................	412,366		
Cotton, &c.,..........................	1,023,086		
Leather,..............................	443,846		
Furniture,............................	204,875		
Carriages,............................	174.310		
Ships,................................	1,184,902		
Houses,..............................	733,067		
Other manufactures,...............	1,503,538		
		$7,102,983	
Deduct for materials one-third,........................		2,334,328	
		$4,768,655	
Manufactures by mills, deducting three-fourths,...		790,398	
Printing, &c., estimated,................................		56,250	
			$5,615,303
III. *Commerce*, 25 per cent on capital,............			1,505,380
IV. *The Forest*,..			1,877,663
V. *Fisheries*,..			1,280,713
VI. *Mines*,..			327,376
Total,..			$26,462,705

ANNUAL PRODUCTS OF INDUSTRY IN NEW HAMPSHIRE.

I. *Agriculture.*			
Horses and mules,............No.	43,892	$2,194,600	
Neat cattle,..........................	275,562	4,133.430	
Sheep,................................	649,264	973,896	
Hogs,..................................	121,671	365,013	
25 per cent of................................		$7,666,939	
is..		$1,916,735	
Poultry,..		107,092	
			$2,023,827

Wheat, ...bush.	422,124	$527,655	
Oats, ...	454,699	160,134	
Maize, ...	1,162,572	796,926	
Other grain, ...	379,880	284,910	
Potatoes, ...	6,206,606	1,241,321	
			$3,010,946
Sugar, ...lbs.	2,162,368	129,742	
Products of dairy, ...		1,638,543	
" orchards, ...		239,979	
Wool, ...lbs.	1,260,517	441,181	
Hay, ...tons	406,107	3,248,856	
Other products, ...		644,678	
			6,342,979
			$11,377,752
II. *Manufactures.*			
Metals, &c., ...	$379,898		
Woollen, ...	795,784		
Cotton, &c., ...	4,290,078		
Hats, ...	190,526		
Leather, ...	712,151		
Paper, ...	152,700		
Carriages, ...	232,240		
Houses, ...	470,715		
Ships, ...	78,000		
Other manufactures, ...	1,235,860		
		$8,437,952	
Deduct for materials one-third, ...		2,812,651	
		$5,625,301	
Manufactures by mills, deducting three-fourths, ...		790,398	
Printing, &c., ...		130,112	
			$6,545,811
III. *Commerce*, 25 per cent on capital, ...			1,001,533
IV. *The Forest*, ...			449,861
V. *Fisheries*, ...			92,811
VI. *Mines*, ...			88,373
Total, ...			$19,556,141

Annual Products of Industry in Vermont.

I. *Agriculture.*			
Horses and mules, ...No.	62,402	$3,120,100	
Neat cattle, ...	384,341	5,764,113	
Sheep, ...	1,681,819	2,522,728	
Hogs, ...	203,800	611,400	
25 per cent of		$12,018,331	
is		$3,006,110	
Poultry, ...		131,578	
			$3,137,688
Wheat, ...bush.	495,800	$619,750	
Oats, ...	2,222,584	888,904	
Maize, ...	1,119,678	746,652	
Other grain, ...	514,190	371,940	
Potatoes, ...	8,869,751	1,773,950	
			4,401,196
Sugar, ...lbs.	4,647,934	278,866	
Wool, ...	3,669,035	1,284,232	
Products of dairy, ...		2,008,737	
" orchards, ...		213,934	
Hay, ...tons	836,739	5,857,173	

Other products,		$697,319	
			10,340,271
			$17,879,155
II. *Manufactures.*			
Metals and machinery,	$161,374		
Woollen,	1,331,953		
Cotton, &c.,	268,430		
Leather,	361,468		
Paper,	214,720		
Carriages,	102,097		
Houses,	344,896		
Ships,	72,000		
Other manufactures,	5,098,653		
		$7,955,591	
Deduct for materials one-third,		2,651,897	
Manufactures by mills, deducting three-fourths,		270,781	
Printing, &c.,		110,950	
			$5,685,425
III. *Commerce*, 25 per cent on capital,			758,899
IV. *The Forest*,			430,224
V. *Mines*,			389,488
Total,			$25,143,191

Annual Products of Industry in Massachusetts.

I. *Agriculture.*			
Horses and mules, No.	61,484	$3,074,200	
Neat cattle,	282,574	5,086,332	
Sheep,	378,226	567,339	
Hogs,	146,221	572,884	
25 per cent of		$9,300,755	
is		$2,325,189	
Poultry,		178,157	
			$2,503,346
Wheat, bush.	157,923	$197,404	
Oats,	1,319,680	527,872	
Maize,	1,809,192	1,356,894	
Other grain,	788,333	591,238	
Potatoes,	5,385,652	1,346,413	
			4,019,821
Wool, lbs.	941,906	329,677	
Products of dairy,		2,273,299	
" orchards,		389,177	
Hay, tons	569,395	5,124,555	
Other products,		1,425,142	
			9,542,450
			$16,065,627
II. *Commerce*, 25 per cent on capital,			7,004,691
III. *Fisheries*,			6,483,996
IV. *Manufactures.*			
Metals and machinery,	$4,717,919		
Woollen,	7,082,808		
Cotton, &c.,	17,823,637		
Hats, &c.,	918,436		
Straw bonnets,	821,646		
Leather,	10,553,826		
Paper,	1,716,630		
Cordage,	852,200		

Carriages,	$803,999		
Furniture,	1,090,008		
Houses,	2,767,134		
Ships,	1,349,994		
Other manufactures,	13,305,878		
		$63,903,617	
Deduct for materials one-third,		21,301,206	
		$42,602,411	
Manufactures by mills, deducting three-fourths,		442,796	
Printing, &c.,		472,850	
			$43,518,057
V. *Mines*,			2,020,572
VI. *The Forest*,			377,354
Total,			$75,470,297

ANNUAL PRODUCTS OF INDUSTRY IN RHODE ISLAND.

I. *Agriculture.*			
Horses and mules, No.	8,024	$401,200	
Neat cattle,	36,891	664,038	
Sheep,	90,146	180,292	
Hogs,	30,659	122,636	
25 per cent of		$1,368,166	
is		$342,041	
Poultry,		61,702	
			$403,743
Wheat, bush.	3,098	$3,875	
Oats,	171,517	60,030	
Maize,	450,498	281,561	
Other grain,	103,990	77,003	
Potatoes,	917,973	227,994	
			650,463
Wool, lbs.	183,830	$65,340	
Products of dairy,		223,229	
Hay, tons	63,449	571,041	
Other products,		285,493	
			1,145,103
			$2,199,309

II. *Manufactures.*			
Metals and machinery,	$1,006,870		
Woollen,	842,172		
Cotton, &c.,	7,564,851		
Hats and bonnets,	178,571		
Leather,	182,110		
Houses,	379,010		
Other manufactures,	2,689,385		
		$12,842,969	
Deduct for materials one-third,		4,280,989	
		$8,561,980	
Manufactures by mills, deducting three-fourths,		20,921	
Printing, &c.,		57,725	
			$8,640,626
III. *Commerce*, 25 per cent on capital,			1,294,956
IV. *Fisheries*,			659,312
V. *Mines*,			162,410
VI. *The Forest*,			44,610
Total,			$13,001,223

Annual Products of Industry in Connecticut.

I. *Agriculture.*			
Horses and mules,..............No.	36,650	$1,732,500	
Neat cattle,............................	238,650	4,145,800	
Sheep,..................................	404,462	806,924	
Hogs,...................................	131,961	527,844	
25 per cent of................................		$7,211,968	
is..		$1,802,992	
Poultry,......................................		176,629	
			$1,979,621
Wheat,..........................bush.	87,009	$108,761	
Oats,...................................	453,262	164,969	
Rye,....................................	737,424	555,568	
Maize,..................................	1,500,441	900,264	
Other grain,............................	336,802	252,598	
Potatoes,...............................	3,414,238	854,559	
			2,836,719
Wool,.............................lbs.	889,870	$311,434	
Products of dairy,............................		1,376,534	
" orchards,...................................		296,232	
Hay,..............................tons	426,704	3,840,336	
Other products,...............................		730,900	
			6,555,436
			$11,371,776
II. *Manufactures.*			
Metals and machinery,..................	$3,559,029		
Woollen,................................	2,494,313		
Cotton, &c.,............................	3,302,059		
Hats and bonnets,......................	886,310		
Leather,................................	2,017,931		
Paper,..................................	541,300		
Carriages,..............................	929,301		
Ships,..................................	428,900		
Houses,.................................	1,086,295		
Other manufactures,....................	3,416,983		
		$18,662,425	
Deduct for materials one-third,...............		6,220,808	
		$12,441,617	
Manufactures by mills, deducting three-fourths,...		135,877	
Printing, &c.,................................		201,469	
			$12,778,963
III. *Commerce*, 25 per cent on capital,......			1,963,281
IV. *Fisheries*,..............................			907,723
V. *Mines*,...................................			820,419
VI. *The Forest*,.............................			181,575
Total,..			$28,023,737

Annual Products of Industry in New York.

I. *Agriculture.*			
Horses and mules,..............No.	474,543	$23,736,150	
Neat cattle,............................	1,911,244	21,823,928	
Sheep,..................................	5,118,777	7,678,165	
Hogs,...................................	1,900,065	5,700,195	
25 per cent of................................		$58,928,438	
is..		$14,757,109	
Poultry,......................................		1,153,413	
			$15,910,522

Wheat,........................bush.	12,286,418	$12,286,418	
Oats,........................	20,675,847	7,753,192	
Maize,........................	10,972,286	6,857,699	
Other grain,........................	7,787,276	5,890,457	
Potatoes,........................	30,123,614	7,530,903	
			$40,318,669
Wool,........................lbs.	9,845,295	3,445,853	
Products of dairy,........................		10,496,021	
" orchards,........................		1,701,935	
Hay,........................tons	3,127,047	28,143,423	
Other products,........................		8,258,838	
			52,046,050
			$108,275,241
II. *Commerce*, 25 per cent of capital,........................			24 311,715
III. *Mines*,........................			7,408,070
IV. *Manufactures.*			
Metals and machinery,........................	$8,060,348		
Woollen,........................	3,537,337		
Cotton, &c.,........................	5,185,968		
Hats and caps,........................	2,914,817		
Leather,........................	6,232,924		
Paper,........................	882,758		
Cordage,........................	792,910		
Musical instruments,........................	472,910		
Spirits,........................	3,592,144		
Carriages,........................	2,364,461		
Furniture,........................	1,971,776		
Houses,........................	7,265,844		
Ships,........................	797,317		
Other manufactures,........................	19,079,759		
		$63,151,273	
Deduct for materials one-third,........................		21,050,424	
		$42,100,849	
Manufactures by mills, deducting three-fourths,...		4,238,320	
Printing, &c.,........................		1,115,345	
			$47,454,514
V. *The Forest*,........................			5,040,781
VI. *Fisheries*,........................			1,316,072
Total,........................			$193,806,433

ANNUAL PRODUCTS OF INDUSTRY IN NEW JERSEY.

I. *Agriculture.*			
Horses and mules,........................No.	70,502	$3,505,100	
Neat cattle,........................	220,202	2,642,424	
Sheep,........................	219,285	438,570	
Hogs,........................	261,443	784,329	
25 per cent of........................		$7,370,423	
is........................		$1,842,606	
Poultry,........................		336,953	
			$2,179,559
Wheat,........................bush.	774,703	$774,703	
Oats,........................	3,083,524	1,233,409	
Maize,........................	4,361,975	2,617,175	
Other grain,........................	2,534,438	1,900,827	
Potatoes,........................	2,072,069	518,017	
			7,044,631
Wool,........................lbs.	397,207	139,022	
Products of dairy,........................		1,328,032	
" orchards,........................		464,066	

Hemp and flax,................tons	2,165¾	$281,547	
Hay,..................................	334,861	3,013,749	
Other products,..		1,759,247	
			$6,985,661
			$16,209,853
II. *Manufactures.*			
Metals and machinery,............	$1 406,997		
Woollen,............................	440,710		
Cotton, &c.,........................	2,321,628		
Hats and caps,......................	1,181,562		
Leather,............................	1,582,746		
Glass,..............................	904,700		
Paper,..............................	569,000		
Carriages,..........................	1,397,149		
Ships,..............................	344,240		
Houses,.............................	1,092,056		
Other manufactures,................	3,412,278		
		$14,653,062	
Deduct for materials one-third,.........................		4,884,354	
		$9,768,708	
Manufactures by mills, deducting three-fourths,...		861,724	
Printing, &c.,...		65,825	
			$10,696,257
III. *Commerce*, 25 per cent of capital,......................................			1,206,929
IV. *Mines*,..			1,073,921
V. *The Forest*,..			361,326
VI. *Fisheries*,..			124,140
Total,..			$29,672,426

ANNUAL PRODUCTS OF INDUSTRY IN PENNSYLVANIA.

I. *Agriculture.*			
Horses and mules,............No.	365,129	$18,256,450	
Neat cattle,........................ ..	1,172,665	14,071,980	
Sheep,..............................	1,767,620	2,651,430	
Hogs,...............................	1,503,064	4,518,192	
25 per cent of..................................		$39,498,052	
is..		$9,877,013	
Poultry,..		685,801	
			$10,565,814
Wheat,.......................bush.	13,213,077	$13,213,077	
Oats,...............................	20,641,819	7,740,682	
Maize,..............................	14,240,022	8,544,013	
Other grain,........................	8,928,508	6,626,480	
Potatoes,...........................	9,535,663	2,383,416	
			38,607,668
Wool,..........................lbs.	3,048,564	1,066,997	
Products of dairy,....................................		3,187,292	
" orchards,..................................		618,179	
Hemp and flax,................tons	2,649¾	344,467	
Hay,................................	1,311,643	11,804,787	
Other products,.......................................		1,985,720	
			19,307,442
			$68,480,924
II. *Mines*,..			17,666,146
III. *Commerce*, 25 per cent of capital,......................................			10,593,368
IV. *Manufactures.*			
Metals and machinery,............	$6,757,665		
Woollen,............................	2,319,061		

Cotton, &c.,	$6,202,133		
Hats and caps,	820,331		
Leather,	3,482,793		
Drugs, &c.,	2,100,074		
Glass,	772,400		
Paper,	887,835		
Carriages,	1,207,252		
Furniture,	1,155,692		
Ships,	668,015		
Houses,	5,354,480		
Spirits,	1,560,046		
Porter, &c.	2,553,194		
Other manufactures,	8,387,737		
		$44,228,708	
Deduct for materials one-third,		13,742,903	
		$30,485,805	
Manufactures by mills, deducting three-fourths,...		2,356.239	
Printing, &c.,		512,235	
			$33,354,279
V. *The Forest,*			1,203,578
VI. *Fisheries,*			35,360
Total,			$131,033,655

ANNUAL PRODUCTS OF INDUSTRY IN DELAWARE.

I. *Agriculture.*			
Horses and mules, ...No.	14,421	$721,050	
Neat cattle,	53,883	646,596	
Sheep,	39,247	58,870	
Hogs,	74,228	222,684	
25 per cent of		$1,649,200	
is		$412,300	
Poultry,		47,265	
			$459,565
Wheat, ...bush.	315,165	$315,165	
Oats,	927,405	370,962	
Maize,	2,099,359	1,259,615	
Other grain,	50,005	37,478	
Potatoes,	200,712	50,178	
			2,033,398
Wool, ...lbs.	64,404	22,541	
Products of dairy,		113,828	
" orchards,		28,211	
Hay, ...tons	22,483	224,830	
Other products,		316,067	
			705,477
			$3,198,440
II. *Manufactures.*			
Metals and machinery,	$350,700		
Woollen,	104,700		
Cotton, &c.,	332,389		
Leather,	166,037		
Gunpowder,	336,000		
Houses,	145,850		
Other manufactures,	581,710		
		$2,017,386	
Deduct for materials one-third,		672,462	
		$1,344,924	
Manufactures by mills, one-quarter,		184,493	
Printing, &c.,		9,462	
			$1,538,879

III. *Commerce*, 25 per cent of capital,..........	$266,257
IV. *Fisheries*,..........	181,285
V. *Mines*,..........	54,555
VI. *The Forest*,..........	13,119
Total,..........	$5,252,535

Annual Products of Industry in Maryland.

I. *Agriculture.*			
Horses and mules,..........No.	92,220	$4,611,000	
Neat cattle,..........	225,714	2,708,568	
Sheep,..........	257,921	381,881	
Hogs,..........	416,943	1,250,829	
25 per cent of..........		$8,952,278	
is..........		$2,238,069	
Poultry,..........		218,765	
			$2,456,834
Wheat,..........bush.	3,345,783	$3,345,783	
Oats,..........	3,534,211	1,413,684	
Maize,..........	8,233,086	4,058,271	
Other grain,..........	800,777	610,582	
Potatoes,..........	1,036,433	259,108	
			10,569,008
Wool,..........lbs.	488,201	170,870	
Products of dairy,..........		457,466	
" orchards,..........		105,740	
Tobacco,..........lbs.	24,846,012	1,739,220	
Hay,..........tons	106,687	1,066,870	
Other products,..........		1,020,712	
			4,560,878
			$17,586,720
II. *Commerce*, 25 per cent on capital,..........			3,499,087
III. *Manufactures.*			
Metals and machinery,..........	$690,155		
Woollen,..........	235,900		
Cotton, &c.,..........	1,692,040		
Hats and caps,..........	153,456		
Leather,..........	150,275		
Paper,..........	198,100		
Carriages,..........	357,622		
Furniture,..........	305,360		
Ships,..........	279,771		
Houses,..........	1,078,770		
Other manufactures,..........	2,779,855		
		$7,921,334	
Deduct for materials one-third,..........		2,640,444	
		$5,280,890	
Manufactures by mills, deducting three-fourths,...		816,812	
Printing, &c.,..........		114,975	
			$6,212,677
IV. *Mines*,..........			1,056,210
V. *The Forest*,..........			241,194
VI. *Fisheries*,..........			225,773
Total,..........			$28,821,661

Annual Products of Industry in Virginia.

I. *Agriculture.*			
Horses and mules,..........No.	326,438	$16,321,900	
Neat cattle,..........	1,024,148	10,241,480	

Sheep,................................	1,293,772	$1,940,658	
Hogs,................................	1,992,155	3,994,310	
25 per cent of................................ ..		$32,498,348	
is..		$8,124,587	
Poultry,..		754,698	
			$8,879,285
Wheat,........................bush.	10,109,716	$10,109,716	
Oats,.................................	13,451,052	5,380,424	
Maize, ...	34,577,591	17,288,795	
Other grain,..........................	1,814,051	1,360,534	
Potatoes,..................	2,944,660	761,165	
			34,900,364
Wool,..............................lbs.	2,538,374	761,512	
Tobacco,..............................	73,347,106	3,767,355	
Cotton, ...	3,494,483	319,558	
Products of dairy,..		1,480,488	
" orchards,..................................		705,765	
Hemp and flax,*...............tons	25,594¼	3,071,310	
Hay,..................................	364,708	2,917,664	
Other products,...		2,282,250	
			15,305,902
			$59,085,821
II. *Manufactures.*			
Metals and machinery,.............	$789,573		
Woollen,..............................	147,792		
Cotton, &c.,..........................	679,312		
Tobacco,..............................	2,406,671		
Leather,..............................	826,597		
Carriages,............................	647,815		
Furniture,............................	289,391		
Ships,................................	136,807		
Houses,...............................	1,367,393		
Other manufactures,................	2,130,483		
		$9,421,734	
Deduct for materials one-third,........................		3,140,578	
		$6,281,186	
Manufactures by mills, deducting three-fourths,..		1,963,850	
Printing, &c.,..		104,212	
			$8,349,218
III. *Commerce*, 25 per cent of capital,..			5,299,451
IV. *Mines.*			
Iron,...		$1,129,247	
Coal,...		1,593,381	
Salt,...		436,404	
Other products,..		162,597	
			3,321,629
V. *The Forest*,...			617,760
VI. *Fisheries*,...			95,173
Total,..			$76,769,032

ANNUAL PRODUCTS OF INDUSTRY IN NORTH CAROLINA.

I. *Agriculture.*			
Horses and mules,.............No.	166,608	$8,330,400	
Neat cattle,..........................	617,371	5,556,339	

* This item is certainly erroneous, if in nothing else, in the product of the county of Lee, which, with a population of 8,441, is stated to produce more hemp and flax—10,468 tons—than any state in the Union, except Virginia. The error probably exceeds $1,000,000.

16

Sheep,	538,279	$682,848	
Hogs,	1,649,716	3,299,432	
25 per cent of		$17,869,019	
is		$4,467,505	
Poultry,		544,125	
			$5,011,630
Wheat, bush.	1,960,855	$1,960,855	
Oats,	3,193,941	1,277,626	
Maize,	23,893,763	9,477,505	
Other grain,	233,936	176,343	
Potatoes,	2,609,239	452,309	
			13,344,638
Wool, lbs.	625,044	156,261	
Cotton,	51,926,190	3,633,863	
Tobacco,	16,672,359	833,618	
Products of dairy,		674,349	
" orchards,		386,006	
Hemp and flax, tons	9,879¾	1,284,367	
Hay,	101,369	810,962	
Other products,		840,147	
			8,619,563
			$26,975,831
II. *Manufactures.*			
Metals and machinery,	$63,039		
Cotton, &c.,	444,721		
Leather,	185,387		
Carriages,	301,601		
Ships,	62,800		
Houses,	410,264		
Other manufactures,	979,022		
		$2,446,834	
Deduct for materials one-third,		815,611	
		$1,631,223	
Manufactures by mills, deducting three-fourths,		388,024	
Printing, &c.,		34,450	
			$2,053,697
III. *The Forest*,			1,446,108
IV. *Commerce*, 25 per cent of capital,			1,322,284
V. *Mines.*			
Gold,		$255,618	
Other minerals,		116,868	
			372,486
VI. *Fisheries*,			251,792
Total,			$32,422,198

Annual Products of Industry in South Carolina.

I. *Agriculture.*			
Horses and mules, No.	129,921	$7,795,260	
Neat cattle,	572,608	4,582,864	
Sheep,	232,981	291,226	
Hogs,	878,532	1,757,064	
25 per cent of		$14,426,414	
is		$3,606,603	
Poultry,		396,364	
			$4,002,967
Wheat, bush.	968,354	$968,354	
Oats,	1,483,208	593,283	

Maize,	14,722,805	$7,361,402	
Other grain,	48,777	37,579	
Potatoes,	2,608,313	452,079	
			$9,412,697
Wool, lbs.	299,070	89,721	
Cotton,	61,710,274	4,628,270	
Rice,	60,590,861	1,514,771	
Products of dairy,		577,810	
" orchards,		55,275	
Hay, tons	24,618	246,180	
Other products,		1,028,742	
			8,138,027
			$21,553,691
II. *Manufactures.*			
Metals and machinery,	$83,531		
Cotton, &c.,	362,830		
Leather,	109,472		
Carriages,	189,270		
Ships,	60,000		
Houses,	1,527,576		
Other manufactures,	492,642		
		$2,825,321	
Deduct for materials one-third,		941,440	
		$1,882,881	
Manufactures by mills, deducting three-fourths,		300,419	
Printing, &c.,		65,615	
			$2,248,915
III. *Commerce*, 25 per cent of capital,			2,632,421
IV. *The Forest*,			549,626
V. *Mines*,			187,608
VI. *Fisheries*,			1,275
Total,			$27,173,536

Annual Products of Industry in Georgia.

I. *Agriculture.*			
Horses and mules, No.	157,540	$9,452,400	
Neat cattle,	884,414	7,075,312	
Sheep,	267,107	407,660	
Hogs,	1,457,755	2,915,510	
25 per cent of		$19,850,882	
is		$4,962,720	
Poultry,		449,623	
			$5,412,343
Wheat, bush.	1,801,830	$1,801,830	
Oats,	1,600,030	644,012	
Maize,	20,905,122	10,462,561	
Other grain,	73,713	58,637	
Potatoes,	1,291,366	322,841	
			13,289,881
Wool, lbs.	371,303	111,391	
Cotton,	163,392,396	11,437,467	
Rice,	12,384,732	309,618	
Products of dairy,		605,072	
" orchards,		156,122	
Hay, tons	16,940	169,400	
Other products,		977,477	
			13,766,527
			$31,468,271

II. *Manufactures.*			
Metals and machinery,............	$144,704		
Cotton, &c.,......................	308,025		
Leather,..........................	123,701		
Carriages,........................	249,065		
Houses,...........................	693,116		
Other manufactures,...............	839,046		
		$2,357,657	
Deduct for materials one-third,......................		785,886	
		$1,571,771	
Manufactures by mills, deducting three-fourths,...		317,179	
Printing, &c.,....................................		65,000	
			$1,953,950
III. *Commerce*, 25 per cent on capital,..............................			2,248,488
IV. *Mines*,..			191,631
V. *The Forest*,..			117,439
VI. *Fisheries*,..			584
Total,..			$35,980,363

Annual Products of Industry in Alabama.

I. *Agriculture.*			
Horses and mules,............No.	143,147	$8,588,820	
Neat cattle,......................	668,018	5,344,140	
Sheep,............................	163,243	244,854	
Hogs,.............................	1,423,873	2,847,746	
25 per cent of....................		$17,025,560	
is................................		$4,256,390	
Poultry,..........................		404,894	
			$4,661,284
Wheat,.....................bush.	828,052	$828,052	
Oats,.............................	1,406,353	562,541	
Maize,............................	20,947,004	8,378,801	
Other grain,......................	58,758	44,091	
Potatoes,.........................	1,708,356	427,189	
			10,240,674
Cotton,.....................lbs.	117,138,823	8,209,717	
Wool,.............................	220,353	66,106	
Products of dairy,................		265,200	
" orchards,.......................		55,240	
Hay,........................tons	12,718	127,180	
Other products,...................		1,071,112	
			9,794,555
			$24,696,513
II. *Manufactures.*			
Metals and machinery,............	$179,470		
Leather,..........................	180,152		
Carriages,........................	88,891		
Houses,...........................	739,871		
Other manufactures,...............	882,449		
		$2,071,333	
Deduct for materials one-third,......................		690,444	
		$1,380,889	
Manufactures by mills, deducting three-fourths,...		306,356	
Printing, &c.,....................................		45,525	
			$1,732,770
III. *Commerce*, 25 per cent on capital,..............................			2,273,267
IV. *The Forest*,...			177,465
V. *Mines*,...			81,310
Total,..			$28,961,325

ANNUAL PRODUCTS OF INDUSTRY IN MISSISSIPPI.

I. *Agriculture.*			
Horses and mules,............No.	109,227	$6,553,620	
Neat cattle,..........................	623,197	3,739,182	
Sheep,..................................	128,367	192,550	
Hogs, ...	1,001,209	2,002,418	
25 per cent of..........................		$12,487,770	
is..		$3,121,997	
Poultry, ...		369,482	
			$3,491,479
Wheat,.........................bush.	196,024	$196,024	
Oats,.....................................	668,624	334,312	
Maize,....................................	13,161,237	5,264,494	
Other grain,............................	13,159	10,298	
Potatoes,................................	1,630,100	407,525	
			6,212,653
Cotton,................................lbs.	193,401,577	15,472,126	
Rice,......................................	777,193	23,315	
Wool,.....................................	175,192	52,559	
Products of dairy,......................		359,585	
" orchards,............................		14,458	
Other products,.........................		868,290	
			16,990,456
			$26,494,565
II. *Manufactures.*			
Metals and machinery,..............	$286,685		
Leather,.................................	118,167		
Houses,..................................	1,175,513		
Other manufactures,.................	568,231		
		$2,121,596	
Deduct for materials one-third,........................		707,199	
		$1,414,397	
Manufactures by mills, deducting three-fourths,...		121,716	
Printing, &c.,..		49,677	
			$1,585,790
III. *Commerce*, 25 per cent of capital,.................			1,453,686
IV. *The Forest*,..			205,297
Total,..			$29,739,338

ANNUAL PRODUCTS OF INDUSTRY IN LOUISIANA.

I. *Agriculture.*			
Horses and mules,............No.	99,888	$5,973,280	
Neat cattle,..........................	381,248	3,049,984	
Sheep,..................................	98,072	147,108	
Hogs, ...	323,229	646,440	
25 per cent of..........................		$9,816,812	
is..		$2,454,203	
Poultry, ...		283,559	
			$2,737,762
Oats and other grain,........bush.	109,225	$54,548	
Potatoes,................................	844,341	217,085	
Maize,....................................	5,952,912	2,976,451	
			3,248,084
Cotton, ...lbs.	152,555,368	10,678,875	
Sugar,....................................	119,947,720	4,797,908	
Rice,......................................	3,604,534	108,136	
Hay,..............................tons	24,651	246,510	

Products of dairy,		$153,069	
" orchards,		11,769	
Other products,		869,262	
			$16,865,529
			$22,851,375
II. *Manufactures.*			
Metals and machinery,	$35,000		
Bricks and lime,	861,655		
Tobacco,	150,000		
Leather,	108,500		
Refined sugar,	770,000		
Tallow candles,	425,000		
Ships,	80,500		
Houses,	2,736,944		
		$5,676,944	
Deduct for materials one-third,		1,892,667	
		$3,784,134	
Manufactures by mills, deducting three-fourths,		176,696	
Printing, &c.,		126,825	
			$4,087,655
III. *Commerce*, 25 per cent of capital,			7,868,898
IV. *Mines*,			165,280
V. *The Forest*,			71,751
Total,			$35,044,959

Annual Products of Industry in Arkansas.

I. *Agriculture.*			
Horses and mules, No.	51,472	$2,573,600	
Neat cattle,	188,786	1,509,188	
Sheep,	42,151	52,699	
Hogs,	393,058	786,116	
25 per cent of		$4,921,603	
is		$1,230,401	
Poultry,		109,468	
			$1,339,869
Wheat, bush.	105,878	$105,878	
Maize,	4,846,632	2,423,316	
Oats and other grain,	196,620	82,232	
Potatoes,	293,608	74,402	
			2,685,828
Cotton, lbs.	6,028,642	$361,718	
Hemp, tons	1,039½	135,135	
Other products,		564,207	
			1,061,060
			$5,086,757
II. *Manufactures.*			
Houses,	$1,141,174		
Other manufactures,	406,578		
		$1,577,879	
Deduct for materials one-third,		525,957	
		$1,051,922	
Manufactures by mills, deducting three-fourths,		82,712	
Printing, &c.,		10,675	
			$1,145,309
III. *Commerce*, 25 per cent of capital,			420,635
IV. *The Forest*,			217,469
V. *Mines*,			18,225
Total,			$6,888,395

ANNUAL PRODUCTS OF INDUSTRY IN TENNESSEE.

I. *Agriculture.*			
Horses and mules,............No.	341,309	$17,070,450	
Neat cattle,.........................	882,857	7,062,956	
Sheep,.........................	741,693	926,991	
Hogs,.........................	2,926,607	4,389,010	
25 per cent of..............................		$29,449,407	
is..		$7,612,352	
Poultry,..		606,969	
			$8,219,321
Wheat,.....................bush.	4,569,692	$3,427,269	
Oats,.........................	7,035,678	1,758,419	
Maize,.........................	44,986,188	11,246,547	
Other grain,.........................	326,307	164,322	
Potatoes,.........................	1,904,370	476,092	
			17,072,649
Products of dairy,..............................		$472,141	
" orchards,..............................		367,105	
Wool,.........................lbs.	1,060,332	265,583	
Tobacco,.........................	29,550,432	1,172,017	
Cotton,.........................	27,701,277	1,662,076	
Hemp and flax,..................tons	3,344½	334,450	
Hay,.........................	31,233	218,631	
Other products,..............................		1,876,207	
			6,368,210
			$31,660,180
II. *Manufactures.*			
Metals and machinery,............	$445,050		
Cotton,.........................	325,719		
Wool, &c.,.........................	27,198		
Hats and caps,.........................	104,940		
Leather,.........................	359,050		
Cordage,.........................	139,630		
Carriages,.........................	219,897		
Spirits,.........................	224,821		
Houses,.........................	427,402		
Other manufactures,...............	1,191,666		
		$3,233,552	
Deduct for materials one-third,......................		1,077,850	
		$2,155,702	
Manufactures by mills, deducting three-fourths,....		255,166	
Printing, &c.,..............................		56,325	
			$2,477,193
III. *Commerce*, 25 per cent of capital,..............................			2,239,478
IV. *Mines*,..............................			1,371,331
V. *The Forest*,..............................			225,179
Total,..............................			$37,973,361

ANNUAL PRODUCTS OF INDUSTRY IN MISSOURI.

I. *Agriculture.*			
Horses and mules,............No.	196,632	$7,865,280	
Neat cattle,.........................	433,875	3,471,000	
Sheep,.........................	348,018	348,018	
Hogs,.........................	1,271,161	1,271,161	
25 per cent of..............................		$12,955,459	
is..		$3,238,865	
Poultry,..		270,647	
			$3,509,512

Wheat,……bush.	1,037,386	$518,693	
Oats,……	2,234,947	335,241	
Maize,……	17,332,524	3,482,505	
Other grain,……	93,727	36,863	
Potatoes,……	783,768	117,565	
			$4,490,867
Products of dairy,……		$100,432	
" orchards,……		90,878	
Wool,……lbs.	562,265	140,564	
Tobacco,……	9,067,913	362,716	
Hemp and flax,……tons	8,010¾	640,860	
Hay,……	49,083	343,581	
Other products,……		804,853	
			2,483,884
			$10,484,263
II. *Manufactures.*			
Metals and machinery,……	$257,600		
Woollen, &c.,……	24,865		
Hats and caps,……	111,620		
Leather,……	298,345		
Carriages,……	97,112		
Houses,……	1,441,573		
Other manufactures,……	…………		
		$3,108,385	
Deduct for materials one-third,……		1,036,128	
		$2,072,257	
Manufactures by mills, deducting three-fourths,…		240,014	
Printing, &c.,……		48,437	
			$2,360,708
III. *Commerce*, 25 per cent of capital,……			2,349,245
IV. *The Forest*,……			448,559
V. *Mines*,……			187,669
Total,……			$15,830,444

ANNUAL PRODUCTS OF INDUSTRY IN KENTUCKY.

I. *Agriculture.*			
Horses and mules,……No.	395,853	$19,792,650	
Neat cattle,……	787,098	9,445,176	
Sheep,……	1,008,240	1,260,300	
Hogs,……	2,310,533	2,310,533	
25 per cent of……		$32,808,659	
is……		$8,202,165	
Poultry,……		536,439	
			$8,738,604
Wheat,……bush.	4,803,152	$2,401,526	
Oats,……	7,155,974	1,788,993	
Maize,……	39,047,120	7,969,424	
Other grain,……	1,347,033	680,602	
Potatoes,……	1,088,085	158,262	
			12,998,807
Products of dairy,……		$931,363	
" orchards,……		434,935	
Wool,……lbs.	1,786,847	446,712	
Tobacco,……	53,435,409	2,137,476	
Hemp,……tons	9,992¼	799,380	
Hay,……	88,306	353,224	
Other products,……		2,386,044	
			7,489,134
			$29,226,545

II. *Manufactures.*			
Metals and machinery,............	$255,106		
Woollen,..........................	151,246		
Cotton, &c.,......................	465,593		
Tobacco,..........................	413,585		
Hats and caps,....................	201,310		
Leather,..........................	732,646		
Cordage,..........................	1,292,276		
Carriages,........................	168,724		
Furniture,........................	273,350		
Spirits,..........................	352,737		
Houses,...........................	1,039,172		
Other manufactures,...............	....		
		$6,624,132	
Deduct for materials one-third,..........		2,208,044	
		$4,416,088	
Manufactures by mills, deducting three-fourths,..		609,484	
Printing, &c.,..........................		66,781	
			$5,092,353
III. *Commerce*, 25 per cent of capital,........			2,580,575
IV. *Mines*,.............................			1,539,919
V. *The Forest*,........................			184,799
Total,..................................			$38,624,191

Annual Products of Industry in Ohio.

I. *Agriculture.*			
Horses and mules,.............No.	430,527	$17,221,080	
Neat cattle,......................	1,217,874	9,728,992	
Sheep,............................	2,028,421	2,535,525	
Hogs,.............................	2,099,746	2,099,736	
25 per cent of....................		$31,585,333	
is................................		$7,896,333	
Poultry,..........................		551,193	
			$8,447,526
Wheat,...................bush.	16,571,661	$8,285,830	
Oats,.............................	14,393,103	2,158,965	
Maize,............................	33,668,144	6,733,629	
Other grain,......................	1,659,884	669,179	
Potatoes,.........................	5,805,021	870,753	
			18,718,356
Wool,....................lbs.	3,685,315	$921,329	
Tobacco,..........................	5,942,275	297,113	
Sugar,............................	6,363,386	381,303	
Products of dairy,................		1,848,869	
" orchards,......................		476,271	
Hemp and flax,...............tons	9,080¼	726,420	
Hay,..............................	1,022,037	4,088,148	
Other products,...................		1,896,666	
			10,636,119
			$37,802,001

II. *Manufactures.*	
Metals and machinery,............	$2,141,807
Woollen,..........................	685,757
Cotton, &c.,......................	435,148
Hats and caps,....................	728,513
Leather,..........................	1,986,146
Paper,............................	350,202
Carriages,........................	701,228
Furniture,........................	761,146
Spirits,..........................	1,265,893

Ships,........................	$522,855		
Houses,........................	3,776,823		
Other manufactures,...........	....		
		$18,036,527	
Deduct for materials one-third,........................		6,012,176	
		$12,024,351	
Manufactures by mills, deducting three-fourths,..		2,217,052	
Printing, &c.,........................		346,680	
			$14,588,091
III. *Commerce*, 25 per cent of capital,........................			8,050,316
IV. *Mines*,........................			2,442,682
V. *The Forest*,........................			1,013,063
VI. *Fisheries*,........................			10,525
Total,........................			$63,906,678

ANNUAL PRODUCTS OF INDUSTRY IN INDIANA.

I. *Agriculture.*			
Horses and mules,............No.	241,036	$9,641,440	
Neat cattle,........................	619,980	4,959,840	
Sheep,........................	675,982	834,939	
Hogs,........................	1,623,008	1,623,008	
25 per cent of........................		$17,069,218	
is........................		$4,267,317	
Poultry,........................		357,594	
			$4,624,911
Wheat,........................bush.	4,049,375	$2,028,687	
Oats,........................	5,981,605	498,467	
Maize,........................	28,155,887	5,631,177	
Other grain,........................	206,655	80,625	
Potatoes,........................	1,525,794	228,868	
			8,467,824
Products of dairy,........................		742,269	
" orchards,........................		110,055	
Sugar,........................lbs.	3,727,795	223,667	
Wool,........................	1,237,919	309,473	
Tobacco,........................	1,820,306	91,015	
Hemp and flax,................tons	8,605½	668,440	
Hay,........................	178,029	712,116	
Other products,........................		1,297,972	
			4,155,008
			17,247,743
II. *Manufactures.*			
Metals and machinery,............	$177,479		
Cotton,........................	135,400		
Wool, &c.,........................	112,141		
Hats and caps,........................	122,844		
Leather,........................	730,001		
Carriages,........................	163,135		
Furniture,........................	211,481		
Spirits,........................	357,427		
Ships,........................	107,223		
Houses,........................	1,241,312		
Other manufactures,................	....		
		$4,556,397	
Deduct for materials one-third,........................		1,518,799	
		$3,037,596	
Manufactures by mills, deducting three-fourths,..		582,283	
Printing, &c.,........................		56,826	
			$3,676,705

III. *Commerce*, 25 per cent of capital,			$1,866,155
IV. *The Forest*,			660,836
V. *Mines*,			80,000
VI. *Fisheries*,			1,192
Total,			$23,532,631

ANNUAL PRODUCTS OF INDUSTRY IN ILLINOIS.

I. *Agriculture.*			
Horses and mules, No.	199,235	$7,969,400	
Neat cattle,	626,274	5,013,192	
Sheep,	395,672	494,590	
Hogs,	1,495,254	1,495,254	
25 per cent of		$14,972,436	
is		$3,743,109	
Poultry,		309,204	
			$4,052,313
Wheat, bush.	3,335,393	$1,667,696	
Oats,	4,988,088	415,667	
Maize,	22,634,211	4,526,842	
Other grain,	228,332	124,346	
Potatoes,	2,025,520	303,828	
			7,038,379
Products of dairy,		428,175	
" orchards,		126,756	
Wool, lbs.	650,007	162,500	
Hemp and flax, tons	1,976¼	158,100	
Hay,	164,932	659,728	
Other products,		1,075,515	
			2,610,774
			$13,701,466
II. *Manufactures.*			
Metals and machinery,	$88,640		
Leather,	247,217		
Carriages,	163,135		
Spirits,	310,336		
Furniture,	84,410		
Ships,	39,200		
Houses,	2,065,255		
Other manufactures,	881,857		
		$3,880,050	
Deduct for materials one-third,		1,293,350	
		$2,586,700	
Manufactures by mills, deducting three-fourths,		604,450	
Printing, &c.,		52,825	
			$3,243,981
III. *Commerce*, 25 per cent of capital,			1,493,425
IV. *Mines*,			293,272
V. *The Forest*,			249,841
Total,			$18,981,995

ANNUAL PRODUCTS OF INDUSTRY IN MICHIGAN.

I. *Agriculture.*			
Horses and mules, No.	30,144	$1,205,760	
Neat cattle,	185,190	1,481,520	
Sheep,	99,618	124,022	
Hogs,	205,890	205,890	
25 per cent of		$3,017,192	
is		$754,298	
Poultry,		82,730	
			$837,028

Wheat,..........bush.	2,157,108	$1,078,554	
Oats,..........	2,114,051	175,337	
Maize,..........	2,277,039	455,408	
Other grain,..........	275,630	148,790	
Potatoes,..........	2,109,205	316,380	
			$2,174,469
Sugar,..........lbs.	2,329,784	$79,877	
Wool,..........	153,375	38,344	
Hay,..........tons	130,805	523,220	
Hemp and flax,..........	755¼	60,420	
Products of dairy,..........		428,175	
" orchards,..........		126,756	
Other products,..........		234,600	
			1,491,392
			$4,502,889
II. *Manufactures.*			
Metals and machinery,..........	$114,073		
Leather,..........	192,190		
Ships,..........	10,500		
Houses,..........	571,005		
Other manufactures,..........	430,181		
		$1,317,949	
Deduct for materials one-third,..........		439,316	
		$878,633	
Manufactures by mills, deducting three-fourths,..		458,091	
Printing, &c.,..........		39,525	
			$1,376,249
III. *Commerce*, 25 per cent of capital,..........			622,822
IV. *The Forest*,..........			467,540
V. *Mines*,..........			56,790
Total,..........			$7,026,290

Annual Products of Industry in Wisconsin Territory.

I. *Agriculture.*			
Horses and mules,..........No.	5,735	$229,400	
Neat cattle,..........	30,269	242,152	
Sheep,..........	3,462	4,327	
Hogs,..........	51,383	51,383	
25 per cent of..........		$527,262	
is..........		$131,815	
Poultry,..........		16,167	
			$147,982
Wheat,..........bush.	212,116	$106,058	
Oats,..........	406,514	33,876	
Maize,..........	379,359	75,872	
Other grain,..........	23,681	13,223	
Potatoes,..........	419,608	62,941	
			291,970
Other products,..........			129,153
			$568,105
II. *Manufactures.*			
Miscellaneous,..........	$102,269		
Houses,..........	212,085		
		$314,354	
Deduct for materials one-third,..........		104,785	
		$209,569	
Manufactures by mills, deducting three-fourths,..		87,748	
Printing, &c.,..........		7,375	
			$304,692

III. *Commerce*, 25 per cent on capital,			$189,957
IV. *Mines.*			
Lead, lbs.	15,129,350	$378,233	
Other minerals,		6,370	
			384,603
V. *The Forest*,			430,580
VI. *Fisheries*,			27,663
Total,			$1,905,600

ANNUAL PRODUCTS OF INDUSTRY IN IOWA TERRITORY.

I. *Agriculture.*			
Horses and mules, No.	10,791	$431,630	
Neat cattle,	38,049	304,352	
Sheep,	15,354	19,192	
Hogs,	104,809	104,809	
25 per cent of		$859,993	
is		$214,998	
Poultry,		16,529	
			$231,527
Wheat, bush.	154,693	$77,336	
Oats,	216,385	32,450	
Maize,	1,406,241	281,248	
Other grain,	10,732	5,912	
Potatoes,	234,063	35,109	
			432,073
Other products,			105,695
			$769,295
II. *Manufactures.*			
Miscellaneous,	$90,224		
Houses,	135,985		
		$226,209	
Deduct for materials one-third,		75,403	
		$150,806	
Manufactures by mills, deducting three-fourths,		23,586	
Printing, &c.,		4,425	
			$179,087
III. *Commerce*, 25 per cent of capital,			136,525
IV. *The Forest*,			83,949
V. *Mines*,			13,250
Total,			$1,182,106

ANNUAL PRODUCTS OF INDUSTRY IN FLORIDA TERRITORY.

I. *Agriculture.*			
Horses and mules, No.	12,043	$722,580	
Neat cattle,	118,081	944,648	
Sheep,	7,198	10,797	
Hogs,	92,680	185,360	
25 per cent of		$1,863,385	
is		$465,846	
Poultry,		61,007	
			$526,853
Maize, bush.	808,974	$404,243	
Oats and other grain,	14,576	6,078	
Potatoes,	264,617	66,154	
			476,475
Cotton, lbs.	12,110,583	$726,632	

Sugar, ...lbs.	275,317	$16,519	
Other products,..		87,758	
			$830,909
			$1,834,237
II. *Manufactures.*			
Miscellaneous,......................	$227,795		
Houses, ...	327,913		
		$555,708	
Deduct for materials one-third,......................		185,236	
		$370,532	
Manufactures by mills, deducting three-fourths,...		47,412	
Printing, &c.,..		16,600	
			$434,544
III. *Commerce*, 25 per cent of capital,..			464,637
IV. *Fisheries*,..			213,219
V. *The Forest*,..			27,350
VI. *Mines*,..			2,700
Total, ...			$2,976,687

ANNUAL PRODUCTS OF INDUSTRY IN THE DISTRICT OF COLUMBIA.

I. *Agriculture.*			
Live stock,......................No.	161,969	....	
25 per cent..		$40,492	
Grain, ...bush.	63,029	46,367	
Other products,..		90,083	
			$176,942
II. *Commerce*, 25 per cent of capital,..			802,725
III. *Manufactures*,..		$1,153,714	
Deduct for materials one-third,......................		387,905	
		$765,808	
Manufactures by mills, deducting three-fourths,...		45,842	
Printing, &c.,..		92,875	
			904,526
IV. *Fisheries*,..			87,400
Total, ...			$1,971,593

Summary of the Annual Products of Industry in the several States, with the proportional amount to each individual of the whole of the free population in each State.

States and Territories.	Value of annual products from							Prop. to each pers'n.	
	Agriculture.	Manufactures.	Commerce.	Mining.	Forest.	Fisheries.	Total.	Wh'le pop.	Free pop.
	Dollars.	*Dollars.*	*Dollars.*	*Dollars.*	*Dollars.*	*Dollars.*	*Dollars.*	*Dolls.*	*Dolls.*
Maine,....	15,856,270	5,615,303	1,505,380	327,376	1,877,663	1,280,713	26,462,705	52	52
N. Hamp.,	11,377,752	6,545,811	1,001,533	88,373	449,861	92,811	19,556,141	68	68
Vermont,.	17,879,155	5,685,425	758,899	389,488	430,224	....	25,143,191	85	85
Mass.,....	16,065,627	43,518,057	7,004,691	2,020,572	377,354	6,483,996	75,470,297	103	102
R. Island,.	2,199,309	8,640,626	1,294,956	162,410	44,610	659,312	13,001,223	110	119
Connect't,	11,371,776	12,778,963	1,963,281	820,419	181,575	907,723	28,023,737	90	90
N. Eng. S.	74,749,889	82,784,185	13,528,740	3,808,638	3,361,287	9,424,555	187,657,294	84	84
N. York,..	108,275,281	47,454,514	24,311,715	7,408,070	5,040,781	1,316,072	193,806,433	79	79
N. Jersey,.	16,209,853	10,696,257	1,206,929	1,073,921	361,326	124,140	29,672,426	79	79
Pennsylv.,	68,180,924	33,354,279	10,593,368	17,666,146	1,203,578	35,360	131,033,655	76	76
Delaware,	3,198,440	1,538,879	266,257	54,555	13,119	181,285	5,252,535	67	70
Maryland,	17,586,720	6,212,677	3,499,087	1,056,210	241,194	225,773	28,821,661	61	76
D. of Col.,	176,942	904,526	802,725	....	....	87,400	1,971,593	45	50
Middle S.,	213,628,160	100,161,132	40,680,081	27,258,902	6,859,998	1,970,030	390,558,303	76	77
Virginia,..	59,085,821	8,349,218	5,299,451	3,321,629	617,760	95,173	76,769,053	62	97
N. Caroli.,	26,975,831	2,053,697	1,322,284	372,486	1,446,108	251,792	32,422,198	44	63
S. Caroli.,.	21,553,691	2,248,915	2,632,421	187,608	549,626	1,275	27,173,536	45	101
Georgia,..	31,468,271	1,953,950	2,248,488	191,631	117,439	584	35,980,363	52	87
Florida, ..	1,834,237	434,544	464,637	2,700	27,350	213,219	2,976,687	54	103
South'n S.	140,917,851	15,040,324	11,967,281	4,076,054	2,758,283	562,043	175,321,836	52	87
Alabama,.	24,696,513	1,732,770	2,273,267	81,310	177,465	....	28,961,325	49	103
Mississip'i	26,494,565	1,585,790	1,453,686	....	205,297	....	29,739,338	79	164
Louisiana,	22,851,375	4,087,655	7,868,898	165,280	71,751	....	35,044,959	99	189
Arkansas,	5,086,757	1,145,309	420,635	18,225	217,469	....	6,888,395	70	88
Tennessee	31,660,180	2,477,193	2,239,478	1,371,331	225,179	....	37,973,360	45	58
S'west. S.,	110,789,390	11,028,717	14,255,964	1,636,146	897,161	....	138,607,378	61	97
Missouri,.	10,484,263	2,360,708	2,349,245	187,669	448,559	....	15,830,444	41	48
Kentucky,	29,226,545	5,092,353	2,580,575	1,539,919	184,799	....	38,624,191	49	64
Ohio, ...	37,802,001	14,588,091	8,050,316	2,442,682	1,013,063	10,525	63,906,678	42	42
Indiana,..	17,247,743	3,676,705	1,866,155	660,836	80,000	1,192	23,532,631	34	34
Illinois,...	13,701,466	3,243,981	1,493,425	293,272	249,841	....	18,981,985	39	39
Michigan,.	4,502,889	1,376,249	622,822	56,790	467,540	....	7,026,390	33	33
Wisconsin	568,105	304,692	189,957	384,603	430,580	27,663	1,905,600	47	47
Iowa, ...	769,295	179,087	136,525	13,250	83,949	....	1,132,106	27	27
N'west. S.	114,302,307	30,821,866	17,289,020	5,579,011	2,958,331	39,380	170,989,925	41	44
Total,..	654,387,597	239,836,224	79,721.086	42,358,761	16,835,060	11,996,008	1,063,134,736	62	73

The following table shows, in centesimal proportions, how the product of each branch of industry in the United States is distributed among the great divisions of the States:

Divisions.	Agricult.	Manufac.	Comm'ce.	Mining.	Forest.	Fisheries.	Total.
New England States,....	11.4	34.3	13.8	9.	20.	78.6	17.6
Middle States,............	32.7	42.	41 6	64.3	40.7	16.4	36.8
Southern States,.........	21.5	6.2	12.3	9.6	16.4	4.7	16.5
Southwestern States,....	16.9	4.6	14.6	3 9	5 3	......	13.
Northwestern States,....	17.5	12.9	17.7	13.2	17.6	.3	16.1
	100.	100.	100.	100.	100.	100.	100.

Table showing in what proportions the several products of industry are distributed, and the proportional value of each product to each person in the great divisions of the States.

EMPLOYMENTS.	N. ENGLAND STATES.		MIDDLE STATES.		SOUTHERN STATES.		SOUTHWESTERN STATES.		NORTHWESTERN STATES.		TOTAL U. STATES.	
	Prop. of prod.	Value to each person.	Prop. of prod.	Value to each person.	Prop. of prod.	Value to each person.	Prop. of prod.	Value to each person.	Prop. of prod.	Value to each person.	Prop. of prod.	Value to each person.
Agricult'e,.	40.	$33.45	54.7	$41.57	80.4	$41.80	79.9	$48.76	66.8	$27.41	61.6	$38.16
Manufact.,.	43.9	37.05	25.6	19.49	8.5	4.46	8.	4.85	18.	7.40	22.5	13.99
Commerce,	7.2	6.05	10.4	7.92	6.8	3.55	10.3	6.28	10.1	4.14	9.2	5.70
Mining,....	2.	1.71	7.	5.31	2.4	1.21	1.2	.72	3.2	1.33	4.	2.47
The Forest,	1.8	1.50	1.8	1.33	1.6	.82	.6	.39	1.7	.71	1.6	.98
Fisheries,...	5.1	4.22	.5	.38	.3	.16	......	....	.2	.01	1.1	.70
Total,...	100.	$84.	100.	$76.	100.	$52.	100.	$61.	100.	$41.	100.	$62.

It appears from the preceding tables, that, notwithstanding the great inequality in the five geographical divisions of the Union, both as to population and extent, there is no considerable difference in the total proportionate value of their annual products, with the exception of those of the Middle States, which are more than one-third of the whole. Of the other four divisions, the New England States, though somewhat the smallest in population, and much the smallest in extent, exceed the other divisions in the value of their annual products.

The agricultural products of the States may be compared in various ways. 1st. As to the proportion which they bear to the agricultural products of the whole Union. 2d. As to the proportion which this branch of their industry bears to the other branches. 3d. As to the average value to each inhabitant. 4th. As to the average value for each one of its territory. 5th. As to the quantities produced.

The three first comparisons are exhibited in the first and third tables. They show that nearly one-third of the agricultural products of the Union are furnished by the Middle States, one-ninth by the New England States, and from about a fifth to a sixth by each of the other three divisions. Thus, four-fifths of the products of the Southern and Southwestern States are agricultural, two-thirds of those of the Northwestern States, more than half of those of the Middle States, and but two-fifths of those of the New England States; that the value of this class of products to each inhabitant is the greatest in the Southwestern States, and the lowest in the Northwestern.

But the greatest diversity is in the average value per acre of their agricultural products, which is principally owing to the great difference among the States in the proportion of their uncultivated lands. Thus:

	Agricultural products.	Area in acres.	Value per acre.
New England States, ...	$74,749,889	42,336,000	$1 76
Middle States, ...	213,628,160	75,168,000	1 84
Southern States,*	139,083,614	133,996,800	1 03
Southwestern States, ...	110,789,390	156,851,200	70
Northwestern States,†	112,964,907	191,904,000	58

The last point of comparison is in the quantities annually produced; and we should make a very false estimate of the agricultural wealth of the different States, if we were to confine our attention to the money value of their several products, and not to regard the quantities produced. A large part of the products of every State are consumed where they are produced; and as to this portion, the greater the cheapness of the products of a State, the greater is its wealth. If the same labour and capital would produce twice as much grain in the Western States as in the Atlantic States, it is obvious that either one-half the labour and capital required in the latter may be saved in the Western States, and diverted to other sources of profit, or that those States may have twice as much as the Atlantic States for consumption. And as to the surplus sent abroad to be exchanged for other products, though the price be but half that in the Atlantic States, yet, if twice the quantity is produced at the same expense, the value produced in both places will be the same. The advantage of the superior fertility of the Western States is not as great as we have supposed, for the purpose of illustration, but it is probably sufficiently great to bring the profits of their agriculture upon a level with those of the Atlantic States.

Of the wheat, Indian corn, and other grain used for bread, and potatoes, the quantities produced by the different great divisions of the States, and the proportion to each inhabitant. are as follows:

GEOGRAPHICAL DIVISIONS.	Population.	Bushels of grain, exclusive of oats.	Propor. to each pers.	Bushels of potatoes.	Propor. to each pers.
New England States,.	2,234,822	12,506,000	5½	35,181,000	15¾
Middle States, ...	5,118,076	89,952,000	17½	42.969,000	8⅓
Southern States, ...	3,279,006	111,080,000	33⅓	9,710,000	3
Southwestern States,.	2,245,602	95,982,000	42¾	6,862,000	3
Northwestern States,.	4,057,313	179,620,000	43½	12,615,000	3

It thus appears, that the proportion of grain to each inhabitant

* The Territory of Florida not included.

† The Territories of Wisconsin and Iowa not included.

in the Western States is eight times as great as it is in New England, and two and a half times as great as it is in the Middle States. If we add the proportion of potatoes to that of the grain, and suppose four bushels of the former equal to one of the latter, then the difference between the Western States and New England will be as 5 to 1, and between the former and the Middle States as $2\frac{1}{4}$ to 1.

It should further be remarked, that about fifteen-sixteenths of the grain and potatoes produced in the United States are consumed at home, either directly, or in the form of animal food, and only one-sixteenth is sent abroad in either of these forms. From this large domestic consumption, we may see how greatly the Western States are benefited by this greater cheapness of production. It may well be supposed that the gain from this source compensates them for their greater distance from market.

The quantity of food annually consumed in the United States by a family of five persons,* after deducting one-sixteenth of the grain for the amount exported, and one-tenth for seed, is as follows:

Indian corn, ...	85 bushels.
Oats, ...	28 "
Wheat, rye, &c., ...	25 "
Potatoes, ...	25 "

The average of domestic animals to each family is:

Horses and mules, ...	$1\frac{1}{6}$
Cattle, ...	4
Sheep, ...	$5\frac{1}{4}$
Hogs, ...	7

To the articles annually consumed by a family, are to be added poultry, to the value of $2 25; pickled fish, one-third of a barrel; rice, 12 lbs.; sugar, 42 lbs.; besides garden vegetables, products of the orchard, and game.

The same, or nearly the same very liberal consumption which is here indicated, may be expected to continue in the United States so long as its population continues thin, compared with the capaci-

* It was not thought necessary to distinguish the families of slaves in this estimate from those of free persons, there being no essential difference between them as consumers of raw produce. If the families of slaves consume somewhat less of animal food, they contain also a greater proportion of children.

ties of the country, and no longer, unless, indeed, the high standard of comfort to the poorest class in this county should prevent that redundancy of numbers which finds its check in disease and destitution. This is a problem which the experience of other nations cannot assist us to solve, since the facility of subsistence which exists here, seems never to have existed in any part of the old continent in any stage of society.

In manufacturing industry, the States differ far more than in agriculture. The New England and Middle States, containing less than two-fifths of the whole population, possess more than three-fourths (76.3 per cent) of the manufactures. The manufactured products of New England exceed those of its agriculture by nearly a tenth. Those of Massachusetts alone exceed in value those of all the Western States together, and are nearly thrice as great as those of the four Southern States united. This diversity is to be referred principally to the different densities of population in the States, and in some degree to the slave labour of one-half of them, which, untutored as it now is, seems suited only to the greater simplicity of agricultural operations.

The cheapness and abundance of provisions and raw materials (including coal) in the Northwestern States, must eventually make them the seats of flourishing manufactures, and this, too, before they have attained that very dense population their fertile soil is destined to support. Even with their present numbers, the census affords evidence of their particular adaptation to this branch of industry. The manufactures of Ohio alone already nearly equal in value those of the four Southern States.

The profits of commerce amount to something more than an eleventh of the whole annual product, if they have not been estimated too high at 25 per cent on the capital employed. They constitute more than a tenth of the whole products in the Middle, the Southwestern, and the Northwestern States; about a fourteenth in New England; and a fifteenth in the Southern States.

Mining contributes but 4 per cent of the whole national product. Nearly two-thirds of the whole (64.3 per cent) are in the Middle States. More than half the remainder is in the Northwestern States.

The products of the forest constitute 1½ per cent of the whole. They are furnished by each division of the States nearly in proportion to the population, except by the Southwestern States, where they are little more than the half of 1 per cent of the products of that division.

The products of the fisheries, the lowest in the scale as to direct gain, barely exceed 1 per cent of the whole, and more than three-fourths of them (78.6 per cent) are contributed by the New England States. From this branch of industry the Southwestern States derive nothing, and the Northwestern next to nothing. It is of far greater importance in a national view, as affording an excellent nursery for seamen, than as a source of gain, except to the New England States, where it yields 5 per cent of their whole annual product.

On comparing the individual States, we find that in agriculture, New York, Pennsylvania, and Virginia, are far before the rest in the value of their products. In manufactures, New York, Massachusetts, and Pennsylvania take the lead. The profits of commerce are greatest iu New York, Pennsylvania, Ohio, and Louisiana; but in proportion to population, Louisiana stands foremost. In mining industry, Pennsylvania equals all the other States except New York, which is second, though not the half of Pennsylvania. Virginia is the third, though not the half of New York. In the products of the forest, the order of precedence is New York, Maine, and North Carolina. In the fisheries, the product of Massachusetts is more than that of all the rest of the Union. New York and Maine are the next highest.

If we distribute the whole annual product in 1840—1,063 millions of dollars—among the whole population, we find that the proportion to each inhabitant is greatest in the New England States, where it is $84; in the Middle States, it is $76; in the Southern, $52; in the Southwestern, $61; and in the Northwestern, $41. The causes of this diversity are to be found yet more in the different densities of population, different degrees of fertility, and different distances from market, than in the existence or absence of slavery, though that also has its influence. It is the difference of distance from market which makes the industry of an individual in the Southwestern States 50 per cent greater than in the Northwestern. It is the difference of fertility which makes the same industry worth $79 in Mississippi, and but $49 in Alabama. The same cause makes the industry of the Southwestern States more productive than that of the Southern States. It is the greater density of numbers in Massachusetts and Rhode Island, and their consequent success in manufactures, which makes industry more productive in those States than it is in New York and Pennsylvania. In the two former, the proportion to an individual is greater than in any other State. In Rhode Island, it is $110, and in Massachusetts, $103. The annual product from manufactures in Rhode Island is very nearly four times that derived from her agriculture.

If we distribute the annual product among the free population exclusively, then the proportion to each individual will be greater in the slaveholding than in the free States, for in several of them the proportion will then be more than doubled. Thus, in South Carolina, it will be raised from $45 to $101 ; in Mississippi, from $79 to $164 ; and in Louisiana, from $99 to $189 ; then the highest proportion in the Union.

The whole of the 1,063 millions annually produced, together with the omitted articles, amounting perhaps to between 40 and 50 millions more, are annually consumed, except a very small portion, which adds to the stock of the national wealth. The progressive increase of this wealth will be considered in the next chapter.

CHAPTER XXI.

THE INCREASE OF WEALTH.

HAVING ascertained the amount of the national income, it would on many accounts be desirable to ascertain also its ratio of increase, and more especially whether it increases at the same rate as the population or at a different rate.

There are obvious reasons why the wealth of an industrious and prosperous community should increase faster than its population. Every year adds to its stock of labour-saving tools and machinery, as well as improves their usefulness. Lands, too, are made more productive by draining, ditching, manuring, and better modes of culture. Both science and practical art are constantly enlarging the quantity of manufactured commodities, and yet more improving their quality. By means of cheaper and quicker modes of transportation, much of that labour which, in every country is expended, not in producing, but in transferring products from place to place, is saved and rendered directly productive: and lastly, the small excess of annual income over annual expense is constantly adding to the mass of capital, which is so efficient an agent of production.

But we must bear in mind that so far as this improvement in the sources of wealth are shared by the whole civilized world, it is not manifested in pecuniary estimates of annual products, supposing the value of the precious metals to be unchanged, since the same portion of them will be constantly representing a greater and greater amount of what is useful and convenient to man. It is only where the increase of wealth of a country is faster or slower than the average that it will be shown in the money value of its annual products compared with its population. It is, then, the relative and not the positive increase of wealth in the United States which we propose to consider.

Had each preceding census furnished the information afforded by the census of 1840, this question had been of easy solution. But this not being the case, we are left to infer the progress of national wealth from such partial indications of it as we are able to derive from other statistical facts.

One of these indications is the progressive increase in the value of the lands and buildings of the several States.

In each of the years 1798, 1813, and 1815, the General Government laid a direct tax, apportioned among them, as the constitution requires, according to their representative numbers. But as the act of Congress authorized the States in 1813 and 1815 to assume the payment of their respective quotas, and thus relieve themselves from the tax, and several of the States availed themselves of this provision, a valuation of the lands in those States not being necessary, did not take place.

The valuations which were made were as follows:

	1798.	1818.
New Hampshire,..	$23,175,046	$36,957,825
Massachusetts,..	83,992,464	149,253,514
Rhode Island,..	11,066,358	24,567,020
Connecticut,..	48,313,434	86,546,841
Vermont, ...	16,723,873	32,747,290
New York,..	100,380,707	265,224,983
Delaware,..	6,234,414	14,218,950
Maryland, ...	32,372,291	106,490,638
North Carolina,..	30,842,372	58,114,952
Tennessee,..	6,134,108	28,748,986
	$359,235,067	$802,870,999

This shows an increase in the value of the lands of 123 per cent in fifteen years, equivalent to a decennial increase of about 68 per cent.

Let us now compare this increase with the increase of population of the same States, in the same period of fifteen years. In 1800 and 1810, their numbers were as follows:

	1803.	1810.
New Hampshire,..	$183,762	$214,360
Massachusetts,..	574,964	700,745
Rhode Island,..	69,122	77,031
Connecticut,..	251,002	262,042
Vermont,..	154,465	217,713
New York,..	586,756	959,049
Delaware,..	64,273	72,674
Maryland,..	341,548	380,346
North Carolina,..	478,103	555,500
Tennessee,..	105,602	264,727
	$2,828,597	$3,701,327

This shows an increase of population of 30.8 per cent., and supposing the increase from 1798 to 1800, and from 1810 to 1813 to be not materially different, we may regard 30.8 per cent as the decennial increase of their numbers. But the decennial increase in the value of their lands was 68 per cent that is, more than twice as great, or nearly as 221 to 100. It may be presumed that those States in which there was no valuation of the lands in 1813 would exhibit the same difference between these ratios.

It is proper to remark that the lands of those States which were valued in 1813, were again valued in 1815, and that the subsequent valuation showed no increase in the total value, and in some of the States an actual falling off. The war, by interrupting foreign commerce, prevented any increase in the total value of landed property, and probably arrested the progress of the national wealth.

Again: The valuation of the lands in Virginia in 1798, under the direct tax law, was $71,225,127, and the same were valued in 1839, under a law of the State, at $211,930,538, showing an increase of value in 41 years of 197.5 per cent. equal to a decennial increase of 31 per cent. The population of the State had, from 1800 to 1840, increased 40.8 per cent., which gives a less average decennial increase than 7 per cent; by which it appears that the value of its lands had increased more than four times as fast as its population, supposing the two valuations made with equal accuracy.

On the other hand, in the State of New York the valuation of its lands, under the direct tax law of 1815, was $266,067,094; and the average valuation of the same lands, for the years 1834, 1835, and 1836, under a law of the State, was $430,751,273. This shows an increase of value, in twenty years, of 61.8 per cent, which is equivalent to a decennial increase of 27.2 per cent. The increase of population of the same State from 1810 to 1830 was 100 per cent, and from 1820 to 1840 was 76.9 per cent. The average between them (88.4 per cent) may be presumed to give the rate of increase from 1815 to 1835, the period in question, which is equivalent to a decennial increase of 37 per cent; and thus, supposing the valuation to have been made on the same principles under the Federal and the State Governments, population would seem to have increased faster than capital in that State, or at least, than capital seeking investment in real estate.

It would seem from the preceding instances that the increase in the value of land has been very different in the different States, even when compared with the increase of population. It has also probably varied at different periods. The great extension of the foreign commerce of the United States during the first decennial term, and the extraordinary demand for their agricultural products caused a rapid rise in the value of their lands. The interruptions to that commerce in the second period, and part of the third, produced a correspondent depression. On the other hand, the depreciation of the currency in most of the States during the war, and in all of them about the year 1835 and 1836, had the effect of enhancing the price of land.

Let us now advert to the progress of commerce, seeing that the growth of national wealth may be expected to manifest itself in an increase of exports and imports. But since they greatly vary from year to year, it will be necessary to take the average of several years.

The average imports for the three years, from March 4th, 1789, to March 4th, 1792, were as follows:

The imports from March 4th, 1789, to December 31st, 1791,...............	$52,200,000
" from December 31st, 1791, to March 4th, 1792, equal to one-sixth of the imports of that year,................................	5,250,000
One-third of......................	$57,450,000
is.....	$19,150,000

The average imports of 1839, 1840, and 1841 are $132,393,000, which shows an increase in fifty years of 692 per cent, equal to a decennial increase of 47 per cent, which is about two-fifths, or 40 per cent more than the average decennial increase of population.

The average annual exports of domestic products from March 4th, 1789, to March 4th, 1792, were $13,500,000, and for the years 1839, 1840, and 1841, the average was $107,937,000, showing an increase of 799 per cent in 50 years, which is equal to a decennial increase of something more than 51 per cent.

Again: The average imports for the years 1819, 1820, and 1821, were $74,720,000, and when compared with those of 1839, 1840, and 1841, an increase is shown of 77 per cent in 20 years, equal to a decennial increase of 33 per cent, which is rather less than the increase of the population in the same period.

The consumption of those commodities which are in extensive, but not in universal use, may also be presumed to indicate the progress of wealth. Of this character are tea, coffee, and wine, all of which, moreover, being imported from abroad, their home consumption can be accurately ascertained.

	From 1808 to 1812.	From 1836 to 1840.
The average quantity annually consumed of Coffee, was......lbs.	16,158,000	96,274,000
" " " " Tea, ...	3,445,932	14,591,000
" " " " Wines, ...gls.	1,737,002	5,422,000

The increased consump. in 30 years of Coffee, 495 p. cent; the decen. increase 81 p. cent.
" " " Tea, 323 " " " 61 "
" " " Wine, 212 " " " 46 "

18

It would seem, then, that from 1808 to 1838 the increased decennial consumption of coffee compared with that of the population, has been as 33 to 81; of tea, 33 to 61; and of wine, as 33 to 46.

It must, however, be remembered, that for the last six years of the term, coffee, which had previously paid a duty of 5 cents per pound, and teas, which had paid an average duty of more than 20 cents per pound, have been free of duty; and that for the same period the duties on wine have been greatly reduced. It is not easy to say how far the increased consumption of these commodities is to be attributed to the changes in the tariff, but it does not probably exceed 20 per cent, and may be much less.

One circumstance which has contributed to diminish the increase both of imports and exports, is the growth of manufactures, which has at once enlarged the home market for the raw materials, and lessened the demand of imports.

Official estimates of the manufactures of the United States were taken both in 1810 and 1820, but there was so many inaccuracies in both, and especially the last, that any inferences drawn from them are to be regarded rather as probable conjectures than well founded estimates.

According to a digest of the returns made by the marshals in 1810 of the manufactures of the United States, they amounted to $127,694,602. A further estimate was afterwards made by the acting Secretary of the Treasury of the omissions, by which the amount was extended to $172,762,676. But inasmuch as there might also be great omissions in the returns of 1840, it would seem safer to compare the returns that were actually made, more especially as Mr. Gallatin had, from those of 1810, estimated the annual amount of manufactures at only 120 millions of dollars.

It seems, however, that each of these estimates contain items that are not comprehended in that of 1840. These, then, will be deducted before the two are compared.

The following articles in the returns of 1810 were not, in 1840, comprehended in the estimate of manufactures, viz:

Amount, according to the marshal's returns,........................			$127,694,602
Fabrics made in families,..............................		$16,491,200	
Products of fulling-mills,..............................		4,117,308	
" of carding-mills,..............................		1,837,508	
Bar and pig iron,..............................		6,081,314	
Tanneries,..............................		8,338,250	
Salt,..............................		1,149,793	
Fish oil,..............................		240,520	
Lead in pigs,..............................		26,720	
			38,332,613
			$89,361,909
Deduct for raw materials one-third,..............................			29,787,329
			$59,574,660
The annual product of the manufactures of 1840, was............			239,752,227
To be deducted, the following articles not comprehended in the digest of 1840, viz :—			
Bricks and lime, two-thirds of....	$9,736,945	$6,491,390	
Houses, two-thirds of..............	41,917,401	28,044,934	
Mill manufactures, one-fourth of.	76,545,246	19,136,311	
			$53,672,635
			$186,079,592

Comparing the same articles of manufacture in 1810 and 1840, the increase, from $59,574,660 to $186,079,592, is 212 per cent in thirty years, or a decennial increase of 46 per cent.

The returns ofmanufactures made by the marshals in 1820 were still more imperfect and inaccurate. In whole counties there were no returns whatever, and in almost all of them there were considerable omissions. In some cases, where capital to a large amount appears to be employed, no product is stated. In not a few large establishments the proprietors refused to answer the marshal's inquiries. In many, it should be added, the manufactures are represented to be in a languishing condition.

The gross annual amount of the manufactures, so far as it can be gathered from such defective returns, appears to be only $36,115,000, and the capital employed in them to $41,507,000. As this branch of industry is known to have been steadily advancing from 1810 to 1815, so great a falling off in five years as is indicated by the returns of 1820, seems to be utterly inadmissible. Without doubt it must have greatly declined after the peace of 1815, which at once raised the price of raw materials and lowered that of manufactures; but after making large allowance for these circumstances and the omissions in the returns of 1820, they do not seem sufficient to account for the great apparent difference, and a part of it seems not improbably to be referred to an over valuation of the manufactures in 1810.

Perhaps the best mode of comparing the manufactures of 1820 with those of 1840 is to compare the number of persons employed in those years; and the rather as this part of the returns is the most complete, and in the most manufacturing States makes some approach to accuracy. The number employed in 1820 was 36,705 men, 5,812 women, and 13,779 children—in all 56,296. The whole number of persons employed in 1840 was 455,668—that is, as 100 to 809; which supposes the extraordinary decennial increase of 284 per cent. After making the most liberal deduction from this estimate for the omissions in the returns of 1820, the remainder shows an advancement in this branch of industry that is without example. As a further evidence of the same fact, we find that while no other branch of our domestic exports has ever doubled since 1820, that of manufactures has increased six fold; that is, from $2,342,000 to $12,868,840 in 1840, and 13,523,072 in 1841.

The increase of the precious metals, or rather of money, would be one of the surest indications of an increase of wealth; but we have no means of ascertaining its amount in the first two or three decennial terms with even an approach to accuracy. In 1791, the estimates of the currency, then almost wholly metallic, varied from nine to sixteen millions of dollars. But in 1821, upon better data, the amount was estimated by the Treasury department at from eighteen to twenty millions. From that time to 1841, the imports of specie and bullion, according to the custom-house returns,

were	$181,589,814
The exports in the same period, were . .	138,085,922
	$43,503,892

This, with the quantity then in the country, estimated at $19,000,000, gives a total of $62,502,892. To this we should add the product of domestic mines, but on the other hand, deduct the quantity wrought into plate and manufactures, or consumed by the wear of the coin.

The quantity of gold and silver manufactured from coin during the twenty years in question, is supposed by those most conversant on the subject not to exceed an average of $500,000 a year. The quantity lost and consumed by the wear of the coin may be set down at one-fourth of 1 per cent a year. The product of the domestic mines, carried to the mint in the same period, has been $6,124,547, and making a moderate allowance for the quantity used by goldbeaters and other manufacturers, we may safely estimate it, in round numbers, at $7,000,000.

On the preceding state of facts, the quantity of specie in the country in 1841 would be as follows:

Amount in circulation in 1821, and since imported,........................		$62,503,892
Product of domestic mines,..		7,000,000
		$69,503,892
Deduct amount manufactured,..............................	$10,000,000	
" " consumed by wear, &c.,..................	2,000,000	
		12,000,000
		$57,503,892

This increase in twenty years, from $19,000,000 to $57,503,892, is equivalent to a decennial increase of 73 per cent, or nearly two-thirds more than the increase of population. Without doubt the quantity of the precious metals in the United States was considerably augmented by the large loans contracted in Europe, but it must be recollected that a large part—it is believed the largest part—of those loans was contracted after 1837, in consequence of the reaction occasioned by the preternatural distension of the currency, and tended rather to check the efflux of specie (which it could not prevent) than to increase its import; and that, whatever was the effect of those loans, it would seem that the equilibrium was restored by the same reaction before 1841, by the fact of the great increase of specie within the last two years.

In this comparative estimate, as well as in all those preceding it, we should take into account the rise which the precious metals have experienced since 1820, by reason of the lessened production of the American mines, and which cannot be much if any short of 10 per cent. If we allow for this additional value, it will convert the $57,503,892 in 1841 to more than $63,000,000, and raise the decennial increase of those metals to something more than 82 per cent.

The result of the preceding comparisons may be seen in the following summary:

Decennial increase of land in 10 States,..	68	per cent.—Of	population,	30.8	per cent.
" " " Virginia,....	31	"	"	7.	"
" " " New York,.	27	"	"	37.	"
" " imports in 50 years,	47	"	"	33.50	"
" " exports "	51	"	"	33.33	"
" " imports in 20 years,	33	"	"	33.33	"
" " exports "	33	"	"	33.33	"
" " imports of tea,	61	"	"	33.33	"
" " " coffee,	81	"	"	33 33	"
" " " wine,	46	"	"	33.33	"
" " manufactures,	46	"	"	33.33	"
" " specie,	82	"	"	33.33	"
	601			371.94	

Which shows the decennial increase of capital and wealth to have been to that of population as 601 to 371.94, or nearly as 50 to 31;

and supposing the decennial increase of population to have averaged 33⅓ per cent, that of wealth has been 53 per cent.

According to the view that has been taken of the resources of these States, their public debts, on the most liberal estimate made of them, bear an insignificant proportion to their means. Supposing the amount of those debts to be 200 millions of dollars, at an interest of 6 per cent, the annual charge is $12,000,000, which is little more than 1 per cent of their income in 1840, and may be presumed to be less than 1 per cent of their present income. But if they were all to provide for the punctual payment of this interest, and thus restore that confidence in the national faith which once existed, or even make an approach to it, the debt could be readily converted at par into a five, or even four per cent stock, and the excess would be sufficient for a sinking fund that would discharge the debt in thirty years or less. In this interval, too, as wealth would be steadily increasing, the burthen would become lighter and lighter, and in twenty-five years, it would bear but a third or a fourth of its present rate on the value of property.

With such ample means of complying with their engagements, the States have not a shadow of excuse for not faithfully fulfilling them. It is true that these debts are distributed among them very unequally, because their affairs have been administered with very unequal degrees of wisdom and forbearance; but even those States which are most encumbered, may provide for the payment of interest by a moderate tax which shall be made to bear on all sources of revenue. Thus the debt of Pennsylvania, estimated at $40,000,000, bears, at 5 per cent, an annual interest of $2,000,000. The income of this State was, in 1840, $131,000,000, and is probably at this time not less than $150,000,000. A nett revenue of only 1⅓ per cent of that income would produce the $2,000,000 required.

But were the burthen yet greater, and the means of discharging them yet less, no State which does not set a higher value on property than integrity, can consent to a violation of the national faith; nor would any right-minded citizen deem the saving thus effected any compensation for the stain of national infamy it would leave behind it. But the public sentiment of the Union, to say nothing of our character abroad, to which we never have been and never ought to be indifferent, is so decided on this subject, that it is impossible the people of any State can permanently resist it. Even the excuses and pretences which were but too successfully urged by those who make a political traffic of their principles when the first stunning effects of the revulsion in 1839 were felt in full force, will soon find no support from any considerable portion of the American people. All men who have at once common sense and common honesty, must see that "repudiation," if warranted by strict law, would not be just; and though it were just, would be neither liberal nor wise.

We confidently trust, then, that the cloud which now fearfully overhangs a few States, and to the distant observer casts a shade over their uncontaminated associates, will soon disappear, and leave the path before us as bright and cheering as that it is our pride to have passed over.

THE END.

APPENDIX.

PREFACE TO THE APPENDIX.

Another census of the United States exhibits their progress in population and wealth from 1840 to 1850. In this period they have experienced some extraordinary changes in their condition, superadded to those which have hitherto marked their course. They have thus gained an accession of territory of more than 800,000 square miles, which has already added two States to the Union, and will, probably, in time, add twelve or fifteen more. By an unprecedented tide of immigration a million and a half of Europeans have found permanent homes in this free and fertile country. Our steam navigation, which had previously traversed all our lakes and great rivers, has been extended to the ocean; and lastly the gold of our California mines produced an influence on the monetary affairs of the world. The result is, that in ten years our population has increased from 17 to 23 millions, that our commerce, manufactures, shipping, and railroads; our religious and charitable institutions; our schools and colleges—everything, in short, which characterizes a civilized community—have increased in a correspondent or yet greater proportion.

The seventh census, in addition to such details as its predecessors have given, has afforded much interesting information relative to our social condition and public economy, which has been made accessible to the popular mind by the valuable publications issued from the census office.

The writer of the following pages has aimed to select and convey in an abridged form the most important facts communicated by this census; accompanying them as heretofore, with such comments as might aid those to whom statistical enumerations were unintelligible or distasteful. He has, moreover, here found the means of confirming or qualifying some of the speculations on which he had previously ventured. In conclusion, he indulges the hope that these authentic exhibitions of our growth and improvement, so gratifying to the pride and love of country, will lead our citizens to greater party forbearance, and give them new incentives to cherish that union to which, under heaven, they owe the blessings they enjoy.

PHILADELPHIA, *January*, 1855.

CONTENTS OF THE APPENDIX.

CHAPTER I.

CENSUS OF 1850.

CHAPTER II.

PROGRESS OF THE POPULATION IN SIXTY YEARS.

CHAPTER III.

PROPORTION BETWEEN THE SEXES.

CHAPTER IV.

IMMIGRATION.

CHAPTER V.

PROBABILITIES OF LIFE.

CHAPTER VI.

THE DEAF, DUMB, BLIND, ETC.

CHAPTER VII.

FUTURE INCREASE OF POPULATION.

CHAPTER VIII.

ATLANTIC AND WESTERN STATES, ETC., COMPARED.

CHAPTER IX.

RELIGION—JUVENILE AND POPULAR INSTRUCTION.

CHAPTER X.

CITIES AND TOWNS.

CHAPTER XI.

THE INDUSTRIOUS CLASSES.

CHAPTER XII.

PAUPERISM AND CRIME.

CHAPTER XIII.

PRODUCTS OF AGRICULTURE.

CHAPTER XIV.

VALUE OF THE ANNUAL PRODUCTS OF INDUSTRY.

PROGRESS OF POPULATION

IN THE

United States.

CHAPTER I.

THE CENSUS OF 1850, BEING THE SEVENTH DECENNIAL ENUMERATION UNDER THE CONSTITUTION.

THIS census differs from every other which preceded it in one important particular. Hitherto the population had been distributed into classes, according to age, sex, and race, by the officers who took the census, but by the act of Congress for taking the seventh census, the census-taker was required to return each individual by name, with his or her sex, age, color, occupation, &c., and left the classification to be made at the seat of government, in the office of the Secretary of the Interior.

This mode was recommended by its promise of greater accuracy, and by its affording materials for additional classes of the individual citizens, according to other points of similarity. It has, however, been found to be attended with the disadvantages of adding largely to the expense, and of requiring a much longer time to complete a digest of the returns. These objections, which, if not obviated, must acquire additional force at each succeeding census, have given rise to a doubt whether the certain inconveniences of the new mode do not outweigh its presumed benefits.

The act also greatly enlarged the field of inquiry. It appointed a Census Board which had the power of prescribing the objects of inquiry, not exceeding one hundred. In the exercise of its authority, this Board augmented the number of agricultural items from twenty-nine to forty-five. It required a valuation of each person's lands, improved and unimproved, and of their implements and machinery; the annual taxes levied in each district; the number of aliens, with the places of their nativity; of paupers; of convicted criminals; of church establishments, with the property of each; and of the public libraries; and, lastly, it aimed at copious details of medical statistics—as the number of deaths within the year preceding the census, the age and color of each person deceased, and the disease of which he died. Though this part of the census is not to be relied on, from the incompetency or carelessness of most of those from whom the census-takers received their information, the seventh census, on the whole, furnishes the materials for a greater stock of statistical information than has probably ever been afforded in a country containing more than twenty millions of people.

The decennial increase in 1850, by multiplication and the accession of Texas, New Mexico, and California, was—

Of the whole population	23,191,876	35.87 per cent.
Of the whites	19,553,068	37.74 "
Of the free colored................	434,495	12.47 "
Of the slaves	3,204,313	28.82 "

The distribution of the different classes under this census, compared with that of 1840, was as follows:—

	In 1840.	In 1850.
The whites amounted to	83.16 per cent.	84.32 per cent.
The free colored................	2.26 "	1.87 "
The slaves.....................	14.58 "	13.81 "

The result of the census of 1850, as to the population of each State and Territory, distributed according to age and sex, white or colored, bond or free, may be seen in the four following tables:—

WHITE POPULATION IN 1850, CLASSED ACCORDING TO AGE AND SEX.

States and Territories.	Under 1. males.	Under 1. females.	1 and under 5. males.	1 and under 5. females.	5 and under 10. males.	5 and under 10. females.
Maine............	7,041	6,915	31,497	30,161	37,765	36,580
New Hampshire...	3,057	3,030	13,660	13,247	17,379	16,833
Vermont..........	3,345	3,226	15,623	15,366	19,437	18,640
Massachusetts.....	11,527	11,463	45,460	44,544	54,148	50,697
Rhode Island......	1,740	1,804	6,939	6,844	7,589	7,611
Connecticut.......	3,851	3,649	16,190	15,908	19,292	19,052
New York........	38,090	37,125	162,659	159,831	187,834	184,305
New Jersey.......	6,401	6,436	26,444	25,687	30,614	39,081
Pennsylvania.......	31,929	31,017	131,268	135,990	157,099	154,424
Delaware.........	983	970	4,191	4,120	5,036	4,882
Maryland.........	6,059	5,962	24,309	24,037	27,558	27,016
District of Columbia	493	506	2,081	1,964	2,451	2,466
Virginia..........	12,026	11,715	57,266	55,190	66,363	63,809
North Carolina......	8,171	7,680	35,721	34,080	40,793	39,407
South Carolina.....	3,313	3,139	17,973	17,084	20,589	19,988
Georgia...........	7,894	7,271	37,844	36,698	42,642	41,118
Florida...........	651	646	3,365	3,139	3,811	3,647
Alabama.........	6,289	5,927	30,241	28,983	34,205	33,485
Mississippi........	4,464	4,209	22,045	20,689	24,404	23,495
Louisiana.........	3,467	3,421	15,380	14,907	16,931	16,274
Texas.............	2,437	2,326	11,133	10,638	12,277	11,317
Arkansas.........	2,817	2,655	12,441	11,944	13,476	12,912
Tennessee.........	11,679	11,247	52,801	50,780	60,471	58,416
Kentucky.........	12,035	11,528	52,441	50,140	59,604	57,315
Missouri..........	10,044	9,529	41,124	39,466	46,356	44,606
Illinois...........	13,546	12,995	58,383	56,436	66,392	63,513
Indiana..........	16,344	15,636	68,294	65,613	79,563	76,369
Ohio.............	28,488	27,707	127,036	123,348	145,958	141,724
Michigan..........	5,462	5,362	25,016	23,775	30,384	28,847
Wisconsin.........	5,279	5,124	20,845	20,045	21,765	20,432
Iowa..............	3,141	2,952	14,302	13,850	15,864	15,095
California..........	148	122	840	784	1,080	1,011
Minnesota.........	66	102	388	363	363	356
Oregon............	161	149	902	835	907	934
Utah..............	220	212	871	863	696	668
New Mexico.......	639	594	3,773	3,792	4,402	4,325
	273,307	264,354	1,198,746	1,160,051	1,372,438	1,331,690

States and Territories.	10 and under 15. males.	females.	15 and under 20. males.	females.	20 and der 30. males.	females.
Maine	36,408	35,188	33,352	33,439	51,456	48,279
New Hampshire	17,426	16,844	16,920	18,821	28,232	28,948
Vermont	18,485	17,609	17,480	16,778	27,431	25,661
Massachusetts	49,129	48,634	48,868	55,044	101,306	107,856
Rhode Island	7,365	7,378	7,172	7,828	14,652	15,192
Connecticut	19,373	18,534	18,527	19,486	35,239	35,050
New York	170,053	167,472	157,151	171,592	308,816	308,392
New Jersey	28,213	26,913	24,294	25,706	42,193	43,152
Pennsylvania	138,633	133,258	116,773	124,483	209,438	206,801
Delaware	4,581	4,342	3,814	3,954	6,354	6,335
Maryland	25,307	24,608	20,767	22,461	40,164	38,173
District of Columbia	2,156	2,235	1,829	2,220	3,523	3,950
Virginia	59,955	57,485	47,638	50,015	77,492	77,559
North Carolina	37,577	35,722	30,178	31,777	46,618	49,630
South Carolina	18,842	18,132	14,732	15,530	23,474	23,833
Georgia	37,075	35,674	28,497	30,085	44,873	43,527
Florida	3,077	2,812	2,338	2,412	4,778	3,727
Alabama	30,145	29,059	24,548	25,215	36,360	35,732
Mississippi	21,105	20,081	15,847	16,157	27,164	23,630
Louisiana	14,103	13,857	10,620	12,498	30,729	24,569
Texas	10,346	9,456	7,836	8,073	16,454	12,311
Arkansas	11,930	11,178	9,059	8,990	15,193	13,238
Tennessee	54,444	51,825	43,870	45,094	64,089	64,537
Kentucky	51,610	49,454	42,115	42,801	69,673	64,506
Missouri	40,589	38,673	32,250	32,299	58,245	40,952
Illinois	58,559	54,301	46,959	45,739	79,465	70,579
Indiana	68,240	64,447	55,477	55,196	86,785	80,349
Ohio	128,101	123,632	107,689	111,126	178,777	168,373
Michigan	25,491	24,040	21,216	21,238	36,186	32,491
Wisconsin	17,571	16,375	14,522	14,217	31,922	26,366
Iowa	13,172	12,137	9,961	10,134	16,702	15,646
California	1,134	813	4,569	877	44,770	1,597
Minnesota	209	263	225	231	1,154	565
Oregon	717	692	677	525	2,375	802
Utah	683	685	659	666	1,264	891
New Mexico	3,678	3,187	3,187	3,833	6,326	6,270
	1,225,575	1,176,554	1,041,116	1,087,600	1,869,092	1,758,469

States and Territories.	30 and under 40. males.	females.	40 and under 50. males.	females.	50 and under 60. males.	females.
Maine	35,935	33,606	27,436	25,802	17,644	17,460
New Hampshire	19,558	20,222	15,837	16,445	11,299	12,372
Vermont	19,766	19,262	15,860	15,212	10,679	10,397
Massachusetts	72,540	70,002	47,696	47,612	28,340	31,293
Rhode Island	10,335	10,191	6,636	7,005	4,047	4,665
Connecticut	25,078	24,251	17,902	18,190	11,845	13,436
New York	216,542	197,333	144,496	128,561	85,440	78,911
New Jersey	30,181	28,151	20,887	19,631	12,796	13,039
Pennsylvania	144,039	133,072	97,558	89,451	58,632	55,919
Delaware	4,605	4,481	3,106	2,948	1,713	1,805
Maryland	29,460	26,685	18,740	17,414	10,647	10,802
District of Columbia	2,679	2,599	1,647	1,633	995	1,056
Virginia	51,451	49,907	36,105	34,756	22,631	22,258
North Carolina	29,340	31,753	20,315	21,922	13,084	14,316
South Carolina	15,534	15,273	10,573	10,603	6,895	6,778
Georgia	28,062	25,534	18,830	17,403	10,891	10,125
Florida	3,558	2,347	2,076	1,410	1,269	810
Alabama	21,862	21,057	15,976	13,721	9,842	7,842
Mississippi	19,061	14,216	11,378	8,776	6,667	4,742
Louisiana	27,451	15,054	13,829	7,529	5,639	3,637
Texas	12,117	7,353	6,939	4,366	3,452	2,117
Arkansas	10,043	7,420	6,056	4,501	3,041	2,186

States and Territories.	30 and under 40. males.	30 and under 40. females.	40 and under 50. males.	40 and under 50. females.	50 and under 60. males.	50 and under 60. females.
Tennessee	38,947	38,361	25,541	25,860	16,269	14,950
Kentucky	45,345	38,672	28,587	25,376	16,995	15,142
Missouri	41,006	30.761	23,540	18,170	12,481	9,594
Illinois	57,178	45,248	34,389	27,683	19,119	14,709
Indiana	57.445	49,853	35,213	32,010	23,538	18,501
Ohio	120,512	107,098	80,204	70,128	43,352	42,520
Michigan	28,120	23,032	19,412	14,809	10,356	7,712
Wisconsin.........	26,086	18,638	14,345	10,428	7,634	5,567
Iowa	13,613	10,451	7,784	5,968	4,115	3,026
California	21,460	986	7,536	453	2,029	182
Minnesota.........	720	251	290	131	129	53
Oregon............	1,343	546	583	274	307	119
Utah..............	761	598	513	404	221	204
New Mexico.......	3,949	3,293	2,407	1,981	1,627	1,243
	1,288,682	1,128,257	840,222	748,566	498,660	459,511

States and Territories.	60 and under 70. males.	60 and under 70. females.	70 and under 80. males.	70 and under 80. females.	80 & under 90. males.	80 & under 90. females.	90 & u. 100. m.	90 & u. 100. fe.
Maine..............	10,493	10,230	5,224	5,247	1,683	1,760	149	180
New Hampshire ...	7,173	8,169	3,905	4,556	1,320	1,731	151	251
Vermont	6,639	6,720	3,521	3,554	1,226	1,165	116	139
Massachusetts	16,743	69,807	7,784	10,003	2,335	3,420	197	393
Rhode Island......	2,443	2,967	1,050	1,510	319	489	38	48
Connecticut	7,408	8,978	3,698	4,754	1,174	1,661	109	202
New York	45,927	43,920	19,947	19,264	5,709	5,877	618	713
New Jersey.......	7,254	7,705	3,126	3,454	888	1,143	72	122
Pennsylvania	31,814	32,224	13,188	13,869	3,344	4,035	335	406
Delaware.........	881	1,005	373	440	76	109	9	15
Maryland..........	5,429	6,008	2,161	2,631	508	749	63	114
District of Columbia	464	537	133	208	35	52	5	8
Virginia...........	12,724	12,711	5,548	5,914	1,659	1,819	228	289
North Carolina.....	7,169	8,407	3,383	3,858	1,054	1,136	135	216
South Carolina.....	3,659	3,809	1,547	1,825	494	623	78	133
Georgia............	6,202	5,508	2,447	2,329	725	797	119	149
Florida	544	376	188	125	40	37	5	8
Alabama...........	4,544	3,795	1,822	1,580	479	490	103	84
Mississippi.........	2,847	2,246	968	860	228	225	35	32
Louisiana..........	2,055	1,678	621	573	126	149	30	29
Texas	1,212	840	365	231	81	63	9	13
Arkansas	1,304	902	414	278	69	82	7	13
Tennessee	8,567	8,234	4,006	3,797	1,231	1,168	180	196
Kentucky	8,904	8,616	3,994	3,620	1,188	1,156	177	180
Missouri	5,206	4,212	1,631	1,340	373	316	50	37
Illinois	7,969	6,441	2,527	2,050	504	434	55	54
Indiana............	10,395	8,846	3,672	3,091	871	796	144	129
Ohio	27,462	23,224	10,790	9,157	2,667	2,349	306	268
Michigan	4,804	3,775	1,593	1,200	317	239	42	25
Wisconsin	3,201	2,339	886	653	177	127	5	13
Iowa..............	1,631	1,261	463	369	97	68	15	9
California	388	69	64	19	15	8	6	2
Minnesota	39	23	17	3	3	2	2	.
Oregon	108	40	16	5	3	.	1	1
Utah	100	94	31	22	1	3	.	.
New Mexico... ...	1,010	684	313	259	194	125	59	28
	264,742	256,480	111,416	112,648	31,243	34,403	3,653	4,499

States and Territories.	100 & upw'ds. males.	100 & upw'ds. females.	Age unknown. m.	Age unknown. fe.	Total males.	Total females.	Grand total.
Maine.............	9	4	613	207	296,745	285,068	581.813
New Hampshire ...	5	6	28	24	155,960	161,496	317,456
Vermont	4	4	26	11	159,658	153,744	313,402
Massachusetts	4	9	1,016	177	484,093	501,357	985,450

States and Territories.	100 & upw'ds. males.	females.	Age unknown. m.	fe.	Total males.	Total females.	Grand total.
Rhode Island......	.	3	15	..	70,340	70,535	143,875
Connecticut	4	2	194	62	179,884	183,215	363,099
New York	33	29	1,174	510	1,544,489	1,503,836	3,048,325
New Jersey.........	4	6	85	71	233,452	232,057	465,509
Pennsylvania......	20	31	664	446	1,142,734	1,115,426	2,258,160
Delaware	.	2	24	14	35,746	35,423	71,169
Maryland	7	10	8	6	211,187	206,756	417,943
District of Columbia	0	0	3	14	18,494	19,447	37,941
Virginia............	28	35	156	128	451,300	443,500	894,800
North Carolina.....	18	43	69	57	273,025	280,003	553,028
South Carolina	58	24	39	42	137,747	136,816	274,563
Georgia	28	27	104	94	266,233	255,339	521,572
Florida	1	1	4	1	25,705	21,498	47,203
Alabama............	10	10	57	41	219,483	207,031	426,514
Mississippi	7	11	67	62	156,287	139,431	295,718
Louisiana	9	12	253	41	141,243	114,248	255,491
Texas	11	12	170	19	84,869	69,165	154,034
Arkansas.	6	4	18	12	85,874	76,315	162,189
Tennessee	28	34	112	102	382,235	374,601	756,836
Kentucky	28	31	108	72	392,804	368,609	761,413
Missouri	12	11	80	51	312,987	279,017	592,004
Illinois	10	5	489	303	445,544	400,490	846,034
Indiana............	18	8	179	132	503,178	470,976	977,154
Ohio	23	22	349	257	1,004,117	950,933	1,955,050
Michigan	5	2	61	59	208,465	186,606	395,071
Wisconsin..........	1	1	112	80	164,351	140,405	304,756
Iowa	.	1	27	27	100,887	90,904	191,881
California	.	.	669	4	84,708	6,927	91,635
Minnesota..........	.	.	....	..	3,695	2,343	6,038
Oregon	.	.	38	27	8,138	4,949	13,087
Utah..............	.	.	....	..	6,020	5,310	11,330
New Mexico.......	19	21	142	1	31,725	29,800	61,525
	357	430	7,153	3,154	10,026,402	9,526,666	19,553,068

FREE COLORED POPULATION IN 1850.

States and Territories.	Under 1. males.	females.	1 and under 5. males.	females.	5 and under 10. males.	females.	10 and under 15. males.	females.
Maine	26	13	64	59	83	75	83	64
New Hampshire ..	7	7	22	23	30	22	24	23
Vermont.........	15	8	41	25	42	34	44	30
Massachusetts	85	114	409	440	459	493	428	433
Rhode Island.....	37	29	164	159	197	194	159	184
Connecticut	74	72	350	360	434	412	397	411
New York	582	539	2,213	2,390	2,666	2,800	2,507	2,619
New Jersey	361	358	1,302	1,395	1,484	1,579	1,498	1,421
Pennsylvania	637	748	2,897	2,911	3,286	3,417	2,900	3,121
Delaware	271	271	1,145	1,140	1,391	1,361	1,232	1,146
Maryland	1,017	998	4,422	4,502	4,950	5,131	4,516	4,582
District of Columbia	125	125	523	511	657	662	534	614
Virginia	695	717	3,403	3,288	3,924	3,911	3,633	3,609
North Carolina....	412	385	1,812	1,837	2,138	2,067	1,907	1,815
South Carolina....	77	78	571	541	695	712	653	634
Georgia..........	44	30	178	165	221	202	203	180
Florida...........	9	16	55	54	70	89	62	55
Alabama	20	29	143	143	160	144	147	154
Mississippi........	8	6	58	61	57	53	56	60
Louisiana.........	191	213	910	931	1,188	1,182	1,059	1,034
Texas	..	2	27	24	38	27	25	19
Arkansas.........	6	5	42	39	35	31	37	36
Tennessee........	81	83	418	423	483	501	440	407
Kentucky.........	101	141	545	530	673	648	501	539

States and Territories.	Under 1. males.	Under 1. females.	1 and under 5. males.	1 and under 5. females.	5 and under 10. males.	5 and under 10. females.	10 and under 15. males.	10 and under 15. females.
Missouri	31	28	110	148	136	143	110	122
Illinois	75	65	331	329	376	371	312	343
Indiana	161	155	772	737	867	915	823	765
Ohio	370	319	1,565	1,493	1,793	1,811	1,572	1,613
Michigan	39	35	177	175	176	169	133	122
Wisconsin	15	6	26	32	50	32	25	37
Iowa	3	3	18	21	29	28	17	20
California	1	2	3	1	4	5	11	20
Minnesota	..	..	..	..	..	2	3	3
Oregon	..	..	23	18	13	19	9	11
Utah	..	..	4	1	1	1	1	1
New Mexico	..	..	..	1	..	..	..	..
Total	5,576	5,600	24,743	24,902	28,806	29,246	26,061	26,247

States and Territories.	15 and under 20. males.	15 and under 20. females.	20 and under 30. males.	20 and under 30. females.	30 and under 40. males.	30 and under 40. females.	40 & under 50 males.	40 & under 50 females.
Maine	69	65	123	127	105	85	69	48
New Hampshire	22	18	41	44	32	35	26	26
Vermont	28	40	66	75	57	32	33	37
Massachusetts	381	448	944	891	704	685	472	485
Rhode Island	153	163	363	339	287	309	180	206
Connecticut	361	397	815	732	543	541	367	389
New York	2,045	2,541	4,556	5,280	3,719	3,911	2,619	2,635
New Jersey	1,174	1,183	2,018	2,101	1,525	1,538	1,049	1,000
Pennsylvania	2,397	2,975	4,607	5,787	3,480	3,792	2,471	2,589
Delaware	1,033	971	1,328	1,522	975	996	683	677
Maryland	3,396	4,015	5,437	6,816	4,344	5,273	3,030	3,625
District of Columbia	394	637	672	1,156	531	763	367	606
Virginia	2,637	2,978	4,298	5,159	2,787	3,344	2,014	2,272
North Carolina	1,520	1,520	2,195	2,581	1,250	1,574	793	1,003
South Carolina	395	495	606	812	474	635	283	356
Georgia	147	171	198	287	131	179	97	96
Florida	36	44	58	64	44	71	29	47
Alabama	115	127	142	226	89	131	95	98
Mississippi	44	38	90	70	49	56	35	41
Louisiana	704	998	1,147	1,761	900	1,474	678	975
Texas	18	24	40	34	23	23	17	19
Arkansas	24	43	43	37	39	31	41	23
Tennessee	307	364	455	497	249	339	236	277
Kentucky	396	459	634	749	492	554	460	489
Missouri	114	79	298	228	205	198	151	136
Illinois	285	292	551	533	353	277	216	198
Indiana	627	625	903	981	561	560	400	371
Ohio	1,332	1,513	2,324	2,457	1,556	1,431	980	961
Michigan	105	104	281	243	252	143	146	76
Wisconsin	27	27	81	56	86	46	26	17
Iowa	18	17	35	37	24	17	11	12
California	72	14	374	29	256	12	111	3
Minnesota	4	2	7	6	4	4	3	1
Oregon	11	10	38	15	20	9	4	5
Utah	3	2	2	2	1	2	..	1
New Mexico	1	..	7	1	5	3	4	..
Total	20,395	23,399	35,782	41,765	26,153	29,052	18,199	19,741

States and Territories.	50 and under 60. males.	50 and under 60. females.	60 and under 70. males.	60 and under 70. females.	70 and under 80. males.	70 and under 80. females.	80 & under 90. males.	80 & under 90. females.
Maine	43	47	29	30	11	13	8	4
New Hampshire	22	29	15	12	8	11	8	8
Vermont	26	27	9	15	8	10	4	5
Massachusetts	284	337	129	158	61	88	29	36
Rhode Island	83	128	58	106	40	51	15	26

States and Territories.	50 and under 60. males.	50 and under 60. females.	60 and under 70. males.	60 and under 70. females.	70 and under 80. males.	70 and under 80. females.	80 and under 90. males.	80 and under 90. females.
Connecticut	237	269	147	161	61	89	25	29
New York........	1,432	1,476	702	820	208	355	100	171
New Jersey.......	715	682	407	439	166	188	63	79
Pennsylvania......	1,467	1,513	744	790	297	357	120	152
Delaware.........	450	480	310	269	143	132	40	52
Maryland.........	2,104	2,252	1,242	1,334	503	605	175	239
District of Columbia	256	353	115	203	52	97	20	67
Virginia	1,259	1,461	794	869	349	432	137	182
North Carolina ...	628	671	337	362	176	210	89	103
South Carolina....	188	281	105	151	47	73	25	41
Georgia..........	62	99	44	67	35	44	8	13
Florida.	16	27	20	23	7	11	6	8
Alabama	63	61	43	36	18	31	13	13
Mississippi	31	33	25	25	17	9	4	6
Louisiana.........	370	683	172	420	87	156	35	87
Texas	14	9	2	2	3	1	1	2
Arkansas	20	22	12	15	12	9	3	1
Tennessee........	205	173	123	144	72	56	29	28
Kentucky.........	458	440	335	334	178	156	62	68
Missouri	108	92	64	56	23	14	5	9
Illinois	171	124	64	74	27	34	9	11
Indiana...........	346	217	166	124	57	52	16	16
Ohio	568	524	413	294	187	138	53	47
Michigan.........	78	40	30	22	10	13	1	3
Wisconsin........	15	13	8	2	3	1	3	..
Iowa............	6	5	1	5	..	2	..	1
California.........	32	4	6	..	2	..	..	..
Minnesota........	..	..	..	..	..	..	..	..
Oregon	2	..	..	..	..	..	..	..
Utah............	2	..	..	..	..	..	..	..
New Mexico......	..	..	..	..	..	..	..	..
Total..........	11,771	12,572	6,671	7,362	2,878	3,438	1,106	1,512

States and Territories.	90 & under 100. m.	90 & under 100. f.	100 & up'rds. m.	100 & up'rds. f.	Age unkn'n. m.	Age unkn'n. f.	Total. males.	Total. females.	Grand Total.
Maine	3	..	..	..	..	..	726	630	1,356
New Hampshire ..	2	2	1	..	..	..	260	260	520
Vermont.........	1	3	1	1	..	1	375	343	718
Massachusetts	7	16	3	3	29	12	4,424	4,640	9,064
Rhode Island.....	1	7	..	..	1	1	1,738	1,932	3,670
Connecticut	5	7	1	3	3	1	3,820	3,873	7,693
New York	24	44	12	14	7	22	23,452	25,617	49,069
New Jersey.......	23	28	3	12	9	9	11,798	12,012	23,810
Pennsylvania	22	60	9	15	35	30	25,369	28,257	53,626
Delaware.........	17	13	2	3	15	5	9,035	9,038	18,073
Maryland.........	45	110	11	48	..	1	35,192	39,531	74,723
District of Columbia	2	11	..	5	..	1	4,248	5,811	10,059
Virginia	51	64	20	35	1	10	26,002	28,331	54,333
North Carolina....	22	20	7	17	2	..	13,298	14,165	27,463
South Carolina....	8	13	3	7	1	..	4,131	4,829	8,960
Georgia	9	14	2	4	1	..	1,375	1,556	2,931
Florida..........	2	4	4	1	..	..	418	514	932
Alabama	5	10	3	5	..	1	1,056	1,209	2,265
Mississippi........	..	1	..	2	..	1	474	456	930
Louisiana.........	11	45	11	21	16	3	7,479	9,983	17,462
Texas	3	..	..	..	..	..	211	186	397
Arkansas	..	2	..	..	..	..	314	294	608
Tennessee........	11	5	7	1	1	4	3,117	3,305	6,422
Kentucky	18	25	6	11	4	5	4,863	5,148	10,011
Missouri	1	4	1	4	4	1	1,361	1,257	2,618
Illinois...........	5	4	1	2	1	2	2,777	2,650	5,436
Indiana..........	7	9	..	6	9	14	5,715	5,547	11,262

States and Territories.	90 & under 100. m.	f.	100 & up'rds. m.	f.	Age unkn'n. m.	f.	Total. males.	females.	Grand total.
Ohio	14	18	5	8	9	11	12,691	12,588	25,279
Michigan	..	..	1	1	2	1	1,431	1,152	2,583
Wisconsin	..	1	..	..	..	.	365	270	635
Iowa	..	..	..	..	..	..	165	168	333
California	..	..	..	..	..	..	872	90	962
Minnesota	..	..	..	..	..	..	21	18	39
Oregon	..	..	..	..	..	..	120	87	207
Utah	..	..	..	..	..	..	14	10	24
New Mexico	..	..	..	..	..	..	17	5	22
Total	319	540	114	229	150	136	208,724	225,771	434,495

SLAVE POPULATION OF 1850, CLASSED ACCORDING TO AGE AND SEX.

	Under 1. males.	females.	1 under 5. males.	females.	5 and under 10. males.	females.	10 & under 15. males.	females.
New Jersey	..	..	..	..	1	2	2	2
Delaware	27	32	155	148	223	178	203	194
Maryland	1,243	1,203	5,961	5,931	6,902	6,712	6,963	6,400
District of Columbia	30	41	165	184	208	287	239	341
Virginia	5,341	5,814	32,419	32,687	35,356	34,897	33,883	32,331
North Carolina	4,022	4,064	21,891	22,043	23,400	23,536	20,711	19,830
South Carolina	4,450	4,744	27,019	28,229	27,069	28,131	24,890	24,825
Georgia	4,730	4,889	27,984	28,070	28,941	28,711	26,834	26,749
Florida	463	451	2,840	2,918	2,889	2,874	2,507	2,442
Alabama	3,992	4,118	25,471	25,687	25,724	25,671	23,190	22,260
Mississippi	3,611	3,788	22,705	23,417	23,240	23,106	20,666	19,812
Louisiana	2,349	2,591	14,260	14,814	14,874	15,009	13,865	13,410
Texas	705	724	4,406	4,366	4,356	4,504	4,152	4,091
Arkansas	540	619	3,475	3,572	3,480	3,546	3,389	3,179
Tennessee	3,452	3,609	17,620	18,075	18,647	19,087	17,889	17,252
Kentucky	3,023	3,245	14,952	15,311	16,761	16,828	15,602	15,203
Missouri	1,365	1,334	6,420	6,684	7,090	6,845	6,492	6,358
Utah	..	..	2	3	2	1	1	3
Total	39,343	41,266	227,745	232,140	239,163	239,925	221,480	214,712

	15 and under 20. males.	females.	20 and under 30. males.	females.	30 and under 40. males.	females.	40 & under 50. males.	females.
New Jersey	5	2	10	1	..	..	2	9
Delaware	219	151	212	213	67	84	31	43
Maryland	5,643	5,466	8,092	7,443	4,269	4,500	2,953	2,931
District of Columbia	207	319	239	325	127	245	91	182
Virginia	25,584	24,659	39,991	36,974	25,435	24,240	18,416	17,514
North Carolina	15,710	15,800	23,969	23,536	13,687	13,927	8,444	8,631
South Carolina	20,521	21,875	31,745	33,472	20,583	22,938	13,138	14,543
Georgia	21,865	23.072	33,959	34,590	19,146	20,427	12,100	13,006
Florida	1.974	2,087	3,878	3,681	2,277	2,312	1,344	1,340
Alabama	18,989	19,871	31,658	31,208	19,635	19,514	11,433	11,779
Mississippi	16,611	17,087	29,915	30,021	18,565	18,986	9,996	9,933
Louisiana	11,151	11,799	26,047	23,971	20,250	18,415	12,690	10,550
Texas	3,175	3,442	5,585	5,683	3,131	3,449	1,750	1,878
Arkansas	2,745	2,765	4,930	4,684	2,528	2,612	1,415	1,421
Tennessee	14,004	14,621	21,709	21,064	11,370	11,984	6,550	7,115
Kentucky	12,370	12,695	19,031	17,627	10,325	10,422	6,520	7,156
Missouri	5,295	5,400	8,623	7,988	3,902	4,300	2,278	2,779
Utah	1	2	2	4	2	..	1	..
Total	176,169	181,113	289,595	282,615	175,300	178,355	109,152	110,780

	50 and under 60.		60 and under 70.		70 and under 80.		80 & under 90.	
	males.	females.	males.	females.	males.	females.	males.	females.
New Jersey	21	38	27	42	17	31	9	7
Delaware.........	20	22	8	11	6	7	..	2
Maryland	1,926	1,850	1,187	1,175	549	510	190	196
District of Columbia	55	129	44	70	12	29	4	8
Virginia	12,138	10,850	7,614	6,981	3,028	3,264	958	1,196
North Carolina....	6,814	6,327	3,637	3,606	1,520	1,665	570	658
South Carolina....	8,771	8,750	5,426	5,502	2,008	2,022	613	638
Georgia.	6,584	6,560	4,585	4,544	1,399	1,430	480	519
Florida..........	895	798	474	397	141	126	45	45
Alabama.	6,368	6,030	3,774	3,451	1,068	959	338	338
Mississippi........	4,854	4,390	3,139	2,839	825	727	288	243
Louisiana	5,955	4,864	3,032	2,388	937	771	319	225
Texas	898	829	373	332	100	93	40	34
Arkansas	653	580	378	339	75	88	30	24
Tennessee........	4,421	4,468	2,050	2,137	719	833	233	287
Kentucky	3,744	3,985	1,819	2,123	621	913	198	255
Missouri	1,136	1,291	535	632	141	220	63	65
Utah..............	1	1	..	..	..	..	..	..
Total..........	65,254	61,762	38,102	36,569	13,166	13,688	4,378	4,740

	90 & under 100.		100 & over.		Unknown.		Total.		Grand Total.
	m.	f.	m.	f.	m.	f.	males.	females.	
New Jersey	2	5	..	..	..	1	96	140	236
Delaware	..	..	1	1	..	..	1,174	1,116	2,290
Maryland.........	41	74	24	31	1	2	45,944	44,424	90,368
District of Columbia	1	3	..	2	..	..	1,422	2,265	3,687
Virginia	263	334	87	184	49	41	240,562	231,966	472,528
North Carolina....	132	202	66	98	8	14	144,581	143,967	288,548
South Carolina....	154	200	81	86	1,288	1,303	187,756	197,228	384,984
Georgia.	142	162	81	79	27	17	188,857	192,825	381,682
Florida..........	22	21	15	14	40	..	19,804	19,506	39,310
Alabama	97	93	65	61	1	..	171,804	171,040	342,844
Mississippi........	85	85	47	73	127	119	154,674	154,626	309,878
Louisiana	81	59	57	66	7	3	125,874	118,935	244,809
Texas............	12	12	6	10	11	14	28,700	29,461	58,161
Arkansas	11	6	9	5	..	1	23,658	23,442	47,100
Tennessee........	82	98	31	47	3	2	118,780	120,679	239,459
Kentucky.........	61	94	28	53	8	8	105,063	105,018	210,981
Missouri	25	25	8	9	11	8	43,484	43,938	87,422
Utah..............	..	..	..	..	..	..	12	14	26
Total..........	1,211	1,473	606	819	1,581	1,533	1,602,245	1,601,490	3,204,313

TABLE SHOWING THE AGGREGATE NUMBER OF WHITES, FREE COLORED PERSONS, AND SLAVES IN THE SEVERAL STATES AND TERRITORIES, ON THE 1ST JUNE, 1850:—

	WHITES.			FREE COLORED.		
States & Territories.	Males.	Females.	Total.	Males.	Females.	Total.
Maine...............	296,745	285,068	581,813	726	630	1,356
New Hampshire ...	155,960	161,496	317,456	260	260	528
Vermont	159,653	153,744	313,402	375	343	714
Massachusetts	484,093	501,357	985,450	4,424	4,640	9,060
Rhode Island......	70,340	73,535	143,875	1,738	1,932	3,670
Connecticut	179,884	183,215	363,099	3,820	3,873	7,693
New York	1,544,489	1,503,836	3,048,325	23,452	25,617	49,069
New Jersey	233,452	232,057	465,509	11,798	12,012	23,810
Pennsylvania	1,142,734	1,115,426	2,258,160	25,369	28,257	53,626
Delaware	35,746	35,423	71,169	9,035	9,038	18,073
Maryland	211,187	206,756	417,943	35,192	39,531	74,723
District of Columbia	18,494	19,447	37,941	4,248	5,811	10,059

States & Territories.	Whites. Males.	Whites. Females.	Whites. Total.	Free Colored. Males.	Free Colored. Females.	Free Colored. Total.
Virginia	451,300	443,500	894,800	26,002	28,331	54,333
North Carolina	273,025	280,003	553,028	13,298	14,165	27,463
South Carolina	137,747	136,816	274,563	4,131	4,829	8,960
Georgia	266,233	255,339	521,572	1,375	1,556	2,931
Florida	25.705	21,498	47,203	418	514	932
Alabama	219,483	207,031	426.514	1,056	1,209	2,265
Mississippi	156,287	139,431	295,718	474	456	930
Louisiana	141,243	114,248	255,491	7,479	9,983	17,462
Texas	84,869	69,165	154,034	211	186	397
Arkansas	85,874	76,315	162,189	314	294	608
Tennessee	382.235	374,601	756,836	3,117	3,305	6,422
Kentucky	392,804	368,609	761,413	4,863	5,148	10,011
Missouri	312,987	279,017	592,004	1,361	1,257	2,618
Illinois	445,544	400,490	846,034	2,777	2,659	5,436
Indiana	503,178	470,976	977,154	5,715	5,547	11,262
Ohio	1,004,117	950,933	1,955,050	12,691	12,588	25,279
Michigan	208,465	186,606	395,071	1,431	1,152	2,583
Wisconsin	164,351	140,405	304,756	365	270	635
Iowa	100,887	90,904	191,881	165	168	383
California	84,708	6,927	91,635	872	90	962
Minnesota	3,695	2,343	6,038	21	18	39
Oregon	8,138	4,949	13,087	120	87	207
Utah	6,020	5,310	11,330	14	10	24
New Mexico	31,725	29,800	61,525	17	5	22
Total	10,026,402	9,523,666	19,553,068	208,724	225,771	434,495

States and Territories.	Slaves. Males.	Slaves. Females.	Slaves. Total.	Grand total.
Maine	......	......	......	583,169
New Hampshire	......	......	......	317,976
Vermont	......	......	......	314,120
Massachusetts	......	......	......	994,514
Rhode Island	......	......	......	147,545
Connecticut	......	......	......	370,792
New York	......	......	......	3,097,394
New Jersey	96	140	236	489,555
Pennsylvania	......	......	......	2,311,786
Delaware	1,174	1,116	2,290	91,532
Maryland	45,944	44,424	90,368	583,084
District of Columbia	1,422	2,265	3,687	51,687
Virginia	240,562	231,966	472,528	1,421,661
North Carolina	144,581	143,967	288,548	869,039
South Carolina	187,756	197,228	384,984	668,507
Georgia	188,857	192,825	381,682	906,185
Florida	19,804	19,506	39,310	87,445
Alabama	171,804	171,040	342,844	771,623
Mississippi	154,674	154,626	*309,878	606,526
Louisiana	125,874	118,935	244,809	517,762
Texas	28,700	29,461	58,161	212,392
Arkansas	23,658	23,442	47,100	209.897
Tennessee	118,780	120,679	239.459	1,002,717
Kentucky	105,063	105,918	210,981	982,405
Missouri	43,484	43,938	87,422	682,044
Illinois	......	......	......	851,470
Indiana	......	......	......	988,417
Ohio	......	......	......	1,980,329

* See census of Mississippi.

States and Territories.	SLAVES. Males.	Females.	Total.	Grand total.
Michigan	......	......	......	397,654
Wisconsin.........	......	......	......	305,391
Iowa	......	......	......	192,214
California	......	......	......	92,597
Minnesota	......	......	......	6,077
Oregon.............	......	......	......	13,294
Utah...............	......	......	.....	11,380
New Mexico.......	......	.. ...	......	61,547
Total...........	1,602,245	1,601,490	3,204,313	23,191,876

The States of Texas and California, and the Territories of New Mexico and Utah, have been acquired since the census of 1840. Though the accession thus acquired to the population is not precisely known, there are authentic data for a near approximation to it. Texas was annexed to the United States in 1845; and two years afterwards, by an official census, its population was 143,205. Supposing its increase to have been nearly as great in these two years when annexation was expected, as it was in the five years succeeding, then its population in 1845 must have been about 100,000. The increase in five years, exclusive of emigrants from the United States, estimating it at 15 per cent, would make the accession from this source 115,000.

The population of New Mexico in 1850 that was exclusively born in the Territory or some other part of Spanish America, was 60,775; the whole of which may be regarded as a further accession to the population of the United States.

Nothing can be added from Utah, it being exclusively in the possession of the Indians before it was occupied by the Mormons.

The population in New or Upper California was, according to Humboldt, 15,600 in 1803; and from the previous rate of its increase, he estimated that it doubled in twelve years. Yet by a census in 1831, it was only 22,995—showing a reduction in the rate of increase to about 50 per cent in twenty-eight years, owing, doubtless, to the troubles consequent on the rupture with the mother country. At this rate, the population at the time of the cession in 1848, would have been about 30,000, but its amount seems to have been considerably less—1st. Because of the 92,507 returned on the gross population in 1850, 62,576 were born in the United States, and 21,802 were born in foreign countries; the whole of the former and a considerable part of the latter had migrated thither between 1848 and June, 1850, attracted by the gold mines discovered in 1848. 2dly. The whole number of females in California in 1850, according to the census, was 7,799. There is no satisfactory reason for supposing that the number of the males much exceeded that of the females. But, supposing it to have been double, the whole population would then be, exclusive of emigrants from the United States, 23,397.

The result of the accessions from these sources in 1850 would be 115,090 + 60,778 + 23,397 = 199,192, which, for the sake of round numbers, we will call 200,000.

The slave population, which from 1830 to 1840 had increased 33 per cent, had, from 1840 to 1850, increased 28.8 per cent—showing a greater ratio in the last ten years of five per cent. A part of this difference admits of a ready explanation. The whole number of slaves in 1850 was increased by the acquisition of Texas; while in 1840 the number had been diminished by the migrations of slaveholders of the United States to that country. The number in Texas at the time of annexation (1845) was about 21,000, which by natural multiplication would have increased to somewhat more than 35,000. This double operation of Texas on the slave population is sufficient for nearly 2½ per cent on the ratio of increase. The residue is to be referred to several circumstances; there have been few cases of manumission in the last ten years, owing partly to a change of public sentiment on this subject in the slaveholding States, and partly to an extension by State legislation of the policy of prohibiting it. The same circumstances contribute to explain the falling off in the increase of the free colored class in the last ten years, from 20.88 per cent to 12.47 per cent. Another cause of the greater increase of slaves is a diminished mortality between 1840 and 1850, both because the Asiatic cholera and yellow fever had been less prevalent in that period, and because there was a greater proportion who had become acclimated in the South. That this class of our population have been better cared for, or have experienced more frequent or more efficient medical treatment, would also contribute to explain the difference; but I am aware of no facts that would much support such an hypothesis.

The males and females of each class were thus distributed according to age:—

1. WHITE POPULATION.

	Males. Per ct.	Females. Per ct.		Males. Per ct.	Females. Per ct.
Those under 5....	14.68	14 95	50 and under 60....	4.97	4.83
5 and under 10....	13.69	13.98	60 " 70....	2.64	2.69
10 " 15....	12.23	12.35	70 " 80....	1.11	1.18
15 " 20....	10.39	11.42	80 " 90....	0.31	0.36
20 " 30....	18.64	18.46	90 " 100....	0.04	0.05
30 " 40....	12.85	11.84	100 and upwards.....	0.04	0.05
40 " 50....	8.35	7.86	Age unknown........	0.07	0.03
				100.00	100.00

2. FREE COLORED.

	Males. Per ct.	Females. Per ct.		Males. Per ct.	Females. Per ct.
Under 5....	14.53	13.51	50 and under 60....	5.64	5.57
5 and under 10....	13.80	12.95	60 " 70....	3.20	3.26
10 " 15....	12.49	11.63	70 " 80....	1.38	1.52
15 " 20....	9.77	10.37	80 " 90....	0.53	0.67
20 " 30....	17.14	18.05	90 " 100....	0.15	0.24
30 " 40....	12.53	12.88	100 and upwards.....	00.5	0.10
40 " 50....	8.72	8.74	Age unknown.... ...	00.7	00.6
				100.00	100.00

3. SLAVES.

	Males. Per ct.	Females. Per ct.		Males. Per ct.	Females. Per ct.
Under 5....	16.67	17.07	50 and under 60....	4.07	3.85
5 and under 10....	14.92	14.98	60 " 70....	2.38	2.28
10 " 15....	13.82	13.40	70 " 80....	0.82	0.85
15 " 20....	10.99	11.31	80 " 90....	0.27	0.30
20 " 30....	18.07	17.64	90 " 100 ...	0.08	0.09
30 " 40....	10.94	11.14	100 and upwards.....	0.04	0.05
40 " 50....	6.81	6.92	Age unknown........	0.12	0.11
				100.00	100.00

As the proportion of children under ten was less in 1840 than it had been in 1830 in all the three classes, so was it less in 1850 than it had been in 1840. Their proportion under that age was—

	In 1840.	In 1850.
Of the whites	31.63 per cent.	28.00 per cent.
Free colored	28.88 "	27.36 "
Slaves	33.93 "	31.60 "

This proportionate diminution of children in the class of whites, may be caused by the greater delay of marriage, an increase of celibacy from any cause, and it may in part proceed from an increased mortality among children, from a greater number having been transported to less healthy regions. It certainly is affected by the increased number of immigrants, who have a larger proportion of deaths. But in the class of slaves, only the second cause, of a greater number removing to a less healthy climate, seems likely to have any influence, unless some gradual and unseen change of manners and sentiments with them also produces postponement of marriage.

The population in the slaveholding States is distributed among the three classes, as follows:—

States and Territories.	Whole population.	Whites.	Free colored.	Slaves.	Per centage. Whites.	F. col.	Slaves.
Delaware	91,532	71,169	18,073	2,290	77.7	19.07	02.05
Maryland	583,083	417,943	74,723	90,368	71.7	12.08	15.05
District of Columbia	51,687	37,941	10,059	3,687	73.4	19.04	07.01
Virginia	1,421,661	894,800	54,333	472,528	62.9	03.08	33.02
North Carolina	869,039	553,028	27,463	288.548	63.6	03.01	33.02
South Carolina	668,507	274,563	8,960	384,984	41.0	01.03	57.06
Georgia	906,185	521,572	2,931	381,682	57.5	00.03	42.01
Florida	87,445	47,203	932	39,310	54.0	01.00	45.00
Alabama	771,623	426,514	2,265	342,844	54.0	01.00	45.00
Mississippi	606,526	295,718	930	309.878	55.3	00.03	44.04
Louisiana	517,762	255,491	17,462	244,809	49.3	03.04	47.03
Texas	212,592	154,034	397	58,161	72.4	00.02	27.04
Arkansas	209,897	162,189	608	47,100	77.3	00.03	22.04
Tennessee	1,002,717	756,836	6,422	239,459	75.5	00.06	23.09
Kentucky	982,405	761,413	10,011	210,981	77.5	01.00	21.05
Missouri	682,044	592,004	2,618	87,422	86.8	00.04	12.08
Total	9,664,656	6,222,418	238,737	3,204,051	64.9	02.46	33.15
The distribution in this class of States in 1840, was					63.41	2.92	33.67

From which it appears that the whites in the slaveholding States have continued to gain on both the colored classes, though the gain of the one and the loss of the other is not quite one per cent. But in seven of the States—North Carolina, South Carolina, Georgia, Alabama, Arkansas, Tennessee, and Kentucky—the slave population has gained somewhat on the whites.

CHAPTER II.

PROGRESS OF THE POPULATION IN EACH STATE, AND IN THE UNION, IN SIXTY YEARS.

THE POPULATION OF EACH STATE AND TERRITORY, AS EXHIBITED BY SEVEN ENUMERATIONS IN SIXTY YEARS, WITH THE DECENNIAL INCREASE OF EACH.

								DECENNIAL INCREASE.					
	1790.	1800.	1810.	1820.	1830.	1840.	1850.	1800.	1810.	1820.	1830.	1840.	1850.
Maine............	96,540	151,719	228,705	298,335	399,455	501,793	583,169	57.16	50.74	30.45	33 89	25.62	16.22
New Hampshire...	141,899	183,762	214,360	244,161	269,328	284,574	317,976	29 50	16.65	13.90	10.03	5.66	11.73
Vermont..........	85,416	154,465	217,713	235,764	280,652	291,948	314,120	80 08	40.95	8.29	19.04	4.02	7.59
Massachusetts.....	378,717	423,245	472,040	523,287	610,408	737,699	994,514	11.76	11 53	10.88	16 65	20.82	34.81
Rhode Island	69,110	69,122	77,031	83,059	97,199	108,830	147.545	0.01	11.44	7.83	17.02	11.97	35.57
Connecticut.......	238,141	251,002	262,042	275,202	297,675	309,978	370,792	5.40	4.40	5.02	8.17	4.13	19.62
	1,009,823	1,233,315	1,471,801	1,639,808	1,954,717	2,234,822	2,234,822	22.13	19.34	12.77	17.77	14.33	22.07
New York........	340,120	586,756	959,049	1,372,812	1,918,608	2.428,921	3,097,394	72.51	63.45	43.14	39.76	26.60	27.52
New Jersey.......	184,139	211,949	245,555	277,575	320,823	373,306	489,555	15.10	15.86	13.04	15.58	16.36	31.14
Pennsylvania......	434,373	602,365	810,091	1,049,458	1,348,233	1,724,033	2,311,786	38.67	34.49	29.55	28.47	27.87	34.09
Delaware.........	59,096	64,273	72,674	72,749	76,748	78,085	91,532	8.76	13.07	0.01	5.50	1.74	17.22
Maryland.........	319,728	341,548	380,546	407,350	447,040	470,019	583,034	6.82	11.42	7.04	9.74	5.14	24.04
Dis. of Columbia ..	......	14,093	24,023	33,039	39,834	43,712	51,687	....	70.45	37.53	20.57	9.74	18.24
	1,337,456	1,820,984	2,491,938	3,212,983	4,151,286	5,118,076	6,624,988	36.15	36.85	28.77	29.20	23.29	29.44
Virginia..........	748,308	380,200	974,622	1,065,379	1,211,405	1,239,797	1,421,661	17.63	10.73	9.31	13.70	2.34	14.67
North Carolina	393,751	478,103	555,500	638,829	737,987	753,419	869,039	21.42	16.19	15.09	15.52	2.09	15.35
South Carolina	249,073	345,591	415,115	502,741	581,185	594,398	668,507	38.75	20.12	21.11	15.60	2.28	12.47
Georgia	82,548	162,101	252,433	340,987	516,823	691,392	906,185	96.37	55.71	35.08	51.57	33.78	31.07
Florida	......	......	......	......	34,730	54,477	87,445	....	....	....	....	56.86	60.52
	1,473,680	1,865,995	2,197,670	2,547,936	3,082,130	3,333,483	3,952,837	26.62	17.77	15.94	20.96	8.16	18.58

PROGRESS OF THE POPULATION IN EACH STATE, AND IN THE UNION, IN SIXTY YEARS.—(CONTINUED.)

THE POPULATION OF EACH STATE AND TERRITORY, AS EXHIBITED BY SEVEN ENUMERATIONS IN SIXTY YEARS, WITH THE DECENNIAL INCREASE OF EACH.								DECENNIAL INCREASE.					
	1790.	1800.	1810.	1820.	1830.	1840.	1850.	1800.	1810.	1820.	1830.	1840.	1850.
Alabama	......	......	*144,317	......	309,527	590,756	771,623	....	....	....	142.00	90.86	30.62
Mississippi	......	8,850	40,352	75,448	136,621	375,651	606,526	....	355.95	86.97	81.08	174.96	61.46
Louisiana	......	......	76,556	153,407	215,739	352,411	517,762	....	....	100.39	40.63	63.35	46.92
Texas	......	......	......	......	......	......	212,592	....	....	....	....	....	....
Arkansas	......	......	......	14,273	30,388	97,574	209,897	....	....	....	112.95	221.09	115 12
Tennessee	35,791	105,602	261,727	422,813	681,904	829,210	1,002,717	195.05	147.84	61.55	61.28	21.60	20.92
	35,791	114,452	378,635	810,258	1,374,179	2,245,602	3,321,117	219.78	230.82	113.99	69.60	63.41	47.89
Missouri	......	......	20,845	66,586	140,455	383,702	682,044	....	....	219.43	110.94	173.18	77.75
Kentucky	73,077	220,955	406,511	564,317	687,917	779,828	982,405	202.35	83.98	38.82	21.90	13.36	25.98
Ohio	......	45,365	230,760	581,434	937,903	1,519,467	1,980,329	....	403.67	151.92	61.30	62.00	30.33
Indiana	......	4,875	24,520	147,178	343,031	685,866	988,416	....	402.67	500.24	133.07	99.94	44.11
Illinois	......	......	12,282	55,211	157,445	476,183	851,470	....	....	349.30	185.17	202.44	78.81
Michigan	......	......	4,762	8,896	31,639	212,267	397,654	....	...	86.80	255.65	570.90	87.34
Wisconsin	......	......	......	......	......	30,945	305,391	....	....	....	....	....	886.88
Iowa	......	......	......	......	......	43,112	192,214	....	....	....	....	....	345.85
	73,077	271,195	699,680	1,423,622	2,298,390	4,131,370	6,379,923	271.11	158.00	103.47	61.45	79.75	54.43
California	......	......	......	......	......	......	92,597	....	....	....	....	....	....
Minnesota	......	......	......	......	......	......	6,077	....	....	....	....	....	....
New Mexico	......	......	......	......	......	......	61,547	....	....	....	....	....	....
Oregon	......	......	......	......	......	......	13,294	....	....	....	....	....	....
Utah	......	......	......	......	......	......	11,380	....	....	....	....	....	....
	......	......	......	......	......	......	184,895	....	....	....	....	....	....
Aggregate	3,929,827	5,305,925	7,239,814	9,654,596	12,866,020	17,069,453	23,191,876	35.01	36.45	33.35	33.26	32.67	35.87

* This number exceeds by 16,416 that recently published at the census office which has followed the first official statement of the census, whereas the number here given conforms to a later official statement. (See *ante*, page 32.)

THE DECENNIAL INCREASE OF EACH OF THE GREAT LOCAL DIVISIONS IN SIXTY YEARS.

INCREASE OF POPULATION FROM AUGUST 1, 1790.

Local Divisions.	10 Years.	20 Years.	30 Years.	40 Years.	50 Years.	60 Years
1. New England States..	122.4	145.8	164.4	193.6	221.3	270 2
2. Middle States with District of Columbia....	136.2	186.3	240.2	310.4	382.7	495.4
3. Southern States......	126.6	149.1	172.9	209.1	226.1	268.2
4. Southwestern States..	319.8	1,058.0	2,264.0	3,839.0	6,174.0	9,279.0
5. Northwestern States..	371.6	857.5	1,948.0	3.145.0	5,654.0	8,730.0
Total of the U. States..	135.0	184.2	245.3	327.4	434.5	490.1

THE DISTRIBUTION OF THE POPULATION INTO THE THREE CLASSES OF WHITES, FREE PERSONS OF COLOR, AND SLAVES, WITH THE DECENNIAL INCREASE OF EACH CLASS.

	1790.	1800.	1810.	1820.
Whites..................	3,172,464	4,304,489	5,862,004	7,861,937
Free colored	59,466	108,395	186,446	233,524
Slaves.	697,897	893,041	1,191,364	1,538,038
Total free	3,231,930	4,412,884	6,048,450	8,195,461
Total colored	757,363	1,001,436	1,377,810	1,771,562

	1830.	1840.	1850.
Whites..................	10,537,378	14,195,695	19,553,068
Free colored	319.599	386,303	434,495
Slaves..................	2,009,043	2,487,455	3,204,313
Total free	10,856,977	14,581,998	19,987,563
Total colored	2,328,642	2,873,758	3,638,808

DECENNIAL INCREASE.

	1800.	1810.	1820.	1830.	1840.	1850.
Whites..........	35.68	36.18	34.12	34.03	34.72	37.74
Free colored......	82.28	72.00	25.25	36.86	20.87	12.47
Slaves	28.1	33.04	29.10	30.62	23.81	28.82
Total free	97.72	37.06	35.05	32.47	34.31	37.07
Total colored ..	32.23	37.58	28.59	31.45	23.41	26.62

THE RELATIVE PROPORTION OF THE THREE CLASSES AT EACH CENSUS FROM 1790 TO 1850.

	1790.	1800.	1810.	1820.	1830.	1840.	1850.
Whites........	80.7	81.1	81.0	81.5	81.9	83.1	84.3
Free colored ...	1.5	2.1	2.6	2.5	2.5	2.3	1.9
Slaves	17.8	16.8	16.4	16.0	15.6	14.6	13.8
Total.......	100	100	100	100	100	100	100

By which the whites have gained and the colored population have lost 3.6 per cent in sixty years, and the free population have gained and the slaves have lost 4 per cent.

CHAPTER III.

PROPORTION BETWEEN THE SEXES.

The seventh census exhibits the same preponderance as its predecessors, of males until the age of 70, with the single exception of the class from 15 to 20, in which, as well as in the census of 1830 and 1840, there is an excess of females of about 5 per cent. In the census of 1850 the difference of the sexes between those two ages is only about $2\frac{1}{2}$ per cent. This concurrence in three different enumerations indicates some general cause for the exception. Can that cause be a greater mortality of males at that age, or is a portion of the females of more than 20 placed in this class? So far as this question is affected by immigration, it tends to increase the proportion of males, as the male immigrants exceed the female at every age. In this census as well as the preceding, after the age of 70 the females exceed the males until the age of 100 is passed, when the males again preponderate. But we could not safely deduce any general law from this last exception, unless we know the several places of birth in these rare cases of longevity.

The number of females for every 100 males in the last census—

Of the white population is..........................	95.0
Of the free colored	108.2
Of the slaves...	99.9

This showing an excess of males in the whites, an excess of females in the free colored, and an equality of the two in the slaves.

In both classes of the colored population the females exceed the males in those who are under one year of age, who are between one and five, and those who are between five and ten. Thus:—

	Free Colored.		Slaves.	
	Males.	Females.	Males.	Females.
Children under 1 year............	5,576	5,600	39,343	41,266
Children between 1 and 5........	24,743	24,902	227,745	232,140
Children between 5 and 10	28,816	29,246	239,163	239,925
Total under 10.................	59,125	59,748	496,251	513,331

Showing an excess of females under ten in both the colored classes of something more that 1 per cent.

In this respect the last census differs from those of 1830 and 1840, in which the males under 10, both of the free colored class and the slaves, exceed the females. In the census of 1820, also, the males in both classes of the colored children under 14 exceed the females. If the census should, from its supposed greater accuracy, be deemed sufficient to overrule the preceding enumerations, a deviation from what appears to be a general law as to sex, seems to merit further inquiry. Supposing the fact established, is it referable to race, or must its cause remain among the unsolved problems of physiology respecting sex?

The white males which, according to the census of 1840, exceed the females 209,424, by the last census exceed them by more than twice the amount—499,736. In like manner the females of the free colored class which in 1840 exceeded the males 7,271, by the last census exceed them 17,044. This increased excess of white males was caused by the great increase of white immigrants, and the increased excess of free colored females was caused by the greater emigration of that class, of which emigrants by far the larger part are males.

CHAPTER IV.

IMMIGRATION.

REGULAR and accurate returns from the custom-house of the number of our foreign immigrants have given us more authentic information on this interesting branch of statistics than we ever before possessed. Their number within the last ten years has not only, as hitherto, been greater than in the preceding decennial term, but the ratio of increase has far exceeded that exhibited by the census of 1840. Between 1830 and 1840 the immigration was not estimated at half a million, and was 136 per cent more than that exhibited by the census of 1830, but between 1840 and 1850 it had reached to between three and four times that amount, as may be seen in the following table:—

	Immigrants.		Immigrants.
To June 1st, 1841..........	83,504	To June 1st, 1846	147,651
" 1842..........	101,107	" 1847	225,182
" 1843..........	75,159	To Sept. 1st, 1848	296,387
" 1844..........	74,607	" 1849	296,208
" 1845..........	102,415	To June 1st, 1850	223,984
Total..........			1,621,275

Taking the average of the immigrants for three years, they were distributed, according to sex and age, in centennial proportions, as follows:—

Males................per cent	58	Number between 20 and 30....	37
Females	42	" " 30 and 40....	16
		" upwards of 40.......	10
	100	" Ages unknown.......	1.5
Number under 10 years of age .	15		100
" between 10 and 20 ...	20.5		

It further appears that although the number of female immigrants is less than that of the males, the proportion of the former within the productive ages, is 25 per cent of the whole number, which exceeds the proportion in the whole white population by 5 to 4. This fact, and the much smaller proportion under ten years of age, (less than one-half,) may compensate, or more than compensate, the supposed greater mortality of foreigners in the first years of their new residence.

For the first time the late census has enumerated the persons in the United States who were not natives. They amounted on the 1st of June, 1850, to 2,240,535, about one-ninth of the white population. Of these—

The natives of Ireland were..........	961,719
" England, Scotland, and Wales	379,093
" British America..........	147,711
" Germany, Prussia, Austria, and Switzerland	598,078
" France..........	54,069
" Sweden, Norway, Denmark, and Russia..........	19,489
" Holland and Belgium	4,161
" Mexico..........	13,317
" Spain, Portugal, and Italy	8,032
" West Indies..........	5,772
" Other countries, including those whose places of birth were unknown	62,411
Total..........	2,240,535

From which it appears that of the foreigners in the United States more than two-thirds are natives of the British dominions, and that more than two-thirds of the remaining third are Germans.

They are very unequally distributed among the States, the Southern and South-western States scarcely containing a fifteenth part, as may be seen by the following table:—

NUMBER OF ALIENS BY BIRTH IN THE DIFFERENT STATES AND TERRITORIES.

State	Number	State	Number
In New York	651,801	In California	22,358
Pennsylvania	294,871	Iowa	21,232
Ohio	218,512	Texas	16,774
Massachusetts	160,909	New Hampshire	13,571
Illinois	110,593	South Carolina	8,662
Wisconsin	106,695	Alabama	7,638
Missouri	72,474	Georgia	5,907
Louisiana	66,413	Tennessee	5,740
New Jersey	58,364	Delaware	5,211
Maryland	55,288	District of Columbia	4,967
Michigan	54,852	Mississippi	4,958
Indiana	54,425	Florida	2,757
Connecticut	37,473	North Carolina	2,524
Vermont	32,831	New Mexico	2,063
Maine	31,456	Minnesota	2,048
Kentucky	29,189	Utah	1,990
Rhode Island	23,111	Arkansas	1,628
Virginia	22,394	Oregon	1,159

But great as is the foreign immigration to the United States, yet with the roving and locomotive propensities of the American people, their emigration from their own respective States to other States is much greater. By the last census it is found that the number of immigrants who are natives of other States is more than four millions, and that, widely separated as are many of the States by distance, emigrants from each State contribute to the population of every other. Though every State has gained and lost inhabitants by this migratory habit, the oldest and first settled States have been the greatest losers, and the new States of course have proportionally gained, as may be seen by the following table:—

DISTRIBUTION OF THE NATIVE FREE POPULATION, WHITE AND COLORED.

States and Territories.	Residing in their native State.	Residing in other States.	Immigrants from other States.
Maine	517,117	67,193	34,012
New Hampshire	261,591	109,878	42,636
Vermont	232,086	145,655	48,880
Massachusetts	695,236	199,582	134,830
Rhode Island	102,641	43,300	21,658
Connecticut	292,653	154,891	39,872
New York	2,151,196	547,218	288,100
New Jersey	385,429	133,381	45,012
Pennsylvania	1,844,672	422,055	169,947
Delaware	72,351	31,965	11,617
Maryland	400,594	127,799	38,322
District of Columbia	24,967	7,269	17,989
Virginia	872,923	388,059	53,231
North Carolina	556,248	283,077	21,502
South Carolina	262,160	186,479	12,653
Georgia	402,666	122,954	115,413
Florida	20,563	4,734	24,757
Alabama	237,542	83,388	182,490

States and Territories.	Residing in their native State.	Residing in other States.	Immigrants from other States.
Mississippi	140,885	......	150,229
Louisiana	145,474	14,779	60,447
Texas	49,160	2,481	87,893
Arkansas	63,206	10,916	97,139
Tennessee	585,084	241,606	170,577
Kentucky	601,764	257,613	139,117
Missouri	277,604	37,824	243,222
Illinois	343,618	45,889	393,313
Indiana	541,079	92,038	390,313
Ohio	1,219,432	295,453	538,124
Michigan	140,618	12,409	200,943
Wisconsin	63,015	3,775	134,897
Iowa	50,380	6,358	120,240
California	6,602	96	63,008
Minnesota Territory	1,334	949 (Territories combined)	2,673
New Mexico Territory	58,421		840
Oregon Territory	3,175		8,817
Utah Territory	1,381		7,974
Total	13,624,897	4,112,681	....

In the preceding numbers there is some variance between the different publications made at the Census-Office. I have followed Mr. De Bow's Compendium as the safest guide.

The last column in the preceding table, which shows the number of free persons who have migrated from the respective States of their birth to other States, should be precisely equal in its total number to the preceding column, but there is a variance of about 1½ per cent by reason of errors which, in such a multiplicity of enumerations, it is almost impossible to avoid.

CHAPTER V.

THE PROBABILITIES OF LIFE.

In executing the act of Congress for taking the Seventh Census, it was intended to have direct evidence of the rate of annual mortality in the United States, as an enumeration was ordered of all persons who had died within the year preceding June, 1850; but that part of the census has been so imperfectly executed as to be valueless. So many deaths have been omitted by the carelessness of the census takers, or rather of their informers, as to show a degree of salubrity such as has never been reached in any country; nor is there that regularity in the errors which would enable us to estimate the comparative mortality of the States—some of the least healthy showing by the returns the smallest number of annual deaths.

The details of the census of 1850, compared with those of the census of 1840, fortunately afford us materials for making this interesting estimate with a near approximation to the truth, as we shall thus see.

It is clear that the difference between the whole population of 1840, and the part of the population of 1850 over ten years of age, would show the number of deaths in ten years, if the country had neither emigration nor immigration. The emigration, however, is insignificant, and the number of immigrants with their increase, we have now the means of ascertaining. But as our numbers in 1850 were augmented by the accession of Texas, New Mexico, and California, as well as by immigration, the population thus acquired must also be deducted. Having found the mortality of the whole population of 1840, that of those who have since come into existence, and are of course under ten in 1850, will be the subject of separate estimate, for which the census also furnishes materials. Let us now see the result:—

Of the whole population of 1850	23,191,877
The whole number under ten is..........................	6,730,044
The number over ten is.................................	16,461,832

To ascertain the number of immigrants to be deducted from the 16,461,832, we must ascertain—1. The number of immigrants under ten on the 1st of June 1850. 2. The number over ten who had died between their arrival and June, 1850. These numbers are exhibited in the following table:—*

	Whole No. of immigrants.	No. of children under ten when they arrived.	No of years to June, 1850.	No. of children under ten June 1, 1850.	No of deaths. to June 1, '50.	No. over ten June 1, 50.
1840–1........	83,504	12,825	9½	642	10,110	72,752
1841–2........	101,107	15,166	8½	2,275	11,105	87,727
1842–3........	75,159	11,274	7½	2,817	7,299	64,043
1843–4........	74,607	11,190	6½	3,916	6,182	65,509
1844–5........	102,415	15,362	5½	6,912	7,068	88,435
1845–6........	147,051	22,057	4½	12,131	8,167	126,753
1846–7........	220,882	33,027	3½	20,867	9,384	190,631
1847–8........	296,387	44,450	2½	24,760	9,135	262,492
1848–9........	296,938	44,540	1½	37,783	5,215	253,940
1849–50.......	223,984	33,597	½	22,270	2,357	199,357
	1,622,034	243,488	..	134,373	76,022	1,411,639

If, then, we deduct from the 16,461,832, the population of 1850 over ten years of age, the number of immigrants over that age equal to 1,411,639, and also the number over ten in the newly acquired territories of Texas, &c., which by computation is about 135,000, the difference will be 14,915,193, which is the number of the survivors of the population of June 1, 1840. As this population was 17,069,453, a deduction of the 14,915,193 survivors shows the number of deaths in ten years to have been 2,154,258, averaging 215,425.8 a year. As in computing the rate of mortality the deaths are compared with numbers beginning with 17,069,453, and gradually descending through the ten years to 14,915,193, we must take the medium between those numbers, which is 15,992,324. Now, if this number be divided by the annual deaths, 215,425.8, it will show the average annual mortality to be 1 in 74.2 in that part of the population which is over ten years of age.

To ascertain the mortality of those under ten, our data are somewhat

* In the computation of deaths contained in the above table, I have, with some hesitation, allowed a somewhat greater mortality than is warranted in the Carlile life tables, those of Quetelet, and others, since I have assumed one-tenth of the children of the immigrants to be under one year, which probably greatly overrates their number at an age when the rate of mortality is far greater than at any other age.

less precise and satisfactory. Two modes of making the estimate present themselves, which lead to different results; and when we shall have more full and reliable data than at present, truth will probably be found to lie between them.

First. If we assume that the mortality of the children under ten, is the same in the United States as in France, according to their respective numbers—and there is no obvious reason why it should be materially different —then, according to the tables which we owe to the patient labors of Heuschling, the number of deaths of the children under ten in the United States, in 1850, was 224,868, exclusive of the children of immigrants between 1840 and 1850. If to this number we add the deaths of the population over ten, 215,425, we have 440,293 for the whole number of deaths in 1850, which exhibits a mortality of 1 in 43.4

Secondly. If, however, we adopt the unsatisfactory data afforded by the seventh census, then we may thus estimate the average mortality. According to that census, the number of white and free colored children who died under one year of age, was 43,055, which, it must be recollected, included the children of immigrants, with the increase of the population generally, for the year 1850. Let us deduct 10 per cent for this portion; for, though the children of immigrants appear not to have exceeded an 11th or 12th of that class, yet, in consideration of the admitted greater mortality, both of immigrants and their children, 10 per cent does not seem too much for their proportion of deaths. If to the number, thus reduced to 38,749, we add the number of slaves who die at that early age, 10,481, we shall have 49,230 deaths of children in the first year after their birth.

What is the number for the other nine years? It may be approximated in this way. The whole number of white persons from 5 to 10 years of age, and from 10 to 15, is 5,106,257, one-tenth of which may be presumed to give the number of those whose age is about ten. If one-tenth of this tenth be deducted (for the children of immigrants,) the remainder 459,563, will exhibit the number of children ten years old in 1850, of the population of 1840.

Their annual number of deaths we will assume to be 1 in 120, which assumes a somewhat greater mortality than is estimated at this period of life by the most approved life tables of Europe. This would be 3,998.7 for the annual deaths of the whites of 10 years of age, and 853.2 for those of the colored race, in all, 4,852. But as there were 49,230 deaths of both classes in the first year of the decade, and 4,852 in the last, the mean —27,041—gives us the annual average deaths of one-tenth of the children under 10, or 270,410 for the whole number. To this, if we add 215,425 for the deaths of persons over ten, we shall have 485,836 for the annual deaths of the population of 1840, and their increase, excluding all accessions from foreign sources.

The population of 1850, with that exclusion, is as follows:—

Gross amount..		23,191,876
From which deduct the immigrants, with their increase, at the rate of 3 per cent per annum from the time of their arrival....	1,840,233	
Accession from Texas, &c...........................	200,000	
	———	2,040,233
		21,151,643

The mean between this number and the 17,069,453, the population of 1840, is 19,110,548, which, divided by 485,836, the total number of annual deaths, we have an average mortality in the year of 39.3 for the whole population, white and colored, bond and free.*

There are two facts by which the preceding estimate would be slightly affected, but which we have no means of ascertaining with precision. These are the immigrants who come into the country overland, and that portion of the colored population who emigrate to foreign countries. But as they tend to counteract each other, they probably little affect the result. A correct estimate of the probabilities of life in these States is of great importance in several of the practical concerns of life; but the knowledge is unattainable without a strict registry of deaths, or more precision and accuracy in this part of the census than has been hitherto exhibited.

By a similar process, the annual deaths of the slaves, together with the number who have been manumitted or have been fugitives abroad, is found to be nearly 7 in 33½ (33.48.) According to the returns of the census, the number of fugitives and manumitted slaves in the year preceding the census was about 3,000, which, if deducted, would not reduce the mortality of the slaves as low as one in 35. But this difference arises from the greater number of deaths in the children. Thus, the number who die in the first year after birth is 10,481, which is nearly one-fourth of the number of white and free colored; while the proportion between the gross amount of the free and the slaves is between a sixth and a seventh. Besides, the deaths of the slaves above 10 is very nearly 1 in 77, which is a less proportion than in the same description of whites, which would be farther reduced by a deduction of the manumitted and fugitives. The greater mortality in the children of slaves is probably not attributable to any difference of race, but solely to the difference between those who have, as most of the whites, and those who want, as must many of the slaves, good nursing and attendance at that tender age. A correspondent excess of deaths is likely to be everywhere found in the indigent classes, especially in the first year after birth.

We have no means of ascertaining the mortality of the free colored class under 10, their deaths in the publications from the census office being blended with those of the whites; but by reason of the number of this class who emigrate, the diminution of the portion over 10, between 1840 and 1850, was as great as 1 in 50.

In the cases of extreme longevity, we continue to perceive a great superiority in the colored classes over the whites, and in the free colored over the slaves, though in both cases less than was shown in the censuses of 1830 and 1840. We perceive, also, a similar advantage of females in advanced age, until it exceeds one hundred years, when the males preponderate.

---

* It may be objected to the above estimate, that it greatly underrates the number of deaths of children under 1 in following the returns of the census, as that class of deaths is not more than one-half the proportion estimated by the life tables of Europe. The error of this part of the census, so grossly inconsistent with other parts, is readily admitted; but it is probably compensated by the rule here adopted (for want of materials for a better) of taking the mean between the deaths of those under 1 and those who are between 9 and 10, since the number who die under 10 is so disproportionately large as greatly to overrate the average annual deaths in the ten years. Notwithstanding the acknowledged error, the number of deaths in persons under ten exceeds those of the European tables of mortality. The result is, therefore, probably not far from the truth.

CHAPTER VI.

THE DEAF AND DUMB, THE BLIND, THE INSANE, AND THE IDIOTIC.

In all the preceding enumerations of those who were deprived of hearing, sight, or reason, the free colored part of the population was confounded with the slaves, and the insane with the idiotic, but in the seventh census they have been separated. The result may be seen in the following table:—

NUMBER OF THE DEAF AND DUMB, BLIND, INSANE, AND IDIOTIC PERSONS IN THE UNITED STATES, JUNE 1ST, 1850.

	Deaf and dumb.			Blind.			Insane.			Idiotic.			Aggregate.
	Whites.	Free col'd.	Sl.	Whites.	Free col'd.	Sl.	Whites.	Free col'd.	Sl.	Whites.	Free col'd.	Sl.	
Maine.....	255	1	..	108	..	..	556	5	..	575	2	..	1.602
N. Hamps'e	180	1	..	132	2	..	378	..	..	350	1	..	1,025
Vermont...	147	1	..	139	1	..	560	..	..	297	2	..	1,147
Massachus's	356	2	..	457	6	..	1,661	19	..	786	5	..	3,292
R. Island...	62	3	..	61	6	..	210	7	..	110	4	..	463
Connecticut	398	6	..	174	12	..	464	6	..	283	4	..	1.347
N. York...	1,256	7	..	1,137	44	..	2,487	34	..	1.644	21	..	6,630
N. Jersey .	184	5	..	178	29	..	370	9	..	406	13	..	1,194
Pennsylv'a.	1,130	15	..	941	28	..	1,865	49	..	1,432	35	..	5,495
Delaware..	48	1	2	25	14	..	48	20	..	74	14	4	253
Maryland .	197	28	25	215	63	45	477	44	25	275	48	68	1,521
D. of Col..	17	2	..	15	8	1	13	9	1	10	3	..	79
Virginia...	540	13	89	497	85	299	864	47	59	890	90	201	3.675
N Carolina.	389	7	75	379	27	155	467	10	33	615	28	151	2,336
S. Carolina.	134	2	22	150	14	134	224	4	21	249	5	94	1,060
Georgia...	208	1	57	224	4	129	294	2	28	515	1	148	1,611
Florida....	13	..	11	15	1	14	9	..	2	28	..	8	101
Alabama..	151	1	58	156	2	138	201	2	30	343	..	133	1,215
Mississippi.	79	1	27	112	..	93	105	..	24	136	2	84	663
Louisiana .	82	3	32	72	2	122	144	11	45	106	6	62	705
Texas.....	49	..	10	61	1	11	37	..	..	93	..	11	273
Arkansas..	80	..	4	78	1	13	60	..	3	103	2	10	354
Tennessee.	334	2	43	383	9	82	380	5	22	756	5	85	2,104
Kentucky .	507	5	51	419	20	113	502	2	23	796	20	91	2,549
Missouri...	263	..	19	191	3	38	249	2	11	325	..	32	1,133
Illinois....	354	2	..	259	5	..	236	2	..	361	2	..	1,221
Indiana....	533	4	..	341	12	..	556	7	..	225	13	..	2,391
Ohio......	905	10	..	630	12	..	1,303	14	..	1,344	17	..	4,235
Michigan...	124	1	..	125	..	..	132	1	..	186	3	..	572
Wisconsin .	69	..	..	63	..	..	54	..	..	92	2	..	280
Iowa	59	..	..	50	..	..	44	..	..	94	..	..	245
California .	7	..	..	1	..	..	2	..	..	7	..	..	17
Minnesota..	..	..	..	..	..	..	..	..	..	1	..	..	2
N. Mexico..	34	..	..	98	..	..	..	..	..	44	..	..	187
Oregon....	..	..	..	2	..	..	5	..	..	4	..	..	11
Utah	..	..	..	..	..	..	5	..	..	1	..	..	6
Total...	9,136	136	531	7,978	429	1,387	14,972	311	327	14,257	348	1,182	50,994

For the sake of better comparing this part of the census with the correspondent parts of the census of 1840, we shall again unite the free colored with the slaves, and the idiotic with the insane. By this comparison it appears that—

OF THE DEAF AND DUMB.

In the white population the proportion in 1840 was as 1 in..............	2,123
" " " 1850 " 1 in..............	2,140
In the colored population the proportion in 1840 was as 1 in............	2,933
" " " 1850 " 1 in............	5,455

OF THE BLIND.

In the white population the proportion in 1840 was as 1 in..	2,821
" " " 1850 " 1 in..	2,450
In the colored population the proportion in 1840 was as 1 in.............	1,509
" " " 1850 " 1 in.............	1,929

OF THE INSANE AND IDIOTIC.

In the white population the proportion in 1840 was as 1 in..............	977
" " " 1850 " 1 in..............	668
In the colored population the proportion in 1840 was as 1 in.............	978
" " " 1850 " 1 in.............	1,929

We here perceive great discrepancies between the last census and that of 1840. In the white population while the number of deaf and dumb is nearly the same, the proportion of the blind has increased about 13 per cent, and that of the insane and idiotic more than 30 per cent. But in the colored race, in all three of the privations, the proportionate number is greatly diminished. In the class of the blind the proportion is reduced more than one-fourth; in the class of the deaf and dumb it is reduced nearly one-half, and in that of the insane and idiotic the reduction is more than one-half.

The suspicions entertained against the accuracy of that part of the census of 1840 which respected the insane of the colored population, have been justified by subsequent investigations, but on the other hand, in correcting the error, the correspondent part of the seventh census seems hardly entitled to our entire confidence. We know that much sensibility was excited by the greater frequency of insanity among the colored race which resulted from that census, and it is possible that the interest thus felt may, in more ways than one, have biased the judgment of the census takers in placing individuals under this class. Though the census of 1840 unquestionably overrated the number of the colored insane in the Northern States, yet when we saw the proportion gradually increase as we proceeded on the Atlantic coast from Georgia to Maine, and in the West from Louisiana to Michigan, it was not to be believed that the diversity was produced by a correspondent variety and gradation of errors; and reasoning on probabilities, we were compelled to admit that there was some solid foundation for the difference exhibited, though it might be greatly exaggerated. We may add that there is intrinsic evidence in favor of the census of 1840 on this point, which that of 1850 does not possess. Nor is this all. That census itself affords grounds for questioning its accuracy. It shows that while in the white population the proportion of the insane and idiotic is as much as 1 in 668, in the colored population it is only 1 in 1,929; and though we cannot admit that in New England, where the colored population shows a small increase, the number of insane and idiotic has fallen from 383 to 45, as the census shows; neither can we readily believe that, contrary to all previous enumerations, the proportion of the white race thus afflicted is three times as great as that of the colored. We must, then, look to future enumerations to decide whether the liability of the last-mentioned race to these mental maladies, which the census of 1840 has confessedly exaggerated in some States, has not been generally underrated by the census of 1850, and whether truth does not occupy a middle point between them.

CHAPTER VII.

ON THE FUTURE INCREASE OF POPULATION.

If we deduct from the population of 1850 the numbers gained by immigration, and by the acquisition of Texas, New Mexico, and California, with their increase to June 1st, 1850, we shall ascertain the present increase by natural multiplication. Thus:—

The whole population was		23,191,876
Deduct the number of immigrants and their increase between 1840 and 1850............	1,840,227	
Gain from Texas and their increase..........	200,000	
		2,040,227
Population exclusive of immigrants..................		21,151,649

The difference between this number and 17,069,453, the population of 1840, showing an increase of 23.9 per cent in ten years, or 2.16 per cent a year. This is far below the ordinary estimates. but it cannot be materially increased without a great reduction in the computed number of immigrants; and if we merely take their number as returned from the custom-house, and allow nothing for their increase, supposing it not more than sufficient to compensate their mortality, then the increase in ten years would be raised only to 25.58 per cent, or 2.32 per cent in one year.

This implies a great diminution in the rate of natural increase, but the census exhibits abundant evidence of the same fact, in accordance with the census of 1840. Thus the number of children under ten of the white population—5,600,586—bears to the white females—9,523,511—the proportion of 58.81 per cent, whereas in 1840 it was 64.63 per cent. If we deduct the immigrants, who, from the greater proportion of adults, tend to lessen the proportion of children, we shall find the same evidence of decrease. Thus by deducting 750,000* for the immigrant females, on the 1st of June, 1850, computed from the custom-house returns and the probable mortality, and 350,000* for the immigrant children, the proportion of the residues of children to females, would be less than 60 per cent—(59.93.)

On examining the rate of increase of the children in the several states, in the last ten years, we do not find the same uniformity of result as was exhibited during forty years, (see *ante*, page 104;) but if some of the States exhibit an increase in the proportion of children, a large majority —20 States out of 29—show a diminution, as may be seen in the following tables.

In six of the States, given below—Massachusetts, Rhode Island, New Jersey, Pennyslvania, Delaware, and Maryland, the proportion of children has increased in the last ten years. What has made these Statese xceptions to the general rule, either in increasing the proportion of their children or in lessening that of their females, is not obvious; but the united increase of the whole five States is but 1.3 per cent.

---

* These numbers, being deduced from data that are partly conjectural, have no claim to accuracy, but no presumable amount of error can materially affect the result.

TABLE SHOWING THE PROPORTION BETWEEN THE WHITE CHILDREN UNDER TEN YEARS OF AGE, AND THE WHITE FEMALES IN TWENTY STATES, IN THE YEARS 1800, 1840, AND 1850.

	1800.		1840.		1850.		Proportion per cent.		
	Females.	Children.	Females.	Children.	Females.	Children.	1800.	'40.	'50.
Maine........	74,069	54,869	247,449	148,846	285,063	163,465	74.0	60.1	57.3
N. Hampshire	91,740	60,465	143,932	70,387	161,496	73,893	65.9	48.5	45.4
Vermont.....	74,580	57,692	144,840	80,111	153,744	82,808	77.3	55.3	53.7
Massachusetts	211,299	124,566	368,351	173,087	501,357	240,835	58.9	46.9	48.0
Rhode Island..	33,579	19,466	54,225	25,384	73,535	36,071	57.9	46.8	49.1
Connecticut ..	123,528	73,682	153,556	71,783	183,215	85,422	59 6	46.7	46.6
New York ...	258,587	195,840	1,171,533	681,091	1,503,836	844,761	75.7	58.1	56.2
New Jersey...	95,600	67,402	174,533	103,302	232,057	138,500	70 5	59.1	59.7
Pennsylvania .	284,627	270,283	831,345	524,189	1,115,426	712,673	71.2	63.0	63.8
Delaware	24,819	15,878	29,302	17,406	35,423	22,135	63.9	59.4	62.4
Maryland	105,676	69,648	159,400	93,072	206,756	120,962	65.9	58.4	61.4
Virginia	252,151	179,761	369,745	240,343	443,500	290,010	71.3	65.0	56.5
North Carolina	166,116	122,191	244,833	162,282	280,003	188,708	73.5	66.2	65.5
South Carolina	95,339	72,075	128,588	86,566	136,816	88,538	75.6	67.3	64.8
Georgia......	48,298	38,248	197,161	150,317	255,329	187,602	81.1	76.2	73.4
Mississippi ...	2,262	1,962	81,818	65,269	139,431	104,688	86.7	79.7	75.1
Tennessee....	44,529	37,677	315,193	234,700	374,601	268,317	84.6	74.4	71.6
Kentucky	88,915	72,234	250,664	204,978	360,609	259,451	83 9	71.9	70.4
Ohio	20,595	18,276	726,762	509,088	950,933	650,416	88.7	73.3	68.4
Indiana.......	2,003	1,645	325,925	248,127	470,976	353,699	82.1	76.1	75.1

If we extend the comparison to all the other States whose population was known in 1840, we shall find in the greater number a correspondent diminution of their natural increase in the last ten years, as may be seen in the following table:—

	1840.		1850.		Proportion per cent.	
	Females.	Children.	Females.	Children.	1840.	1850.
Florida	11,487	8,404	21,498	....	73.2	77.0
Alabama............	158,403	125,547	207,031	16,556	78.9	73.1
Louisiana............	68,716	48,684	114,248	151,346	70.9	67.6
Arkansas	34,363	28,899	76,315	77,268	83.9	80.9
Mississippi...........	118,572	118,572	279,017	260,797	78.8	75.5
Illinois	217,019	165,329	400,490	209,898	76.2	74.3
Michigan............	98,165	69,036	186,606	299,896	70.5	69.2
Wisconsin...........	11,992	8,690	140,405	129,890	72.5	73.8
Iowa.................	18,668	14,562	90,984	71,297	77.5	78,3

The steady diminution in the rate of natural increase thus exhibited by the whole United States, and by most of the individual States, for fifty years, as well as by those States that have afforded the means of making the comparison for a shorter period, shows that the laws of population, as laid down by Malthus, must be considerably modified. It proves incontestably that while in every country the means of attainable subsistence is a necessary element in the increase of its numbers, it is not an all-sufficient cause of such increase, nor so powerful a cause as Malthus seems to suppose; since we find the rate of increase declining in a country and at a period when subsistence is as easily obtained as it ever was, and where the labor of a month—and often that of a fortnight—would be sufficient to procure as much wholesome and palatable food as the laborer consumed in the year. It is clear, then, that moral causes—probably by producing a slight retardation of marriage—constitute the operative check in the United States, and that the extraordinary facility of subsistence which exists here, seems to exert no influence on that check.

It follows from the preceding views that the period of duplication, in our progressive increase, must be steadily increasing, unless the deficiency should be compensated, as it hitherto has been, and sometimes more than compensated, by immigration.

The population of the United States consists principally of two races—the white and the African, and partly of a mixture of the two—the mulatto, which is first specially noticed in the seventh census. Though the natural increase of the colored race, or at least of the servile portion, is greater than that of the whites, yet, by the aid derived from immigration, the white population is always gaining on the colored, so that the proportion, which in 1790 was as 4.19 white to one colored, was, in 1850, 5.37 to one; and the proportion of whites to slaves had increased in the same period from 4.5 to 7.2 to 1.

The opinions which were hazarded in the first part of this work, (page 116,) of the period when slavery would probably terminate of itself in the United States, must now be qualified by important changes in the condition of the United States since 1840. The termination of slavery was, in those speculations, made to depend on the density of population, which again depended on the extent of territory. Since that time the United States have acquired about 800,000 square miles of almost vacant territory, 237,000 of which, being added to the slaveholding States by the annexation of Texas, is one of the contingencies which would tend to prolong the continuance of slavery. With this qualification as to time, the views presented by the author in 1843 remain unchanged, as he has met with neither fact nor argument to affect their soundness.

What may be the increase of the mixed race of mulattoes cannot yet be known, as they have been now enumerated for the first time. Their whole number, in 1850, was 405,754, of whom 159,095 were free, and 246,656 were slaves. There is thus about one mulatto to every eight of the colored population, about one out of twelve of the slaves, and more than one out of two of the free colored. Some physiologists are disposed to regard mulattoes as hybrids, and as exhibiting in their greater shortness of life, the degeneracy of that class; but a comparative table of the blacks and mulattoes in two States—Connecticut and Louisiana, and two cities—New York and New Orleans, disproves this hypothesis.

There is within the limits of the United States a third race—the Indians, who are not considered to be a part of the population. They have no share in the government, and contribute nothing, either by personal service or tax, to its support. They are not amenable to the laws except for crimes, and have no relation to the government, except as grantors of the lands they occupy, and as pensioners, in consequence of those grants. The number in this anomalous condition is estimated at something more than 400,000, a part of whom occupy the territory set apart for them, and seem to be advancing in civilization; but the greater portion continue in their aboriginal habits and pursuits, and though considered to be within the jurisdiction of the States or Territories, are admitted to have the sole property in the soil of their ungranted territory. With regard to the ultimate destiny of this race, those who are advancing in civilization may retain their independence and be finally incorporated with the States of the Union, while those who are still in their savage state may be encouraged by the success of the former to follow their example, or gradually dwindling in number as their lands diminish, the remnant may become paupers and pensioners of the government; or lastly the whole of those who survive their exterminating wars and their free use of ardent spirits, may become gradually amalgamated with the other two races.

CHAPTER VIII.

THE GROWTH OF THE ATLANTIC AND WESTERN STATES—THE SLAVEHOLDING AND NON-SLAVEHOLDING STATES COMPARED.

By the last census it was found that the Western States continued to gain on the Atlantic States, and the States prohibiting slavery or those which permit it, though in a diminished ratio from that which was anticipated in 1840, as may be seen in the following tables of their respective populations, representatives in Congress, and presidential electors, in 1850. As we now have more accurate estimates of the extent of the States and Territories than was before published, and have acquired a large accession of territory since 1840, the areas, as corrected, are here given:—

ATLANTIC STATES.

I. Non-slaveholding States.	Area in sq. miles.	Population.	Representatives.	Electors.
1. Maine	31,755	583,169	6	8
2. New Hampshire	9,280	317,976	3	5
3. Vermont	10,212	314,120	3	5
4. Massachusetts	7,800	994,514	11	13
5. Rhode Island	1,306	147,545	2	4
6. Connecticut	4,674	370,792	4	6
7. New York	47,000	3,097,394	33	35
8. New Jersey	8,320	489,555	5	7
9. Pennsylvania	46,000	2,311,786	21	23
Total	160,747	8,626,851	88	106

II. Slaveholding States.	Area in sq. miles.	Population.	Representatives.	Electors.
1. Delaware	2,120	91,532	1	3
2. Maryland	11,124	583,034	6	8
3. Virginia	61,352	1,421,661	13	15
4. North Carolina	50,704	869,039	8	10
5. South Carolina	29,385	668,507	6	8
6. Georgia	58,000	906,185	8	10
7. Florida	59,268	87,445	1	3
District of Columbia	60	51,687	.	.
Total	272,013	4,679,090	43	57

WESTERN STATES.

I. Non-slaveholding States.	Area in sq. miles.	Population.	Representatives.	Electors.
10. Ohio	39,964	1,980,329	21	23
11. Indiana	33,800	988,416	11	13
12. Illinois	55,405	851,479	9	11
13. Michigan	56,243	397,654	4	6
14. Wisconsin	53,024	305,391	3	5
15. Iowa	50,914	192,214	2	4
16. California	155,980	92,597	2	4
Territories*	1,472,661	92,298	.	.
Total	1,417,991	4,900,369	52	66

* The areas of these Territories are thus given in De Bow's Compendium, on whose authority the areas of the States are also given:—

Indian Territory	71,127	Oregon	185,630
Kansas	114,798	Utah	269,170
Minnesota	166,025	Washington	123,022
Nebraska	335,882		
New Mexico	207,007	Total	1,472,661

II. Slaveholding States.	Area in sq. miles.	Population.	Representatives.	Electors.
8. Louisiana	41,255	517,762	4	6
9. Texas	237.504	212,592	2	4
10. Alabama	50.722	771,623	7	9
11. Mississippi	47.156	606,526	5	7
12. Arkansas	52,198	209,897	2	4
13. Tennessee	45.600	1,002,717	10	12
14. Kentucky	37,680	982,405	10	12
15. Missouri	67,380	682,044	7	9
Total	599,445	4,985.566	47	63

INCREASE OF POPULATION OF THE PRECEDING DIVISIONS OF STATES IN 30 YEARS.

	1830.	1840.	1850.	Decennial increase. 1830.	1840.	18[illegible]0.
Atlantic States	9,188,133	10,686.381	13,305,941	23.8	16.3	24.5
Western States	3,692,569	6,376,972	9.885,935	63.7	73.6	54.5
Non slaveholding States	7,012.300	9.728 922	13,527,220	35.8	38.7	36.2
Slaveholding States	5,848,303	7,334,431	9,664,656	29.9	25.4	31.8

If the same rate of increase should continue with the Atlantic and the Western States respectively, when will the latter attain the preponderance to which they are ultimately destined by reason of their far greater extent of territory? Their respective numbers, which had been in 1840 in the ratio of 60 per cent for the Atlantic States and 40 per cent for the Western States, had changed, according to the census of 1850, to 57.4 per cent for the Atlantic States and 42.6 per cent for the Western; thus showing that as they approached at the rate of only 5.2 per cent in 10 years, it would require three more decennial terms, or be 1880, before the Western States would have a preponderance, which would then be less than 1 per cent.

By this time the progress of railroads, canals, and manufactures, may have so increased their commercial intercourse as to overcome the influence of local jealousy and narrow local interests. Experience may teach the mass of both divisions, that on all great national questions—such, for example, as the policy of supporting a respectable navy—their interests are identical. It must, however, be recollected that the increasing immigration, both foreign and domestic, to the new States and Territories in the West, may accelerate the progress of the Western States beyond the rate here supposed; and that, on the other hand, the States on the Pacific, now reckoned in the Western division, may form a class by themselves, and be neutrals between the other two divisions, or, perchance, incline to throw their weight into the scale of the Atlantic States, under the influence of their commercial connections.

In the other twofold division of the States, growing out of the institution of slavery, it happens that the division which already has the preponderance of numbers, also increases the fastest. What effect this growing ascendancy may have on the agitating and perplexing topic of slavery, cannot now be foreseen. It may infuse a new heat and bitterness in the strife that has been thus engendered; or it may produce more moderation when the disparity is more seen and felt by both parties than at present; or, lastly, in the alternate ebbs and flows which the tides of popular feeling are ever undergoing, the subject that now fills the land with discord, and threatens it with consequences as serious as lasting, may come to be regarded as of no higher concern to the General Government or the American people, than the extent of parental or marital authority in a State, or its penal code, on all of which both man's moral sympathy and his religious creed may be brought to bear as directly as on domestic slavery.

CHAPTER IX.

RELIGION—JUVENILE AND POPULAR INSTRUCTION.

In consequence of the entire freedom of religion in the United States, their different sects are more diversified in tenets and character, and are less unequal in numbers than in any other country. The principal denominations, with the number of churches and value of the property belonging to each, may be seen in the following table:—

Denominations.	No. of churches.	Value of property.	Denominations.	No. of churches.	Value of property.
1. Methodist.......	13,280	$14,822,870	12. Free...........	386	$263,305
2. Baptist	9,375	11,020,855	13. German Reform.	338	975,080
3. Presbyterian....	4,824	14,453,789	14. Dutch Reformed.	330	4,096,880
4. Congregational..	1,706	7,970,195	15. Moravian.......	328	417,667
5. Episcopal	1,450	11,375,310	16. Unitarian	242	3,173,822
6. Roman Catholic..	1,221	9,250,758	17. Menonites.......	113	93,345
7. Lutheran........	1,217	2,884,286	18. Tunkers........	51	37,625
8. Christians.......	863	847,036	19. Jews	30	330,600
9. Friends.........	726	1,713,767	20. Swedenborgian .	16	108,600
10. Union	608	644,715	Minor sects......	418	985,180
11. Universalist. ...	529	1,752,316			
Total..				38,061	$87,328,861

The sects whose churches throughout the Union exceed 1,000, have the following local distribution:—

	Methodist.	Baptist.	Presbyterian.	Congregational.	Episcopal.	R. Catholic.	Lutheran.	Other sects.	Total.
Maine........	199	326	7	180	9	12	...	212	945
N. Hampshire.	103	193	13	176	11	2	...	128	626
Vermont......	146	102	11	175	26	2	...	137	599
Massachusetts.	262	236	15	448	54	41	1	428	1,475
Rhode Island..	23	106	..	21	26	7	...	45	228
Connecticut...	185	114	17	252	104	13	44	14	....
New York....	1,231	781	671	215	279	175	81	700	4,134
New Jersey ..	312	108	149	8	52	22	7	155	813
Pennsylvania .	889	220	775	..	138	139	498	807	3,566
Delaware.....	106	12	26	..	21	3	...	12	180
Maryland.....	479	45	56	..	133	65	40	91	909
Dist. of Colum.	16	6	6	..	6	6	2	4	46
Virginia......	1,025	649	240	..	173	17	50	229	2,383
North Carolina.	784	615	151	..	50	4	49	142	1,795
South Carolina.	484	413	185	1	72	14	41	22	1,182
Georgia......	795	879	97	1	20	8	8	54	1,862
Florida	87	56	16	..	10	5	...	3	177
Alabama......	587	579	162	..	17	5	1	32	1,373
Mississippi....	451	385	143	..	13	9	...	27	1,016
Louisiana.....	125	77	18	..	14	55	...	17	306
Texas........	176	82	45	..	8	13	...	51	341
Arkansas.....	168	114	52	..	2	7	...	19	362
Tennessee....	861	646	363	..	17	3	12	112	2,014
Kentucky	530	803	224	..	19	48	5	216	1,845
Missouri	250	300	125	..	11	65	21	8	880
Ohio	1,529	551	663	100	70	130	260	633	3,936
Indiana......	778	428	282	2	24	63	63	392	2,032
Illinois... ...	405	282	206	46	27	59	42	156	1,223
Michigan.....	119	66	72	29	25	44	12	32	399
Wisconsin.....	110	49	40	37	19	64	20	24	365
Iowa.........	71	20	38	14	5	18	4	23	193
California	5	1	3	..	1	18	...	10	28
Territories....	2	1	2	1	..	79	...	..	94
Total....	13,280	9,375	4,824	1,706	1,459	1,221	1,217	4,979	38,061

It would seem, from the preceding tables, that there is, on an average, a church, or place of worship, for every 610 of the gross population—adults and children; that the average property of each is about $2,300, though some are ten times as rich as others; and that the churches of the Methodists and Baptists united outnumber all the other sects.

These places of worship are distributed in every part of the Union very nearly in proportion to population, showing that the American people, in whose spontaneous action these accommodations for public worship originated and are maintained, exhibit a remarkable uniformity in the spirit of devotion, however great may be the diversity in their manifestations of it, by particular tenets and modes of worship, as may be seen in the following:—

TABLE OF THE NUMBER OF CHURCHES IN EACH OF THE GREAT DIVISIONS OF THE STATES, AND OF THE QUOTAS OF POPULATION ASSIGNABLE TO EACH.

Local divisions.	No. of churches.	Population.	No. of persons to each.
New England States..................	4,607	2,628,116	594
Middle States........................	10,648	6,624,928	660
Southern States.....................	7,399	3,952,538	530
South-western States....	5,065	3,321,117	620
North-western States................	10,853	6,379,923	590

The inequality, small as it is, is increased by the fact that in the Southern States, where the churches are relatively the most numerous, they are probably below the average in the number they can accommodate, and that in the Middle States, where the churches are proportionally the fewest, they are above the average in magnitude.

Of the three classes of PUBLIC SCHOOLS enumerated by the census of 1850, there is no material difference in the number of *Colleges* from the census of 1840, but there is, in the former, a much larger proportion of inferior schools. The proportion of illiterate, however, is about double that in 1840.

This seeming retrograde course, of which instances are so rare in the United States, and which is not in accordance with the great increase of primary schools, may probably be in part attributed to the recent large additions to the number of immigrants—the States which received the greatest number showing also the greatest increase of illiterates—and a part may, perhaps, be ascribed to a smaller number of omissions in this class, now that the census takers are required to return each individval separately.

States.	Universities and colleges.	Students.	Endowment.	Academies.	Scholars.	Endowment.
Maine......................	2	282	$14,000	131	6,648	$51,187
New Hampshire............	1	273	11,000	107	5,321	43,202
Vermont....................	5	464	21,558	118	6,864	48,935
Massachusetts..............	6	1,043	107,901	381	12,774	310,177
Rhode Island	1	150	3,500	46	1,691	32,748
Connecticut................	4	738	53,620	202	6,966	145,967
New England States.........	19	2,950	$211,589	985	40,284	$632,216
New York...................	14	2,673	148,258	853	49,262	810,332
New Jersey.................	4	470	79,700	219	9,569	226,388
Pennsylvania..............	21	3,286	282,205	524	23,751	467,843
Delaware..........	2	144	17,200	65	2,011	47,832
Maryland......	11	992	101,714	225	10,677	242,229
District of Columbia........	2	218	24,000	47	2,333	84,040
Middle States..............	54	7,783	$653,077	1,952	97,603	$1,878,664

States.	Universities and colleges.	Students.	Endowment.	Academies.	Scholars.	Endowment.
Virginia	12	1,535	159,790	303	8,982	234,372
North Carolina	5	513	40,700	272	7,822	187,648
South Carolina	8	720	104,790	202	7,467	205,489
Georgia	13	1,535	105,430	219	9,059	108,983
Florida	.	...	.....	34	1,251	12,089
Southern States	38	4,303	$410,710	1,030	34,531	$748,581
Alabama	5	567	41,255	106	8,290	164,165
Mississippi	11	862	42,400	171	6,628	73,717
Louisiana	5	469	76,250	143	5,328	193,077
Texas	2	165	1,000	97	3,389	39,384
Arkansas	3	150	3,100	90	2,407	27,937
Tennessee	17	1,605	63,507	260	9,517	156,842
South-western States	43	3,817	$227,512	867	35,559	$655,122
Missouri	9	1,809	79,528	204	8,829	143,171
Kentucky	15	1,873	131,461	330	12,712	252,617
Ohio	26	3,621	125,792	206	15,052	149,352
Indiana	11	1,069	43,350	131	6,185	63,520
Illinois	6	442	13,300	81	4,179	40,488
Michigan	3	308	14,000	37	1,616	24,974
Wisconsin	2	75	4,300	58	2,723	18,796
Iowa	2	100	2,000	31	1,051	7,980
California	.	...	.....	6	170	14,270
Territories	1	...	.....	44	894	23,078
North-western States	75	8,497	$413,731	1,128	53,421	$247,246
Total	234	27,159	$1,916,698	6,032	261,362	$4,653,842

States.	Primary schools.	Scholars.	Endowment.	Illiterates.
Maine	1,042	102,815	$315,436	6,282
New Hampshire	2,381	75,642	166,944	3,009
Vermont	2,731	93,457	176,111	6,240
Massachusetts	3,679	176,475	1,006,795	28,345
Rhode Island	416	23,130	100,481	3,607
Connecticut	1,656	71,269	231,226	5,306
New England States	11,905	542,788	$1,996,993	52,780
New York	11,580	675,221	1,472,057	98,722
New Jersey	1,479	78,205	216,992	18,665
Pennsylvania	9,061	413,706	1,414,530	76,272
Delaware	194	8,970	43,861	10,181
Maryland	907	33,254	229,848	41,877
District of Columbia	22	2,169	14,232	4,671
Middle States	23,243	1,211,525	$3,391,520	250,388
Virginia	2,937	67,438	314,025	88,520
North Carolina	2,657	104,095	158,564	80,423
South Carolina	724	17,838	200,600	16,504
Georgia	1,251	32,705	182,231	41,667
Florida	69	1,878	22,386	4,129
Southern States	7,638	223,954	$877,806	231,343

States.	Primary schools.	Scholars.	Endowment.	Illiterates.
Alabama	1,152	28,380	315,002	33 992
Mississippi	782	18,746	254,159	13,528
Louisiana	664	25,046	349,679	24,610
Texas	349	7,946	44,088	10,583
Arkansas	353	8,493	43,763	16,935
Tennessee	2,667	103,651	195,443	78,619
South-western States	5,677	192,262	$1,202,134	118,261
Missouri	2,234	71,429	160,770	36,768
Kentucky	2,667	103,651	211,852	69,706
Ohio	11,661	484,153	743,074	66,020
Indiana	4,822	161,500	314,467	72,710
Illinois	4,054	425,790	349,350	41,283
Michigan	2,714	110,455	169,806	8,281
Wisconsin	1,423	58,817	113,133	6,453
Iowa	742	29,616	51,492	8,153
California	2	49	3,600	5,235
Territories	16	80	15,509	25,994
North-western States	30,335	1,445,540	$2,131,053	370,603
Total	80,991	3,354,173	$9,591,530	1,053,420

The scholars of the three classes are in the following centesimal proportions, by which it appears that the second class and the elementary gained to a small extent, while the college class remained as it was:—

College students	.8
Academical	7.2
Elementary	92
Total	100

But the great source of popular instruction in these States is the periodical press, which has an extent and dispersion known in no other country. Its productions may be classed under the *single sheets* published as newspapers daily, or once, twice, or thrice a week, and *pamphlets* published monthly, semi-monthly, or quarterly. They are thus distributed among the States:—

	Newspapers.			Pamphlets.		
States.	Daily.	Twice or thrice a week.	Weekly.	Monthly.	Quarterly.	Aggregate.
Maine	4	5	39	1	...	49
New Hampshire	.	..	35	3	...	38
Vermont	2	1	30	2	...	34
Massachusetts	22	15	125	32	7	209
Rhode Island	5	2	12	..	...	19
Connecticut	7	4	30	1	2	46
New York	51	21	308	45	3	428
New Jersey	6	..	43	2	...	51
Pennsylvania	24	3	261	19	2	310
Delaware	..	3	7	..	...	10
Maryland	6	4	54	4	...	68
District of Columbia	5	5	8	..	...	18
Virginia	15	12	55	4	...	87
North Carolina	..	5	40	6	...	51
South Carolina	7	5	27	5	...	46

States	NEWSPAPERS. Daily.	Twice or thrice a week.	Weekly.	PAMPHLETS. Monthly.	Quarterly.	Aggregate.
Georgia....................	5	3	37	6	...	51
Florida....................	..	1	9	1	49	10
Alabama....................	6	5	48	..	38	60
Mississippi................	..	4	46	1	35	50
Louisiana..................	11	6	37	..	209	55
Texas......................	..	5	29	..	19	51
Arkansas...................	..	..	9	..	46	9
Tennessee..................	8	2	36	4	428	50
Missouri...................	5	4	45	7	51	62
Kentucky...................	9	7	38	8	310	62
Ohio.......................	26	10	201	27	119	107
Indiana....................	9	2	95	1	68	107
Illinois...................	8	4	84	3	118	261
Michigan...................	3	2	47	6	87	58
Wisconsin..................	6	4	35	1	51	46
Iowa.......................	..	2	25	2	46	20
California.................	4	..	3	..	51	7
Total..............	254	146	1,902	195	19	2,526

These various periodicals have been arranged under the four heads of political, literary, religious, and scientific:—

States.	Political..	Literary..	Religious..	Scientific..	Aggregate.	States.	Political..	Literary..	Religious..	Scientific..	Aggregate.
Maine.....	29	15	4	1	49	Alabama ..	43	12	3	1	60
N. Hampsh.	22	10	5	1	38	Mississippi..	40	10	.	.	50
Vermont...	27	5	3	.	35	Louisiana...	34	19	1	1	55
Massachus.	82	89	24	14	209	Texas......	14	18	2	.	34
R. Island..	12	7	..	.	19	Arkansas ..	6	8	.	.	9
Connecticut.	8	12	4	1	46	Tennessee..	36	7	7	.	50
New York..	263	116	37	12	428	Missouri....	42	17	2	.	61
New Jersey.	44	7	..	.	51	Kentucky..	42	14	5	1	62
Pennsylvan.	198	83	28	1	310	Ohio.......	192	43	21	5	261
Delaware..	8	2	..	.	10	Indiana....	84	21	2	.	107
Maryland...	39	21	6	2	68	Illinois.....	73	23	8	3	107
D. of Colum.	15	3	0	.	18	Michigan ..	39	14	3	2	58
Virginia...	62	15	6	1	87	Wisconsin..	42	3	.	1	46
N. Carolina.	35	10	5	.	51	Iowa......	25	3	1	.	29
S. Carolina.	24	13	3	2	46	California..	..	7	.	.	7
Georgia....	20	24	3	4	51	Territories .	1	3	.	.	4
Florida....	7	..	2	.	10						
Total............							1,907	651	191	53	2,526

The public libraries of the United States seem to be sufficiently numerous, considering how dispersed is the greater part of the population—there being about 1 for each 1,500 of the population. But there is no instance yet of those large and complete libraries which we see in most European countries. No library here has yet reached 100,000 volumes, and but two or three have attained half that number.

These libraries may be arranged under the three heads of *Public* Libraries, provided by the government or by joint-stock companies, *College and Theological* Libraries—and libraries of Sunday and other schools. These, with the number of volumes in each, are thus distributed among the States:—

States.	College and theological libraries.	Volumes.	Public libraries.	Volumes.	School libraries.	Volumes.	Aggregate of libraries.	Volumes.
Maine	17	40,317	77	51,439	142	29,211	236	121,969
N. Hamp .	9	22,425	47	42,017	73	21,317	129	85,759
Vermont..	12	23,860	30	21,061	54	19,720	95	64,641
Massachus.	60	156,157	177	257,737	1,225	270,120	1,462	684,015
R. Island..	8	32,756	25	42,007	62	27,579	96	104,342
Connectic't	11	83,225	42	38,609	111	42,084	164	165,318
N. York...	31	141,577	43	197,229	10,939	1,422,023	11,013	1,760,820
N. Jersey.	6	24,338	77	43,993	43	12,744	128	80,885
Pennsylva.	47	104,411	90	184,686	256	75,192	393	363,409
Delaware .	1	5,000	4	10,250	12	2,700	17	17,950
Maryland..	15	34,642	17	54,750	92	34,650	124	125,042
D. of Col'a.	2	32,500	7	66,100	..	....	9	98,600
Virginia...	16	51,386	16	32,595	17	4,681	54	88,462
N. Carolina	14	25,240	4	2,500	20	3,852	38	29,592
S. Carolina	7	30,964	16	17,758	3	2,750	26	107,472
Georgia ..	9	21,500	3	6,500	26	3,788	38	31,788
Florida...	.	.....	1	1,000	6	1,660	7	2,660
Alabama..	5	7,500	4	3,848	47	9,275	56	26,623
Mississippi	4	10,093	4	7,264	107	4,380	117	21,737
Louisiana..	2	5,000	5	9,800	2	12,000	19	26,809
Texas	1	100	3	2,100	8	2,180	12	4,280
Arkansas .	.	.....	1	250		170	3	420
Tennessee.	5	9,925	9	5,373	23	7,598	34	22,896
Missouri...	4	20,300	13	23,105	70	31,650	97	75,056
Kentucky.	15	34,425	47	49,424	29	4,617	80	79,466
Ohio......	26	59,525	65	65,703	261	63,575	352	186,826
Indiana...	5	9,100	33	35,982	88	13,065	151	68,403
Illinois ...	4	7,800	13	23,105	115	18,704	152	62,486
Michigan .	3	7,900	280	65,116	18	34,927	417	107,943
Wisconsin.	2	1,800	9	12,046	30	7,180	72	21,029
Iowa......	.	.....	4	2,650	4	3,140	32	5,799
Total.....	343	1,484,641	1,217	1,446,015	14,055	2,189,725	15,615	4,636,411

CHAPTER X.

CITIES AND TOWNS.

THE town population has been found, in the last decennial term, as in the preceding, to have increased much faster than that of the country at large, and the excess exhibited by the census of 1850 is much greater than that of 1840. This result admits of a ready explanation. We know that the population of towns receives new accessions from the progress of manufactures, by reason of the variety and subdivision of labor they require; and that the social instinct is ever drawing into the human hive drones as well as bees; but, in addition to these general causes, the extraordinary growth of the cities and towns of the United States since 1840, may be referred partly to the great increase of immigrants, who there find profitable and congenial occupation, and partly to the multiplication of railroads, which so greatly enlarge the intercourse and commerce between town and country. The combined effect of these general and special causes may be seen in the following tables:—

CITIES CONTAINING 100,000 AND UPWARDS.

	1790.	1800.	1810.	1820.	Decennial increase. 1800.	1810.	1820.
Boston	18,038	24,937	33,250	43,298	38.2	33.3	30.0
New York	33,131	60,489	96,373	123,706	82.6	59.3	28.4
Philadelphia	42,520	69,403	94,874	112,772	59.5	32.4	42.7
Baltimore	13,503	26,114	35,583	62,738	93.4	36.7	76.3
New Orleans	.....	.....	17,242	27,176	....	....	57.6
Cincinnati	.....	.....	2,540	9,642	....	....	275.3

	1830.	1840.	1850.	Decennial increase. 1830.	1840.	1850.	Total increase.
Boston	61,302	93,383	136,881	41.9	52.3	46.6	659.7
New York	202,589	312,710	515,547	63.8	53.6	65.6	1,456.0
Philadelphia	161,410	220,423	340,045	43.1	36.6	54.6	699.2
Baltimore	80,625	102,313	169,054	28.5	26.9	65.2	1,152.0
New Orleans	46,310	102,163	116,375	70.7	122.1	13.9	574.4
Cincinnati	24,831	46,338	115,436	75.9	86.4	149.1	4,445.0
			1,393,338				

It would thus seem that in sixty years the increase of New York had exceeded fifteenfold; Baltimore, twelvefold; Philadelphia and Boston, sevenfold; and in forty years that of New Orleans had increased more than sixfold, and Cincinnati more than fortyfold.

CITIES AND TOWNS CONTAINING BETWEEN 10,000 AND 100,000 INHABITANTS.

	1830.	1840.	1850.	Decennial increase. 1840.	1850.
MAINE.					
Portland	12,601	15,218	20,815	20.8	36.8
Bangor	2,868	8,627	14,132	200.8	67.3
			34,947		
MASSACHUSETTS.					
Lowell	6,474	20,796	33,380	221.2	60.5
Salem	13,836	15,082	20,264	9.1	34.4
Roxbury	.....	9,689	18,364	....	89.5
Worcester	.....	7,497	17,049	....	127.4
Charlestown	8,182	11,484	17,216	30.8	57.0
New Bedford	7,592	12,087	16,443	59.2	36.0
Cambridge	.....	8,409	15,215	...	81.0
Lynn	.....	9,367	14,253	....	52.2
Springfield	6,784	10,985	11,766	61.9	7.1
Fall River	.....	6,738	11,524	....	71.0
Taunton	6,042	7,645	10,441	26.5	65.0
			185,955		
RHODE ISLAND.					
Providence	16,833	23,171	41,513	37.7	79.2
Smithfield	.....	9,534	11,500	....	20.0
			53,013		
CONNECTICUT.					
New Haven	10,180	12,960	20,345	27.3	57.0
Hartford	7,076	9,468	13,355	33.8	41.0
			34,700		
NEW JERSEY.					
Newark	10,953	17,290	38,894	57.8	125.0
Paterson	....	7,596	11,334	....	49.2
New Brunswick	....	.....	10,019	....	....
			60,247		

	1830.	1840.	1850.	Decennial Increase. 1840.	1850.
NEW YORK.					
Brooklyn	15,396	36,233	96,838	135.3	173.1
Albany	24,238	33,721	50,763	39.1	89.5
Buffalo	8,653	18,213	42,261	110.0	121.6
Rochester	9,207	20,191	36,403	119.0	80.3
Williamsburg	.....	5,000	30,780	....	515.6
Troy	11,405	19,334	28,785	69.6	48.9
Syracuse	.....	6,500	22,271	....	242.6
Utica	10,183	12,782	17,585	25.5	36.0
Poughkeepsie	.....	10,006	13,944	....	39.4
Lockport	.....	6,500	12,323	....	89.6
Oswego City	.....	4,500	12,205	....	171.0
Newburg	.....	6,000	11,415	....	90.2
			374,613		
PENNSYLVANIA.					
Pittsburg	12,568	21,115	46,601	91.9	93.2
Alleghany	.....	.....	21,262	....	....
Reading	.....	8,410	15,743	....	87.2
Lancaster	.....	8,417	12,369	....	46.9
			95,975		
DELAWARE.					
Wilmington	.....	8,367	13,979	....	66.3
DISTRICT OF COLUMBIA.					
Washington	18.827	23,364	40,001	24.1	71.2
VIRGINIA.					
Richmond	16,030	20,153	27,570	25.7	36.8
Norfolk	9,816	10,920	14,306	11.2	31.0
Petersburg	8,322	11,136	14,010	33.8	25.8
Wheeling	.....	7,885	11,435	....	45.0
			67,321		
SOUTH CAROLINA.					
Charleston	30,289	29,261	42,985	....	46.9
GEORGIA.					
Savannah	7,776	11,214	15,312	44.2	36.9
Augusta	7,885	6,403	11,753	....	83.5
			27,565		
ALABAMA.					
Mobile	3,194	12,672	20,515	296.8	77.7
TENNESSEE.					
Nashville	5,506	6,929	10,478	23.3	51.2
KENTUCKY.					
Louisville	10,341	21,210	43,194	105.1	103.6
MISSOURI.					
St. Louis	5,852	16,469	77,860	181.4	372.8
OHIO.					
Columbus	.....	6,048	17,882	....	195.7
Cleveland	.....	6,071	17,034	....	180.6
Dayton	.....	6,067	10,977	....	80.9
			45,893		

ILLINOIS.

	1830.	1840.	1850.	Decennial Increase. 1840.	1850.
Chicago	.....	4,470	29,960	....	570.3

MICHIGAN.

Detroit	.....	9,100	20,019	....	120.0

WISCONSIN.

Milwaukee	.....	1,700	20,061	....	1,080.0

CALIFORNIA.

San Francisco	.....	.....	34,776	....	....

TOWNS CONTAINING BETWEEN 3,000 AND 10,000 INHABITANTS.

MAINE.

Augusta	8,225	Waldoborough	4,199
Bath	8,026	Eastport	4,125
Gardiner	6,486	Ellsworth	4,009
Biddeford	6,095	Waterville	3,164
Saco	5,798	Lewistown	3,584
Rockland	5,052	Hampden	3,195
Belfast	5,051	Vassalborough	3,099
Hallowell	4,769		
Frankfort	4,232	Total	79,028

NEW HAMPSHIRE.

Portsmouth	9,738	Winchester	3,296
Concord	8,576	Great Falls	3,000
Dover	8,196	Rochester	3,006
Nashua	5,820		
Nashville	3,122	Total	43,748

VERMONT.

Burlington	6,110	Middlebury	3,517
Rutland	3,715		
Total			13,342

MASSACHUSETTS.

Newburyport	9,572	Beverley	5,376
Nantucket	8,452	Northampton	5,268
Lawrence	8,282	Waltham	4,464
Danvers	8,179	Westfield	4,180
Dorchester	7,969	Barnstable	4,901
Gloucester	7,785	Haverhill	3,500
Andover	6,945	Ipswich	3,349
Plymouth	6,024	Clinton	3,113
Marblehead	6,167	North Adams	3,000
Pittsfield	5,872		
Total			112,409

RHODE ISLAND.

Newport	9,563
North Providence	7,680
Total	17,243

CONNECTICUT.

New London	8,991	Waterbury	5,137
Bridgeport	7,560	Middletown	4,230
Danbury	5,964	New Milford	4,058
Stonington	5,431	Litchfield	3,953
Stamford	5,000		
Total			50,324

NEW YORK.

Auburn	9,548	Oswego City	4,769
Schenectady	8,921	Kingston	4,500
Elmira	8,166	Catskill	5,454
West Troy	7,564	Whitehall	4,726
Watertown	6,810	Penn Yan	3,000
Ithaca	6,909	Cohoes	4,229
Hudson	6,286	Rome	4,000
Johnstown	6,131	Canandaigua	3,500
Waterloo	3,000	Amherst	4,153
Geneva	6,000	Amsterdam	4,128
Ogdensburg	6,500	Seneca Falls	3,600
Bingamton	5,000	Sag Harbor	3,600
Lansingburg	5,752	Yonkers	4,160
Plattsburg	5,618	Sing Sing	3,000
Little Falls	4,855		
Total			153,879

NEW JERSEY.

Camden	9,479	Elizabethtown	4,000
Jersey City	6,856	Morristown	3,300
Trenton	6,461	Salem	3,052
Rahway	6,006	Princeton	3,021
Woodbridge	5,141		
Burlington	4,536	Total	51,352

PENNSYLVANIA.

Harrisburg	7,834	Carlisle	4,581
Pottsville	7,515	Allentown	3,778
Easton	7,250	Birmingham	3,732
Yorktown	6,863	Mauch Chunk	3,722
Germantown	6,209	Chambersburg	3,336
Norristown	6,024	Danville	3,302
Erie	5,850	Hawley	3,000
West Philadelphia	5,571	Tamaqua	3,060
Carbondale	4,945	Westchester	3,172
Frankfort	5,346		
Total			95,089

MARYLAND.

Cumberland	6,073	Annapolis	3,011
Frederickstown	6,028		
Hagarstown	3,829	Total	18,921

DISTRICT OF COLUMBIA.

Georgetown	8,366

VIRGINIA.

Alexandria	8,734	Winchester	3,857
Portsmouth	8,121	Wellsburg	3,000
Lynchburg	8,071		
Fredericksburg	4,061	Total	35,844

NORTH CAROLINA.

Wilmington	7,264	Raleigh	4,518
Newbern	4,681		
Fayettesville	4,646	Total	21,109

SOUTH CAROLINA.

Columbia	6,060

GEORGIA.

Columbus	5,942	Rome	3,000
Macon	5,720		
Madison	3,516	Total	18,178

ALABAMA.

City	Population
Montgomery	8,728
Tuscaloosa	3,500
Total	12,228

MISSISSIPPI.

City	Population	City	Population
Natchez	4,434	Holley Springs	3,500
Aberdeen	5,000		
Vicksburg	3,678	Total	16,612

LOUISIANA.

City	Population
Baton Rouge	4,500

TEXAS.

City	Population	City	Population
Brownsville	4,500	San Antonio	3,488
Galveston	4,177		
Total			12,165

TENNESSEE.

City	Population	City	Population
Memphis	8,841	Clarksville	3,000
Chatanooga	3,500		
Total			15,341

KENTUCKY.

City	Population	City	Population
Newport	5,895	Hopkinsville	3,500
Covington	9,408	Frankfort	3,308
Maysville	3,840		
Total			25,951

MISSOURI.

City	Population	City	Population
St. Joseph	5,000	Jefferson City	3,000
Weston	3,775		
Carondelet	3,775	Total	15,550

ILLINOIS.

City	Population	City	Population
Quincey City	6,902	Alton	3,885
Galena	6,004	Warsaw	3,009
Peoria	5,095		
Springfield	4,558	Total	29,853

INDIANA.

City	Population	City	Population
Madison	8,012	Indianapolis	3,197
New Albany	8,181	Terre Haute	4,051
La Fayette	6,129		
Fort Wayne	4,282	Total	34,948

OHIO.

City	Population	City	Population
Zanesville	7,929	Mansfield	3,557
Chilicothe	7,100	Circleville	3,411
Steubenville	6,140	Newark	3,654
Springfield	5,108	Piqua	3,277
Portsmouth	4,011	Akron	3,266
Massillon	4,009	Fulton	3,224
Toledo	3,829	Marietta	3,175
Mount Vernon	3,711	Xenia	3,024
Lancaster City	3,483		
Total			71,908

WISCONSIN.

Racine	5,107
Kenosha	3,458
Total	8,565

MICHIGAN.

Ann Arbor	4,858	Ypsilanti	3,051
Grand Rapids	3,147		
Adrian	3,006	Total	11,062

IOWA.

Council Bluffs	3,000

CALIFORNIA.

Maryville	8,000	Stockton	4,000
Placerville	5,625	San Jose	3,500
Sonora	4,000		
Total			25,125

NEW MEXICO.

Santa Fe	4,846

The preceding table partakes, in some degree, of the inaccuracy in the list of towns of 2,000 inhabitants in 1840, in consequence of the practice prevailing in some of the States of not distinguishing between their towns and townships, (see *ante* page 133.) But the rural population returned with that of the towns has been excluded, wherever the means could be obtained of making the discrimination; and it is believed that there is scarcely any town here named whose numbers in congregated dwellings do not amount to 3,000.

AGGREGATE OF THE POPULATION OF THE TOWNS IN THE UNITED STATES CONTAINING 3,000 PERSONS AND UPWNRDS ON THE 1ST OF JUNE, 1850.

States.	Towns of 10,000 persons and upwards.	Towns between 10,000 and 3,000.	Total.	Proportion of town population in each State.
Maine	34,947	79,028	113,975	4.2 per cent.
New Hampshire	13,932	44,748	58,680	29.0 "
Vermont	.....	13,342	13,342	4.2 "
Massachusetts	322,796	112,409	435,205	44.1 "
Rhode Island	53,013	17,243	70,256	48.9 "
Connecticut	34,700	50,324	85,024	22.7 "
New England States	459,388	327,094	786,482	28.8 "
New York	890,160	153,879	1,044,039	33.7 "
New Jersey	60,247	51,352	111,599	22.8 "
Pennsylvania	436,020	95,089	531,109	24.6 "
Delaware	13,979	.....	13,979	17.9 "
Maryland	169,054	18,991	188,045	32.2 "
District of Columbia	40,001	8,366	48,367	.... "
Middle States	1,609,461	317,677	1,927,138	29.0 "
Virginia	67,321	35,844	102,165	7.2 "
North Carolina	.....	21,109	21,109	2.4 "
South Carolina	42,985	6,060	49,045	5.2 "
Georgia	27,565	18,178	45,743	5.0 "
Southern States	137,871	81,191	219,062	5.5 "

States.	Towns of 10,000 persons and upwards.	Towns between 10,000 and 3,000.	Total.	Proportion of town population in each State.
Alabama.................	20,515	12,228	32,743	4.2 per cent.
Mississippi................	.....	16,612	16,612	2.7 "
Louisiana................	116,375	4,500	120,875	23.3 "
Texas	.....	12,165	12,165	5.8 "
Tennessee................	10,478	15,341	15,819	2.4 "
South-western States	147,368	60,846	208,214	6.2 "
Kentucky............. ...	43,194	25,951	69,145	8.9 "
Missouri	77,860	15,550	93,410	13.7 "
Ohio......................	161,329	71,908	233,237	18.6 "
Indiana....................	......	34,948	34,948	3.5 "
Illinois....................	29,963	29,853	59,816	7.0 "
Michigan...................	20,019	11,062	31,081	7.8 "
Wisconsin.................	.....	8,565	8,565	2.8 "
Iowa	.....	3,000	3,000	1.5 "
North-western States.....	332,365	200,837	533,202	8.15 "
California.	34,776	25,125	59,901	58.6 "
New Mexico..............	.....	4,846	4,846	7.8 "
	34,776	29,971	64,747	.... "
Total..................	2,721,229	1,017,616	3,738,845	16.1 "

It appears from the preceding tables that in the last ten years the towns containing 10,000 inhabitants and upwards had more than doubled, both in number and population; and that the population of the towns containing between 10,000 and 3,000 in 1850 somewhat exceeds that of the towns containing between 10,000 and 2,000 in 1840. If we add to the former the towns of from 2,000 to 3,000 inhabitants, the number will be more than double that of the same description of towns in 1840. The town population which in the enumerated towns is now 16.1 per cent of the whole, would then be augmented to more than 20 per cent. But to produce this average there is a great diversity among the States from Rhode Island and Massachusetts, whose cities and towns contain between 40 and 50 per cent of their whole population respectively, to the States of Mississippi and North Carolina, whose towns contain probably less than 5 per cent of their whole town population.

CHAPTER XI.

THE INDUSTRIOUS CLASSES.

We are presented with an interesting subject of speculation when we look at the various modes in which the members of a civilized community, in seeking to provide for themselves and their families, administer to the wants and gratifications of others. In this way, nearly every individual in the human hive is impelled by the strongest instincts of his nature to be at once busy and useful.

Of the free population in 1850, amounting to 19,987,563, the number of males above fifteen years of age who were employed in different branches of industry was 5,371,876. Supposing the number of females, who in their appropriate employments are at least as industrious as the males, to be equal, then the industrious class of both sexes above fifteen amount to 10,743,562. The difference between this number and that of the whole free population is 9,243,811. If from this residue we deduct the tenants of the poorhouses, hospitals, jails, and penitentiaries, the superannuated and the children under fifteen, all of whom are either too young to work, are already employed or qualifying themselves for future employment, the remainder, constituting the voluntary idle and unproductive class, would be an inconsiderable portion of the community, as may be thus seen:—

Whole number, after deducting the working classes		9,243,811
Children under fifteen by the census	8,173,896	
Persons over seventy by the same	308,686	
Paupers by the same	50,352	
In hospitals for the insane, blind, &c., by the same	50,994	
In State prisons and penitentiaries, by the same	5,646	
In jails and houses of correction	7,444	
		8,597,018
Whole number of idle class		646,793

It would thus seem that the whole number of the idle class of both sexes between the ages of fifteen and seventy is less than 3 per cent, or one person in thirty-three of the free population; and though the labor to which man is inevitably destined is occasionally excessive or irksome, yet in the main his bread is sweetened as well as moistened by the sweat with which it is earned.

Their whole 5,371,876 are distributed at the census office into 325 different occupations, which have been afterwards condensed into the following ten more general divisions, nearly correspondent to the classification made of the occupations in England, viz.:—

1. Commerce, trade, manufacturing, and mechanic arts and mining.
2. Agriculture.
3. Labor not agricultural.
4. Army.
5. Sea and river navigation.
6. Law, medicine, and divinity.
7. Other pursuits requiring education.
8. Government civil service.
9. Domestic servants.
10. Other occupations.

The distribution among the States and Territories may be seen in the following:—

TABLE OF THE EMPLOYMENTS OF THE FREE MALE POPULATION OVER FIFTEEN YEARS OF AGE IN 1850.

	Commerce, manufactures, mining, etc.	Agriculture.	Labor not agricultural.	Army.	Sea and river navigation.	Law, medicine, and divinity.
Maine	38,247	77,082	26,833	114	15,669	2,212
New Hampshire	27,905	47,440	14,253	38	778	1,642
Vermont	17,063	48,328	22,997	....	159	1,827
Massachusetts	146,002	55,669	57,942	72	19,598	4,702
Rhode Island	21,004	8,482	9,295	....	2,033	556
Connecticut	38,653	31,881	16,813	....	4,801	1,614
New York	312,697	313,980	196,613	1,462	23,243	14,258
New Jersey	46,544	32,834	38,383	....	4,351	1,751
Pennsylvania	266,927	207,495	163,628	101	9,064	9,954
Delaware	5,633	7,884	6,663	....	743	251
Maryland	47,616	28,588	32,102	67	9,740	2,059
District of Columbia	6,128	421	2,535	91	186	330
Virginia	52,675	108,364	48,338	274	3,263	4,791
North Carolina	20,613	81,982	28,560	....	1,659	2,263
South Carolina	13,205	41,302	8,151	....	346	1,829
Georgia	20,715	83,362	11,505	18	282	2,815
Florida	2,380	5,977	2,666	423	708	357
Alabama	16,630	68,638	7,683	....	807	2,616
Mississippi	12,053	50,284	6,067	....	292	2,329
Louisiana	32,879	18,639	15,264	45	4,263	1,827
Texas	7,327	25,299	6,194	584	321	1,368
Arkansas	4,296	28,942	5,684	33	106	911
Tennessee	23,432	118,979	17,559	....	258	3,363
Missouri	30,098	65,561	20,326	305	2,471	2,893
Kentucky	36,598	115,017	28,413	204	1,027	3,811
Ohio	142,687	270,362	92,765	....	4,109	9,001
Indiana	45,318	163,229	29,854	....	1,725	4,229
Illinois	36,232	141,099	29,778	....	1,644	3,307
Michigan	22,375	65,815	15,602	143	1,220	2,007
Wisconsin	20,526	40,980	13,196	77	561	1,477
Iowa	9,255	32,779	5,392	71	163	1,077
California	69,007	2,059	3,771	149	617	876
Minnesota	656	563	751	163	4	68
New Mexico	1,054	7,956	6,209	655	2	45
Oregon	1,007	1,704	511	289	130	99
Utah	828	1,581	622	...	18	26
Total	1,596,265	2,400,583	993,620	5,370	116,341	94,515

	Other occupat'ns requiring education.	Government civil service.	Domestic servants.	Other occupations.	Total.
Maine	1,727	419	232	125	162,711
New Hampshire	1,425	305	47	31	94,564
Vermont	1,563	129	34	127	92,226
Massachusetts	5,371	1,566	1,375	2,972	295,300
Rhode Island	881	176	774	269	43,471
Connecticut	2,162	189	220	677	97,010
New York	11,104	4,985	6,324	3,628	888,294
New Jersey	2,457	373	404	1,663	128,740
Pennsylvania	10,830	3,719	4,431	4,495	680,644
Delaware	581	124	69	113	22,061
Maryland	2,442	963	1,021	278	124,876
District of Columbia	436	559	507	16	11,209
Virginia	5,622	1,491	79	1,978	226,875
North Carolina	3,447	570	46	247	139,387
South Carolina	3,161	372	149	34	68,549
Georgia	3,942	416	15	173	123,343

	Other occupat'ns requiring education.	Government civil service.	Domestic servants.	Other occupations.	Total.
Florida	302	258	12	42	13,135
Alabama	3,638	325	42	97	100,467
Mississippi	3,380	377	69	231	75,082
Louisiana	2,444	811	308	488	77,168
Texas	996	677	....	90	42,856
Arkansas	676	110	....	27	46,785
Tennessee	3,589	705	10	345	168,240
Missouri	3,147	767	1,458	1,149	128,175
Kentucky	4,420	902	212	471	191,075
Ohio	8,263	1,218	1,167	1,219	550,792
Indiana	3,031	677	184	449	248,096
Illinois	2,071	701	376	151	215,350
Michigan	1,092	337	220	167	108,978
Wisconsin	800	185	191	145	78,139
Iowa	425	103	10	46	49,315
California	198	130	710	123	77,631
Minnesota	37	59	15	20	2,336
New Mexico	58	206	1,292	1	17,478
Oregon	48	40	40	6	3,874
Utah	48	12	....	....	3,135
Total	95,814	24,966	22,243	22,159	5,371,876

The following fivefold division of the various occupations seems to separate those who are most essentially different: 1st, those whose industry is chiefly exerted in mental labor; 2d, those who are employed in producing useful raw materials; 3d, those who change the form of those materials by manufacture or handicraft; 4th, those who aid in transferring the raw or manufactured article from person to person or place to place; and, 5th, those who belong to neither of the preceding classes, or partly to one and partly to another. We will notice each of these general divisions separately, with the principal occupations belonging to each:—

FIVEFOLD DIVISION OF THE OCCUPATIONS OF THE FREE MALES ABOVE FIFEEEN IN THE UNITED STATES, ETC.

I.—MENTAL INDUSTRY.

	Number employed.		Number employed.
Students	42,340	Editors	1,372
Physicians and surgeons	49,755	Civil engineers	512
Professors and teachers	30,550	Architects	591
Clergymen	26,842	Other occupations	1,844
Lawyers	23,939		
Public officers	10,268	Total	179,023

II.—PRODUCERS.

	Number employed.		Number employed.
Farmers	2,363,938	Fishermen	9,025
Miners	77,410	Ironfounders	9,271
Planters	27,055	Oystermen	2,244
Iron furnaces	14,437	Quarrymen	1,902
Weavers	31,872	Hunters and trappers	619
Coal miners and colliers	17,385	Nurserymen	335
Lumbermen	20,070	Other occupations	2,911
Gardeners, &c.	8,144		
Total			2,544,771

III.—MANUFACTURES.

	Number employed.		Number employed.
Carpenters	181,671	Watchmakers	2,901
Cordwainers	130,473	Chandlers	2,388
Blacksmiths	99,708	Confectioners	3,871
Masons and bricklayers	63,392	Nailmakers	2,046
Tailors	52,069	Bookbinders	3,414
Coopers	48,694	Boatbuilders	2,086
Cabinet-makers	37,339	Dyers, &c.	3,241
Weavers	31,872	Engravers	2,208
Wheelwrights	30,693	Paper munufacturers	2,971
Painters and glaziers	28,166	Paper-hangers	2,572
Millers	27,795	Rope and cord makers	2,200
Machinists	24,095	Sailmakers	2,182
Saddlers	22,779	Sash and blind makers	2,025
Butchers	17,733	Caulkers	1,915
Bakers	14,256	Basketmakers	1,841
Stonecutters	14,076	Tuners	1,823
Printers	14,740	Piano-makers	1,822
Ship carpenters	14,565	Comb-makers	1,782
Sawyers	11,974	Carvers and gilders	1,742
Clockmakers	11,812	Boiler-makers	1,581
Brickmakers	11,514	Wagon-makers	1,550
Millwrights	9,613	Pattern-makers	1,374
Tinsmiths	11,747	Woodcutters	1,322
Tobacconists	10,823	Agricult'al implement mak'rs.	1,313
Joiners	12,672	Plumbers	1.304
Coachmakers	14,049	Broom-makers	1,244
Molders	7,237	Shingle-makers	1,285
Spinners	5,692	Trimmers	1,238
Iron-workers	5,008	Brush-makers	1,227
Brewers	4,854	Morocco dressers	1,223
Potters	4,155	Carpet-makers	1,218
Gunsmiths	3,843	Clock-makers	1,181
Glass manufacturers	3,237	Riggers	1,115
Woolcombers	3,206	Trunk-makers	1,161
Turners	3,823	Salt-makers	1,026
Gold and silver smiths	3,082	Woolen manufacturers	1,037
Stovemakers	3,747	Lime burners	1,013
Jewelers	5,111	Block and pump makers	1,973
Tanners, &c.	14,988	Other occupations	119,256
Total			1,229,609

IV.—MERCHANTS AND TRANSPORTERS.

	Number employed.		Number employed.
Merchants	100,752	Barkeepers	5,479
Mariners	70,603	Booksellers	1,720
Boatmen	32.454	Drovers	1,999
Grocers	24,479	Milkmen	2,328
Teamsters	15,469	Storekeepers	3,747
Carters	13,879	Clothiers	3,780
Railroad men	4,831	Auctioneers	1,890
Porters, &c.	3,185	Pilots	2,015
Brokers	2,555	Dealers	4,684
Bankers, &c.	1,927	Other occupations	3,226
Apothecaries	6,139		
Total			316,053

V.—MISCELLANEOUS.

	Number employed.		Number employed.
Laborers	909,786	Dentists	2,923
Clerks	101,325	Artists	2,023
Servants	22,243	Apprentices	1,847
Innkeepers	22,476	Woodcutters	1,222
Barbers	61,013	Actors	722
Soldiers	5,149	Boarding-house keepers	2,554
Agents	6,264	Refectory keepers	3,226
Ostlers	4,029	Telegraph officers	544
Musicians	2,606	Gate keepers	1,168
Livery stable keepers	2,741	Other occupations	3,561
Total			1,102,422

THE PRECEDING DIVISIONS, IN CENTESIMAL PROPORTIONS, ARE AS FOLLOWS:—

I.	179,023	persons constitute about	3	per cent.
II.	2,544,777	"	48	"
III.	1,229,607	"	24	"
IV.	316,053	"	6	"
V.	1,102,422	"	19	"
	5,731,876		100	

But if the miscellaneous class be distributed among the three classes employed in production, manufacture, and Commerce, according to their respective numbers—which is probably not wide of the truth—then the two classes of producers and manufacturers will comprehend seven-eighths of the whole, while three-fourths of the other eighth are employed in Commerce and transportation, and the remaining fourth, or about one-thirtieth of the whole are sufficient to discharge the functions of civil government, of juvenile instruction, and the learned professions.

We may see the progress of manufactures generally, from 1820 to 1850, in the following:—

TABLE OF THE PERSONS EMPLOYED IN MANUFACTURING ESTABLISHMENTS IN EACH STATE IN 1820 AND 1840, AND ALSO IN 1850, IN THOSE PRODUCING OVER $500 EACH.

	1820.	1840.	1850.
Maine	7,643	21,879	28,078
New Hampshire	8,600	17,826	27,092
Vermont	8,484	13,174	8,445
Massachusetts	33,454	85,176	165,938
Rhode Island	6,091	21,271	20,881
Connecticut	17,541	27,932	47,770
New York	60,038	173,193	199,349
New Jersey	15,941	27,004	37,311
Pennsylvania	60,215	105,883	146,766
Delaware	2,821	4,060	3,888
Maryland	18,640	21,879	30,124
District of Columbia	2,184	2,278	2,176
Virginia	32,336	54,147	29,109
North Carolina	11,844	14,322	12,444
South Carolina	6,091	10,325	7,000
Georgia	3,557	7,984	8,378
Florida	....	1,779	991
Alabama	1,412	7,195	4,936
Mississippi	650	4,157	3,179
Louisiana	6,041	7,565	6,437
Texas	....	....	1,066
Arkansas	179	1,172	903

	1820.	1840.	1850.
Tennessee	7,860	17,815	12,032
Missouri	1,952	11,100	16,850
Kentucky	11,779	23,217	24,385
Ohio	18,956	65,265	51,489
Indiana	3,229	20,590	14,342
Illinois	1,007	13,185	12,065
Michigan	650	6,890	9,290
Wisconsin	....	1,814	6,089
Iowa	....	1,629	1,707
California	....	....	3,964
Minnesota	....	....	63
New Mexico	....	....	81
Oregon	....	....	317
Utah	....	....	51
Total	349,247	791,545	944,991

While manufacturing industry appears, by the preceding table, to have considerably increased in the New England and Middle States, in nearly all the others it was less in 1850 than in 1840, by reason, no doubt, of other branches of industry having become more profitable.

The important manufactures of cotton, wool, and iron, are distributed among the States, according to the following tables:—

COTTON MANUFACTURES, 1850.

	Value of raw material.	No. of hands employed.	Value produced.
Maine	$1,573,110	3,739	$2,596,356
New Hampshire	4,839,429	12,122	8,830,619
Vermont	114,415	241	196,160
Massachusetts	11,289,309	28,730	19,712,461
Rhode Island	3,484,579	10,875	6,447,120
Connecticut	2,500,062	6,186	4,257,522
New York	1,985,973	6,320	3,591,989
New Jersey	666,645	1,712	1,109,524
Pennsylvania	3,152,530	7,663	5,322,262
Delaware	212,068	838	538,439
Maryland	1,165,579	3,022	2,120,504
Virginia	828,375	2,963	1,486,384
North Carolina	531,903	1,619	831,342
South Carolina	295,971	1,019	748,338
Georgia	900,419	2,272	2,135,044
Florida	30,000	95	49,920
Alabama	237,081	715	382,260
Mississippi	21,500	36	30,500
Arkansas	8,975	31	16,637
Tennessee	297,500	891	510,624
Kentucky	180,907	402	273,439
Missouri	86,446	155	142,900
Ohio	237,060	401	394,700
Indiana	900,419	95	44,200
Total	34,835,036	87,286	61,869,184

WOOLLEN MANUFACTURES, 1850.

Connecticut	$3,325,709	5,488	$6,465,216
Maine	495,940	624	753,300
New Hampshire	1,267,329	2,127	2,127,745
Vermont	830,684	1,393	1,572,161
Massachusetts	8,671,671	11,130	12,770,565
Rhode Island	1,463,900	1,758	2,381,825

WOOLLEN MANUFACTURES, 1850.

	Value of raw material.	No. of hands employed.	Value produced.
New York	3,838,292	6,674	7,030,604
New Jersey	548,367	898	1,164,446
Pennsylvania	3,282,718	5,726	5,321,866
Delaware	204,172	140	251,000
Maryland	165,568	362	295,140
Virginia	488,899	668	841,013
North Carolina	13,950	30	23,750
Georgia	30,392	78	88,750
Texas	10,000	8	15,000
Tennessee	1,675	17	6,310
Missouri	16,000	25	56,000
Kentucky	205,287	318	318,319
Ohio	578,423	1,201	1,111,027
Indiana	120,486	216	205,802
Illinois	115,367	178	206,572
Michigan	43,402	129	90,240
Iowa	3,500	7	13,000
Wisconsin	32,630	25	87,992
Total	25,755,678	39,252	48,207,545

IRON MANUFACTURES, 1850.

	IRON CASTINGS.		
Maine	$112,570	244	$265,000
New Hampshire	177,060	374	371,710
Vermont	160,603	381	450,831
Massachusetts	1,057,904	1,546	2,235,035
Rhode Island	258,267	800	728,705
Connecticut	351,369	949	981,400
New York	2,393,768	5,925	5,921,980
New Jersey	177,060	803	686,430
Pennsylvania	2,422,467	4,782	5,354,481
Delaware	153,852	250	267,462
Maryland	259,190	761	685,000
Virginia	297,014	816	674,416
North Carolina	8,341	15	12,867
South Carolina	28,128	155	87,683
Georgia	172,530	39	46,200
Alabama	102,085	212	271,126
Mississippi	50,570	112	717,400
Louisiana	75,300	347	342,500
Tennessee	90,035	261	264,325
Missouri	133,114	297	336,495
Kentucky	295,533	558	744,316
Ohio	2,372,467	2,758	3,069,350
Indiana	66,918	143	149,430
Illinois	172,330	332	441,185
Michigan	91,865	337	279,697
Wisconsin	86,930	228	216,195
Iowa	2,524	17	8,500
Texas	8,400	35	55,000
California	8,530	3	20,740
Total	10,346,265	23,589	25,108,155

	WROUGHT-IRON.		
New Hampshire	$11,575	9	$20,400
Vermont	83,094	79	127,886
Massachusetts	2,430,533	2,524	2,908,952
Rhode Island	112,123	222	223,650
Connecticut	517,554	394	847,196

	WROUGHT-IRON.		
	Value of raw material.	No. of hands employed.	Value produced.
New York	2,305,441	2,130	3,758,547
New Jersey	566,865	935	1,079,576
Pennsylvania	5,698,563	6,591	9,224,256
Delaware	35,410	47	38,200
Maryland	412,050	468	771,431
Virginia	531,325	1,131	1,098,252
North Carolina	50,089	262	331,914
Georgia	4 136	27	12,384
Alabama	3,355	34	7,500
Tennessee	585,616	786	670,618
Missouri	24,509	101	68,700
Kentucky	180,800	183	299,700
Ohio	193,148	276	127,849
Indiana	4,425	22	11,760
Total	13,524,777	16,248	22,629,271

Of all the facilities to internal Commerce and transportation, no one has increased like railroads in the United States.

	Miles.		Miles.
In 1830 the railroads extended...	41	In 1845 the railroads extended...	4,511
In 1835 " " ...	918	In 1850 " " ...	7,355
In 1840 " " ...	2,167		

THE NUMBER OF CANALS AND RAILROADS IN THE UNITED STATES IN 1854, IS THUS GIVEN IN DE BOW'S COMPENDIUM, PAGE 189:—

	Miles of Canal.	RAILROADS. Miles in operation.	Miles in progress.	Cost.
Maine	50	417	90	$13,660,645
New Hampshire	11	512	24	16,185,254
Vermont	...	422	59	14,116,195
Massachusetts	100	1,283	48	55,602,687
Rhode Island	...	50	...	2,614,484
Connecticut	61	221	...	20,857,357
New York	989	2,345	564	94,523,785
New Jersey	147	408	29	11,536,505
Pennsylvania	936	1,464	987	58,494,675
Delaware	14	16	43	600,000
Maryland	184	597	30	26,024,620
Virginia	189	673	1,180	12,720,421
North Carolina	13	249	223	4,106,000
South Carolina	50	575	374	11,287,093
Georgia	28	884	445	16,084,872
Florida	...	43	...	600,000
Alabama	51	221	659	3,636,208
Mississippi	...	155	436	3,070,000
Louisiana	101	117	119	1,131,000
Texas	...	...	72	....
Tennessee	...	388	695	7,800,000
Missouri	...	50	963	1,000,000
Kentucky	486	233	452	4,909,990
Ohio	921	2,367	1,578	44,927,058
Indiana	367	1,127	748	22,400,000
Illinois	100	1,262	1,945	25,420,000
Michigan	...	601	...	13,842,279
Wisconsin	...	178	200	3,800,000
Iowa	...	...	480	....
Total	4,798	17,317	12,526	$489,603,128

It seems, from the preceding table, that of the 4,798 miles of canal, nearly one-half, or 2,270, is in the Middle States; and that of the 17,317 miles of railroad completed in 1854, about five-twelfths, or 5,034 miles, are in the same States. The average cost of the roads is about $40,000 per mile, though in the Southern and Southwestern States they have averaged less than half that cost.

We may here notice the shipping of the United States, by which the whole of their Commerce with foreign countries is carried on, (except an insignificant portion with the British possessions on the Northeast, and with Mexico on the Southwest,) and a large part of that of the States with each other. It is of three descriptions:—

1st. The Registered Tonnage, which is the exclusive vehicle of the foreign trade, and which is therefore subjected to stricter regulation.

2d. The Enrolled Tonnage, which is employed principally in the coasting trade and the fisheries.

3d. The Licensed Tonnage, comprehending vessels of 20 tons and less, which is employed partly in the coasting trade and partly in the fisheries. The progress of tonnage from 1800 to 1850, may be seen in the following:—

TABLE OF THE TONNAGE OF THE UNITED STATES, BOTH REGISTERED AND ENROLLED AND LICENSED, IN QUINQUENNIAL PERIODS FROM 1800 TO 1850.

	Registered tonnage.	Enrol'd and licensed tonnage.	Total.
1800	669,921	245,929	972,492
1805	749,341	301,366	1,140,368
1810	984,269	371,114	1,424,683
1815	854,294	435,066	1,368,127
1820	619,047	661,118	1,280,166
1825	700,787	722,323	1,423,110
1830	576,475	615,301	1,191,776
1835	885,321	939,118	1,824,940
1840	899,764	1,280,999	2,180,764
1845	1,095,172	1,321,829	2.417,002
1850	1,585,711	1,949,743	3,545,450

Thus showing nearly a fourfold increase in half a century.

THE WHOLE TONNAGE WAS THUS DISTRIBUTED AMONG THE STATES IN 1850:—

	Tons.
Maine	501,422
New Hampshire	23,096
Vermont	4,530
Massachusetts	685,442
Rhode Island	44,480
Connecticut	113,087
New York	944,349
New Jersey	80,300
Pennsylvania	258,939
Delaware	16,720
Maryland	193,087
District of Columbia	17,011
Virginia	74,071
North Carolina	45,219
South Carolina	36,072
Georgia	21,690
Florida	11,273
Alabama	24,158
Mississippi	1,828
Louisiana	250,090
Texas	4;573
Tennessee	3,776
Kentucky	14,820
Missouri	28,908
Illinois	21,242
Ohio	62,462
Michigan	38,145
Oregon	1,063
California	17,592
Total	3,545,450

Of which more than four-fifths are owned in the New England and Middle States, and one-third by Maine and Massachusetts.

CHAPTER XII.

PAUPERISM AND CRIME.

In the most fortunate and best regulated community a portion will be found who are unable to earn a subsistence by their own efforts, and another portion who violate the rights of others; in other words, no country is exempt from poverty and crime. In considering these drawbacks from the benefits of civilization, our notice will at once show their amount and the means adopted by the laws for their correction.

The relief afforded to the destitute by individual contribution is too minute and irregular to be estimated by statistics. Our attention will, therefore, be confined to those who are relieved by public charitable establishments.

According to the returns of the seventh census, the number of paupers in the United States on the 1st of June, 1850, was 50,353, which is equal to about 1 for every 40,000 of the free population. Somewhat more than a fourth of them are foreigners, and they are thus distributed among the several States:—

States.	Natives.	Foreign.	Total.	States.	Natives.	Foreign.	Total
Maine	3,209	326	3,515	Florida	58	4	62
New Hampshire	1,998	186	2,184	Alabama	306	9	315
Vermont	1,565	314	1,879	Mississippi	245	12	257
Massachusetts	4,059	1,490	5,549	Louisiana	76	30	106
Rhode Island	492	204	696	Texas	4	...	4
Connecticut	1,463	281	1,744	Arkansas	67	...	67
New York	5,755	7,078	12,833	Tennessee	577	14	591
New Jersey	1,339	239	1,578	Missouri	251	254	505
Pennsylvania	2,654	1,157	3,811	Kentucky	690	87	777
Delaware	240	33	273	Ohio	1,254	419	1,673
Maryland	1,681	320	2,001	Indiana	446	137	583
Virginia	4,356	102	4,458	Illinois	279	155	434
North Carolina	1,567	13	1,580	Michigan	248	181	429
South Carolina	1,113	180	1,293	Wisconsin	72	166	238
Georgia	825	29	854	Iowa	27	17	44
Total					36,916	13,437	50,353

The annual cost of supporting these paupers is $2,954,806, equivalent to $58 to each pauper.

Besides these public charities, in all the cities many of the poor are relieved by permanent charitable societies.

The information as yet derived from the seventh census respecting criminals is of a very limited character. The following table exhibits the number of convictions within the year preceding, the number imprisoned on June 1, 1850, distinguishing the foreigners from the natives:—

States.	No. of convictions within the year. Natives.	Foreign.	Total.	No. in prison, June 1, 1850. Natives.	Foreign.	Total.
Maine	284	460	744	66	34	100
New Hampshire	66	24	90	28	5	33
Vermont	34	45	79	64	41	105
Massachusetts	3,366	3,884	7,250	653	583	1,236
Rhode Island	309	287	596	58	45	103
Connecticut	545	305	850	244	66	310
New York	3,962	6,317	10,279	649	639	1,288
New Jersey	346	257	603	198	92	290
Pennsylvania	564	293	857	296	115	411
Delaware	22	....	22	14	...	14

States.	No. of convictions within the year. Natives.	Foreign.	Total.	No. in prison, June 1, 1850. Native.	Foreign.	Toial.
Maryland	183	24	207	325	72	397
District of Columbia	....	....	132	...	...	46
Virginia	98	9	107	291	22	313
North Carolina	634	13	647	647	43	690
South Carolina	32	14	46	21	15	36
Georgia	72	8	80	36	7	43
Florida	33	6	39	9	2	11
Alabama	117	5	122	69	1	70
Mississippi	49	2	51	45	1	46
Louisiana	197	100	297	240	183	423
Texas	15	4	19	5	10	15
Arkansas	24	1	25	35	27	62
Tennessee	73	8	81	276	12	288
Missouri	242	666	908	55	125	180
Kentucky	126	34	160	41	11	52
Ohio	689	154	843	102	31	133
Indiana	150	25	175	41	18	59
Illinois	127	189	316	164	88	252
Michigan	273	386	659	139	102	241
Wisconsin	105	162	267	26	35	61
Iowa	2	1	3	5	...	5
California	1	...	1	35	27	62
Minnesota	1	1	2	...	1	1
New Mexico	104	4	108	37	1	38
Oregon	5	...	5	5	...	5
Utah	6	3	9	6	3	9
Total	12,856	13,691	26,679	4,925	2,457	7,428

The following table of persons in jails and penitentiaries, was made up at the Census Office from the population returns; and though not agreeing with the preceding,* it is here inserted, partly because it is more likely to be accurate, and partly because it distinguishes the sexes, and the white from the colored population :—

States.	Whites. Males	Females	Native	Foreign	Total	Colored. Males	Females	Total	G. total
Maine	79	..	62	17	79	..	..	..	79
New Hampshire	89	2	77	14	91	..	..	..	91
Vermont	69	..	39	30	69	..	..	..	69
Massachusetts	389	..	264	125	389	42	..	42	431
Rhode Island	35	..	21	14	35	3	..	3	38
Connecticut	136	10	117	29	146	27	3	30	176
New York	1,310	70	835	545	1,380	230	21	251	1,631
New Jersey	117	6	86	37	123	48	1	49	172
Pennsylvania	322	6	205	123	328	94	9	103	431
Delaware	1	..	1	...	1	4	1	5	6
Maryland	110	5	81	34	115	99	21	120	235
District of Columbia	25	2	17	10	27	18	10	28	55
Virginia	128	2	119	11	130	65	4	69	199
North Carolina	11	1	12	...	12	2	..	2	14
South Carolina	31	1	19	13	32	..	..	..	32
Georgia	88	1	85	4	89	..	..	..	89
Florida	12	..	12	...	12	..	..	..	12

* Some of the discrepancy arises from the fact that the last table includes slaves, which were not comprehended in the first. Notwithstanding this, the proportion of crime is much less in the slave-holding States, even in the native population. According to Mr. Bow's statement (see compendium, page 16,) the number of criminals in those States is less than one-third of the whole, or 988 out of 3,259.

States.	Whites. Males	Females	Native	Foreign	Total	Colored. Males	Female	Total	G. total
Alabama	116	1	21	97	117	2	..	2	119
Mississippi	85	..	80	5	85	1	..	1	86
Louisiana	191	4	89	106	195	54	12	71	266
Texas	5	..	2	3	5	1	..	1	6
Arkansas	37	..	37	...	37	1	..	1	38
Tennessee	188	1	180	9	189	6	1	7	196
Missouri	165	..	107	58	165	1	..	1	166
Kentucky	147	..	126	21	147	15	..	15	162
Ohio	359	3	291	71	362	41	3	44	406
Indiana	131	..	106	25	131	15	..	15	146
Illinois	127	..	85	42	127	8	1	9	136
Michigan	111	..	73	38	111	16	..	16	127
Wisconsin	27	..	8	19	27	3	..	3	30
Iowa	2	..	2	...	2	..	..	..	2
Total	4,643	115	3,259	1,499	4,758	801	87	888	5,646

CHAPTER XIII.

THE PRODUCTS OF AGRICULTURE.

Of all the pursuits of human industry, that of agriculture, which so multiplies the fruits of the earth, is the most important in the eyes of the statesman and philosopher. It affords all the materials to manufactures; contributes largely to those of commerce, and, more than all, it furnishes food to man. It thus determines the numbers, wealth, and strength of all large communities, and constitutes the only solid and permanent basis for their prosperity.

Under the most improved system of husbandry, its products are greatly affected by the seasons, and a diminution of the crop produces, in much greater proportion, an enhancement of price. This evil is greatly mitigated in modern times by the extension and improvement of the commerce between nations, but it is not remedied; and though it very rarely happens that an individual in a civilized community dies of actual starvation, yet in seasons of scarcity members slowly perish from an insufficiency of wholesome food.

From this dire calamity the United States are now entirely exempt, and in future times, when their population becomes dense, they have a defense against it which few countries possess. They cultivate two kinds of grain —wheat and Indian corn—which are equally palatable and wholesome, and which, ripening at different times of the year, and requiring a difference of seasons, it rarely happens that they both fail in the same year; and thus the deficiency in some places is compensated by the abundance in others.

These products having been distributed under nearly the same heads by the census of 1850 as by that of 1840, they can be readily compared, and the progress of the country in most of the items can be seen. The number of live stock and the quantity of the principal agricultural products in 1850, may be seen in the following table:—

States.	Horses.	Asses and mules.	Milch cows.	Working oxen.
Maine	41,721	....	......	.....
New Hampshire	34,233	55	133,556	83,893
Vermont	61,057	19	94,277	59,027
Massachusetts	42,216	218	146,128	48.577
Rhode Island	6,168	1	18,698	8,189
Connecticut	26,879	49	85,461	46,988
New York	447,014	963	931,324	173,909
New Jersey	63,955	4,089	118,736	12,070
Pennsylvania	350,398	2,259	530,224	61,527
Delaware	13,852	791	19,248	9,797
Maryland	75,684	5,644	86,856	34,135
District of Columbia	824	57	813	104
Virginia	272,403	21,483	317,619	89,513
North Carolina	148,693	25,259	221,799	37,309
South Carolina	97,171	37,483	193,244	20,507
Georgia	151,331	57,379	334,223	73,286
Florida	10,848	5,002	72,876	5,794
Alabama	128,001	59,895	227,791	66,961
Mississippi	115,460	54,547	214,231	83,485
Louisiana	89,514	44,849	105,576	54,968
Texas	76,760	12,463	217,811	51,285
Arkansas	60,197	11,559	93,151	34,239
Tennessee	270,636	75,303	250,456	86,255
Missouri	225,319	41,667	230,169	112,168
Kentucky	315,682	65,609	247,475	62,274
Ohio	463,397	3,423	544,499	65,381
Indiana	314,299	6,599	284,554	49,221
Illinois	267,653	10,573	294,671	76,156
Michigan	58,506	70	99,676	55,350
Wisconsin	30,179	156	64,339	42,801
Iowa	38,536	754	45,704	21,892
California	21,719	1,666	4,280	4,790
Minnesota	860	14	607	655
New Mexico	5,079	8,654	10,635	12,257
Oregon	8,046	420	9,427	8,114
Utah	2,429	325	4,861	5,266
Total	4,336,719	559,331	6,385,094	1,700,744

States.	Other cattle.	Sheep.	Swine.
Maine	......	......	......
New Hampshire	125,890	451,577	54,598
Vermont	114,606	384,756	63,487
Massachusetts	154,143	1,014,122	66,296
Rhode Island	9,375	44,296	19,509
Connecticut	80,226	174,181	76,472
New York	767,406	3,453,241	1,018,252
New Jersey	80,455	160,488	250,370
Pennsylvania	502,196	1,822,357	1,040,366
Delaware	24,166	27,503	56,261
Maryland	98,595	177,902	352,911
District of Columbia	123	150	1,635
Virginia	669,137	1,310,004	1,829,843
North Carolina	434,402	595,249	1,812,813
South Carolina	563,935	285,551	1,065,503
Georgia	690,019	560,435	2,168,617
Florida	182,415	23,311	209,453
Alabama	433,263	371,880	1,904,540
Mississippi	436,254	304,929	1,582,734
Louisiana	414,798	110,333	597,301
Texas	61,018	100,530	692,022
Arkansas	165,329	91,256	836,727
Tennessee	414,051	811,591	3,104,800

States.	Other cattle.	Sheep.	Swine.
Missouri	449,173	762,511	1,702,625
Kentucky	442,763	1,102,091	2,891,163
Ohio	749,067	3,942,929	1,964,770
Indiana	389,891	1,122,493	2,263,776
Illinois	541,209	894,043	1,915,907
Michigan	119,471	746,435	205,847
Wisconsin	76,293	124,896	159,276
Iowa	69,025	149,966	323,247
California	253,599	17,574	2,776
Minnesota	740	80	734
New Mexico	10,085	377,271	7,314
Oregon	24,188	15,382	30,235
Utah	2,489	3,262	914
Total	9,698,069	21,723,220	30,354,213

States.	Value of live stock.	Value of slaughtered animals.	Bushels of wheat.	Bushels o rye.
Maine	$9,705,726	$1,646,773	226,259	102,916
New Hampshire	8,871,901	1,522,873	185,658	183,117
Vermont	12,643,228	1,861,336	635,955	176,233
Massachusetts	9,647,710	2,500,924	31,211	481,021
Rhode Island	1,532,637	667,486	49	26,409
Connecticut	7,467,490	2,202,266	41,762	600,893
New York	73,570,409	13,573,883	13,121,498	4,148,182
New Jersey	10,679,291	2,638,552	1,601,190	1,255,578
Pennsylvania	41,500,053	8,219,848	15,367,691	4,816,169
Delaware	1,849,281	373,665	482,511	8,066
Maryland	7,997,634	1,954,809	4,494,689	226,014
District of Columbia	71,643	9,638	17,370	5,509
Virginia	33,656,659	7,502,986	11,212,616	458,930
North Carolina	17,717,647	5,767,866	2,130,102	239,563
South Carolina	15,060,015	3,502,637	1,066,277	43,790
Georgia	25,728,416	6,339,762	1,088,534	53,750
Florida	2,880,058	514,685	1,027	1,152
Alabama	21,690,112	4,823,485	294,044	17,261
Mississippi	19,403,662	3,636,582	137,990	9,606
Louisiana	11,152,275	1,458,990	417	475
Texas	10,412,927	1,116,137	41,729	3,108
Arkansas	6,647,960	1,163,313	169,639	8,047
Tennessee	29,978,016	6,401,765	1,619,386	89,137
Kentucky	29,661,436	6,462,598	2,142,822	415,073
Missouri	19,887,580	3,367,106	2,981,652	44,268
Illinois	24,209,258	4,972,286	9,414,575	83,364
Indiana	22,478,555	6,567,935	6,214,458	78,792
Ohio	44,121,741	7,439,243	14,487,351	425,918
Michigan	5,808,734	1,328,327	4,925,889	105,871
Wisconsin	4,897,385	920,178	4,286,831	81,253
Iowa	3,689,275	821,164	1,530,581	19,916
California	3,351,058	107,173	17,328	......
Minnesota	92,859	2,840	1,401	125
New Mexico	1,491,629	82,125	196,516	......
Oregon	1,876,189	164,530	211,913	106
Utah	546,968	67,985	107,702	210
Total	$544,180,516	$111,703,142	100,485,944	14,188,813

States.	Bushels of Indian corn.	Bushels of oats.	Lbs. of rice.
Maine	1,750,056	2,181,637	....
New Hampshire	1,573,670	973,381	....
Vermont	2,032,396	2,307,734	....
Massachusetts	2,345,490	1,165,146	....
Rhode Island	539,201	215,232	....

8

States.	Bushels of Indian corn.	Bushels of oats.	Lbs. of rice.
Connecticut	1,935,043	1,258,738	....
New York	17,858,400	26,552,844	....
New Jersey	8,759,704	3,378,663	....
Pennsylvania	19,835,214	21,538,156	....
Delaware	3,145,542	664,518	....
Maryland	10,749,858	1,242,151	....
District of Columbia	65,230	8,134	....
Virginia	35,254,319	10,179,144	17,154
North Carolina	27,941,051	4,052,078	5,465,868
South Carolina	16,271,454	2,322,155	159,930,613
Georgia	30,080,099	3,820,044	38,950,691
Florida	1,996,809	66,586	1,075,090
Alabama	28,754,048	2,965,696	2,312,252
Mississippi	22,446,552	1,503,288	2,719,856
Louisiana	10,266,373	89,637	4,425,349
Texas	6,028,876	199,017	88,203
Arkansas	8,893,939	656,183	63,179
Tennessee	52,276,223	7,703,086	258,854
Kentucky	58,672,591	8,201,311	5,688
Missouri	36,214,537	5,278,079	700
Illinois	57,646,984	10,087,241	....
Indiana	52,964,363	5,655,014	....
Ohio	59,078,695	13,472,742	....
Michigan	5,641,420	2,866,056	....
Wisconsin	1,988,979	3,414,672	....
Iowa	8,656,799	1,524,345	....
California	12,236	....	....
Minnesota	16,725	30,582	....
New Mexico	365,411	5	....
Oregon	2,918	61,214	....
Utah	9,899	10,900	....
Total	592,071,104	146,584,179	215,313,497

	Pounds tobacco.	Bales cotton of 400 lbs. each.	Pounds wool.	Bushels peas & beans.
Maine	....	......	1,364,034	205.541
New Hampshire	50	......	1,108,476	70,856
Vermont	....	......	3,400,717	104.649
Massachusetts	138,246	......	585,136	43,709
Rhode Island	....	......	129,692	6,846
Connecticut	1,267,624	......	497,454	19,090
New York	83,189	......	10,071,301	741,546
New Jersey	310	......	375,396	14,174
Pennsylvania	912,651	......	4,481,570	55,231
Delaware	....	......	57,768	4,129
Maryland	21,407,497	......	477,438	12,816
District of Columbia	7,820	......	525	7,754
Virginia	56,803,227	3,947	2,860,765	521,579
North Carolina	11,984,786	73,845	970,738	1,584,252
South Carolina	74,285	300,901	487,233	1,026,900
Georgia	423,924	499,091	990,019	1,142,011
Florida	998,614	45,131	23,247	135,359
Alabama	164,990	564,429	657,118	892,701
Mississippi	49,960	484,292	559,619	1,072,757
Louisiana	26,878	178,737	109,897	161,732
Texas	66,897	58,072	131,917	179,350
Arkansas	218,936	65,344	182,595	285,738
Tennessee	20,148,932	194,532	1,364,378	369,321
Kentucky	55,501,196	758	2,297,433	202,574
Missouri	17,113,784	......	1,627,164	46,017
Illinois	841,394	......	2,150,113	82,814
Indiana	1,044,620	14	2,610,287	35,773

	Pounds tobacco.	Bales cotton of 400 lbs. each.	Pounds wool.	Bushels peas & beans.
Ohio	10,454,449	......	10,196,371	60,168
Michigan	1,245	......	2,013,283	74,254
Wisconsin	1,268	......	253,963	20,657
Iowa	6,041	......	373,898	4,775
California	1,000	......	5,320	2,292
Minnesota	....	......	85	10,002
New Mexico	8,467	......	32,901	15,688
Oregon	325	......	29,686	6,566
Utah	70	......	9,222	289
Total	199,752,655	2,409,093	52,516,959	9,219,901

	Irish potatoes.	Sweet potatoes.	Bushels buckwheat.	Bushels barley.
Maine	3,436,040	......	104,523	151,731
New Hampshire	4,304,919	......	65,265	70,256
Vermont	4,951,014	......	209,819	42,150
Massachusetts	3,585,384	......	105,895	112,385
Rhode Island	651,629	......	1,245	18,875
Connecticut	2,689,725	80	229,297	19,090
New York	15,398,368	5,629	3,183,955	3,585,059
New Jersey	2,207,236	508,015	878,934	6,492
Pennsylvania	5,980,732	52,172	2,193,692	165,584
Delaware	240,542	65,443	8,615	56
Maryland	764,939	208,993	103,671	745
District of Columbia	28,292	3,497	378	75
Virginia	1,316,933	1,813,634	214,898	25,437
North Carolina	620,318	5,095,709	16,704	2,733
South Carolina	136,494	4,337,460	283	4,583
Georgia	227,379	6,986,428	250	11,501
Florida	7,828	757,226	55	......
Alabama	246,001	5,475,204	348	3,958
Mississippi	261,482	4,741,795	1,121	228
Louisiana	95,632	1,428,453	3	......
Texas	94,645	1,332,158	59	4,776
Arkansas	193,832	788,149	175	177
Tennessee	1,067,844	2,777,716	19,427	2,737
Kentucky	1,492,487	998,179	16,097	95,343
Missouri	939,006	335,505	23,041	9,631
Illinois	2,514,862	157,433	184,504	110,795
Indiana	2,083,337	201,711	149,749	45,483
Ohio	5,057,769	187,991	638,069	354,358
Michigan	2,359,897	1,177	472,917	75,249
Wisconsin	1,402,077	879	79,876	209,692
Iowa	276,120	6,243	52,516	25,093
California	9,292	1,000	......	9,712
Minnesota	21,145	200	515	1,216
New Mexico	3	....	100	5
Oregon	91,326	....	......	......
Utah	43,968	60	332	1,799
Total	65,747,896	38,268,148	8,956,912	5,167,015

	Value orchard produce.	Gallons wine.	Value produce of garden.	Pounds butter.
Maine	$342,865	724	$122,387	9,243,811
New Hampshire	248,543	344	56,810	6,977,056
Vermont	513,255	659	18,853	12,137,980
Massachusetts	463,995	4,688	600,020	8,071,370
Rhode Island	63,994	1,013	98,298	995,870
Connecticut	175,148	4,269	196,874	6,498,119
New York	1,761,950	9,172	912,047	79,766,094
New Jersey	607,268	1,811	475,242	9,487,218

	Value orchard produce.	Gallons wine.	Value produce of garden.	Pounds butter.
Pennsylvania..............	$723,389	25,580	$688,714	39,878,418
Delaware..................	46,574	145	12,714	1,055,308
Maryland..................	164,051	1,431	200,869	3,806,160
District of Columbia........	14,843	863	67,222	14,872
Virginia..................	177,137	5,408	183,047	11,089,359
North Carolina..............	34,348	11,058	39,462	4,146,290
South Carolina..............	35,108	5,880	47,286	2,981,850
Georgia..................	92,776	796	76,500	4,640,559
Florida..................	1,280	10	8,721	371,498
Alabama..................	15,408	220	84,821	4,008,811
Mississippi..................	50,405	407	46,250	4,346,234
Louisiana..................	22,359	15	148,329	683,069
Texas..................	12,505	19	12,354	2,344,900
Arkansas..................	40,141	35	17,150	1,854,239
Tennessee..................	52,894	92	97,183	8,139,585
Kentucky..................	106,230	8,093	303,120	9,947,523
Missouri..................	514,711	10,563	99,454	7,834,359
Illinois..................	446,049	2,997	127,494	12,526,543
Indiana..................	324,940	14,055	72,864	12,881,535
Ohio..................	695,921	48,247	214,004	34,449,379
Michigan..................	132,650	1,654	14,738	8,065,878
Wisconsin..................	4,823	113	32,142	3,633,750
Iowa..................	8,434	420	8,848	2,171,148
California..................	17,709	58,055	75,275	705
Minnesota..................	......	......	150	1,100
New Mexico..................	8,231	2,363	6,679	111
Oregon..................	1,271	......	90,241	211,464
Utah..................	......	......	23,868	83,309
Total..................	$7,723,186	221,249	$5,280,030	313,345,306

	Pounds cheese.	Tons hay.	Bushels clover.	Bush. other grasses.
Maine..................	2,434,454	755,889	9,647	9,214
New Hampshire..................	3,196,563	598,854	829	8,072
Vermont..................	8,720,834	866,153	760	14,936
Massachusetts..................	7,088,142	651,807	1,002	5,083
Rhode Island..................	316,508	74,818	1,328	3,708
Connecticut..................	5,363,277	516,131	13,841	16,628
New York..................	49,741,413	3,728,797	88,223	96,493
New Jersey..................	365,756	435,970	28,280	63,051
Pennsylvania..................	2,505,034	1,842,970	125,050	53,913
Delaware..................	3,187	30,159	2,525	1,403
Maryland..................	3,975	157,956	15,217	2,561
District of Columbia........	1,500	2,279	3	.....
Virginia..................	436,292	369,098	29,727	23,428
North Carolina..................	95,921	145,653	576	1,275
South Carolina..................	4,976	20,925	376	30
Georgia..................	46,976	23,449	132	428
Florida..................	18,015	2,510	......	2
Alabama..................	31.412	32,685	138	547
Mississippi..................	21,191	12,504	84	523
Louisiana..................	1,957	25,572	2	97
Texas..................	95,299	8,354	10	.....
Arkansas..................	30,088	3 976	90	436
Tennessee..................	177,681	74,091	5,096	9,118
Kentucky..................	213,954	113,747	3,230	21,481
Missouri..................	203,572	116,925	619	4,346
Illinois..................	1,278,225	601,952	3,427	14,380
Indiana..................	634,564	403,230	18,320	11,951
Ohio..................	20,819,542	1,443,142	103,197	37,310
Michigan..................	1,011,492	404,934	16,989	9,285
Wisconsin..................	409,283	275,662	483	5,093

	Pounds cheese.	Tons hay.	Bushels clover.	Bushels other grasses
Iowa	209,840	89,053	342	2,096
California	150	2,083	......	.....
Minnesota	....	2,019	......	.....
New Mexico	5,848	......	......	....
Oregon	36,980	373	4	22
Utah	30,998	4,805	2	.....
Total	105,535,893	13,838,642	468,978	416,831

	Pounds hops.	Tons hemp.	Pounds flax.	Bushels flaxseed.	Pounds silk cocoon.
Maine	40,120	....	17,081	580	252
New Hampshire	257,174	....	7,652	189	191
Vermont	288,023	....	20,852	939	258
Massachusetts	121,595	....	1,162	72	7
Rhode Island	277	....	85	...	...
Connecticut	554	....	17,928	763	328
New York	2,536,269	4	940,577	57,963	1,774
New Jersey	2,153	....	182,965	16,525	23
Pennsylvania	22,088	44	530,397	41,728	285
Delaware	348	....	11,174	904	...
Maryland	1,870	63	35,686	2,446	39
District of Columbia	15	....	......	...	...
Virginia	11,506	139	1,000,450	52,318	517
North Carolina	9,216	39	593,796	38,196	229
South Carolina	26	....	333	55	123
Georgia	261	....	5,387	622	813
Florida	14	....	50	..	6
Alabama	276	....	3,921	69	167
Mississippi	473	7	665	26	2
Louisiana	125	....	......	...	29
Texas	7	....	1,048	26	22
Arkansas	157	15	12,291	321	38
Tennessee	1,032	595	368,131	18,904	1,923
Kentucky	4,309	17,787	2,100,116	75,801	1,281
Missouri	4,130	16,028	527,160	13,696	185
Illinois	3,551	150	160,063	10,787	47
Indiana	92,796	....	584,469	36,888	387
Ohio	63,731	....	446,932	188,880	1,552
Michigan	10,653	....	7,152	519	108
Wisconsin	15,930	....	68,393	1,191	...
Iowa	8,242	....	62,660	1,959	246
California	....	....	......	...	...
Minnesota	....	....	......	...	...
New Mexico	....	....	......	...	...
Oregon	8	....	640	...	...
Utah	50	....	550	5	...
Total	3,497,029	34,868	7,709,676	562,312	10,843

	Pounds maple sugar.	Hogsheads cane sugar.	Gallons molasses.	Pounds beeswax & honey.	Value domestic manuf.
Maine	93,542	....	3,167	189,618	$513,599
New Hampshire	1,298,863	....	9,811	117,140	393,455
Vermont	6,349,357	....	5,997	249,422	267,710
Massachusetts	795,525	....	4,693	59,508	205,333
Rhode Island	28	....	4	6,347	26,495
Connecticut	50,796	....	665	93,304	192,252
New York	10,357,484	....	56,539	1,755,830	1,280,333
New Jersey	2,197	....	954	156,694	112,781
Pennsylvania	2,326,525	....	50,652	839,509	749,132

	Pounds maple sugar.	Hogsheads cane sugar.	Gallons molasses.	Pounds beeswax & honey.	Value domestic manufac.
Delaware	......	....	50	41,248	38,121
Maryland	47,740	....	1,430	74,802	111,828
District of Columbia	......	....	.....	550	2,075
Virginia	1,227,665	....	40,322	880,767	2,156,312
North Carolina	27,932	....	704	512,289	2,086,522
South Carolina	200	671	15,904	216,281	909,525
Georgia	50	1,642	216,150	732,514	1,838,968
Florida	......	2,750	352,893	18,971	75,582
Alabama	643	8,242	83,428	897,021	1,934,120
Mississippi	......	388	18,318	397,460	1,164,020
Louisiana	255	226,001	10,931,177	96,701	139,232
Texas	......	7,351	441,918	380,825	266,984
Arkansas	9,330	....	18	192,338	638,217
Tennessee	158,557	248	7,223	1,036,572	3,137,790
Kentucky	437,405	284	30,079	1,158,019	2,459,128
Missouri	178,910	....	5,636	1,328,972	1,674,705
Illinois	248,204	....	8,354	869,444	1,155,902
Indiana	2,921,192	....	180,325	935,329	1,631,039
Ohio	4,588,209	....	197,308	804,275	1,712,196
Michigan	2,439,784	....	19,823	359,232	340,947
Wisconsin	610,976	....	9,874	131,005	43,624
Iowa	78,407	....	3,162	321,711	221,292
California	......	....	.....	......	7,000
Minnesota	2,950	....	.....	80	.....
New Mexico	......	....	4,236	2	6,033
Oregon	......	....	24	......	.....
Utah	......	....	58	10	1,392
Total	34,252,436	247,577	12,700,896	11,853,644	27,493,644

The proportion of the principal articles of food mentioned in the preceding tables which is consumed by a family of five persons, is nearly the same as it was in 1840, (see *ante*, 198,) though the year preceding 1850 was an unfavorable one for wheat.

THE QUANTITIES CONSUMED IN 1840 AND 1850 WERE AS FOLLOWS:—

	1840.	1850.
Indian corn .... bushels	85	100
Oats	28	29
Wheat, rye, &c	25	24
Potatoes	25	20

THE PROPORTION OF DOMESTIC ANIMALS TO EACH FAMILY WAS—

	1840.	1850.
Horses and mules	1.16	1.05
Cattle	4.00	3.09
Sheep	5.25	4.07
Hogs	7.00	6.05

From which it would appear that the proportion of vegetable food was greater in 1840 than in 1850, and that of animal food less, but in a smaller proportion.

CHAPTER XIV.

VALUE OF THE ANNUAL PRODUCTS OF THE UNITED STATES.

We have not, as yet, as ample materials for estimating the annual income of the nation as were afforded by the census of 1840; but by taking the estimate for 1840 as a guide, with such aid as the late census affords, we may arrive at a result not remote from the truth.

We will estimate the products of industry for 1850 under the same six heads as those of 1840, in the following order:—1. Agriculture. 2. Mining. 3. Manufactures. 4. Commerce. 5. Fisheries. 6. The forest.

1. Agriculture. Of this source of the national wealth, which exceeds all the rest united, we have full details of the quantities, and the only room for uncertainty is in the valuation. In that which is here made, we shall aim to give the value of each product at the place where it is produced. This is always below, and sometimes far below, the market price, which, in so extensive a country as the United States, is often greatly enhanced by the cost of transportation.

The value of this class of products will be found to exceed that of 1840 far more than the increase of the population, not so much from the increase in quantity, which in several important items has actually decreased, but from a general enhancement on the prices of 1840. The products of 1850 are thus valued:—

	Production.	Price.	Value.
Indian corn..... ....bushels	592,071,104	$0 50	$296 085,552
Live stock, ¼th of the value ($544,180,516)	....	.....	136,045,128
Wheat. .... bushels	100,485,949	0 90	90,437,350
Cotton..........................bales	2,469,093	32 00	79,010,976
Hay ....tons	13,838,642	10 00	138,386,420
Oats ....bushels	146,584,179	0 35	51,304,462
Butter.........................pounds	313,345,893	0 18	56,402,154
Irish potatoes..................bushels	65,797,896	0 40	26,319,158
Sweet potatoes	38,268,148	0 50	19,134,074
Wool..........................pounds	52,516.959	0 30	15,755,087
Tobacco............	199,752.655	0 06	11,985,159
Cane sugar...............	247,577,000	0 04	9,913,080
Rye.........................bushels	14,168,813	0 70	9,918,169
Cheese.........................pounds	165,535,893	0 05	8,216,794
Orchard products—value of by the census returns...................... ...	....	.....	7,723,186
Market gardens—value of	....	.....	5,280,560
Buckwheat...................bushels	8,956,912	0 60	5,741,804
Hemp...........................tons	34,871	120 00	4,184.520
Barley..................... bushels	5,167.015	0 75	3.875.250
Peas and beans	9,919,901	0 75	7,439.175
Rice ....pounds	215,313,497	0 02	4.306,270
Molasses.......................gallons	12.700,991	0 20	2,540,179
Maple sugar...................pounds	34,253.346	0 05	1,712.674
Clover and other grass seeds.....bushels	925,589	3 00	2,776,767
Beeswax and honey ....pounds	14,853,790	0 15	2,228,061
Hops, flax and flaxseed, wine, and silk cocoons, as estimated at the census office.	....	.....	3,293,314
Total..			$1,000.005,116

To the preceding may be added—

Milk and eggs, allowing two cents a day, or $7 30 a year for the average consumption of a family.....	$33,860,000	
Fodder afforded by the blades of the Indian corn, at the moderate allowance of ten pounds of fodder to the bushel of corn, is 5,920,711,040 pounds, which at 50 cents per 100 pounds	29,603,555	
Wood sold, in proportion to that of 1840, 6,785,188 cords at $2½.....	16,962,965	
Annual addition to the live stock, 3 per cent........	16,325,415	
Home-made goods, deducting one-half for raw material	13,746,122	
Poultry, in the proportion of that of 1840..........	12,458,876	
Feathers, allowing a bed for every three persons of the annual addition to the population, 300,000, at $10..	3,000,000	
		125,956,927
Total..		$1,125,962,043

The preceding valuation of the products of agriculture shows an increase of 70 per cent on that of the products of 1840, which is about double of that of the population, and no one is likely to think it too high. It had, indeed, been easy to have swelled this estimate, on plausible grounds, from 10 to 20 per cent higher, but, besides that the writer wished to guard against that natural bias which, in estimates of national resources, so generally and sometimes so egregiously overrates them, the latter part of this little work would not have been congruous with the former, nor have shown the real progress of the country, unless the estimate of 1850 had been made with the same caution and moderation as had characterized that of 1840.

2. Mining. The materials which the seventh census have as yet furnished to the public, for estimating the products of mining and manufactures are—1. The number of males employed in mining and manufacturing. 2. The joint product of mining, manufactures, and the mechanic arts. 3. The number employed in manufacturing establishments in the years 1820, 1840, and 1850.

In the statement of the industrious classes the number of miners is 77,416. In the account of the joint product of mining, manufactures, and the mechanic arts, the whole number of hands employed is 948,991, and the whole annual product is $1,013,336,463. Supposing the product of mining to be in proportion to the number of hands employed, it would be about $80,000,000 annually. This is nearly double of that estimated for 1840, which was $42,358,000, and is probably very short of the truth, considering how the mining of coal, iron, and lead have increased since 1840. The mining of California will make a vast alteration to this item.

3. Manufactures. These, which have fallen off in some of the States, as has been mentioned, have continued to increase in others, and the whole number employed in manufacturing establishments has risen from 791,247 in 1840 to 944,991—showing an advance of less than 20 per cent in ten years. But the value produced would seem to be in a far larger proportion, since the product of mining, manufactures, and the mechanic arts are together more than $1,000,000,000; and if this amount be apportioned among the three, according to the number of operatives they severally employ, more than three-fourths seem to be occupied in manufactures; but the precise proportion cannot be ascertained, as, on this subject, one part of the census is not in accordance with another. There is, however,

abundant evidence to show a great proportional increase, as may be seen in the following comparison between some of the principal manufactures of 1840 and those of 1850:—

I. MANUFACTURES OF COTTON.

	1840.	1850.
Capital invested	$51,102,359	$74,500,931
Persons employed	72,119	82,286
Value produced	$46.350,453	$61,869,184

II. MANUFACTURES OF WOOL.

Capital invested	$15,765,124	$28,118,650
Persons employed	21,342	39,252
Value produced	$20,696,999	$43,207,545

III. MANUFACTURES OF PIG-IRON, IRON CASTINGS, AND BAR-IRON.

Capital invested	$20,432,131	$51,796,055
Persons employed	30,497*	60,285
Tons of pig-iron produced	286,903	563,755

There are no sufficient materials for comparing the separate products of iron castings and bar-iron. The whole sum produced from the three descriptions of iron manufacture in 1850 were as follows:—

Pig-iron	$12,748,727	
Iron castings	25,108,155	
Wrought-iron	22,629,271	
		$60,476,153
From which must be deducted for the cost of the raw materials as follows:—		
Pig-iron	$7,005,298	
Iron castings	10,346,265	
Wrought-iron	13,542,727	
		30,876,340
Total produce of iron manufactures		$29,600,813

For the want of details of other manufactures, we must be content to take the statement made at the census office of the united product of manufactures, mining, and the mechanic arts—

Which was	$1,013,336,453
From which we will deduct for raw materials one-third† as the cost	337,778,817
Product of mining, manufactures, and the mechanic arts for 1850	$657,557,636
The product of mining and manufactures in 1840 was	282,000,000

4. COMMERCE. The materials for ascertaining the profits, or even extent of the Commerce of the United States, afforded by the last census, are yet more imperfect than those branches of industry that have been

* This includes men employed in mining.

† In the details of principal manufactures, given in Mr. De Bow's Compendium—180-182—the value of the raw materials is stated to be more than half that of the finished product. As this is at variance with the rule generally adopted both in England and this country, which allows only one-third, I have considered the larger allowance to be a mistake, occasioned probably by the census takers having included the raw materials *on hand* with those *worked up* in the manufactured articles, and have accordingly adopted the usual course of allowing one-third for the raw materials. It is true that in the progressive improvement of manufactures, the increased substitution of machinery, tends to lessen the proportion of human labor on manufactures, but their increased fineness and delicacy tends also to lessen the proportion of the raw material.

considered—(see De Bow's Compendium, page 183.) But we have indirect evidence that the increase from 1840 to 1850 has been greater than that of 1840.

In the first place, the whole domestic tonnage has increased in that time from 2,094,379 tons in 1840 to 3,535,454 tons in 1850—showing an increase of 75 per cent. The foreign tonnage *entered* in 1840 was 712,363 tons; in 1850 it was 1,775,623. The same tonnage *cleared* was 706,486 tons in 1840, and 1,758,214 tons in 1850. In the next place there has been a great increase of the steam tonnage, both in the foreign and coasting trade, in the same period; and generally speaking steam vessels make two voyages to one made by sail vessels. The great increase of railroads is a further evidence of the same increase of commerce; fourthly and lastly, the amount of imports retained for home consumption had risen from $88,951,297 in 1840, to $163,186,207 in 1850. From these facts, we seem warranted in putting down the profits of commerce to double the estimated amount in 1840, that is to $159,442,000.

Even this sum may seem quite too little for the profits of more than 100,000 merchants, returned by the census, besides those of other occupations who belong to this class. It must, however, be recollected that merchants obey that well-known law in political philosophy, that wherever the profits of any branch of business are irregular and sometimes very great, the illusive influence of hope will tempt an over-proportion of persons to engage in it, by which its profits will be reduced below the average; and, in some cases, so far below that the whole loss from blanks will exceed the whole gain from prizes. The adventurers to California, both in mining and commerce, probably afford a striking illustration of the truth and force of this principle. The average profits of commerce are, therefore, inferior to those of less tempting occupations.

5. The Fisheries. These are stated in the returns of the seventh census at $10,000,000, which is nearly $2,000,000 less than the same source of wealth was estimated in 1840.

6. The Products of the Forest. The unwonted increase of the cities, railroads, and shipping, justify us in doubling this source of wealth since 1840. It would then be $33,670,000. The result of the preceding estimate would be as follows:—

Products of agriculture	$1,125,162,000
" manufactures, mining, and the mechanic arts	657,557,000
" Commerce	159,442,000
" the fisheries	10,000,000
" the forest	33,670,000
Total	$1,985,831,000

This is 74 per cent on the whole annual product in 1840. It is equal to $87 to each individual of the whole population, and to $100 to each one of the free population.

The following table is taken from Mr. De Bow's Compendium of the seventh census. The valuation of the real and personal estate is compiled from the returns of the census takers, to which he has added another valuation, exhibiting a juster estimate. The revenue, expenditures, and debts of the several States for 1852 are derived from other sources.—(See Compendium, page 190.)

TABLE OF THE REAL AND PERSONAL ESTATE OF THE STATES AND TERRITORIES IN 1850, AND OF THE REVENUES, EXPENDITURES, AND DEBTS OF THE STATES IN 1852.

States and Territories.	Real estate.	Personal estate.	Total.	True valuation.
Maine	$64,336,119	$32,463,434	$96,799,553	$122,777,571
New Hampshire	67,839,108	27,412,488	95,251,596	103,652,825
Vermont	57,320,369	15,660,114	72,980,483	92,205,049
Massachusetts	349,129,932	201,976,892	551,106,824	573,342,286
Rhode Island	54,358,231	23,400,743	77,758,974	80,508,794
Connecticut	96,412,947	22,675,725	119,088,672	155,707,980
New York	564,649,649	150,719,379	715,369,028	1,080,302,216
New Jersey	153,151,619	....	153,151,619	153,151,619
Pennsylvania	427,865,660	72,410,191	500,275,851	729,144,998
Delaware	14,486,595	1,410,275	15,896,870	18,855,803
Maryland	139,026,601	69,536,956	208,563,566	219,217,364
Dist. of Columbia	14,409,413	1,774,342	16,183,765	16,723,619
Virginia	252,105,824	130,198,429	382,304,253	391,646,438
North Carolina	71,702,740	140,368,673	212,071,413	226,800,472
South Carolina	105,737,492	178,130,217	283,867,709	288,257,694
Georgia	121,619,739	213,490,486	335,110,225	335,425,714
Florida	7,924,588	15,274,146	23,198,734	23,198,734
Alabama	78,870,718	162,463,705	241,334,423	228,204,332
Mississippi	65,171,438	143,250,729	208,422,167	228,951,130
Louisiana	176,623,654	49,832,464	226,456,118	233,998,764
Texas	28,149,671	25,414,000	53,563,671	55,362,340
Arkansas	17,372,524	19,056,151	36,428,675	39,841,025
Tennessee	107,981,793	87,299,565	195,281,358	207,454,704
Missouri	66,802,223	31,793,240	98,595,463	137,247,707
Kentucky	177,013,407	114,374,147	291,387,554	301,628,456
Ohio	337,521,075	96,351,557	433,872,632	504,726,120
Indiana	112,947,740	39,922,659	152,870,399	202,650,264
Illinois	81,524,835	33,257,810	114,782,645	156,265,006
Michigan	25,580,374	5,296,852	30,877,223	59,787,255
Wisconsin	22,458,442	4,257,083	26,715,525	42,056,595
Iowa	15,672,332	6,018,310	21,690,642	23,714,638
California	16,347,442	5,575,731	21,923,173	22,161,872
Minnesota	97,363	164,725	262,088	262,088
New Mexico	2,679,486	2,494,985	5,174,471	5,274,867
Oregon	3,997,332	1,066,142	5,063,474	5,063,474
Utah	337,866	648,217	986,083	986,083
Total	$3,899,226,347	$2,125,440,562	$6,024,666,909	$7,066,562,966

States and Territories.	Revenue.	Expenditures.	Debts.
Maine	$744,879	$624,101	$471,500
New Hampshire	141,686	149,890	74,399
Vermont	185,830	183,058	48,436
Massachusetts	598,170	674,622	6,259,930
Rhode Island	124,944	115,835	....
Connecticut	150,189	137,327	8,000
New York	2,698,310	2,520,932	22,623,838
New Jersey	139,166	180,614	71,346
Pennsylvania	7,716,552	6,876,480	41,524,875
Delaware	....	....	30,000
Maryland	1,279,953	1,360,458	15,260,667
District of Columbia	....	....	....
Virginia	1,265,744	1,272,382	13,573,355
North Carolina	219,000	228,173	977,000
South Carolina	532,152	463,021	3,144,931
Georgia	1,142,405	597,882	2,801,972
Florida	60,619	55,234	2,800
Alabama	658,976	513,559	3,983,616
Mississippi	221,200	223,637	7,271,707
Louisiana	1,146,568	1,980,911	11,492,566
Texas	140,688	156,622	5,725,671

States and Territories.	Revenue.	Expenditures.	Debts.
Arkansas.....................	$68,412	$74,076	$1,506,562
Tennessee.....................	502,126	623,625	3,776,856
Missouri.....................	326,579	207,656	857,000
Kentucky.....................	779,293	674,697	5,726,307
Ohio.....................	3,016,403	2,736,060	15,520,768
Indiana.....................	1,283,064	1,061,605	6,712,880
Illinois.....................	736,030	192,940	17,500,000
Michigan.....................	548,326	431,918	2,307,850
Wisconsin.....................	135,155	136,096	12,892
Iowa.....................	139,681	131,631	81,795
California.....................	366,825	925,625	2,159,403
Minnesota.....................	....	....	....
New Mexico.....................	....	....	....
Oregon.....................	....	....	....
Utah.....................	....	....	....
Total.....................	$27,068,925	$24,628,666	$191,508,922

To the preceding table, which may be considered only an approximation to the truth, it may be added that the debt of the general government together with the debts of the several States were, in June, 1850, about $150,000,000, equal to something more than $10 to each individual of the whole population, or less than $12 to each one of the free population; and that the whole annual expenditure of the Federal and State treasuries, is less than $3 to each citizen of the Republic.

To conclude: we have seen in the preceding brief and imperfect sketch of the United States, as exhibited by the census of 1850, that they have increased in ten years from 17,000,000 to 23,000,000, and that their advancement in agriculture, manufactures, and commerce, in the means of education and religious instruction, and those of commercial and social intercourse, has been in a far greater ratio. The seventh census will enable us to see hereafter whether to the rapid development of our numbers, wealth, and power, we shall add the rarer praise of lessening our share of pauperism, crime, and the cost of civil government.

www.ingramcontent.com/pod-product-compliance
Lightning Source LLC
LaVergne TN
LVHW010227110826
845151LV00004B/1205

* 9 7 8 1 4 2 5 5 2 6 6 9 6 *